MW00775145

HOLISTIC EDUCATION

An Analysis of Its Ideas and Nature

The FOUNDATIONS OF HOLISTIC EDUCATION *Series*

For more information contact the Foundation for Educational Renewal

Holistic Education

An Analysis of Its Ideas and Nature

by Scott H. Forbes

Foreword by John Wilson

THE FOUNDATIONS OF HOLISTIC EDUCATION SERIES, VOLUME VIII

A Solomon Press Book
FOUNDATION FOR EDUCATIONAL RENEWAL, publishers
P.O. Box 328, Brandon, VT 05733

Forbes, Scott H.
Holistic Education: An Analysis of Its Ideas and Nature
Foundation for Educational Renewal

ISBN 1-885580-15-0

Copyright © 2003 by Scott H. Forbes

Library of Congress Cataloging-in-Publication Data

Forbes, Scott H. (Scott Hall), 1948–
   Holistic education: an analysis of its ideas and nature/by Scott H. Forbes
     p. cm. – (The foundations of holistic education series ; v. 8)
   "A Solomon Press Book."
   Includes bibliographical references and index.
   ISBN 1-885580-15-0
     1. Alternative education. 2. Education—Philosophy. 3. Learning,
   Psychology of. I. Title. II. Series.

LC46.3.F67 2003
371.04–dc21

2003051381

All rights reserved.

No part of this book may be reproduced, stored in a retrieval system,
or transmitted in any form or by any means, electronic, mechanical,
photocopying, microfilming, recording, or otherwise, without written
permission from the publisher.

For information contact the publisher:

Foundation for Educational Renewal
P.O. Box 328
Brandon, VT 05733   U.S.A.
Phone: 800-639-4122   Fax: 802-247-8312
http://www.great-ideas.org

10   9   8   7   6   5   4   3   2   1

Book design by Raymond Solomon
Cover design and painting by Sidney Solomon
Typesetting by Eve Brant in Garamond and Bodoni fonts.
Printed in the United States of America

To my parents

Foreword

I am very pleased to be able to commend this book to what I hope will be a very wide range of readers. It took its origins from a doctoral thesis for which I supervised the author, and from which—as commonly with supervisions, not only at Oxford University—I learned at least as much as I taught. It is, to the best of my knowledge, the best (perhaps the only) attempt to give the idea and practice of holistic education a serious philosophical underpinning, and it may be worth saying a little about why that is important.

Educational theories have always been generated by various feelings, attitudes and intuitions entertained by theorists and practitioners, from Plato to Dewey and beyond. The list is almost endless: Socrates and Isocrates, Locke, Kant, Montessori, Steiner, Freire and many others. Various schools and other educational institutions have risen, and fallen, based upon such intuitions: A.S. Neill's school Summerhill is a contemporary example. Their rise and fall has been largely a function of their appeal or lack of appeal to contemporary culture and society, in which certain vaguely-formulated ideals become fashionable or salient: "back to basics," or "progressive education," or "inclusion," or (in the UK) "the comprehensive ideal" (now much less fashionable than it was in the 1960s). There will be talk from time to time of "liberation" or "freedom," of "behavioral objectives" or "basic skills," of "education for change" or "education for the new millennium." These fashions or climates of opinion come and go; and it has to be admitted that philosophers, psychologists, sociologists and other academic theorists do little (one may sometimes feel, hardly anything) to stabilize the position. There is no established corpus of educational knowledge, as there is such a corpus in natural science, so that educational theory seems not much more than a plaything for partisan prejudice.

Holistic education arose in part from a reaction against certain types of schooling, which were seen as too narrow, or too fragmented, or in some way failing to take due account of the student's real or inner self. As this book shows, that general reaction goes back a long way, at least as far as Rousseau. But if it is to be more than just a reaction of protest, defining itself only negatively and by contrast with some enemy (perhaps "traditional schooling"), it has to be shown that it represents a coherent ideal which can be justified in the light of reason. That is what I take the main message of this book to be: to show that holistic education is not just a practice that happens to appeal to people of a particular temperament, but something which is required for doing justice to the concept of education itself.

That involves, first of all, giving a coherent definition or account of what holistic education is, or what "holistic education" means: no easy task, but one which the author manages to accomplish. A clear account of this kind is worth infinitely more than any general talk of "freedom" or "spirituality." We can now, whatever our personal feelings, confront an educational ideal which is adequately described and circumscribed, and which is based on more than mere intuition or some general feeling of dissatisfaction with contemporary schooling. The author puts together the various insights of past and current thinkers into a manageable package which can be evaluated. That in itself is a considerable step forward: at least we know what we are talking about.

The author then tries to demonstrate, in my judgment successfully, why this ideal must commend itself to any serious student or practitioner of education. That requires a good deal of hard philosophical argument, which will at least free the reader from too narrow an interpretation of the concept marked by "education." The door is thus philosophically opened to allow us to enter on the more substantive questions of just what holistic education consists of, both in theory and practice: in particular, what findings of psychology and social science shed light on it. That then sheds light on and makes sense of the actual practices of holistic education, practices which might otherwise appear diffuse and unfocussed, but which can now be seen as representing a coherent ideal.

That kind of methodology or heuristic procedure is required for any educational theory or ideal; and the author's deployment of it would be valuable even if he had not made out an overwhelmingly strong case for this particular ideal. For that reason even those antagonistic to the notion of holistic education may profit by it: even an extreme traditionalist would need to employ a similar methodology in order to defend his position coherently. At least the author shows what is required to make out an intellectually respectable case for any educational ideal or theory; and that may, in one way, be at least as important as the particular case he makes.

As the author would himself be the first to admit—indeed, to emphasize—no single book can make such a case complete. That is because books in themselves can only do so much. There is, inevitably and rightly, an interplay between the theory of holistic education and its practice. The theory sheds light on the practice: it enables us to identify, via the use of certain general concepts, just what features of the practice are important. But equally the practice itself generates experiences and insights which shed light on these general concepts, and modify and enlarge them. As Kant puts it, "Experience without concepts is blind, and concepts without experience are empty."

That has important practical consequences. Now that we have—I believe, for the first time—a clear account of what holistic education is, we have something which can be seriously researched. Empirical research tells us little or nothing unless it is geared in the first place to a clear set of concepts, which is why such research has not availed to advance our educational knowledge and practice to any great extent. (To take an obvious example, empirical research into moral education, however interesting in itself, has to be geared to a clear account of what "morally educated" means, and hence to the logically necessary goals of moral education: otherwise it appears merely as a series of dislocated facts or "findings") So it is to be hoped that this book will spark off a considerable number of empirical research projects, which will tell us in more detail exactly what the results of holistic education are in terms of student outcomes.

It is also to be hoped that politicians, administrators and other policymakers will take the ideal of holistic education on board, and facilitate it in practice: again, not just as a fashionable "movement" or "school of thought," but as a coherent ideal which has to be taken seriously. That is asking a lot: politicians and administrators are not naturally open to educational ideals in general, being more concerned with (as people say) more "practical" issues, usually financial or economic. But they need to remember something often forgotten: the fact that billions of dollars are spent on education, yet without any real assurance that they are well spent, or that people are any better educated than they were. The ultimate test of any educational system must be in terms of values and ideals, which is why they need serious inspection.

That point is relevant not only to educationalists. For inevitably the ideal of holistic education is based ultimately upon a certain picture of human nature and the human condition; and that is relevant to the life of any and every human individual. It is, by and large, an optimistic picture; and if I diverge from the author at any point, it is that he sometimes seems to make insufficient allowance for certain endemic difficulties in the human condition from which we may never be entirely able to break free. A dose of St. Augustine, or the classical Greek tragedians, or perhaps of Freud might be salutary here; but I shall not pursue the point. For on any account an immense amount can be done, as now it is not done, to educate not only our students but ourselves holistically: and that must at least give grounds for some optimism. It is not too much to say that we can learn to live holistically, both within ourselves and in our personal relationships; and that is something to which any individual needs to pay attention.

Rightly the author makes no attempt to brainwash or indoctrinate the reader into an acceptance of holistic education, as if it were a kind of religion that depended on blind faith. He uses the tools of reason and not of rhetoric. In our ongoing discussions over the years neither he nor (I hope) I have tried to convert, but only to persuade. That style of interaction (whether or not we always succeeded in adhering to it) is perhaps of more fundamental importance to educational theory—indeed to most human enterprises—than anything else. To share one's views and debate them with rigor and without personal animus is a precondition for any serious intellectual advance: without that, we have only the blind confrontation of one ideal with another—what Plato distinguishes as "eristic" rather than "dialectic." It is perhaps that, at bottom, which has prevented much progress being made in such human enterprises as education, morality, politics, and religion: we cling to our own intuitions rather than take the responsibility of subjecting them to the discipline of reason and the criticism of other people. This book may serve as an exemplar of that procedure, as of much else. I hope it will meet with the success that it richly deserves.

—John Wilson, Senior Research Associate
University of Oxford Department of Education

Acknowledgments

Mary Zimbalist must be acknowledged as a prime mover in this study having been undertaken. Without her support and encouragement, it would not have occurred.

I wish to thank John Wilson for the many years he gave to discussing this project with me, and for his often inspired advice.

I would like to thank Richard Pring for his thought provoking contributions.

I am most grateful to Professor Basil Bernstein and Dr. Anthony Storr who were kind and generous in their support and encouragement.

My thanks also go to Patricia English for her friendship, feedback and encouragement throughout this long project, to Robin Martin for her excellent editorial help, to Isabelle Brent for her support, understanding and thoughtful contributions, and to Ron Miller for his friendship and belief in this project.

Contents

Note to the Reader

*T*his book is arranged so that it can be read in different ways for different purposes. The three sections can be read separately if the reader has only an interest in a general overview of holistic education (Section I), only an interest in the philosophical precedents of holistic education (Section II), or only a sociological analysis of holistic education (Section III). There is a very extensive appendix for Section II as the authors of the intellectual precedents are wonderfully articulate, and many of their works, or works about them, are now quite rare, so that the inclusion of these quotations could be of interest to a scholar of holistic education. These quotations are not necessary, however, for an understanding of the authors, so they have been excluded from the main text to leave it less cluttered for the casual reader.

CHAPTER 1

Introduction

*T*here is no doubt that holistic education exists (at least in name) as a widespread institutionalized endeavor. Over the last several decades the number of education initiatives that describe themselves as holistic has dramatically increased as parents, students, and educators feel that an alternative to mainstream education is needed. While thousands of schools have been created world-wide that describe themselves as alternative or holistic,[1] there are uncounted special programs claiming to be holistic which are called into non-holistic schools so that students can engage in learning that these schools do not normally cover. There are still more education initiatives which describe themselves as holistic outside of schooling altogether (out of school hours, out of term times, or as substitutes for schooling, e.g., homeschooling).

To describe and promote holistic education, several journals have emerged (e.g., *Holistic Education Review*, *ΣΚΟΛΕ*, *Paths of Learning*, etc.) and University departments have been created (e.g., Holistic and Aesthetic Education at the Ontario Institute for Studies in Education at The University of Toronto, The Holistic Teaching/Learning Unit at The University of Tennessee at Knoxville). There are many books describing education programs or schools which claim to be holistic, one book which traces the origins of holistic education,[2] several books which describe holistic curricula,[3] and many which describe the need for a more holistic approach to education; but there is no book which attempts to construct a coherent account of all these initiatives and ideas.

WHAT HOLISTIC EDUCATION COVERS

Unfortunately, this field is extremely diverse and there is no element of which one can say, 'If it has X it is holistic; and if it doesn't, it isn't'. As no consensus exists as to what 'holistic education' means, my task is to give it a clear meaning by identifying a clear group of elements—beliefs, feelings, principles, and general ideas (hereafter called 'notions')—which seem basic and central to holistic education. Some of the elements would exist to some extent in all schools and programs claiming to be holistic, although in few (if any) schools or programs would we see all of them. In this, what will be examined is similar to what philosopher Ludwig Wittgenstein described as 'family resemblances'.

> ...we see a complicated network of similarities overlapping and criss-crossing: sometimes overall similarities, sometimes similarities of detail.
> I can think of no better expression to characterize these similarities than "family resemblances"; for the various resemblances between members of a family: build, features, colour of eyes, gait, temperament, etc. etc. overlap and criss-cross in the same way.[4]

Wittgenstein gave as an example of family resemblance the notion of games. There seems to be no single criterion which determines if an activity is a game (e.g., there need not be competition—there are cooperative games, there need not be different sides—there is solitaire, etc.); but rather an overlapping set of characteristics, any combination of which may be present in a game.

In trying to elucidate the elements of the family resemblance of holistic education, one must take one step back from any particular expression of holistic education to see if we can understand what *most* people engaged in holistic education will mean *most* of the time when they use that expression. It might then be possible to pick out elements of schools or programs that are holistic in nature; and, still further, perhaps it would be possible to see in what way a school or program could be changed to make it more or less holistic.

Holistic education frequently claims that it wants to, 1) educate the whole child (all parts of the child), 2) educate the student as a whole (not as an assemblage of parts), and 3) see the child as part of a whole (society, humanity, the environment, some spiritual whole, etc.) from which it is not meaningful to extract the student. This seemingly simple statement hides an extraordinary number of complexities and ambiguities: e.g., what is the whole child? (what parts does the child contain?); what does it mean to educate those parts?; how could such education occur?; if a child is part of a whole from which he or she can't be meaningfully extracted, where does the child end and the non-child begin so that some boundaries to the educational intention can be established?

While it will take the whole of this book to describe and elucidate the field of holistic education, some brief comments may be needed to orient the reader who knows nothing of this approach to pedagogy. Arguably, most forms of education have as their *raison d'être* either enculturation or preparation for work. Holistic education has as its goal the fullest possible human development (described more fully beginning on page 17) with fitting into society and vocation having secondary importance. If such full development is seen as including 'right' relationships to the environment and consciousness (as is the case with many New Age paradigms) then ecology and meditation have importance in approaches to holistic education arising from those paradigms. If the paradigms are more Christian (as was the case with holistic educators of two hundred years ago or Montessori), or Theosophical (e.g., Rudolf Steiner), or some combination of Eastern and Western theologies (e.g., American Transcendentalists of the mid 1800's) then their views of full human development and consequent approaches to holistic education reflect those paradigms.

ACCOMPLISHING THE PURPOSES OF THIS BOOK

To accomplish the purposes of this book, which is to construct a coherent account of holistic education that would include as many of its various forms, initiatives and ideas as is possible, a two pronged approach is taken—examining both the thoughts and actions of holistic educators. Any attempt to individually elucidate the various forms of holistic education would be inadequate and instantly obsolete as they are too numerous, new ones are continuously being created, and existing forms often change radically. How then is one to begin to establish the "family resemblance" of holistic education?

As with many living organisms, establishing the *genus* of holistic education can be assisted by examining its principal elements. For educational approaches, there are two broad categories of elements that one could choose: the *thinking* in and of an educational approach, or the *doing* in and of an educational approach. It seems appropriate in trying to establish a new *genus* of pedagogy that both categories be examined. Hence, in this book the *thinking* of holistic education is examined through a philosophical exploration of its intellectual precedents, while what holistic education *does* is explored using the discipline of sociology. Section I of this book gives an overview of holistic education. Section II explores what holistic education *thinks* by examining its intellectual precedents. Section III explores what holistic education *does* using some tools of the sociology of education as propounded by Basil Bernstein.

There needs to be some organizing principle for Sections I and II because the educational notions contained therein have spanned almost two and a half centuries, several languages, and even more countries. I believe there are three principal questions which can be useful for organizing the notions of any educational approach and which, consequently, also serve as a convenient basis for organizing the educational notions in Sections I and II. They are: 1) What does an educational approach claim is the goal of education? 2) What does an educational approach claim needs to be learned in order to achieve its goal? 3) What does an educational approach claim facilitates or causes the needed learning?

In Section I these three questions will serve to elucidate a presentation of the principal notions in holistic education. These principal notions are only put in very general terms as an attempt to describe what *most* adherents of holistic education claim *most* of the time for holistic education, and with the understanding that these adherents are many and extremely varied. These principal notions presented in Section I also serve as a summary of the notions for the authors of holistic education's intellectual precedents, which follow in Section II. This may at first appear to be a backward way of proceeding—first a summary of the intellectual precedents, and secondly details of what has been summarized. However, on reflection there seems little choice, as we must have a clear general overview of what we will be examining in the intellectual precedents before we can examine these particulars.

This approach should also serve the purpose of establishing the *genus* of holistic education. Like the biological sciences, which observe categories of elements in several species (e.g., the flowers of several plants), attempt to find similarities, then trace their ancestry back to a common source and in so doing establishing a *genus*; so must we proceed. We can use the three organizing questions to establish general notions of holistic education, trace the notions back to their origins and see how they have changed over time. Hence the importance of holistic education's intellectual precedents for establishing holistic education as a distinct and legitimate form of pedagogy. Some present forms of holistic education will find resonance with early enunciations of a notion, while other forms will find later expressions of that same notion to more closely represent their approach to education. However, in seeing the theme of which they hold variations allows a family resemblance to begin to be established and thus the *genus* of holistic education to be established.

In Section II holistic education's intellectual precedents are traced through the works of Rousseau, Pestalozzi, Froebel, Jung, Maslow and Rogers. These authors (excluding Jung) are the most often cited and quoted by holistic educators as the originators of the central notions of holistic education, and a good case has been made for the influence of their work on the current thinking in holistic education.[5] These men, as a group, will from here on be called the "Authors," not just because their writing has been so widely cited, but also because they are often seen as the authorities on which these notions rest. However, not all the work of these authors is relevant to holistic education.

While some advocates and writers on holistic education agree with the inclusion of Jung in this list, to others this may seem curious. There are several reasons why Jung should be on this list: Jung was, if not the first, then at least the popularizer of the notion that the locus of the religious is the psyche; a notion widely held in holistic education. Jung was also the popularizer of notions linking Eastern religions, Western religions and the psyche, allowing him and others since him to see what they claim are 'larger truths' behind the dogma and culturally bound expressions of religion. The importance of this to holistic education is discussed in several of the following sections of this book. Jung also saw and inspired others to see biological, psychological, and religious 'evolution' as merged and a human imperative. This imperative lies behind much of the fullest possible human development that many holistic educators feel is the goal of education. In short, Jung's work lies behind much in the views of what it means to be human that are held by proponents of holistic education, and views of what it means to be human are central to views of education.

Some readers may find it curious that educators such as Montessori, Steiner, Dewey or some others are not included amongst the Authors, but these others cannot be counted as philosophical originators of key notions in holistic education. Maria Montessori was certainly original in her creation of teaching technique and even the development of size appropriate school furniture, but she was an inheritor of the educational philosophies of Rousseau, Pestalozzi, and Froebel. Rudolf Steiner was original in both his philosophies and techniques of education, but he has had little to no influence on other forms of holistic education, and cannot therefore be considered part of holistic education's intellectual precedents. While John Dewey said many things that seem to have come directly from Rousseau, Pestalozzi and Froebel (whose work he read, knew, and quoted) he also put forward many other ideas that were original. However, these original notions of Dewey are not relevant for holistic education, and consequently his work is not included.

The Authors are not assumed to be the first people to have had the ideas examined here; in fact, they almost certainly were not. Obviously, there is no way of knowing who first thought of something, and tracing these notions as far back into the past as possible risks being a pursuit of the ideas for its own sake and a sterile intellectual exercise. The Authors are selected because they are acknowledged by most advocates of holistic education to have been highly influential in creating the principal notions in holistic education. So, Rousseau is seen as a source for the thinking in holistic education, yet Rousseau himself refers to and gives credit to Plotinus, Plutarch, Plato, Aristotle, Locke, etc., for many of the ideas admired by holistic educators. However, it was Rousseau who assembled the various thoughts and presented them in a form that holistic educators feel speak to them. It is Rousseau, therefore (rather than Plotinus, Plutarch, etc.), who is considered as providing part of the intellectual precedents for holistic education.

Similarly, tracing the intellectual precedents for what are called "democratic schools" need not pursue the idea of democracy back over two millennia. These schools (which sometimes describe themselves as holistic) take as their precedents the New England town meetings in colonial America, and they model many of their features on such meetings. One could trace the notions of democracy to Pericles, and indeed some of the colonial Americans would have been familiar with Pericles and democracy in ancient Greece. However, there seems little point in tracing the thinking in democratic schools back to ancient Greece since this is not something that the schools themselves usually do.

There is also another important factor in determining whom to acknowledge as a source of current thinking in holistic education, and that is whether the advocates wish to be associated with a potential source. For example, it is arguably true that Hitler popularized vegetarianism in Germany during a certain era, but present-day German vegetarians may understandably not wish to acknowledge Hitler as an inspiration for their beliefs. Similarly, holistic education, which usually tries to distance itself from particular creeds or religious dogmas, may not want to acknowledge some important Christian thinkers, even though these thinkers said things with which holistic educators would agree and these Christian thinkers clearly had an influence on the intellectual climate in which the Authors lived. The exceptions to such lack of acknowledgement by holistic educators are some mystical Christian writers like St. John of the Cross, Jan Van Ruysbroeck, Julian of Norwich, or the anonymous author of *The Cloud of Unknowing*.

The notions examined in Section II need to be seen as both a collection and an evolution. For example, Pestalozzi was such an ardent admirer of Rousseau (who he claimed was "the turning point between the old and new worlds of education"[6]), that his early attempts at education were almost a "paint by numbers" application of Rousseau's *Emile*. He even named his only son after Rousseau. Froebel was a student and early promoter of Pestalozzi, even though he eventually broke with him. Yet,

> ...far from merely echoing what was said before them, each of these [Authors] subjected existing ideas to scrutiny and modification... Any criticism, however, was designed not to reject the basic proposition, but to ensure that this new approach to education was soundly based or wisely interpreted.[7]

In this sense, there is an evolution.

Yet there is also the fact that three distinct disciplines (philosophy, pedagogy, psychology) are represented by the Authors and at least the psychology cannot be seen as evolving from the first two. At the same time, many of the holistic educators who take up the notions examined here will never have read the Authors except in decontextualized quotes or small excerpts. Consequently, the very real differences that exist in the works of these Authors tend to disappear within the everyday understanding held by holistic educators about the Authors' original works. A collection of similar sounding notions that seem to echo each other remains; and it is in this sense that it is a collection. This is especially important to remember as holistic education does not exist in a single form. As mentioned earlier, holistic education can be identified, like Wittgenstein's "family resemblances," through a collection of characteristics not all of which will always be present, but which, as a collection, are distinct.

The task of examining the thinking in holistic education in Sections I and II seems methodologically *sui generis*, although it is not without parallel. It has a parallel in making sense of movements or styles of thought such as 'romanticism' or 'socialism', and in this sense is similar to an examination of the history of ideas. Yet, the task here seems a bit more complex as the notions central to holistic education are a confluence of several notions from different eras and different disciplines, and have only fairly recently been called 'holistic education'. Thus, while the task is similar to that of asking, "What is romanticism?" or "What is socialism?" it is also quite different for several reasons. Perhaps most notably, movements like 'romanticism' or 'socialism' 1) have fairly distinct historical starting points, 2) have been called 'romanticism' and 'socialism' from fairly early on in their existence, and 3) the main contributors to those movements felt they were engaged in 'romanticism' or 'socialism'. Holistic education has no such luxuries.

Nonetheless, the present task has resonance with Isaiah Berlin's examination of romanticism, fascism, utopianism,[8] etc., and is therefore a philosophical task in the way it was proposed by Berlin. This book, however, does not attempt to critique the ideas as they appeared in history, as this would not serve to elucidate the nature of present day holistic education.

Like many of the early adherents of 'romanticism' or 'socialism', advocates of holistic education often identify themselves through opposition—what they are against, or what they are not—and their writings are often polemicized. One needs to get beneath the rhetoric (e.g., equality, fraternity, authenticity, naturalness, etc.) to see the characteristics of the fundamental notions. Perhaps the only criteria for the success of this task is analogous to those of psychological or literary interpretation: 1) That its adherents (like the patient in psychotherapy) acknowledge the interpretation as being a fair representation of their experience or view, and 2) That the notions described are reasonably coherent, thereby making sense of the rhetoric and laying it open to criticism.

Despite Section I being about holistic education in general, examples of what is being said will often be taken from the Authors rather than from the literature of holistic education. There are several reasons for this. Firstly, the Authors as a group are wonderfully articulate and took great pains to make their thought explicit. Unfortunately, this does not always characterize the writings of modern holistic educators whose ideas, while often just as valid, are frequently less clear. Secondly, this book is most interested in establishing the *genus* of holistic education, and reference to those who generated its notions (the Authors) seems more useful than any particular modern expressions of those notions. Thirdly, despite my efforts to know as much as possible about the various present-day forms of holistic education, many such forms are in continuous flux, and anything that may be valid at the time of writing may be inaccurate by the time this goes to press.

Sociology was developed as a social science to understand how groups of people and institutions act. Sociology of Education, as a separate branch of sociology came into its own in the latter half of the twentieth century, and probably one of its most controversial and thought provoking proponents was Basil Bernstein. His last work serves the task of this book particularly well in that it serves as a basis for understanding how the institutions of holistic education act. Section III, therefore, stands apart from the more philosophical Sections I and II in that this third section uses the tools of sociology. Section III also stands apart from the first two in that I had the great good fortune of being able to consult with the authority (Basil Bernstein) on many occasions for this book, while no such checking with the six preceding Authors of Sections I and II was possible.

THE EMIC (OR INSIDER'S) PERSPECTIVE

The criteria for success mentioned above are also held by Yvonna S. Lincoln in describing what is required for social research on "nonmainstream concerns and issues" of "individuals and groups...described as marginal...."[9] Certainly holistic education is, by virtue of it being a form of alternative education, such a nonmainstream group. Clearly, in view of the number of students exposed to some form of holistic education and the dearth of research on holistic education, holistic education has been marginalized; and participants in holistic education usually feel themselves to be outside the mainstream. Lincoln makes the case that marginalized groups are often "defined and circumscribed by texts which take as their point of departure the 'normal'"[10] and, as a consequence, fail to understand or accurately represent the very group they purport to study. Lincoln concludes her remarks with the view that without the views of the marginalized groups, "we will probably not have a full critique of the social order"[11] which impoverishes society as a whole. Lincoln proposes that for the study of such marginalized groups, the emic (insider) perspective is preferable to the etic (outsider) perspective, and that all accounts should seek internal validity through validation by those who are the object of the research.

The philosophic importance of an emic perspective in social science was emphasized by Peter Winch as early as 1958 by making the case that

> even if it is legitimate to speak of one's understanding of a mode of social activity as consisting in a knowledge of regularities, the nature of this knowledge must be very different from the nature of knowledge of physical regularities.[12]

Studying the activities of an engineer, he gives as an example, is not the same as the engineer studying an engine. One must be inside the "mode of social activity" to understand it.

As someone who has worked for more than thirty years in holistic education, speaking with those attracted to it (e.g., parents, students, interested guests, etc.) I believe I can justifiably claim the emic perspective. The school at which I did almost all of my teaching and served as principal was founded by J. Krishnamurti who, along with Rudolf Steiner and Maria Montessori, are the founders of the oldest continually existing schools considered by most to be holistic. The first school founded by J. Krishnamurti that continues to exist was started in 1924. As the Brockwood Park Krishnamurti Educational Centre (the holistic school at which I worked) was the only one founded by Krishnamurti between India and California, and because he resided there for almost six months of the year (during twelve years of my tenure), it attracted a great diversity of people interested in holistic education from all over the world. It was especially a magnet for European interest. This gave me contact with a far greater number and variety of people than a teacher or principal in comparable private schools might enjoy, and demonstrated the extent (both in number and geography) of the growing interest in holistic education.

During my twenty years at Brockwood, I came to know a great many holistic education initiatives. The feeling amongst those involved with such initiatives was similar to those of the staff in my school; namely, that what we were attempting was very experimental and therefore fragile, and the glare of publicity or research was best avoided.

The small experiences of publicity or research, which many of these holistic schools had, reflected Lincoln's contention that marginalized groups see such publicity and research as being unable to accurately represent their views and experiences. Consequently, almost no one outside of these schools knows what such education is thinking or doing. Often even the existence of such schools is unknown to those who live in the same area. Frequently those who work in holistic schools only know in any depth about other schools of the same variety, e.g., Steiner schools of other Steiner schools, Democratic schools of other Democratic schools, etc. Therefore, some work seems needed that would allow holistic education to be located within the field of education as a whole, and which would give a basis (e.g., the family resemblances) for holistic schools to compare and contrast what they think and do which is not tied to the rhetoric of their normal presentation.

Holistic education is, as explained above, not a single initiative, but a broad range of initiatives that share family resemblances. Having witnessed the increase in both variety and number of holistic education initiatives, including journals and university departments dedicated to the subject, it seems clear that an attempt to make coherent what these initiatives are thinking and doing as a generic form of pedagogy is long overdue. An intellectual work is needed for this field in which most people involved have only a sense or 'feel'.

To avoid the dangers of too personal a perspective, I have sought confirmation of my work (as a form of triangulation) with five other people who have a longstanding involvement with holistic education. The confirmation by these individuals (founders of holistic schools, writers on holistic education, holistic school head, and a university professor) has been important to me in satisfying Lincoln's criterion that work on the 'silenced' be felt by them to be an authentic 'voice'.

SOCIAL ISSUES AND INDIVIDUAL DIFFERENCES IN HOLISTIC EDUCATION

This book does not deal with many of today's social issues (gender, race, disability, social injustice) which some readers may feel are concerns of holistic education. This omission is partly because such issues do not appear in any illuminative way in the writing of those authors quoted for the intellectual precedents nor do they appear in the sociological analysis of Basil Bernstein referenced in Section III. Some social issues do appear in the Author's works in ways that were relevant for the time in which they wrote, but present-day readers would not be satisfied by these approaches to such issues. For example: 1) Rousseau addressed the education of girls in ways that are an anathema to most people concerned with the education of girls today, but they were revolutionary for his time; 2) Pestalozzi spent most of his life creating schools for the poor, seemingly out of compassion, and felt their education should be like that of the more advantaged children, but he never addressed corrective measures of economic inequity and social justice; and 3) Bernstein gives attention to the identity constructions of minority groups in his referenced work, but only to describe them—a process activists dismiss by likening it to the description of water for someone drowning. The omission of today's social issues in this book is also partly because these issues form a negligible part of most holistic education literature, a fact that has been repeatedly criticized by a frequent contributor to conferences and articles on holistic education, David Purpel.[13] Perhaps this is because many supporters of holistic education today believe that 'the greater encompasses the lesser', i.e., that there can be no social justice without a sense of morality, and there can be no morality without an adequate notion of Ultimacy (see page 17); so that education for social justice without a prior education for Ultimacy puts the cart before the horse. Many modern supporters of holistic education also contend that with the respect for the individual which holistic education advocates, education is necessarily sensitive to the situation of each student. Consequently, issues arising from stigma, disadvantage, or personal trauma are met at the level at which each victim must meet them rather than at the level of social activism.

Finally, it also seems important to explain some of the terminology that follows. While the word "man" is used in many quotes and some of the text referring to the quotes, it does not necessarily refer to gender. Rousseau did specifically state that the education he proposes in *Emile* is for boys, although his brief discussion on education for girls makes many similar points. For Rousseau then, "man" sometimes referred to males and at other times to humankind. Pestalozzi and Froebel were concerned with the education of both sexes and very little of their work (and certainly none of their fundamental concepts) distinguishes between genders. In their work, the word "man" does mean "humankind," and as all of the translations of their work predate concerns with sexism in language, and as I wish to rely heavily on quotations in order to allow the Authors to speak for themselves, some of the text in this book may appear to show a similar lack of concern.

This, however, is not true, and efforts are made, whenever it doesn't detract from the Authors, to be sensitive to this important modern issue. There is also use of the word "race" in many of the quotes from Pestalozzi and Froebel, but in all instances they are referring to the human race. The twentieth century Authors, having become sensitized by history to race issues often used the word "specieshood," but this term was not in use at the time of most of the translations of the earlier Authors.

SECTION I

CHAPTER **2**

Ultimacy As the Goal of Education

*T*he goal of holistic education is best encapsulated by the term "Ultimacy." First coined by Paul Tillich,[14] "Ultimacy" as a term has been used by several writers but often in slightly different ways. "Ultimacy" will be used in this book in its broadest sense meaning both: 1) the highest state of being that a human can aspire to, either as a stage of development (e.g., enlightenment), as a moment of life that is the greatest but only rarely experienced by anyone (e.g., grace), or as a phase of life that is common in the population but usually rare in any particular individual's life (e.g., Maslow's peak-experience); and 2) a concern or engagement that is the greatest that a person can aspire to (e.g., being in service to something sacred). These two meanings can overlap or intertwine, sometimes causally (e.g., being concerned with the sacred might be seen as bringing about a religious state, or entering an ultimate state might be seen as service to the sacred). This description of Ultimacy does not have the details that many readers might like to see. In this, we are probably best served by Maslow who, describing the many terms modern psychology uses to convey what we are calling Ultimacy, felt that it is not only impossible to define very exactly what is meant by the ultimate state, but that such definitions are also not desirable,

...since a definition which does not emerge easily and naturally from well known facts is apt to be inhibiting and distorting rather than helpful, since it is quite likely to be wrong or mistaken if made by an act of the will, on a priori grounds. Its meaning can be *indicated* rather than defined, partly by positive pointing, partly by negative contrast, i.e., what it is *not*.[15]

More details will emerge in the following chapters with which the reader can flesh out this rather austere description.

The term "Ultimacy" is not just convenient for our purposes. It also seems necessary to use a slightly unorthodox word for the following reasons: A term is needed that denotes both an end-state and a process, not just interchangeably but also as both.[16] A term is also needed that can encompass religious as well as psychological notions. Ultimacy for holistic education is often at least quasi-religious, if not overtly religious, and yet usually the notions belong to no particular religion. Many aspects of Ultimacy also fall within theories of human development, and are therefore psychological. Finally, most terms in common usage that denote what we are calling Ultimacy are already part of a tradition (often very rich) that has promoted one particular view. Such common terms are, therefore, connotatively loaded in a way that is not helpful to the present task of creating a new understanding.

NOTIONS OF ULTIMACY IN HOLISTIC EDUCATION

That there are notions of Ultimacy in most (if not all) cultures and subcultures seems a fairly simple assertion. Without such notions it would be impossible for a culture to have heroes, saints or human exemplars, and most (if not all) cultures seem to have at least one of these. The nature of a culture's exemplars reveals a great deal about that culture. They indicate the values in that culture (e.g., exemplars by virtue of wisdom, goodness, religiosity, physical beauty, abilities in war, capacities to accumulate wealth indicate that those qualities are valued), as well as have pronounced determining effects on that culture (i.e., members of a culture tend to emulate their exemplars). It has been argued that our modern Western cultures have particularly impoverished exemplars.[17] Whether the details of the Authors' notions or the various holistic education notions of Ultimacy are 'true' cannot be a subject for this book, even though such 'truth' was of great concern to the Authors and their critics and is of equal concern to the various proponents of holistic education.

In most forms of holistic education and in all of the Authors' writings, there is a fusion of ends and means, as will be evident in all the aspects of Ultimacy examined in the following pages. It is similar to the fusion that is sometimes found in religions (e.g., an act is "charitable" only if performed in a "charitable" way, doing "good" is being "good," etc.). As such, notions of Ultimacy often bridge (or perhaps blur) the distinction between the process of achieving the endpoint, the experience of the endpoint, and the endpoint itself.

THE IMPORTANCE GIVEN TO ULTIMACY IN HOLISTIC EDUCATION

Even if all that has been said of Ultimacy above is true, one could rightly ask, "What difference does it make? Can't we just get on with living and ignore Ultimacy? There seem to be many adherents of religions (who therefore accept, at least implicitly, notions of Ultimacy) who don't appear to give Ultimacy that much importance in their daily living; why does holistic education give Ultimacy such importance in daily life?" These questions, indeed, *should* be asked as all the Authors felt that achieving or approaching Ultimacy is not only arduous but often onerous. For example, "He [Jung] liked to quote Thomas á Kempis to the effect that suffering is the horse which carries us fastest to wholeness."[18] Some modern notions of Ultimacy initially appear to contend that approaching Ultimacy is not arduous or onerous bur rather "natural" and effortless. Yet, usually upon questioning as to why, then, is Ultimacy so rarely achieved, the answer (echoing Rousseau) is that what is "natural" and therefore *should* be effortless is corrupted, constrained, or prevented by social or cultural forces (like conditioning). In this argument, the arduous and onerous qualities are simply displaced to being what is necessary to counter these inhibiting factors, but they are nonetheless present.

If it is true that achieving or approaching Ultimacy is onerous or arduous yet necessary, then the importance of achieving or approaching Ultimacy can only lie in the view that *not* doing so is somehow worse. If *not* achieving or approaching Ultimacy is worse than achieving or approaching it, then it must be worse for our health, our psyches, our "spirits," our material success, something completely outside of ourselves but which affects us (e.g., the environment, society), or for some combination of these. If our well-being (of health, psyches, etc.) is what gives importance to Ultimacy, then either: 1) there is something about the nature of well-being that is best served by approaching Ultimacy, despite its arduous or onerous nature (like the well-being of physical fitness requires arduous and, some might say, onerous exercise), or 2) there is something about human nature which requires Ultimacy, and without it our natures or purposes are thwarted with subsequent suffering of some sort. The first position, which seems to be held by many people today, begs the questions as to why approaching Ultimacy serves well-being. The answer to this could lie in the second proposition, which was adopted by all the Authors.

In this second view Ultimacy is seen as central to human nature so that ignoring it is to ignore a major (perhaps *the* major) and integral part of ourselves. From this it follows that if we do not develop Ultimacy, we do not develop into what we are meant to be—we never develop fully, but remain only partial entities. This would be analogous to an acorn seedling (a metaphor used by both Pestalozzi and Froebel) always being cut or lacking the nutrients and never becoming more than some small bush. The acorn never becomes what it was intended to be, never plays out its natural part in the environment, and never comes to full fruition. Normal healthy development is seen as thwarted without Ultimacy and the result is deformity, sickness, stunted growth, and/or chronic flaw. If success in human life means achieving what we were meant to achieve or the most we are capable of achieving, then success in life is blocked with such stunted growth. It is acknowledged that achieving some worldly success may be advantaged by such maldevelopment (hence the deliberately stunted growth in the past of people destined to be chimney sweeps or jockeys); however, in what the Authors consider to be success at what it means to be a human being, such lack of development is a hindrance. Hence, to approach being a saint or a hero of virtue (as opposed to heroes of race tracks, chimneys, war, or making money), with all the "healthy" success that is consequent to that approach, requires a concern for Ultimacy. There is a social aspect to this position. For those who give primacy to Ultimacy, full human development is seen as not only needed for an individual, but for society as a whole. Societies need fully developed humans, because it is the heroes of virtue (rather than the heroes of any function, e.g., sweeping chimneys or conducting war) who are seen as the well-spring of cultural and social renewal.

In these issues the Authors seem to have ignored or simply denounced a contention made by Hume in his "Treatise on Human Nature" (and supported by many subsequent philosophers) that an *ought* cannot be derived from an *is*; that what is desirable for humans cannot be discerned from facts about their nature. It is only Maslow who directly addresses this issue even slightly (but without mentioning Hume) and might provide a perspective that at least puts this issue aside if not resolves it. (See the discussion on page 184.) This is an important point for most proponents of holistic education, because they usually start with claims about the nature of people (either from experiences of 'self-discovery' or from conviction) and from such claims move to views of Ultimacy.

The nature of the importance given to Ultimacy by the different Authors reveals characteristics of their notions of Ultimacy that are often only implicit. Sometimes one gets the impression that, for the Authors, these characteristics are self-explanatory (e.g., for Froebel, Ultimacy had a direct connection to Christian salvation—which was not true for the modern Authors), while for other Authors there is the impression that explicating their notions of Ultimacy is a distraction from their educational concern. Aside from the above generalizations, it is difficult to make a more substantive case for the importance of Ultimacy without first establishing more about human nature and the characteristics of human well-being, as well as establishing some of the characteristics of Ultimacy that correspond to these.

ULTIMACY IN RELATION TO VIEWS OF HUMAN NATURE

While there is reason to assume that other entities may share aspects of Ultimacy with humans (e.g., plants and animals in the wild faithfully follow "nature's call"—one of Rousseau's aspects of Ultimacy[19]), Ultimacy *in toto* is seen as uniquely human. It is not, however, just being unique to humans that gives Ultimacy its normative function (humans are also the only entities that drive cars, play violins, etc.). Ultimacy is seen as describing the best, the most, the finest, etc., which *only* humans can be; the maximum development of those capacities that together make up a human being. As such, Ultimacy defines what it means to be human for the Authors; which, however, does not imply that humans, as they usually live, achieve the best, the most, etc. Instead of defining the human condition as it is daily lived by most people, Ultimacy is seen more as an end point on a continuum of qualities along which humans live. However, as approaching Ultimacy is seen as generating well-being, and as all species are seen as naturally tending towards their well-being, Ultimacy ends up as the goal towards which all people are naturally drawn. By establishing the goal of humanity, Ultimacy also indicates the trajectory of a purposeful and natural development, and hence its importance for education.

This understanding of human nature goes against the dominant traditional view of the Western world. If Ultimacy defines the goal 1) toward which humans are naturally going, 2) is natural to humans (at least as a potential if not a latency), 3) is driving the force of development of our species, and 4) is objectively and unequivocally good (as it is seen by the Authors); then it follows that humans are naturally good and tending toward the good, and not sinful and tending toward evil. Furthermore, if goodness is innate, then humans are not dependent on intervention from any outside agent (either metaphysical or human) to have contact with goodness or Ultimacy. For many, it naturally follows that a person need only listen to or be sensitive to that which is within. Such listening and sensitivity is usually seen as an individual activity that cannot be engaged in for one person by someone else. The question then arises, "Will everyone who hears correctly and senses accurately, hear and sense the same thing?" The answer, according to the Authors and most forms of holistic education, seems to be "yes" and "no." There are general features of Ultimacy which all people have in common (e.g., discovering more fully who one is), but each person is also unique (e.g., each person's talents are different); therefore what each person discovers is both the same and different. This militates against education to fit an externally derived model of who a person *should* be, and sees the teacher as helping students find and actualize who they *are*. The Authors, in different ways, contend that this point has implications for questions of authority, freedom and the social order, as well as for damage to full human development which they all felt is associated with prescribed learning.

There are two important implications of this perspective of Ultimacy in relation to human nature. These implications are usually only implicit in much holistic education literature, and just as usually explicit in all the Authors.

1) As Ultimacy refers to some absolute or end point, if the challenges of Ultimacy are satisfied, then the lesser challenges are seen as

automatically satisfied. It amounts to saying that the greater encompasses the lesser (e.g. by understanding the way a whole engine works, one understands the role each separate part plays). The converse is not true; taking care of the lesser things does not necessarily add up to taking care of the greater ones. This may take the form of understanding the greater things so that lesser things can be undertaken more meaningfully (if not, in fact, better) which, in turn, makes a greater contribution to the performer's well-being as well as society's. There is also an implication that the more the whole is understood, the easier it is to make sense of the parts. In this there is a similarity to Systems Theory and Gestalt Psychology.

2) Ultimacy is seen as being reflected in what we might think of as primary human values (e.g., compassion, integrity, etc.) and these values are always good. There are also secondary human values (e.g., efficiency, hard work, etc.) that can and should be good, but are not necessarily so as they are context dependent. However, secondary values in association with primary values ensure that the secondary values are good (e.g., with compassion, efficiency will not be ruthless, which it might otherwise be). This implies that even the smallest of human or social activities must be approached with Ultimacy in mind, and by extension, with reference to education, that all education must be approached at the level of Ultimacy rather than at more superficial levels. The Authors do not suggest that what one might call non-ultimate concerns can be neglected (i.e., learning a skill or technique does have its own importance), only that, without Ultimacy, non-ultimate concerns will most likely have very little meaning (e.g., learning to write beautifully but having nothing to say).

ULTIMACY AS AN ASPECT OF RELIGIOUSNESS

As discussed above, the Authors saw Ultimacy as having extreme importance in people's lives—perhaps (after the needs of survival) penultimate importance. Mention has been made in the discussion above about the religious nature of some notions of Ultimacy, and this calls for further elaboration. To pursue this, a distinction needs to be made between *religions* and *religiousness*.

The Authors all felt that religions (as generally practiced, and even generally conceived) are too removed from the religiousness they felt is an aspect of Ultimacy. Consequently, the Authors (in different ways and to different extents) felt the need to create new senses of religiousness to get away from the inadequacies of traditional religions, including the limitations and conflicts they saw generated by and inherent in religions.

The new senses of religiousness the Authors discuss, however, are in all cases claimed by the Authors not to be new at all, but to be closer to the religiousness that lies at the origins of the "great and true" religions; a religiousness which has been forgotten, lost, or corrupted over time. As such, they felt that they were not being schismatic or contradicting the truths of existing religions, simply being truer to them than convention. This is probably the claim of most heretical and schismatic movements in history.

Such sentiments are certainly evident in many holistic education contentions having to do with what is usually described as "spiritual." Many proponents of the "spiritual" in holistic education eschew attempts to clarify or define too exactly what they mean by that term. They often claim that such attempts narrow or pervert a *sense* of what is "spiritual" into an *idea* of what is "spiritual," a trap that has corrupted most religions. In this they are true descendents of the Authors.

The early Authors distinguished *religiousness* from *religion* by allying themselves with what they believed to be the divine in nature—what they took to be naturally divine, and therefore in existence before humans. All of the early Authors are lamentably vague on exactly what they meant by *divine*, but we can deduce from their work that they believed the divine to be inherent in humans as it is inherent in all of nature. The divine seemed to have been for these early Authors more evident in nature than in people, although perceiving the *divine within* was the responsibility of each individual. The twentieth century Authors allied themselves with that which is in individuals that can sense, experience, or perceive the divine. The aspect of humans that can sense the divine is, in itself, seen as related to that which is divine—which these later Authors generally see as associated with the psyche or consciousness. This aspect amounts to the manifestation in humans of the divine which acts as a bridge to that which is divine and not in humans.

As the Authors claimed they were concerned with that which lies at the origins of all religions, and that which is in humans that is related to the divine, they made universal claims which they felt are beyond the limitations of time and place inherent in religions.

Holistic education's current attempts to also make claims about *religiousness* that is beyond any single *religion* have a new imperative. Our world is seen as having become so global and so pluralist that a person versed in only one expression of religious values is viewed as ethically and metaphysically inarticulate, and this is a potential problem. Religious wars are seen as wars over expressions rather than over fundamental "truths." Holistic education often promotes what some have called "secular-religiousness"— "secular" in that no religion is followed, but "religious" in that what is "sacred," or "divine," or "spiritual" is given great importance. Any ritual, ceremony, rite or icon from any religion has equal importance to those of any other religion or to any created by participants themselves. The importance of ritual, ceremony, rite or icon comes from the role these play in helping an individual approach Ultimacy rather than from their relation to dogma. Consequently, an icon created by an individual that plays a significant role in what that individual perceives to be an experience of Ultimacy is far more important than a culturally revered icon that plays no such role. To proponents of any single religion, this seems like heresy; a problem faced by all the Authors.

All of the Authors stated or implied that they came to their notions of religiousness from their own experiences and not from speculation, belief, or persuasion. It was a direct experience of religiousness that they felt gave them their authority to speak about it. Furthermore, they felt that other people (for some Authors, all other people) can experience this religiousness themselves. Such universality of potential acquisition was fundamental to the Authors, and is fairly common in holistic education—no one is inherently more likely to have a religious experience, and no single approach to Ultimacy which is suitable for one person is necessarily suitable for another.

An important aspect of the religiousness of Ultimacy rests in the notions of wholeness or oneness that are seen to lie at the origins of humanity. These notions seem to exist in three general forms:

1) Chronological notions. These presume that there was a time in history when people lived in wholeness or oneness. This historic state is our original state and, as such, is truer to our natures than the non-whole or multiplicity of states in which we currently generally live. This is supported especially by Rousseau and Pestalozzi.

2) Etiological notions. These claim that our individual origins, or each of our first causes, lie in a non-manifested state (or pre-manifestation state) of oneness or wholeness (e.g. God, Atman, etc.) and that we become fragmented either at birth or soon therafter. This view was principally held by Froebel, Pestalozzi and Jung.

3) Ontological notions. These argue that wholeness or oneness was, is and remains the foundation of our being and therefore the

fundamental state of our being; we just don't generally know it or live it. Jung, Maslow and Rogers expressed this point of view.

These categories are not mutually exclusive (as indicated by some Authors being listed in more than one category). For example, both Jung and Maslow were fascinated by the religiousness of pre-modernized indigenous peoples which they felt revealed the religiousness of the pre-modern world and, therefore, of the major religions (which all have pre-modern origins). This would be a chronological notion which Jung and Maslow do not otherwise display. Nevertheless, the primary thrust of the notions of wholeness or oneness of the Authors do, in the main, fall into one, or at most two, categories. In most holistic literature concerned with "spirituality" all three of these notions are generally conflated.

As the state of wholeness or oneness is seen as more original, truer and more authentic than non-whole or non-one states, and as people who experience such states confirm this perspective (as the Authors themselves attest), it naturally follows that there is a value in regaining, retaining, or re-perceiving such wholeness or oneness. This is usually spoken of with words that derive from *union* (e.g., unity, unite, unification, unison, etc.) or in terms that connote an ending of fragmentation (that results in union). These notions seem to exist in two forms:

1) Unification *of.* This involves the unification of different parts or aspects; e.g., faculties (Rousseau, Pestalozzi), "head, heart, and hand" (Froebel), the conscious and unconscious (Jung), feeling and thinking (Maslow and Rogers).

2) Unification *with.* This involves the unification of the individual with something outside of themselves or that is part of a larger self; e.g., with God (Froebel, Pestalozzi), with humanity at large (all of the Authors), *Unus Mundus* (Jung, Maslow).

In all cases, the wholeness or oneness that results from the unification conceived was seen by the Authors as an aspect of Ultimacy and as a form of religiousness. This unification for advocates of holistic education is even implied in the word "holistic" and which is often spelled "wholistic."

There is a complexity in examining notions of union which stems from the fact that terms deriving from "union" exist as nouns, verbs, and adjectives. Consequently, these terms describe states of being, actions, and qualities; and the relationships between these are anything but easily enunciated. For example, there are claims that the pre-existing unity thought to exist within a person must be seen by the person in order to bring about unification. One might ask, "If unity or wholeness already exists, what new unity or wholeness is there after such unification?" Similarly, there is thought to be a oneness of the universe, yet people seeing that they are one with the universe are seen as bringing about a oneness in themselves. Again, this can be seen as paradoxical. Although there are such paradoxes (which have been dealt with in some traditional esoteric literature), there are not necessarily any substantive contradictions. Close readings of the Authors' works show them often deliberately resolving these potential contradictions. The problems arise partly because there seem to be aspects, or what might be thought of as levels, of union (e.g., oneness with family, society, or humanity; a consciousness of unity is seen as different from the inherent unity that exists without that consciousness, etc.), and partly because of the problems inherent in any discussion in which ends and means are not entirely distinguishable.

CHAPTER 3

What Needs to Be Learned

*I*t seems safe to say that education is about learning and that learning involves the acquisition of knowledge. However, as Rousseau said, we can't know everything, we can't even know everything that is known to other people, so we need to choose what knowledge to acquire. It follows from this that we need to ask if all knowledge is of the same nature and, if not, do the different kinds of knowledge have different values? The answer to the first question for the Authors was clearly no; all knowledge is not the same.

One thing that distinguishes the Authors is that they did not categorize knowledge by its contents or by the mental processes that different contents require, unlike many modern philosophers of education. Knowledge of numbers was not seen by the Authors as different in any important sense from knowledge of words. However, the Authors did distinguish knowledge on the basis of how and why it is acquired.

The Authors and holistic education have two kinds of knowledge which they feel have preeminent importance: experiential knowledge and competence. Conceptual clarity about these two forms of knowledge was only clearly enunciated in the last half of the twentieth century, so that the early Authors and holistic educators have struggled to explain (often with limited success) what they mean. To understand, therefore, what holistic education feels needs to be learned, we must take the time to fully understand these two concepts of knowledge.

28

EXPERIENTIAL KNOWLEDGE

The Authors considered knowledge acquired from experience to be fundamentally different from knowledge acquired through abstractions or representations. Consequently, knowledge of how to sail a boat and knowledge of how to ride a bicycle, if both sets of knowledge are acquired only from books, are seen as fundamentally the same; while knowledge of how to sail a boat from a book is seen as fundamentally different from the same knowledge contents when acquired through experience. In holistic education this distinction is sometimes made using terms such as "authentic learning," "situated learning," or "experiential learning."

One of the claims made for experience is that it is the only way in which some kinds of knowledge can be acquired. While it is easy to understand this for some mundane examples (e.g., knowledge of colors[20]), it is more difficult to understand it for others. Knowing love may be a good example. A person may know *about* love from books, movies, other people's accounts, etc.; but they can only know *of* love from experiencing it. While this distinction is made by a few modern philosophers (e.g., John Wilson) it is as common in holistic education as it is foreign to mainstream education. What gives this distinction such importance for holistic education is the perception that experiential knowledge has a relation to Ultimacy. Such a relationship of knowledge from experience to Ultimacy is certainly made by the Authors—the "the divine within," "compassion," "*Unus Mundus*," "Being," etc., can only be known from experiencing them. As Ultimacy for holistic education has extraordinary importance, and most knowledge needed for Ultimacy can only be gained through experience, experiential knowledge as a class of knowledge assumes great importance; and this begins to answer the question as to the relative value of different kinds of knowledge for holistic education.

Experiential knowledge usually also distinguishes itself from the types of knowledge found in mainstream education on the basis of why that knowledge is acquired. An impulse to learn arising from within the learner (e.g., out of interest, or need) was seen by the Authors as resulting in a fundamentally different kind of knowledge from that which is acquired due to a secondary motivation (e.g., a reward or fear of punishment), even though both kinds of knowledge may ostensibly appear similar in the description of their contents. Consequently, knowledge of how to measure the angles of a triangle learned out of curiosity was seen by the Authors as fundamentally different from the same knowledge acquired in order to pass a test. This is partly due to the way in which curiosity is seen. Curiosity is not seen as generally being about disjointed information, but is instead interwoven with aspects of a student's life or world that have meaning to the student. Therefore, in the example above, curiosity about the angles of a triangle comes because a student wants *to do* something with that information or that information is part of some larger understanding that has meaning for the student. As such, it is part of the child's experience of the world.

The ascendance of experience (over the representative) for holistic educators is often justified by them in terms which clearly echo the early Authors whose position was seen to have been at least partly a "revolt against the traditions of the Renaissance or Revival of Learning … [which] had led to the enthronement, in all schools, of *book knowledge*."[21] For Rousseau, Pestalozzi, and Froebel, book knowledge is not knowledge that happens to be in books, but rather knowledge acquired from books. It is knowledge acquired from representations of things, rather than from direct experience of the things themselves. For the Authors, as well as for many holistic educators, "the word is not the thing,"[22] and to know the words which represent something is not the same as experientially knowing that thing itself. Because representative or abstracted knowledge was seen by the Authors as removed from the actual world (by virtue of its representative nature), it is not only different from knowledge that stemmed from "engaging with, and constructing, the world,"[23] it also plays a different role in life, and consequently has a very different value.

The values of the different kinds of knowledge seem derived from two criteria: the relation of the kind of knowledge to Ultimacy, and the usefulness of the knowledge in meeting the challenges of living. As mentioned briefly above, some knowledge necessary for Ultimacy can only be acquired from experience (e.g., Pestalozzi's "divine within," Maslow's "Being-knowledge," etc). Another kind of knowledge that is important for Ultimacy can be categorized as knowledge of the use of capacities required for Ultimacy (e.g., the capacities to see, sense, and listen 'within'—to either the divine or the psychological; being present or the capacity to only "exist where we are"[24]). It could be claimed that these are capacities rather than knowledge of the use of capacities, but 'competence' as a knowledge concept (as elucidated by Basil Bernstein, described below) bridges this seeming divide.

Experiential knowledge was also more valuable for the Authors because they perceived it as having greater pragmatic value. Even though knowledge from experience and knowledge from representations may appear to be the same on the basis of their contents (e.g., how to sail a boat from experience or from books) the Authors stated or implied that knowledge which originates in life can move to abstractions or concepts and then easily find application in experience again; whereas knowledge acquired from abstraction is difficult to apply to life, tending to remain only as abstractions. Therefore, all abstractions used to communicate knowledge (e.g., books, maps, numbers, and even words) were eschewed by the Authors for experiences that could lead to the same knowledge content. Modern holistic educators find support for this in the work of Montessori, Dewey, Piaget, and constructivist learning theory in which children are given materials and opportunities to learn something specific, but are left to discover what there is to learn rather than instructed in what to learn. It is only after learning from experience has occurred that the knowledge should be articulated by the teacher; a process which adds a representational knowledge dimension to the experiential knowledge base.

Of course, few holistic educators and none of the Authors would deny that children must be prepared to function in society, which implies acquiring certain academic skills and non-experiential knowledge. Some knowledge simply cannot be learned experientially (e.g., the square root of three). However, apart from Jung who seems not to have addressed this issue, all the Authors believed that such knowledge is of a much lower order than either experiential knowledge or competence; and they implied, if not stated, that acquiring representational knowledge occurs easily if the kind of learning they cared most for is given priority. It is a case of the greater encompassing the lesser.

COMPETENCE

The second kind of knowledge that holistic education promotes is called competence, and has been most effectively discussed by Basil Bernstein. This kind of knowledge should not be confused with what commonly passes by that name but which Bernstein feels is nothing more than a collection of generalized skills and which, therefore, would be more accurately called "generic performances."[25] A more complete discussion of competence occurs in Section III, but a small introduction is required here in order to understand holistic education.

Bernstein claims that competence as a knowledge concept solidified in the 1960s as a result of the work of Chomsky, Piaget, Lévi-Strauss, Garfinkle, Dell Hymes, and Wittgenstein.[26] However, the concept is evident, at least in an embryonic form, in the work of all the Authors and so goes back two hundred years before Bernstein feels the concept was explicated. In brief, competence refers to knowledge which is "the acquisition of...procedures"[27] rather than facts or ideas, and is of a general nature. Bernstein claims that competence has three essential characteristics: 1) it contains "procedures for engaging with, and constructing the world," 2) it is "intrinsically creative and tacitly acquired in informal interactions,"[28] and 3) it adheres to five elements of social logic described by Bernstein (and discussed beginning on page 218 .). The examples Bernstein gives of competence as a form of knowledge are the linguistic competence of Chomsky, the cognitive competence of Piaget, the cultural competence of Lévi-Strauss, the members/social competence of Garfinkle, and the communicative competence of Dell Hymes. If holistic education also promotes a form of competence, it will be necessary to describe what kind of competence that is.

For Bernstein, competence as a kind of knowledge is an important consideration as he wishes to distinguish what he feels are two very different kinds of education: competence based pedagogy and performance based pedagogy. Interestingly, all of the Authors (and subsequent supporters of holistic education) similarly contrast their approach to pedagogy with the mainstream pedagogy promoted in their time and place. Essentially they saw mainstream education as performance based pedagogy, in which students are expected to master certain performances (of reading, writing, math, etc.) with the display of performance as the basis for assessment. Competence based pedagogy involves the much more difficult to assess "procedures for engaging with, and constructing the world" which are "intrinsically creative and tacitly acquired in informal interactions."[29]

It may be easier for the reader to grasp the difference between performance based pedagogy and competence based pedagogy with the use of a metaphor. Consider the traditional education of Australian aboriginal children. Their instruction was informal but rigorous. It was acquired tacitly by engaging with and constructing their world aided by adults. The procedures they needed to learn were not broken up into performances which were abstracted from real life and learned separately. Assessment was not of a display of performances. Rather, when the child came of age and the adults thought the child was ready, the aboriginal child went alone into the desert on a "walk-about" for six months or longer. Survival was proof that the child had learned what was needed, and the child "graduated" into adulthood.

While all the Authors and the major branches of holistic education promote some procedures unique to their particular vision of competence, there is a core of procedures that most of them seem to share. This core of procedures unites the Authors and unites holistic education, and it is this core of procedures which makes the competence of holistic education distinct from that of Chomsky, Piaget, etc. While these procedures need to be discussed separately, it is a mistake to see them as separate. The Authors certainly saw these procedures as interdependent, often as two faces of the same coin. While each Author (and many forms of holistic education) has slightly different versions of these procedures, they generally have the following characteristics in common:

1) *The exercise of good judgment.* This involves a complex and subtle relationship to the world. It involves being able to see clearly the matters about which a judgment is to be made as well as the context of those matters. It also requires having sufficiently comprehensive and coherent values which serve as a basis of judgment. The exercise of good judgment also involves the quality of "resilience," an ability to make good judgments in bad circumstances. It has only been in the last ten years that the word "resilience" has been used to describe a quality or capacity that educators and child psychologists have tried to define and study. Nevertheless, versions of this capacity have long been recognized (and called by a variety of other names) and have been a central concern of holistic education. Resilience involves being able to face setbacks, overcome obstacles, persevere when success is not in sight, etc. This quality is evident in certain people, seems to be acquired, and should be a concern of education since dealing successfully with the substantive challenges of life seems to require it. All of the Authors gave it (by other names) prominence in their view of what education should help children learn, and saw it as related to having good judgment.

2) *The ability to be free.* While there are certain political connotations to the freedom promoted by the Authors and holistic education, it is not political freedom that is most highly valued. Freedom from psychological authorities is generally discussed in far greater depth, and this generally includes freedom from destructive conditioning, habits, and opinions (even one's own). Consequently, there is a correlation between such freedom and what is often translated as "liberation" in many Eastern religious texts.

3) *The ability to discover and refine values.* The emphasis in this is on "discovering" and "refining." To simply absorb or take on the values

of another person, religion, culture, etc. is thought of as counterproductive. Values are not thought of as arbitrary or relative, but as rooted in either the nature of humans, life or something more universal. As values are thought of as having such roots, they are able to be discovered, and being discovered have a far greater meaning to the discoverer. Also, acquisition of values through discovery avoids the impingement of freedom which the imposition of values (through training, conditioning, etc.) necessarily involves.

Learning to love was seen by all the Authors and is generally acknowledged by holistic education to be a cornerstone to discovering and refining values. While romantic love played an important and separate part in Rousseau's approach to education, for the most part holistic educators promote love in a more generalized form. Love of one's family, of children, and of fellow humans (or even all other sentient beings as in Buddhism), and compassion are seen as indispensable to a real understanding of the world and of oneself. Many of the early holistic educators presaged a modern understanding of social development: that love is related to empathy, and empathy is necessary for social development and an internalization of values needed for pro-social behavior.

As will be seen later, love is also the foundation for the pedagogic relationship of holistic education; rather than the respect, admiration or even fear many teachers have tried to engender.

4) *Meta-learning.* This refers to learning how to learn, and more specifically, learning how oneself, as an individual, learns. People are seen as learning in a variety of different ways, and one needs to understand one's own learning processes in order to be responsible for learning. This is seen as essential for becoming an independent learner and the much-trumpeted 'life long learning'. It is only by being responsible for one's own learning that a person is seen as being able to learn judgment, have freedom, discover and refine values, etc.

5) *Social-ability.* This is not sociability and does not indicate conviviality. It refers to ability in social contexts, with "ability" indicating successful negotiation of the context while simultaneously living according to one's greatest truths (i.e., approaching Ultimacy). Social-ability also does *not* refer to, what are often called, "social skills," which generally implies artfulness with the semiotics of a culture and therefore great immersion in that culture. The Authors indicated that social-ability implies being *in* a society but not *of* it; a distinction which the Authors felt most people do not maintain. Many of the Authors, when they indicated a stage of development in which such social-ability can

be learned, felt this is learned later in life than the other characteristics of competence. Before it is learned, the Authors felt, a child must be protected from being overwhelmed or taken in by the very social elements through which they will eventually need to learn to negotiate with integrity. Social-ability seems to have features that are unique amongst the other procedure of holistic education competence. It is the only procedure that is not predominantly intrapsychic, referring instead to a person's relationship with the extrapsychic. However, that relationship was perceived by the Authors to be determined by the intrapsychic. As such, social-ability is seen as determined by the other characteristics previously listed.

As these core procedures of a competence envisaged by the Authors and holistic education have similarities (though they can not be said to be identical), it seems appropriate to propose a term to denote this particular kind of competence. All of these views of competence are linked to common notions of "wisdom" and are seen as significant to approaching Ultimacy. For this reason, it would seem reasonable to call this form of competence "sagacious competence," indicating its nature and to distinguish it from the other competences (e.g., Chomsky's, Piaget's, etc.) mentioned above. It is the Authors' link between sagacious competence and Ultimacy that gives their work importance for today's holistic educators to the extent that it is those aspects of the Authors' work (i.e., the link between sagacious competence and Ultimacy) that are most referred to in holistic education literature. None of the Authors are adopted completely by holistic education today, and the list of what holistic educators do not try to emulate in the Authors' work would be long.

More detailed discussion of the distinction between performance based pedagogy and competence based pedagogy is reserved for Section III. It must suffice for now to say that the five procedures of holistic education competence listed above cannot be construed as performances; cannot be learned through any combination of skills, facts, or concepts; and cannot be assessed through any single or series of performances. They were seen as being learned only through experience, and exposure to them through representations (e.g., maxims, precepts, aphorisms, etc.) prior to an experience of them was thought by the Authors to inhibit the development of competence. As a consequence, pedagogy based mainly on the transfer of information, skills or concepts, was seen as more than merely inadequate; it was seen as inhibiting the needed learning. While there can be experiential knowledge which does not lead to sagacious competence (e.g., learning how to ride a bicycle), the Authors insisted that sagacious competence cannot be acquired without experiential knowledge. Therefore, the relationship between experiential knowledge and competence seems in significant ways to be synergistic; they derive their importance to the question of "what needs to be learned?" from their existence as a compound entity that has relevance to approaching Ultimacy.

CHAPTER 4

What Facilitates
the Needed Learning

*F*rom the examination of what holistic education believes needs to be learned, the question naturally follows: "How does such learning come about?" For the Authors this is not a question about what *causes* the needed learning, as the causal dynamic seems rarely to be implied. Rather it is a question of what *facilitates* the needed learning. This distinction is important. The answer to what might facilitate the needed learning seems two-fold, as there are two major categories of facilitating factors: 1) aspects of the students, and 2) aspects of the teachers. Some educators may find it curious that neither facilities nor learning materials are seen by the Authors as necessary to facilitate the needed learning, although two of them (Pestalozzi and Froebel) saw some materials as helpful. There is technically a third factor that facilitates the needed learning; namely, family members, especially mothers. This is especially marked in the work of the early Authors as they were writing at a time when there was very little early childhood education except by mothers. There was no public education and only the wealthy could turn their children over to nannies and tutors. However, what is said of teachers in this analysis is also said of parents and other family members as well, so that leaving out aspects of family as a separate category does not exclude anything important.

In general, most of the aspects of the students that facilitate the needed learning are seen as fixed by nature, while most of the aspects of teachers that facilitate the needed learning are the result of the teachers' agency. The students have inherent learning processes (including stages of development fixed by nature), and intrinsic motivation (also fixed by nature), although the more mature elements of motivation are seen to be partly of the students' agency. Yet even such agency is not entirely left to the students as the Authors see, for the most part, that it is up to the teachers to inspire such motivation.

The aspects of the teachers that facilitate the needed learning are more complex, and for the most part involve both the teachers' understanding, and their acting on such understanding. Teachers are seen as needing to understand four elements: 1) the individual students and their needs, 2) the correct pedagogic process, 3) the correct pedagogic relationship, and 4) the importance of their own self-development. The only aspects of the teachers that facilitate the needed learning that are seen as partially fixed by nature are some subtle and often esoteric elements of the correct pedagogic relationship, although it is within the agency of the teacher to act in ways which engage those aspects.

In examining holistic education there is a frequent conflation of elements. We can't, for example, discuss the learning process without some discussion of the learner. In exploring what facilitates the needed learning, much that is in both of the previous two chapters (Ultimacy and what needs to be learned) is necessarily interwoven. One sees, for example, that one can't very well discuss what facilitates the needed learning without reference to what needs to be learned or what the goal of that learning is. All of the Authors have this same problem, which reflects the holistic nature of their approach to education.

It is in the discussions by the Authors of what facilitates the needed learning that the Authors most frequently juxtaposed their notions of education with what they felt occurred in the mainstream education of their time. For many holistic educators, this is interesting because much of what the Authors were against has remained part of mainstream education to this day. The Authors often seem to use this juxtaposition as though they could only fully show what they were for by indicating what they were against. This 'location through opposition' is also true for many people involved in holistic education today; however, unlike the Authors, many in holistic education do not 'positively locate' their pedagogy by spelling out what they are for. To say simply that "we are against grades" or "we are against coercion" doesn't say what is being promoted.

ASPECTS OF STUDENTS THAT FACILITATE
THE NEEDED LEARNING

The Authors claim that the aspects of the students that facilitate the needed learning are inherent. There are two such aspects which all the Authors discuss: 1) an inherent learning process, and 2) inherent motivation. The Authors felt that learning is not an alien activity, but rather a capacity which people are born with and which develops as people mature. The various Authors see both the inherent learning process and inherent motivation slightly differently, and these differences are reflected in different approaches to holistic education, but these differences provide little conflict. Similarly, one can find in a single holistic school the learning process described in Piagetian terms as well as Vygotskyian terms—real differences with no necessary conflict. However, in general the inherent learning process is seen as moving from the simple to the complex, and doing so in stages. Inherent motivation is seen as originating in the simple need to survive and developing through social needs to a "natural" need for Ultimacy (discussed previously).

Inherent Learning Process

All the Authors agree that humans have inherent learning processes which develop until at least early adulthood (with the later Authors contending it is life-long) and that these inherent learning processes can be utilized, ignored, or violated by education. Unsurprisingly, the Authors feel that education should utilize these inherent processes.

While there are some differences between the Authors as to the nature of the inherent learning processes, they agree that wanting to learn is so much a part of being human that it forms part of the definition of what it means to be human. The Authors also seem to agree that the inherent learning processes develop in stages, although they have different descriptions of these stages, and different ages at which the stages occur. This difference in descriptions of the stages has to be seen in the light of the Authors living in very different historical contexts and having different foci. While all of the Authors have Ultimacy as their goal, they focus on different elements in a child's development to identify the stages. Consequently, although the stages of development identified by the Authors differ, they are not contradictory. For example, Rousseau largely identified the ability to form different kinds of concepts (e.g., geometrical vs. historical concepts) as the basis for the stages of development. Pestalozzi and Froebel agreed with Rousseau but added some abilities to engage in certain kinds of academic operations (e.g., singing, drawing, writing, etc.). Jung, Maslow and Rogers principally identified elements of the developing psyche. Similarly in holistic education, those who look at neurological development see the stages of development differently from those who look at "spiritual" development.

What is agreed upon is that the inherent learning processes follow laws that are both general and particular. The stages of development of the inherent learning process have a sequence that is common for almost all people (i.e., stage one comes before stage two, etc.) and this sequence constitutes a general law. However, the laws are also particular to each individual in that these stages proceed at idiosyncratic paces, and often have idiosyncratic expressions. No two children just because they are of the same age should be expected to have their inherent learning processes at the same stage of development, and no two students whose learning processes are at same stage of development should be expected to express those stages in the same way. Hence, in many holistic schools, students are grouped by perceived learning stage (and, therefore, with a learning process affinity) rather than by chronological age.

Another point of agreement between the Authors is that if either the sequencing or the pacing of the student's inherent learning processes are violated, damage to the student occurs—perhaps lasting damage. Long before Freud, Froebel warns:

> Wounds and lacks in childhood are never recouped and remain wounds. Look to the scars on our own souls to see the truth of this.[30]

What is important to the Authors is that the inherent learning processes in the students have a chance to develop fully, and all of the Authors contend that how this is to be done cannot be known beforehand. They also seem to agree that any information acquired as knowledge is very much of secondary importance to the development of the learning processes.

From the above it follows that the curriculum planning and grading by age of mainstream education are incompatible with holistic education. What is required instead is a much more tailored form of education that follows and fits the individual child's development; which all the Authors agree is a far more demanding role for a teacher than that which they perceived to generally exist in mainstream education.

Inherent Motivation

Like the inherent learning processes, the Authors claimed that people are inherently motivated to acquire the needed learning. Also like the inherent learning processes, this motivation can be harnessed or violated, nourished or crippled. The use of secondary motivation (e.g., money, grades, gold stars, public praise, etc.) for all the Authors is either dismissed as ineffectual or denounced as damaging. It is interesting to note the amount of research that supports their view, yet how little impact such research has had on education in general.

From Rousseau's natural *amour de soi* to Maslow's hierarchy of needs and homeostasis, people are seen as being naturally motivated to acquire the needed learning. However, this motivation is seen as being able to operate only under ideal conditions and, unfortunately (due to various reasons depending on the Author), these conditions do not generally exist. These reasons range from Rousseau's belief that man has developed through civilization beyond the reach of natural impetuses and responses, to Maslow's contention that a person's upbringing deafens him to the inner calls.

The conclusion of all the Authors is that the inherent aspects of the students, which should naturally facilitate the needed learning, are no longer sufficient, so that teachers become necessary. There is not unanimous agreement on this conclusion amongst holistic educators. Some (following A.S. Neill) contend that children need only be left to their own devices, and they will naturally come to what is best for them.

ASPECTS OF TEACHERS THAT FACILITATE THE NEEDED LEARNING

Unlike the aspects of the students that facilitate the needed learning which are inherent, the aspects of the teachers that facilitate the needed learning need to be acquired. The Authors see teachers as needing to acquire different understandings: 1) of students and their needs, 2) of the correct pedagogic practice, 3) of the correct pedagogic relationship, and 4) of the importance of their own self-development.

This topic necessarily intertwines in the Authors' writings with their discussions of Ultimacy, the needed learning, and aspects of the students that facilitate the needed learning. Nevertheless, all the Authors made deliberate efforts to communicate the role of the teachers as all were involved in teaching teachers (or teaching therapists whose role is educative); therefore all were especially concerned to communicate what they saw as the special role of the teacher in the students' acquisitions of the needed learning.

Teachers' Understanding of Students and their Needs

All the Authors felt that teachers need to understand generalities about students, but they were all adamant that such understanding is only the basis for the more important particular understanding of each student as an individual. The Authors were insistent that education is always of individuals and not of amalgams (e.g., "classes" or "student bodies").

The Authors claimed that each person has an inherent and unique self (at least as a potential or latency). If this is not the case, then the self must be the product of inheritance, or conditioning ("construction," either personal or social), in which case it cannot be related to that which is unconditional (which they all contend is an aspect of Ultimacy). However, if people have unique inherent selves, then it follows that each has a unique form into which that person should develop. Such a unique form, for the Authors, is determined by nature, God, destiny, etc. but never by people. Consequently, any attempt to determine the form into which another person develops is necessarily a corruption. Furthermore, as the unique intrinsic form of everyone is seen as related to the fullest possible development, it is also related to approaching Ultimacy. Consequently, the Authors saw the attempt to determine the form another person should develop into as not just a corruption, but as a sacrilege as well. Other people (e.g., a teacher) may facilitate the development of a student's inherent form or true self, or they can pervert and/or hinder such development.

Teachers' Understanding of the Correct Pedagogic Process

The teachers' understanding of the correct pedagogic process must obviously be part of what would facilitate the needed learning. Obviously also, from all that has been said, the correct pedagogic process must be determined by the Authors' notions of what needs to be learned and make most use of those aspects of students that facilitate the needed learning.

A distinction needs to be made between notions of a pedagogic *process* and details of a pedagogic *practice*. It is the difference between the nature of pedagogic activities and the exact form those activities take. Rousseau made this distinction and claimed that the details of practice must vary with each student according to their temperament and context, and were of little importance. He gives the details of his imaginary practice with Emile as examples, but warns that they are not to be imitated blindly. Pestalozzi and Froebel wrote a great deal about both the process and the details of their evolving practices as they were trying to instruct teachers for particular contexts. However, that context no longer exists and it is only their notions of the process that have relevance for holistic education. The modern Authors gave greater emphasis to the processes in their work than to the details of practice. However, all of the Authors felt that the correct pedagogic process was following nature, both human nature in general and the nature of the individual student in particular. All of the Authors also felt that a large part of the correct pedagogic process is simply preventing damage (Rousseau's "negative education") rather than the determining, shaping role they all saw as existing in most approaches to education.

The inherent learning processes are seen as naturally elaborating from the simple to the subtle and complex. The correct pedagogic process must elaborate with the learning process, following it rather than determining it. In this the students are seen as needing to be active co-determiners of the pedagogic practice (and perceive themselves as such) because: 1) such a role facilitates the needed development of certain aspects of students (e.g., responsibility, freedom, self-expression); and 2) it ensures that the pedagogic practice reflects the students' natures, allowing them to unfold. What was important for the Authors is the elaboration of the learning process in the students, not what is learned (although learning what is needed for successful negotiation in society had unquestioned value for them), because it is the elaboration of the learning process that is linked to Ultimacy. Learning something extremely subtle requires a learning process that is extremely subtle. As Ultimacy, for the Authors, requires balance and unity, the learning processes and the pedagogic processes must also be balanced and have harmony as they elaborate. For the Authors this means avoiding over-development in any sphere as the process elaborates. One of the over-developments that all the Authors felt existed in most approaches to the education of their day was an over-emphasis on intellectual development at the expense of the social and emotional. It may surprise some modern holistic educators that this common complaint of theirs has been made for almost two hundred and fifty years.

Teachers' Understanding of the Correct Pedagogic Relationship

For holistic education the correct pedagogic relationship is an indispensable part of the correct pedagogic process, yet it is distinct enough to merit a separate discussion. We know from research that certain kinds of mechanical learning, often called training (like the training of animals), can be accomplished with fear. However, for learning that requires internalized understanding, meaning-making, or any kind of creativity, fear cannot be part of the learning process. Not only can fear not be present, but positive feelings of empathy and even affection must exist between the teacher and the student as it is only this kind of relationship which can act as a conduit for our deepest learning. Goethe is often quoted as saying, "We only learn from those we love," and this is echoed by all of the Authors. Besides being a conduit for meaning, affection is also spoken of as providing the security needed for the daring act of really questioning and being vulnerable to new understandings. To "not know" is insecure, but it is also necessary for learning.

Being treated with affection and empathy by a person with far greater social power (e.g., a teacher) is also thought of as the way a student learns to similarly treat others with less social power. As such, the correct pedagogic relationship is seen as laying an important foundation for social life and social justice. The all too common bullying that is found in schools (by the Authors in their day as well as by holistic educators now) is not seen as behavior that is inherent in youth, but as a demonstration of learned social interaction: all too often learned in the pedagogic relationship. The pedagogic relationship is not just part of the context of learning, it is an important part of the content as well.

The correct pedagogic relationship also requires trust in the students' inherent goodness. It would be difficult, at best, to have affection and empathy for an entity seen as inherently evil or sinful (which still exists as a vestige from our medieval European past). It would also be difficult, if not impossible, to give students the freedom they need to unfold into their unique selves (as discussed above) if they can not be trusted. Trust (or distrust) is also seen as generating the same feeling in the other party, and a teacher who isn't trusted is ineffectual.

Part of the way in which teachers show trust is to present themselves honestly (within the bounds of what is socially appropriate), without pretence or affectation. This is much more difficult than it might initially appear. Teaching is a social role; and not "playing" a role, not projecting an image, not presenting a persona is a real challenge. However, some things can only be learned in relationship, and those things are almost always contained in the relationship (e.g., learning affection from an affectionate relationship, learning to question oneself and being open to change from someone doing those things, etc.). If the pedagogy is to extend beyond the superficial, then the pedagogic relationship must equally extend beyond the superficial.

Unlike many relationships in which the nature of the relationship is seen as the responsibility of all the participants, the correct pedagogic relationship was seen by all the Authors as being only in the purview of the teachers. While this may seem obvious when dealing with infants, the Authors maintained this perspective even for students who are adult.

Teachers' Self-Development

While the Authors all felt that the students' learning processes need to be linked to the correct pedagogic process, they also felt that both of these are linked to the self-development of the teachers. Part of what a student experiences in education is the teacher, and what the student experiences of the teacher is what the teacher actually *is*, not what the teacher pretends or intends to be. It follows for all the Authors that if an important part of the students' experiential learning is their experience of the teachers, then a sure way of improving the nature of the students' learning is to improve the nature of what they experience. This means the improvement of teachers.

Teacher improvement can, however, mean many things. It can mean improvement in teaching skills, and all the Authors advocated this. However, improved teaching skills is not what any of the Authors felt was most important. They all felt that the most significant aspect of teacher improvement was personal development, not unlike the development intended for students.

Notions of self-development for the early Authors seem to revolve mostly around the development of virtue, morals, and religiousness. For the later Authors, notions of the psychological and religious fuse (as seen in the previous discussion on Ultimacy), and notions of development revolve around development of the psyche—a multiplicity of notions of development reflected in various forms of holistic education today. For all the Authors, however, the teachers' self-development was seen as an essential element in the students' education. Like the pedagogic relationship in which the nature of what is communicated is embedded in the nature of the exchange itself, teachers are seen as only being able to accomplish with the students what they are able to accomplish with themselves. This contrasts sharply with training in which the trainer need not be able to accomplish what he is training others to do (e.g., an Olympic swimming coach need not be an Olympic swimmer). There is an implication that, as what needs to be learned is the synergistic compound of experiential knowledge and sagacious competence, teachers should have their own experiential learning of sagacious competence present when engaging with students. The Authors imply that the teachers experiencing their own development is a principal way in which the students (vicariously or by way of empathy) can gain important lessons in development. In its simplest form, this is experiential learning through seeing someone else experience something, but in its more subtle forms this is a communication through sharing experiences in which the teachers directly contribute to the students' development by their own self-development. As love between the students and the teacher is seen by the Authors as a special conduit for certain kinds of learning, so too the teachers' deliberate self-development combined with the natural development of the young generates another important conduit for learning.

Summary of Section I

While the details of what all the Authors felt is the goal of education were different, the notions are all similar in that they can be described by the term "Ultimacy." These notions seem not to contradict one another so much as reflect the different times in which the Authors lived and wrote. This is seen even in the translations of the same work that appeared at different times (e.g., the earlier translations of Froebel sound more conventionally Christian than later translations of the same piece). Similarly, the different notions of Ultimacy in holistic education often reflect only the culture of their constituency (e.g., Japanese holistic schools versus California holistic schools), current fads (e.g., native American mythology, or EST), or the inclinations of a predominance of the staff (e.g., toward Sufism, or Transcendental Meditation), etc. It is even common for holistic schools to move through a variety of notions of Ultimacy much as an individual might in trying to "find themselves."

The various notions of Ultimacy are all seen as having great importance by their adherents because Ultimacy is viewed as fundamental to human nature. Humans are seen as constituted so that their well-being (at least psychologically and physiologically if not materially) depends on approaching or achieving Ultimacy. The extent to which a person achieves it is seen by the Authors as determining the extent of that person's meaningful success in life, or the extent to which that person has succeeded in living meaningfully (an equation most holistic educators would make). This stems from the Authors' views of "meaningful" and relates to their views of the sacred which, in all cases, is imbedded in a state of being or a religiousness, and not in any particular religion. The latter was felt by the Authors to be bound by time and culture, dogmatic, and (for some) of suspicious origin or intent. Religiousness, on the other hand, was felt by the Authors to be in nature (including human nature), universal, and with no permanent form. The Authors believed that people can come upon religiousness through their own experience (as they felt they had) and that such experiences are ones of unity (wholeness, oneness, or an ending of fragmentation) and harmony or balance. In the twentieth century, Ultimacy within the individual became clearly sited in the psyche, and consciousness was seen as the locus of union, wholeness, and balance that could lead to the universal. Such Ultimacy, because it is related to what is ultimately and universally religious, is beyond the purview of conventional science; and since such Ultimacy is also seen as inherent in human nature, it follows that the study of humans cannot be confined to the limitations of conventional science or logic.

If, as will be shown, the Authors contend that an individual's relationship to Ultimacy determines that individual's success in life, then it follows that they would also see Ultimacy as establishing the trajectory of intended development for younger people, and therefore as what should be the principle concern of education. This sets their views of education apart from others who see the principal goal of education as preparation for earning a living, citizenship, or entering a cultural discourse. And this is precisely why the Authors are seen by proponents of holistic education to establish their intellectual precedents. The confluence of the purpose of life and the purpose of education and the link of both with Ultimacy is the cornerstone of holistic education.

The answer to the question, "What does holistic education contend needs to be learned?" is two fold: 1) experiential knowledge, and 2) sagacious competence. Of course, there are also minor answers as well, which some approaches to holistic education would have in common (e.g., the skills necessary for earning a living, relationship skills, etc.) and others which would be unique to a particular approach to holistic education (e.g., Vipassana meditation).

Some things—often the most important—can only be known from experience (e.g., Rousseau's "man's estate," Pestalozzi's "the divine within," Jung's "*Unus Mundus*," Maslow's "self-actualization," etc.). Things which can only be known through representations (e.g., the square root of three, the distance to the moon, etc.) may have pragmatic value, but they tend not to have as much significance for meaningful daily living or for approaching Ultimacy.

Experiential knowledge was generally seen by the Authors to have greater value than non-experiential knowledge because they saw it as more "real," "significant," "meaningful," "veridical," etc. The reasons for this greater meaningfulness is that the Authors saw experiential knowledge as: 1) being more easily applicable to life, 2) involving more than just the intellect (i.e., the heart, unconscious, etc.), and 3) resulting from being discovered rather than being received, and therefore connected with more aspects of each learner's life. These same reasons for the value of experiential knowledge are repeatedly found in the literature of holistic education and are supported by countless anecdotes.

Integrally related to notions of experiential knowledge are notions of self-knowledge. This is partly because it is only through experience that one can know the self, and partly because the self is always what does the experiencing. Perspectives on the nature of self evolved dramatically during the more than two hundred and fifty years that spanned the Authors' lives,[31] so it shouldn't surprise us that there are differences in the Authors' portrayals of the self. What is surprising are the similarities in their notions. They all felt that the self is essentially inherent and needs to be discovered, not constructed. They also felt that emotional development is an important element of such discovery, partly because emotions were seen as an aspect of the self and partly because the emotions were seen as a gateway to understanding deeper aspects of self. Self-knowledge was also seen as a cornerstone of social development. On the simplest level this is true because people must know themselves to know how they are affected by and affect others. On a more subtle level, the Authors all contended that self-knowledge leads to a lessening of the separation between oneself and others through compassion or a sense of "oneness" with humanity.

Competence is the second form of knowledge which holistic education feels needs to be learned. Competence (as the word is used in this book) is a tacitly acquired compound of procedures. This compound needs to be thought of as a single entity, even though it can be seen to be composed of distinct elements. An example of this is the act of speaking which can be thought of as a single action but which is composed of several elements (e.g., thinking, remembering words, framing sentences, expelling air from the lungs, manipulating the tongue, etc.). The form of competence promoted by holistic education is being called sagacious competence because of its relationship to what has traditionally been thought of as wisdom.

An aspect of both experiential knowledge and competence which has great significance is the manner in which they need to be acquired. Different kinds of knowledge require different forms of acquisition; learning about the atmosphere of Mars can be done by reading a book, while learning how to ride a bicycle cannot be done by reading. Experiential knowledge and competence are such completely different kinds of knowledge to the knowledge that preoccupies mainstream education, that they require a different form of pedagogy; hence the distinction made by holistic educators, all the Authors, and Bernstein between what Bernstein called competence based pedagogy and performance based pedagogy.

The question, "what facilitates the needed learning" rather than "what causes it" avoids causal questions which the Authors eschewed. Like the maxim, "You can lead a horse to water but you can't make him drink," the Authors claimed that a teacher can provide opportunities for meaningful understanding, but can't make students meaningfully understand. In this regard, the Authors made distinctions between "real" (or situated, concrete, etc.) knowledge and "non-real" (or abstract, representational, etc.) knowledge; between knowing with one's head and knowing with one's heart, hand, or, better still, with one's whole being. This non-causal learning militates against the model of teachers and schools as agents and students as the objects of agency.

Aspects of the students themselves facilitate the needed learning but, this is saying more than that the nature of the vessel determines what can be put into it (e.g., molten metal can't be put into a porcelain bowl, or fine sand into a rough sieve, etc.). Students have agency in needed learning, and most of what gives them agency is inherent. Students have inherent learning processes and inherent motivation. The inherent learning process is seen as an innate human tendency to absorb information needed for meaningful living, and then to group and characterize such information as generalizations or abstractions. Such a natural formation of abstractions is seen as allowing the application of abstractions to the concrete. An increasing complexity of the learning process (i.e., absorbing information, generalizing, applying generalities to particulars, etc.) develops by stages. While the Authors felt that the sequence in development generally held for everyone, the pacing and expression of stages must, of necessity, be idiosyncratic as everyone is a unique individual.

The motivation which is seen as inherent is intrinsically related to the inherent learning process as this is what motivates the process to absorb the needed learning and organize it. Such motivation (notions of which were described by all the Authors, from Rousseau's *amour de soi* to Maslow's hierarchy of needs) is part of being human.

Allowing the inherent learning processes and motivation were seen by the Authors as necessary for balanced and natural growth. The imposition of artificial learning processes or motivation (i.e., rewards and punishments) were seen as distorting. To continue the horticultural metaphor favored by the early Authors, a tree artificially stimulated to grow with fertilizers for too long will not have the strength or the root structure to survive when such stimulation is removed or the environment becomes unusually challenging.

Unlike the aspects of the students, the aspects of the teachers that facilitate the needed learning are acquired. What is most important to acquire, however, is understanding not techniques or procedures. In this, the understanding to be acquired by the teachers mirrors the experiential learning and sagacious competence described as that which needs to be learned by the students. While some of what the teachers must understand involves 'head knowledge' (e.g., the stages of development), much of it involves constantly understanding anew, or discovering, the individual student. This constant understanding anew or discovery of the students is seen as important to engage in with the students so that the students can learn to do it by themselves. This militates against trying to determine what a student "should be" (except in the most general terms).

The teachers' understanding of the correct pedagogic process is largely one of preventing damage to the students' inherent learning processes and motivation. It is not a process which has intentions to 'shape'. Like the students' learning processes, it moves from simple to complex. Part of the correct pedagogic process is that the students need to be agents in the process and need to perceive themselves as such. The Authors felt this is the only way students can learn important elements of sagacious competence (e.g., exercising good judgment, freedom, etc.). The correct pedagogic process also ensures balance in development rather than specialization (seen by the Authors as socially sanctioned imbalance).

An essential aspect of the correct pedagogic process is the pedagogic relationship. This is a relationship of mutual affection and empathy, and as such, is part of what needs to be learned. But the pedagogic relationship is a result of what the teacher *is*, which makes the teacher's self-development a major responsibility of the teacher. The Authors all indicate that what a teacher *is* is a large part of what that teacher teaches. A teacher's character is part of what a student experiences, and in experiential learning, as one wants to deepen what the student experiences, there is a necessary concern for deepening the teacher. As such, the development of teachers both reflects and facilitates what needs to be learned.

An Analysis of the Ideas of Holistic Education Through Examining Six Founding Authors

Introduction to Section II

*I*n this section the work of the six Authors who make up the intellectual precedents of holistic education is examined in historical order. No attempt is made at a complete synopsis of their work but only those aspects of their work which have relevance for holistic education. Consequently, for each author, there is an examination only of the notions explicated in the previous section. Hence, for each Author there is an examination of their notion of Ultimacy including the relationship of Ultimacy to human nature and Ultimacy as an aspect of religiousness. In exploring each Author's views of what needs to be learned, there is also an examination of their views of experiential knowledge and competence. In trying to understand what each Author says about what facilitates the needed learning, there is an exploration of the aspects of the students they felt facilitated the needed learning and the aspects of the teachers that facilitate the needed learning.

As we are exploring the intellectual precedents of holistic education, we are looking for the first instance of a notion or for significant variations. Many of the Authors repeat what previous Authors had said (and in fact often quote them), so there would be a tedious repetition if all of their views on the above list of topics were covered. Therefore, only when there is a new variation or a different emphasis is an Author's view explicated. Consequently, more attention is given to Rousseau who formulated the greatest number of original notions with regard to holistic education. As Pestalozzi developed Rousseau's work, and Froebel developed Pestalozzi's work, subsequent chapters on these Authors are shorter. With Carl Jung, the new discipline of psychology is broached, so that many original notions first appear which find their way into holistic education. There is also a very different approach to psychology with Maslow and Rogers (humanistic psychology), and many new notions absorbed by holistic education are introduced in the Maslow chapter. However, for the purposes of holistic education Maslow was very similar to Rogers, so that, many of the comments which both of them hold are found in the chapter on Maslow simply because Maslow is discussed first. Consequently, the chapter on Rogers (as it follows the one on Maslow) is shorter, but Rogers' contribution to holistic education is at least as significant as Maslow.

All the variations of the notions found in the Authors for the topics listed above can be thought of as the "gene pool" for the "family resemblances" of holistic education. It is the blending of these "genes" which gives modern forms of holistic education their rich variance while still allowing them to be recognizable.

CHAPTER 5

Jean-Jacques Rousseau

A BIOGRAPHICAL SKETCH
OF JEAN-JACQUES ROUSSEAU
(28 JUNE 1712 – 2 JULY 1778)

R ousseau's life combined intellectual brilliance with squandered opportunity, great admiration with relationship failure, longing for stability with continual upheaval. The negative aspects of his life are often a point of criticism to modern commentators, yet this may well be unjust and uninformed as there is every reason to believe he was the victim of a clinical personality disorder which would have been diagnosed today but which was unknown in his time.

Rousseau's mother died at his birth, and he was left in the care of his egocentric and violently tempered father. In fact, from the little we know of Rousseau's father, he also displayed the fury and relationship difficulties that plagued Rousseau and, as such personality disorders often have a hereditary component, the case for Rousseau having something like oppositional-defiant disorder is strengthened. In any event, Rousseau's erratic sometime-watchmaker father had to flee Geneva when Rousseau was about eight as a consequence of threatening someone with a sword (which according to his social class he was not allowed to wear, but which, for the sake of pretence, he often sported).

Rousseau spent the next six years as an unwanted orphan in his mother's family (who despised his father) during which time he was badly treated and humiliated. Rousseau applauds his father's upbringing and education of him because it was mostly *laissez-faire,* and Rousseau remembers his childhood with his father as happy compared to his time with his mother's family. He was an avid reader as a child, but he was mostly self-taught.

Due to his 'bookishness' he was apprenticed to a notary at the age of 14, but this failed for some reason lost to history. He was then apprenticed to a coppersmith who ruled him with iron discipline and harsh punishment. At the age of 16 he escaped from this regime by running away and simply wandered around France and Sardinia.

Although a Protestant, he was eventually taken in by some Catholic priests at Consignon in Savoy (a duchy which included, in Rousseau's time, Sardinia, Sicily, parts of France, and parts of Italy) and was eventually turned over by them to Madame de Warens. She was a Baroness living in Annecy (part of Savoy) with both a remarkable method and a remarkable success rate for converting young Swiss Protestant males to Catholicism. She had herself been a Swiss Protestant, married a Swiss Baron who she fleeced for most of his money before running away to France with the gardener's son where she became Catholic. What is significant about Madame de Warens for Rousseau is not just his temporary conversion to Catholicism, nor the fact that he later returned to her household and educated himself there for eight years, but that he probably first heard from her the views that humans are naturally good and that nature itself is good. As a child Warens had studied with a collection of Protestant mystical ministers who had assembled in Bern, Switzerland, and who were a counter to the stern Calvinists in Geneva. Rousseau held and made famous their views about human nature. Eventually, Rousseau and Warens became lovers (which seemed common with her converts), and she sent Rousseau to study Catholicism in Turin where he converted. However, Rousseau argued with Warens about her sexual activity, which he felt was at odds with her religion, and he left her. This is just one of many relationships with famous people which started extremely well, who could have permanently supported Rousseau, but with whom the relationship disintegrated.

Rousseau became a servant in various households, and he was accused of theft in one of them, but none of these lasted for very long. After more wandering, in 1730 he returned to the household of Madame de Warens who had moved to Chambery. There he remained for eight years as a minor assistant in the house, but was mainly a student, studying music, nature, Latin and English languages, French and German philosophy, chemistry, and mathematics.

For several years he seemed to have been a music tutor, and in 1742 he went to Paris to try out his opera *Les Muses Galantes*. Much to his chagrin, it failed. He took a job copying music, and eventually became secretary to Madame Dupin, a Parisian socialite. Through her, Rousseau met and eventually became friends with Diderot, Grimm, and other intellectuals who had gathered in Paris and were writing the *Encyclopédie*. This endeavor was an important arena for political radicalism and anticlerical views, and was famous for attacking the opinions of the establishment. This fit perfectly with the vituperation and scathingly argumentative tendency that marked Rousseau's personality disorder, which combined with his beautiful prose made him a celebrity. His contributions to the *Encyclopédie* were about music, and he was a significant reforming influence in both popular culture and in the court (acknowledged by many important musicians including Mozart). Nevertheless, his proposal for a new system of musical notation was rejected by the Academy of Sciences, which Rousseau took as a personal attack.

For a year and a half spanning 1743 to 1744, Rousseau had the prestigious and lucrative position of secretary to the French ambassador to the doge of Venice, after which he returned to Paris. Leaving such a wonderful position after such a short time, and knowing Rousseau's history, one presumes there was a spat.

In 1749, on a walk to Vincennes to visit Diderot (who was imprisoned there for his anticlerical writing), Rousseau had what he described as an epiphany. He suddenly saw modernity in a way that was the opposite of how he had previously seen it and as it was generally seen. Rather than progress, he saw it as corruption that was ruining humanity. This led him in the following year to write the first of several prize-winning essays for the Academy of Dijon, *Discours sur les Sciences et les Arts* (*Discourse on the Sciences and Arts*). In this essay Rousseau first goes into print with themes that were to reappear in several of his later and more popular works: the virtue of going back to nature, the noble savage, that humans are good by nature and corrupted by society with the more sophisticated societies being the most corrupt.

At this time in Rousseau's life, he had substantial contact with the French court, which only exacerbated his views of human corruption. This contact was mostly due to his work with music, and his popularity increased substantially in 1752 with the success of his operetta, *Devin du village* (*The Village Fortuneteller*). Despite his success, and the ease with which he could have made a living as a court composer, he stopped writing music after, and, perhaps, because of this success.

During this period in Paris he began what was to be his only lasting relationship: an affair with his laundress, Thérèse Levasseur. This was an age in which illicit liaisons with people of much lower social standing were common, usually fleeting, publicly unacknowledged, and illegitimate offspring were not thought of as the children of the father. In this Rousseau was no exception. Rousseau fathered five children with Levasseur, all of whom were put up for adoption. Rousseau has been charged with being heartless by modern commentators, but this is to ignore the convention of the time as well as the poverty, wandering exile, and constant upheaval in which Rousseau lived. What was unconventional for his day about this relationship is that Rousseau eventually married Levasseur in 1768, ten years before his death.

In 1753 Rousseau wrote *Discours sur l'Origine et les Fondements de L'inégalité Parmi les Hommes* (*Discourse on the Origins and Fundamentals of Human Inequality*), his second prize winning essay for the Academy of Dijon which solidified his reputation as a writer and philosopher. In this essay which was of particular interest to Marx and Lenin, Rousseau criticizes the inequalities of society but, unlike his two later admirers, Rousseau did not believe that any return to the original free and happy state of "natural man" was possible.

Rousseau returned to Geneva in 1754 and was welcomed as a prodigal son of the city. He was feted as a famous intellectual, for renouncing the Catholicism to which he had converted and returning to the Calvinism of his youth, and for proudly and publicly proclaiming himself a "citizen of Geneva." He brought Levasseur with him, but he introduced her as a nurse he needed for unspecified medical reasons. This produced whispered comment and knowing glances, but it was accepted as part of the welcome return of this famous man of letters in this otherwise intellectually drab city. His welcome, however, was soon worn out by his personality problems, and in 1756 he had to move and so went to live in a cottage in the woods of Madame d'Epinay who had agreed to support him. There he fell passionately and violently (but unrequitedly) in love with the Countess d'Houdetot which, along with his growing paranoia and acerbic nature cost him his remaining friends and support. Again Rousseau had to move, this time to live in the park of the Duke of Luxembourg at Motmorency where he managed not to offend anyone to the extent that he was able to stay there until 1762. A significant aspect of Rousseau's passion for d'Houdetot is that it formed the basis for Rousseau's first novel *Julie ou la nouvelle Heloise* published in 1761. This novel about love made impossible by differences of social class was the most popular in his life time, tremendously advanced the cause of Romanticism, and made him a darling amongst the wealthy sophisticated women who were to support him as a fugitive.

1762 saw the publication of Rousseau's most incendiary work, and caused him to become a fugitive from both Switzerland and France. *Du Contrat Social* (*The Social Contract*) begins with the famous lines, "Man is born free, but he is everywhere in chains…." This work which was to inspire revolutionaries in the American colonies and later in France was first burned in Geneva which also issued a warrant for his arrest. *Emile ou de L'education* (*Emile or On Education*) written that same year was ordered burned in France by the parliament (under pressure from the church), and a warrant for his arrest was issued in France. This did no good for a man already suffering from feelings of persecution and paranoia. He fled to Neuchâtel in present-day Switzerland, but which was then under the jurisdiction of Prussia. There he remained until the local population (again incited by the church) rioted against him and attacked his house. Rousseau then fled to Isle St. Pierre in Lake Bienne (again in modern Switzerland) which was then under an independent government centered in Berne. Rousseau was there for a short time before he again had to flee when Berne ordered him to leave.

Rousseau was saved by the English philosopher David Hume who offered him refuge in his home and secured for Rousseau a lifetime pension from King George III. Rousseau was now financially secure, respected for his intellectual work, and admired for offending the French. Any sane man would have been grateful, kept his peace with his new supporters, and lived out the rest of his life in the security of his good fortune. But Rousseau's personality disorder afforded him no such luxury. He soon quarreled with and offended Hume and his other new found friends. He saw plots against him everywhere he looked and came to violently dislike everyone around him. After only about a year, he returned to France incognito to be with Levasseur, whom he had come to feel was the only person that he could trust. She was indeed the only person who seemed able to put up with his chronic pathology. The following year, in 1768, they married.

In 1770, Rousseau was officially pardoned and allowed to return to Paris. He had begun autobiographical works when he was with Hume, and these he continued until his death. These works were partly inspired by the work of Montaigne, whom he greatly admired, and partly to counter the charges he imagined were leveled against him by those he imagined were his enemies. As usual, he eventually offended all his acquaintances in Paris, and in 1778 he fled to Ermenonville as a guest of the Marquis de Girardin, where he died soon after arriving.

ROUSSEAU'S NOTION OF ULTIMACY

Of all the Authors, Rousseau was the least explicit about the characteristics of Ultimacy—perhaps anticipating the conflict between the notions of Ultimacy in *Emile* and those of the Church that would soon after its publication cause him to have to flee for his life.

Rousseau's name for a person who is "all that a man should be,"[32] or the greatest to which we can aspire is "natural man," without defining exactly what those terms mean. In brief, even though Rousseau felt that modern man had passed the point of no return to a state of pre-civilization, he promoted being "a savage made to inhabit cities."[33] This state of being required emotional development (in a very Rogerian way), full development of our physical capacities, self-reliance, a healthy curiosity, an ability to be *in* society but not *of* it, rationality, judgment, and virtue. Rousseau's various religious conversions did not affect his basic Christian outlook, and he never saw any necessity to explain why a religious life, or God (or Ultimacy) is important.

Ultimacy in Relation to Rousseau's View of Human Nature

Rousseau had no single term to denote Ultimacy, but he equated it with being "a man,"[34] and "man's estate." A person, no matter how humble his social status, who "...rises to the station of man, which so few men know how to do,"[35] was seen by Rousseau as a far greater being than a social luminary (like a king) who has not so risen. Fulfilling the common callings related to "man's estate" allows all the lesser callings to be fulfilled[36] (in keeping with the discussion earlier about the greater encompassing the lesser). He spoke of his fictional student, Emile, as an "apprentice man" and said that this apprenticeship is "harder and longer" than any apprenticeship to a craft.[37] Rousseau gave the reader no clear definition of "man" or "man's estate," and no idea of what a person is who isn't a "man" (except that the non-man is corrupted). Instead, we are left to see a picture emerge of the young Emile as he develops and acquires the qualities of "a man." The reader is told that people are, by nature, good because Nature is good[38] and that it is humans who corrupt things. "Everything is good as it leaves the hands of the Author of things; everything degenerates in the hands of man."[39] Unfortunately, since Rousseau saw modern humans as creatures of civilization, he believed it was no longer possible simply to leave human formation in the hands of nature[40]—we are conditioned by civilization from the moment we are born. This insight runs contrary to the more radical child-centered holistic educators.

In a remarkable statement that seems to stand out, Rousseau reiterated his view of goodness, but extended it, in a very Buddhist way, to include more than people and nature.

> I always return to my principle, and it provides me with the solution to all my difficulties. I study what is, I seek its cause, and I finally find that what is, is good.[41]

Rousseau's version of listening to or sensing that which is within is, again, not as clear as one would like it to be. He pleads, "O man, draw your existence up within yourself..."[42] and he exhorts the reader to study and know the limits of the human condition, and to see and know human passions, but he is lamentably short on how this is to be done. He provides one hint when he exhorts teachers to teach students to engage in what would be called (in modern day meditation jargon) being "aware of the present," which he feels is "nature's order."[43] Rousseau gave great importance to this for several reasons. Firstly, he condemns as a form of cruelty,

> that barbarous education which sacrifices the present to an uncertain future, which burdens a child with chains of every sort and begins by making him miserable in order to prepare him from afar for I know not what pretended happiness...[44]

Rousseau also felt that such education helps to establish, in human existence, one of the greatest sources of misery;[45] "We no longer exist where we are; we only exist where we are not."[46] This is only one of many instances of Rousseau having Buddhist-like notions about desire and mental projection.

Ultimacy As an Aspect of Religiousness for Rousseau

Rousseau's religiousness is summed up in what he called natural religion, and which can be seen as related to the "natural law" whose history traces as far back as the ancient Greeks.[47] As with so many of the Romantics who followed Rousseau, nature can be thought of as a gateway to the divine; God's word (scripture) is replaced by God's work (nature) as the most reliable and direct communication with the sacred. While Rousseau saw mainstream religions as products of cultures and, therefore, subject to the limitations and misunderstandings of cultures, "natural religion," as he saw it, is free of such conditioning and other forms of authority.[48] For Rousseau, being free of authority is an important aspect of freedom, which is itself important for Ultimacy. Rousseau felt that a person who would "shake off the yoke of opinion in everything"[49] (a form of freedom from authority for Rousseau), and who would seek what is universally true rather than simple cultural truisms, has the "good use of his faculties"[50] to guide him; and reason would lead such a person to natural religion. Rousseau's natural religion is a religiousness more than a religion; it refuses dogma and has a sense of morality rather than a code of one.[51] Rousseau's declarations to this effect were surprisingly strong in view of the fact that heretics were still being put to death in France at that time, and it is not surprising that Rousseau had to flee France after *Emile* was published because of the religiousness the book propounds.

For Rousseau, unification and wholeness take the form of harmony and balance, perhaps as a result of his study of the classics and the emphasis placed on balance by some of the ancient Greeks. This is first evident in Rousseau's claim that we are "formed by three masters,"[52] namely nature, men and things. Only a child raised with those three in union can be in harmony with himself and the world.

Rousseau especially emphasized the importance of physical exercise for harmony and balance, and would have a gymnasium central to every school.[53] He cited support for this from "the ancients," "Montaigne...the wise Locke, the good Rollin, the learned Fleury, the pedant Crousaz" who differed on many other things but who all saw the wisdom of this.[54]

> It is a most pitiable error to imagine that the exercise of the body is harmful to the operations of the mind, as if these two activities ought not to move together in harmony and that the one ought not always to direct the other![55]

Rousseau felt that harmonious physical, intellectual, and emotional development is essential for the individual's development as a whole person in his own right. He saw it as required for material success ("to work like a peasant and think like a philosopher...."[56]), and also for becoming a good citizen. Rousseau claimed that craftsmen in Paris were trained to use only their hands (which leaves them unprepared to be good citizens and only partially formed as humans), while in Geneva craftsmen also had "training of head and the heart" which are required to become a good person (whom "one can present anywhere") and to become a good citizen.[57] Rousseau's emphasis on "exercising the senses, the mind, and the strength…"[58] is a theme of unification that was to be substantially developed by Pestalozzi and Froebel.

One final element in Rousseau's notions of balance is his view that man's weakness and much of his misery comes from "the inequality between his strength and his desires."[59] He believed that keeping desires balanced with strengths and circumstances allows a person to be strong, happy, and wise.

WHAT NEEDS TO BE LEARNED FOR ROUSSEAU

Rousseau's View of Experiential Knowledge

Rousseau was alone among the Authors in demonstrating any familiarity with the epistemological arguments that have raged between rationalists (e.g., Descartes, Spinoza, Liebniz) and empiricists (e.g., Bacon, Locke), and he came down solidly with the empiricists. Rousseau partially took John Locke's position (to whom he refers in several instances) that knowledge is derived either from experience or from logical deductions from other knowledge. The previous knowledge, however, itself derives originally from experience.

Rousseau's simple epistemology, stated briefly, is as follows: Before adolescence (for Rousseau, the stage when reason develops), people can directly receive for themselves only sensations or images of actual objects. The relationships that a young person sees between actual objects are "notions of objects,"[60] and these constitute what he called "simple ideas."[61] Therefore, the images of horses in relation to images of dogs shows horses to be bigger, and from this is derived the simple idea that horses are bigger than dogs.

> At first our pupil had only sensations. Now he has ideas. He only felt; now he judges; for from the comparison of several successive or simultaneous sensations and the judgement made of them is born a sort of mixed or complex sensation which I call an idea.[62]

Any ideas that a young person has other than these are received ideas, and not known directly; and these, for Rousseau, amount to beliefs rather than knowledge, and they can never be more than pale reflections of what needs to be learned.[63] More than even Locke, Rousseau gave primacy to experience; probably one of the reasons he is so often given such importance in the genesis of Romanticism and its cousin in the visual arts, Impressionism.

From Rousseau's notion of the first ideas emanating from sensation he derived his whole epistemology. As sensations or experiences are judged and compared to form ideas, simple ideas are compared and judged to form complex ideas.

> It is by the number of these ideas that the extent of our knowledge is measured. It is their distinctness, their clarity which constitutes the accuracy of the mind. It is the art of comparing them among themselves that is called *human reason*. Thus what I would call *sensual* or *childish* reason consists in forming simple ideas by the conjunction of several sensations, and what I call *intellectual* or *human reason* consists in forming complex ideas by the conjunction of several simple ideas.[64]

Unsurprisingly, Rousseau extended his notions of comparing ideas as a basis for reason to using it as a basis for evaluating people's intelligence. "The greater or lesser aptitude at comparing ideas and at finding relations is what constitutes in men greater or lesser intelligence."[65]

Rousseau also distinguished between knowledge that is useful or non-useful,[66] and between what Pestalozzi will later call "unreal" or "real" knowledge (which for Rousseau means both knowledge of what he considers "real," and knowledge which is "really" acquired, as opposed to knowledge which is just memorized). For knowledge to be really acquired it must be discovered, not given. This naturally affects teaching.

> ...his [the teacher's] task is less to instruct than to lead. He ought to give no precepts at all; he ought to make them be discovered.[67]

Rousseau felt that children, as part of a healthy self preservation which he called *amour de soi*, naturally want to discover because they are interested in all things surrounding them which affect their well-being. A child's "first study is a sort of experimental physics relative to his own preservation,"[68] and to divert this proper study with abstractions is to ruin such a proper and natural course of study. The young person should be allowed to develop his natural curiosity and to develop his senses by developing his interest in the sense relations he has with his world. This is not only what a young person is made by nature to do, it also gives him the only solid basis for the later acquisition of knowledge from reason which is possible at an older age. Without that basis, Rousseau believed, a person cannot really *know* things.

> Since everything which enters into the human understanding comes there through the senses, man's first reason is a reason of the senses; this sensual reason serves as the basis of intellectual reason. Our first masters of philosophy are our feet, our hands, our eyes. To substitute books for all that is not to teach us to reason. It is to teach us to use the reason of others. It is to teach us to believe much and never to know anything.[69]

Rousseau's method of using the senses as a basis for forming abstractions is to judiciously put a child in contact with natural objects and events.[70] As the child gives attention to such phenomena, he naturally (according to Rousseau) becomes curious about them. Rousseau frequently insisted that "to feed his curiosity, never hurry to satisfy it"[71] —one of the many errors of the pedant. Not only does this give the child the opportunity to really *know* things, but it has the other very important benefit of helping the child learn to ask and answer his own questions. Knowing how to ask good questions is at least as important as knowing answers. For Rousseau, asking one's own questions also provides a basis for freedom from authority and judiciousness, both of which are aspects of Ultimacy and important objects of education and indicators of competence.

One reason for the importance Rousseau gave to the cultivation of the senses is that he felt the "well-regulated use" of all the senses leads to "a sort of sixth sense called *common sense*"[72] which he likened to intuition. The sensations of the sixth sense "are perceptions or ideas,"[73] but, unfortunately, he does not elaborate further.

As Rousseau gave such primacy to experiences, it is not surprising that he repeatedly pleaded with teachers to give their lessons "more in actions than in speeches";[74] lessons which a child can more easily remember but also, as discussed earlier, can more easily apply.[75] This is as true for moral education as it is for intellectual education. Rousseau insisted that, "There is no moral knowledge which cannot be acquired by another's or one's own experience."[76] A person learns from another's experience through empathy which is vicariously experiencing the experiences of others. After a lesson has been *felt*, a teacher can summarize it verbally, and this, for Rousseau, is the proper use of words: they come after the 'real knowledge' of experience to summarize and so form the first level of abstraction. Such an abstraction can then be related to other abstractions (similarly formed) which together form "complex ideas." The foundation, however, is always experience.

Many necessary experiential moral lessons occur naturally in games. So scathing was Rousseau about the possibility of 'real' education being acquired through words in the classroom that he insists that the child learns more in the schoolyard than the class.[77] Consequently for moral education (as well as physical education), Rousseau called for schools to create "gyms or places for corporeal exercise" which he felt are far more effective than the use of "so many vain and pedantic precepts, which amount to nothing more than lost words."[78]

Rousseau resolved one issue that has caused contention between the more and less radical child-centered holistic educators; he did not feel that students should just be left to their own devices to learn from whatever experiences occurred. He insisted that experiences should be deliberately determined or engineered (to the extent possible) by the teacher as an indispensable teaching tool.[79] Rousseau would even engineer quite humiliating experiences to have Emile learn the lesson of humility. "Make him feel it, or he will never know it."[80] Rousseau insisted, however, that he would endure the same suffering with his student and not heartlessly leave him on his own; an aspect of Rousseau's notions of the pedagogic relationship. Knowledge was seen by Rousseau as being very personal (as it needs to be acquired through personal experience), but the teacher is there to determine to a certain extent what experiences are available, and to help the student learn more from the experiences than the student might do if left entirely to himself. For instance, the teacher is able to assist by summarizing with maxims or drawing links to related experiences thereby helping in the formation of abstractions or making connections. The teacher is not there to burden the child with precepts, morals, responsibilities, and maxims that, in any case, Rousseau felt are impossible for the child to comprehend when they are divorced from experience. The teacher is there to see the opportunities in everyday events and conversation that allow the needed learning to be anchored in the student's life. For this reason, prescribed studies are not possible, although a loose curriculum content is. For instance, a teacher might feel that it is important for the student to learn the value of honesty, but must wait for the opportunity to make use of the student's experiences for that lesson to be learned.

Perhaps because he was a writer, Rousseau saw the dangerous power of words and books; especially the danger of confusing the word with what the word represents. He went as far as saying, "I hate books. They only teach one to talk about what one does not know."[81] Rousseau did not condemn books per se (he praises them elsewhere), but he pointed to the difference between knowledge acquired from experience and its much inferior surrogate acquired through representations, and he condemned the human tendency to confuse the two.[82] Rousseau felt that this confusion is especially rife in education in which "we stuff children's heads with words which have no meaning"[83] instead of giving them meaningful experiences, with the result that "we produce only babblers."[84] It is not, however, only words that Rousseau condemned, but any representation used as a basis for knowledge (e.g., maps and globes) when substituted for experience of the real world.[85]

As part of experiential knowledge, the emotional element was also very important to Rousseau who used the words "sentiment," "passions," "desires," and "emotions" interchangeably. He commented that,

> …our true masters are experience and sentiment, and man has a good sense of what suits man only with respect to those relations in which he himself has actually participated.[86]

Consequently, Rousseau told teachers to, "make the language of the mind pass through the heart, so that it may make itself understood."[87] Rousseau felt that this inclusion of an emotional component is necessary because people are not "all mind,"[88] and the other aspects of people must be engaged in order to acquire what needs to be learned.

Although emotions are an important part of experience, Rousseau observed that actual physical engagement occurs prior to emotions. Simple emotions are available to everyone since, by the end of early childhood, everyone has had the physical engagements necessary to have experienced the emotional components attached to them (e.g., fear from physical pain). Complex emotions require complex experiences (with their emotional components), so that education is "pure stupidity"[89] when it tries to make students feel sentiments for which they do not have the experiential base. This, Rousseau felt, is what goes on in the mainstream study of art or literature when students are expected to relate to complex adult emotions, for which they do not yet have the experiential basis that would make such emotions intelligible.

Of course, not all emotions are pleasant, and Rousseau does not hesitate to say that suffering is important to experience and that he would be distressed if Emile "grew up without knowing pain."[90] Rousseau would have Emile know suffering (within very defined limits) for several reasons. One reason is that a person's own suffering is the basis for knowing the suffering of others, which is the foundation of empathy, compassion and social development.

Another reason that Rousseau wanted Emile to know suffering was to learn the "law of necessity." Rousseau felt that there are immutable laws governing humans as well as matter (e.g., desire, gravity). To ignore these laws brings inevitable disaster, and learning them while young through experiencing the consequences is far better than learning them when older and suffering greater consequences (e.g., falling off small things as an infant is better than falling off large things as an adult). In his discussions of the law of necessity, Rousseau deals with another type of experiential knowledge as well—self-knowledge.

Rousseau felt that the law of necessity was in some matters general (e.g., the passions in everyone follow similar laws) while in other matters it is particular to the individual and his condition. Part of what Rousseau meant by knowing oneself was to know the limits of one's condition: "study and know these limits,"[91] for no one can be happy who does not know this and subsequently restrains his desires to what is possible within these limits. Rousseau encouraged people to "extend the law of necessity to moral things,"[92] and championed an asceticism not unlike a Buddhist form of detachment as a basis for values.

Some of Rousseau's notions of emotions have a curiously modern ring; they are part of the self that must be known, not suppressed or rejected. It is clear from his writings that Rousseau placed great emphasis on his own self-knowledge (increasingly as he grew older—see his *Confessions*).[93] Rousseau gave no clear definition of 'the self', but he implied enough to provide an outline sketch. Some of Rousseau's notions of self are evident in the two forms of self-love he held to exist: *amour de soi* and *amour-propre*. For Rousseau, *amour-propre* is akin to pride, the kind of self-love which, in excess, is hubris; whereas *amour de soi* consists of the self-love that is the basis of self-preservation and is thus a natural and necessary part of our constitution. Therefore, like all things natural, he felt *amour de soi* is good.

> The love of oneself [*amour de soi*] is always good and always in conformity with order. Since each man is specially entrusted with his own preservation, the first and most important of his cares is and ought to be to watch over it constantly. And how could he watch over it if he did not take the greatest interest in it?[94]

The relation of *amour de soi* to *amour-propre* is complex, as is their role in human experiences; but a brief account is necessary to understand Rousseau's notions of self-knowledge. Rousseau felt that, "we have to love ourselves to preserve ourselves; and it follows immediately from the same sentiment that we love what preserves us."[95] This extends to our loving those who preserve us (e.g., parents, family, etc.) and "this is how the gentle and affectionate passions are born of [*amour-de soi*]."[96]

Rousseau felt that when a person gets old enough to compare himself with others, he automatically wants to be superior in such comparison, and this is where *amour de soi* gives rise to pride or *amour-propre*.[97] Another way in which *amour de soi* generates *amour-propre* occurs when the imagination acts incorrectly, such as when people want to preserve their self-images, confusing these with their real selves.

By itself, *amour-propre* (like emotions, but unlike *amour de soi*) is neither good nor bad, but becomes the one or the other by application.[98] *Amour-propre* can be of beneficial use (e.g., pride in doing something well, or generating self-esteem). However, Rousseau warns, "*Amour-propre* is a useful but dangerous instrument. Often it wounds the hand making use of it and rarely does good without evil."[99] He explained that in seeing the suffering of others with *amour de soi*, the self extends to others and compassion is born. Seeing the same suffering with *amour-propre* leads to contempt or to what today is usually called by its German name, *schadenfreude* (happiness at seeing the misery of others).

Rousseau's notions of *amour de soi* also elucidate his understanding of the emotions as part of the self. *Amour de soi*, Rousseau claimed, is "the source of our passions, the origin and the principle of all the others."[100] All the passions we have are modifications of this first and natural passion, which is love of ourselves, and therefore all passions can be said to be natural in origin. Unfortunately, the original natural passion can be so augmented by unnatural forces that it changes into something no longer natural and not good for us. The difference between these passions is simple for Rousseau.

> Our natural passions are very limited. They are the instruments of our freedom; they tend to preserve us. All those which subject us and destroy us come from elsewhere. Nature does not give them to us. We appropriate them to the detriment of nature.[101]

For Rousseau, imagination is another aspect of experience that plays an important role with the passions, and thus also with experiential knowledge. He felt that in nature's order "the senses wake the imagination," while in a sensually corrupt and precocious society "the imagination wakes the senses."[102] Natural passions quite naturally stir the imagination. When, however, imagination is the source of passions, then imagination has reversed nature's order and the passions that result from this reversal are destructive. Therefore, it is not the passions themselves that are wicked; their nature is determined by their origin and application.[103] Hence, Rousseau did not support the suppression of passion, an activity seen as virtuous in his day.

> I would find someone who wanted to prevent the birth of the passions almost as mad as someone who wanted to annihilate them; and those who believed that this was my project up to now would surely have understood me very badly.[104]

Rousseau also held that it is wrong to distinguish good from bad passions "in order to yield to the former and deny oneself the latter."[105] Passions are in themselves good because,

> Our passions are the principal instruments of our preservation. It is, therefore, an enterprise as vain as it is ridiculous to want to destroy them—it is to control nature, it is to reform the work of God. If God were to tell men to annihilate the passions which He gives him, God would will and not will; He would contradict Himself. Never did He give this senseless order. Nothing of the kind is written in the human heart. And what God wants a man to do, He does not have told to him by another man. He tells it to him Himself; He writes it in the depths of his heart.[106]

Yet the problem remains of dealing with the destructive effects of some passions. Rousseau's solution lies with imagination. Rousseau felt that man must have an understanding of natural and right relationship with others; he must then see the role passions have in relationships; and then "order all the affections of the soul according to these relations."[107] The way this ordering is to be accomplished is not through any form of suppression, but through directing the imagination and staying in the order of nature. Part of Emile's education was learning such mastery of his imagination.

Learning such mastery is not only valuable because it avoids the destruction that would follow from its absence, it is also valuable because of its role in the acquisition of virtue. For Rousseau, a person can be good without being virtuous. It is in self-mastery (in which mastery of the imagination plays a part) that virtue is achieved.[108] Rousseau told Emile,

> Now be really free. Learn to become your own master. Command your heart, Emile, and you will be virtuous.[109]

There is one final role for the imagination in passions, and it broaches the topic of social development. Rousseau claimed that all people experience suffering, and although we may see the suffering of others, "to see it without feeling it is not to know it."[110] It is imagination that allows a person to feel the suffering of others[111] and this empathy, eventually, can give rise to compassion. Consequently, Rousseau encouraged teachers, as a necessary part of social development, to "arouse the first emotions of nature [*amour de soi*] and to develop his [the student's] heart and extend it to his fellows."[112]

Competence for Rousseau

Closely related to Rousseau's perspectives on experiential knowledge as the foundation of what needs to be learned are his descriptions of competence versus performance based pedagogy and the characteristics of the kind of competence he valued.

Rousseau felt that the reason education had come to place so much emphasis on representations (i.e., books and words) rather than real knowledge was because the presentation of knowledge had come to be valued[113] over the acquisition of real knowledge. This distinction is mirrored in the differences in the knowledge concepts of "performance" and "competence" that are discussed extensively in the third section of this book. The latter can be thought of as the real knowledge discussed earlier, a knowledge complex that forms an active part of a person's ability to meet the challenges of life, while "performance" can be thought of as knowledge acquired in order to display its acquisition (e.g., learning something to pass a test).

Competences can not be reduced to a set of skills in which a person can be trained as one might train a dog or program a robot. While none of the Authors used the terms "competence" or "performance" to identify knowledge concepts, the Authors certainly had the concepts and made it central to their writing on education. Rousseau was the first, and certainly one of the most articulate, proponents of (what shall henceforth be called) competence over performance, and in doing so became an icon for holistic education. Rousseau felt that performance based pedagogy depended on representations and abstractions for its displays, and that such learning was devoid of any emotional engagement on the part of the student. Rousseau claimed that it is much easier to "present a showy display of the instruction"[114] than to instruct a child in anything truly useful (in which Rousseau includes moral and social learning that informs behavior). He acknowledged that competence based pedagogy does not make the teacher's "…talents conspicuous from the outset nor make an impression on fathers. But it is the only one fit for succeeding."[115] This does, however, depend on what is meant by succeeding, and for Rousseau, succeeding is, as discussed previously, becoming a "natural man" and "all that a man should be"—achieving Ultimacy.

Rousseau gave no definitions of what we are calling competence based pedagogy or performance based pedagogy, but he frequently described the differences. These differences are evident in Rousseau's frequent juxtaposition of Emile's education with what he saw as mainstream education. He contrasted, for example, knowing by heart with knowing by experience, being able to read well in books with being able to read "in the book of nature," Emile having his mind in "his head" with the mainstream student having it "in his tongue," memory with judgment,[116] and teaching science with helping the child develop the mindset "fit for acquiring it [science]."[117] Rousseau blamed the self-interest of teachers for the emphasis on performance based pedagogy. It is only through giving performances of knowledge that the teacher can show off his skills, and in this way the student himself becomes a performance for the teacher.

> A preceptor thinks of his own interest more than of his disciple's. He is devoted to proving that he is not wasting his time and that he is earning the money he is paid. He provides the child with some easily displayed attainments that can be showed off when wanted. It is not important whether what he teaches the child is useful, provided that it is easily seen. He accumulates, without distinction or discernment, a rubbish heap in the child's memory. When the child is to be examined, he is made to spread out his merchandise. He displays it; satisfaction is obtained. Then he closes up his pack again and leaves. My pupil [Emile] is not so rich. He has no pack to spread out. He has nothing to show other than himself.[118]

Rousseau shows his disinterest in performance based pedagogy by insisting that the amount of knowledge a child has is of very little importance.[119] Rousseau was far more interested in students learning how to question and acquire by themselves the knowledge which each student needs and wants than he was in the acquisition of any particular knowledge. Certainly becoming an expert in one subject is harmful to the child's overall development, and it is this overall development that generates the ability to meet the challenges of living. By not giving Emile facts or answers (which Rousseau repeatedly proclaimed are of slight importance) and by not demanding the acquisition of specific knowledge, Rousseau rejected the possibility of performance based pedagogy. Instead, Rousseau presented Emile with objects and situations that he felt might generate certain kinds of learning and, in so doing, loosely directed Emile's learning.[120] Such steering can only work if the student is a self-motivated learner, but for Rousseau motivation to learn is inherent in young people. Sometimes, Rousseau indicated that he knew what he wanted Emile to learn (e.g., some aspect of geometry), while at other times he seemed less sure what Emile would learn, only that he would learn something (as one might expect a person to learn by taking a trip around the world without knowing exactly what would be learned).

Rousseau also contrasted competence with performance in his discussion of art education. He claimed that a child can draw or paint a better likeness if the child copies another drawing or painting; and if the product is important (as it is in performance based pedagogy) then that is the best way to proceed. Rousseau, however, was not interested in the product. He was interested in training the hand and the capacity to see, in increasing the child's contact with nature since he felt this is related to an appreciation of something sacred—nature. Consequently, he insisted on Emile drawing from nature.[121]

Characteristics of Competence Promoted by Rousseau

Examining Rousseau's notions of judgment and values is complicated by the fact that there was no word in eighteenth century French that can be directly translated into the modern term 'values' in the sense the word is used in such modern expressions as 'values education'. The nearest eighteenth century French equivalent is *vertu*. *Vertu* is sometimes used by Rousseau to denote "virtue" and sometimes to denote "values." The difficulty is further increased because a close reading shows that both meanings can fuse even within a single sentence. This is perhaps explained by seeing that, for Rousseau, the man of virtue has values and the acquisition of values leads to virtue.

Rousseau presented Emile as valuing certain things and, as Emile is

Rousseau's ideal man, it is evident that Rousseau felt everyone should have similar values and criteria for establishing values. Such values follow from the virtue of commitment to self-preservation and well-being (which he saw as truly useful), and this commitment comes naturally from an uninhibited *amour de soi*. When it is understood that Rousseau included compassion and social responsibility within 'utility', it becomes less of an instrumental concept.

> It is by their palpable relation to his utility, his security, his preservation, and his well-being that he ought to appraise all the bodies of nature and all the works of men. Thus, iron ought to be much more valuable in his eyes than gold, and glass than diamonds.[122]

Rousseau included morals amongst the virtues to be acquired, but, for him, morality did not mean following prescribed behavior. Among other considerations, moral conduct meant acting with the emotional mastery discussed previously, being free of opinion and authority, having a "healthy heart" (which included compassion for others), "good sense," "courage," "wisdom," and "reason,"[123]

Virtue, for Rousseau, required struggle, and he claimed that much of the education which Emile received was to make him physically, mentally, emotionally, and socially strong, so that Emile could prevail in the struggle for virtue. Rousseau felt that strength is partly necessary to "arm man against unexpected accidents,"[124] but its most important role is as part of the complex struggle of gaining virtue. Rousseau said to his imaginary student,

> My child, there is no happiness without courage nor virtue without struggle. The word *virtue* comes from *strength*. Strength is the foundation of all virtue. Virtue belongs only to a being that is weak by nature and strong by will. It is in this that the merit of the just man consists; and although we call God good, we do not call Him virtuous, because it requires no effort for Him to do good.[125]

Rousseau believed that it is only strength derived from struggle that gives goodness its real value. Without strength, goodness is too fragile, conditional, dependent on emotions and often self-serving. The strength of emotional mastery is the strength of virtue.

> …he who is only good remains so only as long as he takes pleasure in being so. Goodness is broken and perishes under the impact of the human passions. The man who is only good is good only for himself.[126]

Judgment, for Rousseau, also requires strength, as well as the acquisition of values (the criteria of judgment). Therefore, for Rousseau, a judicious person needs the qualities previously listed under strength and values. It is the development of judgment which Rousseau claims as a principal aim of his education.[127] He felt his fictional character's education was a success because of Emile's judiciousness and because Emile himself values this quality highly.[128] Rousseau claimed that, by the age of fifteen, the amount of intellectual knowledge a child acquires in mainstream education will be equivalent to what Emile has learned through Rousseau's competence based pedagogy,

> ...but with the difference that your child's knowledge will be only in his memory, while mine's will be in his judgement.[129]

In this quote and several others that are similar, it is evident that Rousseau saw what he called judgment as related to a concept of knowledge rather than an activity of deciding. Judgment is a form of competence that Rousseau felt develops from experiential knowledge and self-knowledge, and it is indispensable in life. Judiciousness with regard to the physical world is important for survival and safety. Judiciousness with regard to the social world is important for both well-being (as we are social entities) and because we learn from observing others and need to judge well what we see. Such judiciousness involves not being deluded by conventional social indicators, but judging men "only by the condition of their hearts..."[130] Rousseau claimed that such judgment requires insight, intuition, and sensitivity; and this involves not just the intellect but also "a heart sensitive enough to conceive all the human passions and calm enough not to experience them"[131]—self-knowledge and emotional mastery.

Judgment, however, requires more than these elements. It also requires freedom. A person who is not free of influences that can pervert insight, intuition, sensitivity, etc., cannot judge well. Rousseau frequently stated that Emile does not value the prejudices of others,[132] or even those of his own making; "he does not know what routine, custom, or habit is," and "never follows a formula..."[133] We hear Emile declare that he will be free anywhere he goes because, "all the chains of opinion are broken for me..."[134] It is not so much the things outside of the mind that enslave people, it is the inner authorities. This is noteworthy in view of Rousseau's political writings.

In a series of statements that resemble those about homeostasis in the twentieth century, Rousseau claimed that in giving a child liberty that child will come to do what is good for him.

> In leaving him thus master of his will, you will not be fomenting his caprices. By never doing anything except what suits him, he will soon do only what he ought to do; and although his body is in continuous motion, so long as he is concerned only with his immediate and palpable interest, you will witness developing all the reason of which he is capable much better and in a way much more appropriate to him than it would in purely speculative studies.[135]

A consequence of leaving a student "master of his will" is that the teacher has no tools for motivation other than inspiring interest, which exists only when the child derives pleasure or utility from the learning.[136] Rousseau described the importance of a young child learning how to be attentive, but "attention ought always to be produced by pleasure or desire, never constraint" because "it is never as important that he learn as that he do nothing in spite of himself."[137] To learn to act "in spite of himself" is to learn to violate *amour de soi*, the natural order, freedom, and is what permits evil. Learning to do things "in spite of himself" is also learning to be gullible in the future to all those whose abuse (through persuasion, authority, etc.) will require such rejection of *amour de soi*.

Another aspect of learning freedom is learning to not be dependent on others, so Rousseau avoided assisting Emile too much.

> The only one who does his own will is he who, in order to do it, has no need to put another's arms at the end of his own; from which it follows that the first of all goods is not authority but freedom. The truly free man wants only what he can do and does what he pleases. That is my fundamental maxim. It need only be applied to childhood for all the rules of education to flow from it.[138]

Rousseau did feel that one form of dependence is positive—love— and this stems from being a human and not God. In one of several statements, which sound as though they could have come from a Buddhist tract, Emile discussed his love of Sophie.

> If I were without passions, I would, in my condition as a man, be independent like God himself; for I would want only what is and therefore would never have to struggle against destiny. At least I have no more than one chain. It is the only one I shall ever bear, and I can glory in it. Come, then, give me Sophie, and I am free.[139]

Interestingly, Rousseau felt that giving a child freedom to do as he pleases (and experiencing the consequences), allows a child to learn another dependence. This is our dependence on the law of necessity, and paradoxically this law shows us that we cannot just do what we please.

> The irrepressible law of necessity always teaches man early to do what does not please him in order to prevent an evil which would displease him more. Such is the use of foresight, and from this foresight, well or ill controlled, is born all human wisdom or all human misery.[140]

Rousseau believed that one cannot teach foresight to a child, but instead must allow the child to learn foresight from experiencing the law of necessity. As with all attempts to teach a child behavior construed by adults to be good, trying to teach foresight will generally only produce reaction and rebellion, which too often generates the opposite of the intended lesson.[141]

Learning the law of necessity was, for Rousseau, a very important element of what needs to be learned in education. Rousseau gave Emile "well-regulated freedom"[142] by which he meant that Emile had freedom within the confines of what Rousseau thought was safe, and conducive to his well-being and learning. Emile was allowed to make his own mistakes (as long as they did not endanger him) and to take actions that had unpleasant consequences. Having freedom but facing the consequences was the way Emile learned "dependence only on things," which is how one learns the law of necessity and follows "the order of nature in the progress of…education."[143] Paradoxically, following these laws makes one free.[144] These laws are

> …the eternal laws of nature and order… For the wise man, they take the place of positive [governmental] law. They are written in the depth of his heart by conscience and reason. It is to these that he ought to enslave himself in order to be free. The only slave is the man who does evil, for he always does it in spite of himself. Freedom is found in no form of government; it is in the heart of the free man. He takes it with him everywhere. The vile man takes his servitude everywhere. The latter would be a slave in Geneva, the former a free man in Paris.[145]

As with all the Authors and others who have seen freedom as an aspect of what we have called sagacious competence, Rousseau does not conflate non-dependence with independence. As a consequence of our being social entities and the law of necessity, people cannot be independent. Rousseau claimed that Emile's "...maxim was always to learn to do without the help of others in regard to everything he could do himself,"[146] and this extended to an important form of non-dependence: learning to learn by himself. This has several important consequences, such as depending less on authorities, giving less to the opinions of others, and, as a consequence, not getting "accustomed to servile submission."[147] From this there follow several other benefits according to Rousseau. One benefit is advancing in learning only at one's own rate rather than a rate determined by another, which means that the knowledge acquired is more likely to be appropriate to the condition and circumstances of the learner. Another benefit is that learning progresses only by making one's own connections which generates meaning, rather than accepting the connections and meaning of someone else[148] (which links to the earlier discussion of 'real' and 'non-real' knowledge, which shall be elaborated further in the chapters on Pestalozzi and Froebel).

For Rousseau, knowing facts discovered by someone else is never as valuable as discovering facts oneself,[149] and from this it follows that learning how to learn is one of his central characteristics of competence. "The goal is less to teach him a truth than to show him how he must always go about discovering the truth."[150] However, learning how to learn by oneself, according to Rousseau, requires that a person learns about their individual learning processes: meta-learning. It is partly to develop meta-learning that Emile is allowed to follow his own interests to such a large extent—what he learns is not as important as *that* he learns and *how* he learns, and *that* he learns *how* he learns. Rousseau frequently claimed that Emile does not acquire vast amounts of knowledge, "but what he has is truly his own." Rousseau also claimed that,

> Emile has a mind that is universal not by its learning but by its faculty to acquire learning: a mind that is open, intelligent, ready for everything, and, as Montaigne says, if not instructed, at least able to be instructed.[151]

Rousseau felt that such a universal mind is especially important in moral questions and questions of judgment, as these areas often have no established answers. Therefore, one must be able to find them.[152] For Rousseau, the ability to find the right questions, frame them, and find one's own answers is the only way to approach morality and judiciousness, and such skill must be deliberately learned. Meta-learning, for Rousseau, involves a person consciously seeing how they are learning and how their mind is functioning so that it remains "open, intelligent, and ready for everything."

Rousseau believed that without judgment a person can not know directly what is worth learning. Without values as criteria for establishing worth, a person can not judge. Without freedom to form criteria and freedom from the coercive effects of opinion, authorities, beliefs, etc., a person is not in a position to exercise judgment. Such judgment, values and freedom can not be taught but they can be learned, and much of it, Rousseau believed, comes from self-motivated learning and learning to learn. The result of this learning is not knowledge as seen in schools, but knowledge as competence.

Rousseau presented several pictures of Emile who, as the ideal man, develops the competence Rousseau would have us all develop. Hence, we can see what Rousseau's competent person would be like. Rousseau called Emile "my pupil" and then corrected himself to show Emile's link with Ultimacy by saying, "or rather nature's,"[153] and described him as being "self-sufficient" and not turning to others for answers. Emile as an adolescent becomes judicious, pragmatic, practical, resourceful, a self-motivated learner, with foresight, physical strength, and self-knowledge of what suits him.[154] By the time Emile reaches almost the end of his education he is,

> ...well formed, well constituted in mind and body, strong, healthy, fit, skillful, robust, full of sense, reason, goodness and humanity, a man with morals and taste, loving the beautiful, doing the good, free from the empire of cruel passions, exempt from the yoke of opinion, but subject to the law of wisdom and submissive to the voice of friendship, possessing all the useful talents and some of the agreeable ones, caring little for riches, with his means of support in his arms, and not afraid if lacking bread whatever happens.[155]

Rousseau felt that social-ability becomes intelligible to young people only very late in their development, at the end of adolescence. The attempt to teach it earlier (as it cannot be properly understood) requires the imposition of rules, habits, and opinions which are a violation of the child's nature. In fact, in the nearest Rousseau came to defining a person's "nature," he described it as "dispositions" before they have been "constrained by our habits" or "corrupted by our opinions."[156] To reduce the impact of the habits and opinions of society, Rousseau recommended using the law of necessity to guide children, which "can be expanded and contracted"[157] around the child by the wise teacher, instead of imposing social laws which a child cannot really understand[158] and which inevitably corrupt the child's nature.

Social-ability is necessary to learn because "to live in the world, one must know how to deal with men,"[159] as the intention of Rousseau's education was to help people live in society, not isolated in nature.

> But consider, in the first place, that although I want to form the man of nature, the object is not, for all that, to make him a savage and to relegate him to the depths of the woods. It suffices that, enclosed in a social whirlpool, he not let himself get carried away by either the passions or the opinions of men, that he see with his eyes, that he feel with his heart, that no authority govern him beyond that of his own reason.[160]

Emile was to be "the natural man living in the state of society" who, following his *amour de soi*, must know how to preserve himself, which means knowing how to deal with other people and "to live, if not like them, at least with them."[161] What is different about Emile, is that he has been raised according to the immutable laws of nature and for Ultimacy, and therefore raised for himself, not for society. Rousseau felt (as did the other Authors) that an education in which a person is raised for himself is incompatible with an education in which a person is raised for others (i.e., for society).

> But what is to be done when…instead of raising a man for himself, one wants to raise him for others? … Forced to combat nature or the social institutions, one must choose between making a man and making a citizen, for one cannot make both at the same time.[162]

Rousseau insisted that development for nature and development for society follow "contrary routes," and that if we try to follow both we are "forced to divide ourselves" and "follow a composite impulse which leads us to neither one goal or the other," and in the end we aren't "good either for ourselves or for others."[163] Rousseau did feel that being good for others—contributing positively to society—is important. However, Rousseau felt being good for others can only come from compassion and never duty, and compassion cannot be taught but can be learned through the education he promoted. While Rousseau believed that privileged people have a greater social debt,[164] all people have a social responsibility and, if properly educated (in which *amour de soi* extends to include others), will naturally meet this responsibility from a properly developed sense of extended self.

Rousseau contended that education for others cannot produce the same result. Such education may produce people who engage in fine acts and have good intentions, but in such people social responsibility must necessarily conflict with self-interest (which is more primary), with the result that meeting social responsibilities is always contingent on the self being either appeased or suppressed.

Rousseau implied that institutions also have a form of self-interest. Hence, the intention of state education is to preserve the state (by producing workers, soldiers, nationalism, conformist behavior, etc.), and that what is good for the state must necessarily take precedence over what is good for the individual. Good parents, on the other hand, care primarily for the well-being of their individual children. If such care for the individual is fully pursued, it produces a person who is also good for society through being compassionate and having a developed sense of social responsibility. State education intending to produce good citizens cannot, Rousseau felt, produce good individuals because, of necessity, education for good individuals gives primacy to *amour de soi* which cannot be the intention of the state.

In summarizing Rousseau's conception of knowledge and education, Boyd makes a statement with which all the Authors would probably agree and which is in keeping with competence based education.

> An educational system that places emphasis on preparation for adult life places more emphasis on what is taught than on predilections and aptitudes. An educational system that stresses development of the individual child puts more emphasis on the distinctive view of life taken by the child over the subjects. The actual child gets more attention than the future man, and what he learns is personal.[165]

ASPECTS OF STUDENTS THAT FACILITATE THE NEEDED LEARNING FOR ROUSSEAU

For Rousseau, students have learning processes that are natural and do not require the intervention of adults. However, he believed that, without interfering in these natural processes, the teacher had a great deal to do. Rousseau saw the student's learning processes as a product of *amour de soi* in that the student has a natural wish for self-preservation and well-being, hence a natural wish to learn anything that is useful for self-preservation and well-being. As the *soi* (self) of which one has *amour* can extend beyond the boundary of the skin (through compassion, morality, social responsibility, etc.), so the healthy and natural development of the self's utility, preservation and well-being become a natural foundation for learning social and moral duties[166] and for acquiring a love of order and the public good.[167] Rousseau warned teachers that these natural learning processes can very easily be violated, because they have a natural sequence, which can be violated by approaching things out of their proper order. This is done, for instance, when trying to teach social and moral duties before *amour de soi* has developed to the point of extending itself. Rousseau believed that children must feel their rights before they can feel their duties.[168] Rousseau contended that, without the correct foundation that comes from respecting the student's natural learning processes, what should bring compassion only brings arrogance, and the student's education would be for nothing.[169] Such perversion of the natural learning processes also occurs when we use reason with children too early in their development.[170]

Rousseau saw children's play as an expression of this natural learning process. It is in play that he felt children (like most animals) try to explore and understand their world; a theme taken up and greatly expanded by Pestalozzi and Froebel. Rousseau felt that education should emulate as well as make use of children's play.

> ...it ought always to be borne in mind that all this [education] is or ought to be only a game, an easy and voluntary direction of the movements nature asks of children, an art of varying their play to render it more pleasant to them without the least constraint ever turning it into work. Really, what will they play with that I cannot turn into an object of instruction for them?[171]

This he contrasted with what he felt occurred in the mainstream education of his day where teachers

> feel that, no matter what, they just have to teach them [students] this or that always find it impossible to succeed without constraint, without quarreling, and without boredom.[172]

Rousseau felt that the result of violating the student's natural learning processes is the creation of distorted and un-natural man. Because of the "constraint," "quarreling," and "boredom," a student naturally feels "aversion, disgust, and distaste" for his education,[173] and, as a consequence, the teacher must use "fear, covetousness, envy, pride" and other "passions that serve as instruments for common education."[174]

It is worth noting that what Rousseau meant by "play" did not necessarily indicate ease or effortlessness, and he frequently disparaged all that is otiose. Rigor, toughness, endurance, and the ability to exert oneself were seen by Rousseau as important, and he ensured that these qualities entered into the play of Emile, (much as a mountaineer might find his form of "play" includes the most grueling and demanding efforts).[175]

Rousseau felt that following the natural learning processes in students leads to the natural man because a person develops in a manner that is true to his nature. He also felt that this is the way in which a person leads a happy life. In describing his approach to educating Emile, Rousseau remarked,

> I kept to the road of nature while waiting for it to show me the road of happiness. It turned out that they were the same and that, by not thinking about it, I had followed the road of happiness.[176]

One of the most important aspects of the inherent learning processes is that, for Rousseau, they exist within the context of distinct stages of development—hence the five books of *Emile* which correspond to those stages. Rousseau's insistence, as discussed previously, on the cultivation of the senses in early childhood (which he felt was universally ignored by mainstream education[177]) was due to his belief that there are distinct stages in human development, with each stage needing to be successfully completed before the next is engaged. A principal that Rousseau claimed is central to *Emile* it that it causes damage to a child to treat that child as though the child is in a more advanced stage than is actually the case.

> My whole book is only a constant proof of this principle of education.[178]

Rousseau felt that teachers have to know the characteristics of these stages (which hold for people in general), yet be sensitive to the progress of the individual through those stages as these vary tremendously with the individual. The principle importance of these stages is that they determine what a person is capable of learning naturally, and Rousseau felt that he "cannot exhort the governor [tutor/teacher] too much to be sure that his proofs match the pupil's capacity to understand them."[179] Consequently, for Rousseau, the teacher should know the dynamics of the different stages of development, the characteristics of different types of learning,[180] and have a willingness to "not displace ages any more than seasons. One must be oneself at all times and not battle against nature."[181] Unfortunately, Rousseau claimed, most people

> ...concentrate on what it is important for men to know without considering what children are in a condition to learn. They are always seeking the man in the child without thinking of what he is before being a man.[182]

The results of such ignorance and of forcing learning before it is time are "defects of body and of mind."[183] Rousseau felt that whatever faults his book may have in devising learning for the different stages, he is accurate in identifying the stages, and that this may be the main contribution his book makes to education.[184] Yet Rousseau believed the stages of development had to be more than merely acknowledged; they had to be valued. He claimed that "each age, each condition of life, has its suitable perfection, a sort of maturity proper to it"[185] and that rather than hurrying a child to maturity, we should "be humane with every station, every age...love childhood, promote its games, its pleasures, its amiable instinct...."[186]

Rousseau insisted that,

> Nature wants children to be children before being men. If we want to pervert this order, we shall produce precocious fruits which will be immature and insipid and will not be long in rotting. We shall have young doctors and old children. Childhood has its ways of seeing, thinking, and feeling which are proper to it. Nothing is less sensible than to want to substitute ours for theirs, and I would like as little to insist that a ten-year-old be five feet tall as that he possess judgement.[187]

Rousseau believed that pushing children ahead of their time was the result of the teacher's or parent's egotism in the pretence of creating prodigies, but that the damage to children was lasting. He warned that, contrary to the common opinion, "harm is not in what the pupil does not understand but is in what he believes he understands,"[188] but actually doesn't; a harm generated by "false" knowledge that is very difficult to undo. Rousseau cited the results of religious instruction to children as an example. Not only are children not capable of understanding theology,[189] but also such study becomes an act of sacrilege by preventing an eventual true understanding.

The great evil of the deformed images of the divinity which are drawn in the minds of children is that they remain there all their lives; when the children become men, they no longer conceive of any other God than that of children.[190]

For Rousseau, the attempt to learn before one is capable of understanding produces learning without knowing, and links this topic with the discussion of "real" or "unreal"/"false" knowledge. He claimed that at the age of fifteen Emile

did not know whether he had a soul. And perhaps at eighteen it is not yet time for him to learn it; for if he learns it sooner than he ought, he runs the risk of never knowing it.[191]

It is real and certain knowledge that is needed for Ultimacy, not "performance" or the mere show of knowledge. The proper study of childhood stems from the senses, and only at young adulthood should one attempt to know anything of the religious. Rousseau felt that it is "simple to rise from the study of nature to the quest for its Author [God]"[192] which is a natural progression and one more likely to give students "real knowledge."

Rousseau held that it was only after puberty—a "second birth" (when most education ended in 18th century Europe), that the faculty of reason has matured and that a more substantial education can begin because with reason education "takes on true importance."[193] This for Rousseau, was the last stage of the student's learning processes marked by physiological changes. The remaining changes were marked by developments of character, in the moral, social, and emotional domains.

As well as the inherent learning processes as one aspect of the student that facilitates the needed learning, Rousseau, like all of the Authors, also stresses another aspect of the student that facilitates this learning—inherent motivation.

Rousseau's View of Inherent Motivation

For Rousseau, the foundation of motivation was rooted in *amour de soi*, which is constantly seeking ways to be preserved, extended and satisfied.

The innate desire for well-being and the impossibility of fully satisfying this desire make him constantly seek for new means of contributing to it. This is the first principle of curiosity, a principle natural to the human heart, but one which develops only in proportion to our passions and our enlightenment.[194]

It is important to remember, however, that *amour-propre* can be a surrogate for *amour de soi* and Rousseau warned of the former becoming a source of motivation. Rousseau believed that reason is the correct and safe "guide of *amour-propre*" so that before a child reaches the age of being able to employ reason well, *amour-propre* should be avoided assiduously.[195] It must especially be avoided as a source of motivation. Consequently, Rousseau felt it was important that a child do nothing out of wanting to receive the praise or avoid the criticism of others; nothing, in short, out of what today is called 'secondary motivation'. Of course, this excludes obedience as a motivation for children, and from this "it follows that they can learn nothing of which they do not feel the real and present advantage in either pleasure or utility."[196] Rousseau frequently stressed that the "advantage" needs to be "present" for the child.

> It is inept to demand that they apply themselves to things one tells them vaguely are for their own good (without their knowing what that good is) and to things they are assured they will profit from when they are grown up (without their taking any interest now in that alleged profit, which they would not be able to understand).[197]

Reiterating part of the discussion on freedom, a child who is conditioned always to ignore his own feelings and sense of what is right to do is robbed of developing "good sense," accustoming "him to always be led," and preparing him to be "a machine in others' hands. You want him to be docile when little: that is to want him to be credulous and a dupe when he is grown up."[198] However, Rousseau felt that as long as a child responds "only to what nature asks of him, …then he will do nothing but good."[199]

Consequently, Rousseau warned teachers that it was not up to them to decide what students should learn, it was up to the students. However, as so often with Rousseau, things are not simple. Rousseau felt that it was up to the teacher to "skillfully give birth" to the students' desires to learn things which, as Rousseau demonstrated, does not exclude the use of ruses and deceptions.

> …you should be well aware that it is rarely up to you to suggest to him what he ought to learn. It is up to him to desire it, to seek it, to find it. It is up to you to put it within his reach, skillfully to give

birth to this desire and to furnish him with the means of satisfying it. It follows, therefore, that your questions should be infrequent but well chosen; since he will put many more questions to you than you to him...[200]

For Rousseau, a principal example of ignoring inherent motivation as a facilitator of the needed learning can be seen in the mainstream approach to learning reading and writing. Rousseau felt that, when a person begins to appreciate human relations,

> The art of speaking to and hearing from absent people, the art of communicating our feelings, our wills, our desires to them at a distance without a mediator is an art whose utility can be rendered palpable to all ages.[201]

Instead of such utility being made obvious, children are forced to learn reading and writing, which then become onerous tasks, and all manner of devices and methods need to be invented to help a child learn what he would rather not do. Rousseau claimed that if the desire to learn is instilled, the child will practically learn by himself.

ASPECTS OF TEACHERS THAT FACILITATE THE NEEDED LEARNING FOR ROUSSEAU

In addition to the aspects of the student being critical to facilitating the needed learning, throughout *Emile*, Rousseau also indicates many aspects of the teachers which facilitate this learning, namely, their understandings of the students, the pedagogical process, and the pedagogic relationship, as well as the teacher's own self development.

Teachers' Understanding of Students and their Needs for Rousseau

Rousseau was convinced that each child is different and, as a consequence, each child needs to be approached differently.

> One must know well the particular genius of the child in order to know what moral diet suits him. Each mind has its own form, according to which it needs to be governed; the success of one's care depends on governing it by this form and not by another. Prudent man, spy out nature for a long time; observe your pupil well before saying the first word to him. [202]

As the "form" for each person is different, the details of education for any particular child must also differ, with the consequence that Rousseau felt that it was impossible to stipulate what children, in general, should learn or when they should learn something.[203] In fact Rousseau believed that, "it is of little importance whether he learns this or that, provided that he get a good conception of what he learns and the use of what he learns."[204] What was important for Rousseau was the development of the person, and such development, Rousseau believed, had little to do with developing specific knowledge. He insisted that the differences between children has to be respected as these are the basis for true development, and these differences are the consequence of differences in character, disposition, geographic location, and social position. He felt there are too many possible permutations of these to allow any intelligent discussion.[205] What Rousseau felt he could discuss were general principles of learning, and general progression in human development. Rousseau did not want the acquisition of knowledge confused with the development of capacities. The rate at which the development of capacities occurs must be natural, according to Rousseau, and can not be speeded up by a teacher without damage to a child, but it can be slowed down without risk (by delaying contact with stimuli). Rousseau advocated such slowing down for sexual development; a development he felt was artificially stimulated by society.[206] Such slowing down, however, is not slowing down the natural development of a child, but rather slowing down artificially accelerated development so that nature can take its proper course. Rousseau's general rule for timing seemed to be to give all instructions "sooner or later as the peaceful or turbulent nature of the pupil accelerates or delays the need."[207]

While Rousseau said that teachers have to study carefully each of their charges because what is taught necessarily "depends on the genius peculiar to each pupil, and the study of that genius depends on the occasions one offers each to reveal himself," Rousseau did not suggest that some careful objective study of a child (as one might carefully study a plant) was sufficient. The subjective experiences of a child are also very important (as seen in the discussion of experiential knowledge), and he claimed these are beyond adult comprehension. The teacher must know the student, but there is a severe limit to such knowledge.

> None of us is philosophic enough to know how to put himself in a child's place.[208]

Teachers' Understanding of
the Correct Pedagogic Process for Rousseau

With Rousseau's notions of nature, it isn't surprising that his basic premise of the correct pedagogic practice is to follow nature. He counseled teachers to "always remember that you are the minister of nature, and you will never be its enemy."[209] The sense throughout Rousseau's work is that if nature is allowed to act on its own without disturbance, it will make a person into a Natural Man. However, with the development of civilization, undisturbed natural processes are no longer possible. The teacher's job, therefore, is to understand what Nature wants (signs of which, Rousseau felt, abound in Nature as well as in the nature of humanity), make an alliance with the forces of nature, and help bring about what nature would have produced if it had not been thwarted by civilization. Rousseau counseled teachers to "leave nature to act for a long time before you get involved with acting in its place, lest you impede its operations."[210] In a sense, much of the correct pedagogy is thwarting harmful effects.

Such thwarting, instead of going towards something, seems to be the principle reason Rousseau described his education as "negative education." Rousseau felt that the surest way of reaching Ultimacy was to teach nothing that is not called for by the child for the first twelve years of the child's life.

> To form this rare man [natural man], what do we have to do? Very much, doubtless. What must be done is to prevent anything from being done.[211]

This is very difficult to achieve in society, and very difficult for a teacher, because a teacher is judged by the student's learning of performances and not by preventing inappropriate learning. Yet this is what Rousseau felt was necessary and amounts to a "doing everything by doing nothing."[212]

As a consequence of Rousseau's notions of developmental stages (with the corollary that engaging in learning prematurely causes damage), Rousseau was more concerned with preventing damage than making progress. He was certain that the learning forces inherent in people insures that they will learn what they need (for "utility" or "pleasure") quickly and easily if such learning is not ruined by premature exposure. What was necessary was prevention, "securing the heart from vice and the mind from error," rather than "teaching virtue" and knowledge.[213] Rousseau felt that the end result of such prevention is a highly educated and wise young adult, and it is the end product that was important for Rousseau, not the intermediary stages.

Rousseau said that one of his important maxims was "that usually one gets very surely and quickly what one is not in a hurry to get."[214] Rousseau was indifferent whether Emile learned how to read before the age of fifteen, though he was certain that Emile would learn well before that age because Emile would see its utility and want to learn it. Rousseau was convinced that if he tried to teach Emile to read before the natural motivation was in place, then the activity would be made onerous to Emile. If reading was made onerous for him, then even if Emile achieved a high level of reading, reading as an activity would be ruined for him. This, Rousseau felt, is too often the result that "positive" education achieves. Consequently he says provocatively, "Dare I expose the greatest, the most important, the most useful rule of all education? It is not to gain time but to lose it."[215]

Rousseau claims that from birth to the age of twelve is the most fragile time of life when a person is most vulnerable to the damage of "errors" and "vices." Rousseau felt that "the only instrument for destroying" such damage was reason, but a child hasn't reached the age of reason before twelve, and therefore has no means of combating such damage. For Rousseau, doing nothing educationally but avoiding error and vice is enough of an accomplishment.

> You know, you say, the value of time and do not want to waste any of it? You do not see that using time badly wastes time far more than doing nothing with it and that a badly instructed child is farther from wisdom than the one who has not been instructed at all. You are alarmed to see him consume his early years in doing nothing. What? Is it nothing to be happy? Is it nothing to jump, play, and run all day? He will never be so busy in his life. ...Therefore, do not be overly frightened by this alleged idleness. What would you say of a man who, in order to profit from his whole life, never wanted to sleep? You would say, "That man is crazy; he does not gain time for his joy; he deprives himself of it. To flee sleep, he races toward death." Be aware, then, that we have here the same thing that childhood is reason's sleep.[216]

Negative education has other aspects as well. Rousseau felt that much moral education can only be approached negatively. Rousseau claimed that the most important moral lesson is "never to harm anyone," and that all notions of doing good must be subordinate to this or they are "dangerous, false, and contradictory,"[217] as can often be seen by the most wicked of men who often try to do good in a limited way or to a limited group. Rousseau believed that "the most sublime virtues are negative,"[218] and although he doesn't list many, there is enough in his text to imagine he might have had the list of Judeo-Christian "thou shalt not" in mind. In his *Social Contract* Rousseau stated simply, "I will never say enough that good education must be negative. Prevent vices from forming and you will have done enough for virtue."[219]

Even intellectual progress is to proceed by a negative approach. Rousseau claimed that it was better for Emile to take pride in "not falling into error" about something, than in "knowing the truth" of that thing;[220] to know he didn't know is better than to mistakenly think he did know, and a surer way of avoiding folly. "To be wise one must discern what is not wise."[221]

One of the tools that Rousseau believed a teacher should use to facilitate the needed learning is, as mentioned previously, what he called the "law of necessity." Most simply, this may be considered as combining the rules which govern the physical universe (e.g., physics, chemistry), human dynamics (e.g., *amour de soi* being the source of all passions), and human relations (e.g., compassion requires empathy). Rousseau felt that it is obviously important for people to understand such laws. Consequently, understanding that there is a law of necessity, as well as understanding what some of those laws are, must be included in education. It is equally important, but far less obvious, that it is these laws which should serve as the basis for childhood discipline. For Rousseau this has several advantages, which he demonstrated by the example of a child lying.

1) A child cannot understand the reasons for prescriptions against lying because moral concepts are beyond his development. However, he can well understand that he is no longer believed because of past lying, and he can see the disadvantage of not being believed especially if he is wrongly accused of something and his protestations of innocence are not believed.[222]

2) If a child is punished for lying (for violating a prescription), he will generally feel that his punishment comes from the punisher who is, as a consequence, seen as the source of his discomfort rather than seeing his lying as the source. The child is, therefore, simply estranged from his punisher, and should this punisher be the teacher, it is anti-educational as the teacher is a person with whom the student should have a good relation.

3) If the consequences of actions come from people (e.g., punish-

ment or rewards) rather than things which follow the law of necessity, a child learns that what is important is the impressions received by those who can reward and punish, with the consequence that the positions of authorities are elevated and the art of dissembling is (unintentionally) encouraged.

For Rousseau, therefore, the teacher needs to understand that the experience of the consequences of the law of necessity "ought to take the place of law for"[223] the student.

The teacher ought not train the student to follow commands but to understand the consequences of actions. The student ought also to not learn to issue commands, but learn to limit his desires to what he can do for himself and so learn the limits of his own strength. Rousseau understood that children cannot do many things for themselves which they need, but feels that such things must be distinguished from doing things for children that they simply want, because a lack of such distinction can give a child an inaccurate sense of his strength, his place in the world, his relations, and his freedom. Due to the law of necessity, such false learning will eventually rebound on the child and continually rebound until accurate senses of strength, place, relations, and freedom are acquired; potentially a prolonged and very painful process. What must be avoided is "an excess of rigor and an excess of indulgence."[224] This is what Rousseau called "well-regulated freedom," which he succinctly described as the student doing "only what he wants; but he ought to want only what you want him to do."[225] Thus, the teacher's understanding of the correct pedagogic process must be embedded in giving a child freedom but within a context the teacher controls (with the context exerting the "law of necessity") that should steer the child in the direction the teacher feels is most apposite.

> All the instruments [for governing children] have been tried save one, the only one precisely that can succeed: well-regulated freedom. One ought not to get involved with raising a child if one does not know how to guide him where one wants by the laws of the possible and the impossible alone. The sphere of both being equally unknown to him, they can be expanded and contracted around him as one wants. One enchains, pushes, and restrains him with the bond of necessity alone without his letting out a peep. He is made supple and docile by the force of things alone without any vice [from reacting to the teacher] having the occasion to germinate in him...[226]

To reinforce Emile's understanding of the law of necessity, Rousseau had as Emile's first book *Robinson Crusoe* as this is the story of a man who needs give no importance to anything but this law. Yet the law of necessity has implications that go far beyond survival, and Rousseau hoped Emile would begin to understand these implications. The law of necessity establishes the "true relations of things" rather than the artificial relations of society, and understanding true relations is the beginning of the formation of judgment.[227] The law of necessity is also the beginning of moral understanding. Rousseau would have the teacher gradually move his instruction from understanding the law of necessity, to seeing what is useful, to finally seeing "what is suitable and good," because what is useful, suitable and good is necessary.[228] In this way, morality finds its rightful place; it is an extension of the law of necessity and not some duty or obligation, and a person with that understanding of morality will remain moral even when it is difficult, while the person who sees morality as duty or obligation will not.

Linked in Rousseau's mind with the law of necessity is learning these laws (whenever it is safe) from experience. For Rousseau then, the correct pedagogic practice is one in which the child experiences the law of necessity in safety, although not always in comfort.

To learn what is truly necessary, Rousseau insisted on the importance of preventing the formation of habits in children. Habits, he felt, are artificial needs and confuse a child's understanding of the law of necessity, so that even the most basic habits should be avoided.

> Food and sleep too exactly measured become necessary for them at the end of the same spans of time, and soon desire no longer comes from need but from habit, or, rather, habit adds a new need to that of nature. That is what must be prevented.
> The only habit that a child should be allowed is to contract none.[229]

While Rousseau would govern the child by expanding and contracting the law of necessity around him, he would also "choose the time, the place, and the objects most favorable to the impression I want to make."[230] The "time" refers not just to the stage of development of a child, but to whether the child is in a frame of mind to learn something. The "objects" refer to those things that a judicious teacher will put in front of a child to excite his curiosity or stimulate his activities. The "place" refers to the context of a lesson (Rousseau sometimes used "place" as one of the "objects") which has importance for a child's ability to make connections between his life and the lesson or between lessons. Much in *Emile* describes Rousseau's application of these three variables (time, objects, and place),[231] but with only a superficial understanding of Rousseau, one could accuse him of shaping a student through the application of stimuli rather than assisting Nature in its unfolding of the student's inherent nature.

The "objects" with which Rousseau would have surrounded a student must be simple enough for him to understand, amusing or useful enough to be of interest and, in the teacher's mind at least, linked to other objects that together might form elements of a complex understanding. Rousseau would not, however, explicate that complex understanding for the child, as this is just the kind of abstraction he felt a child should not be subjected to. This is one of the instances in which Rousseau exhibited an unexplicated notion of pre-conscious cognition. Rousseau believed that if objects and experiences "are connected with one another by some sort of deduction..." students can easily and naturally "order them in their minds and recall them when needed,"[232] thereby generating their own, and therefore, appropriate abstractions. In this way a teacher can avoid the conflation of learning words (that Rousseau was so against) with the learning of things, and avoid the danger of *amour-propre* (from performance/representational learning, rather than competence) that often follows.[233]

As the student gets older, the "objects" include other people and their situations. When the student is young, Rousseau would have only those people around who would not corrupt the student. Yet, Rousseau insisted that if a child is brought up in society, then he must begin early to get "some idea of the relations of man to man and of the morality of human actions."[234] To avoid corruption that might come from too much direct exposure, Rousseau felt it is better to first show the student "men from afar, to show him them in other times or other places...."[235] Rousseau proposed this as the appropriate time for the study of history, as it allows for the study of people, but with a helpful objectivity that automatically comes from the peoples of history coming from another time and often another place. The history Rousseau would start with is biography.[236]

Thus, as the student gets older, Rousseau would have the student directly experience different kinds of people. Rousseau suggested that a young person regularly engage in charitable acts, partly because "it is in doing good that one becomes good; I know of no practice more certain."[237] Another reason for this is that Rousseau felt it is important for young people to understand human nature, but not just human nature in abstraction; human nature and the application of action to human nature.

However, Rousseau believed that the practice of exposing the student to humans in need must be judiciously done. The point is to learn about people and to develop empathy. Great care must be taken that the student "must be touched and not hardened by the sight of human miseries."[238]

Rousseau put as a maxim for the correct pedagogic processes in social development that,

> It is not in the human heart to put ourselves in the place of people who are happier than we, but only in that of those who are more pitiable.[239]

From this Rousseau felt it followed that instead of simply studying the glories and greatness that has been the lot of others, a child should also see the "sad sides" of others.[240]

Rousseau held as a second maxim that,

> One pities in others only those ills from which one does not feel oneself exempt.[241]

From this Rousseau felt it followed that a student must see others less fortunate as not "alien to him"[242] but as different only in fortune, and that good fortune is precarious and fickle. Rousseau would have the student not just hear about this, but "let him see, let him feel the human calamities."[243]

Teachers can extend a student's exposure to actual objects to what Rousseau called "facts." He didn't seem to ask any of the questions modern philosophers might ask about the nature of facts, but seems to be satisfied with a simple definition of facts as "things" and "events." Rousseau's pedagogic practice is to expose the student to things that he can verify with his senses. He would have the younger student verify one sense with another, e.g., seeing that a straw half in water looks like it bends at the point of entry, but then pulling it out and seeing that it isn't bent. For older students he would have them "learn to verify the relations of each sense by itself without need of recourse to another sense";[244] a kind of critical thinking in which each impression is doubted and checked for its inner validity. This level of validation, Rousseau felt, is necessary for the development of judgment, as it is a safeguard against illusion and self-delusion.

Rousseau would also have the student in the early years exposed only to "facts" about history and social relations, without any opinions. Rousseau felt that,

The worst historians for a young man are those who make judgements. Facts! Facts! And let him make his own judgements. It is thus that he learns to know men. If the author's judgement guides him constantly, all he does is see with another's eye; and when that eye fails him, he no longer sees anything.[245]

Such avoidance of opinion is especially difficult with regard to the teacher's own opinions, as facts and opinions are so easily mixed together in our minds. This is another reason to avoid what Rousseau felt were mainstream notions of teaching, and to allow the child to experience things as much as possible on his own. Rousseau believed that there was a time for the teacher to give his own opinion; but, it was more important to first allow the child to develop judgment and to give the child the necessary experience of freedom (which for Rousseau included freedom from opinions). Thus, the time for the teacher to give opinions was only after the child had formed his own judgments.[246] The dangers of public opinion were even more severe.

But if you begin by instructing him in public opinion before teaching him to appraise it, rest assured that, whatever you may do, it will become his, and you will no longer be able to destroy it. I draw the conclusion that to make a young man judicious, we must form his judgements well instead of dictating ours to him.[247]

Rousseau summarizes in one elegant sentence several of his notions about the pedagogic process necessary for facilitating the needed learning.

Set these contrasts side by side, love nature, despise opinion, and know man.[248]

Rousseau also had a great deal to say about the correct pedagogic practices for learning about the passions (which combine many modern notions of desire and emotion). Rousseau was convinced that sexual activity before early adulthood was premature and damaging to morals, character and body. He would prefer to keep a child ignorant of such matters until late adolescence, but was realistic about the practicality of this in society. Since innocence wasn't possible, education at an early age was necessary.

It is important here to leave nothing to chance; and if you are not sure of keeping him ignorant of the difference between the sexes until he is sixteen, take care that he learn it before he is ten.[249]

Rousseau ridiculed those who want to "guide the young soberly" by making "love disgusting to them and would gladly make it a crime for them to think of it at their age, as though love were made for the old."[250] Rousseau felt that the hearts of young people know this is a lie, and because it is contrary to Nature it can never work. He proposed instead to talk to the young about love as "the supreme happiness in life, because in fact it is"[251] and to show the rightful place of sex as the ally of love in order to "disgust him with libertinism."[252] Rousseau claimed that the passions must be conquered, but this can only be done with the passions themselves—akin to fighting fire with fire. He claimed that part of the correct pedagogic processes is understanding that "it is always from nature itself that the proper instruments to regulate nature must be drawn."[253]

Even though Rousseau stated that what a child learned was not important, he did feel that general academic areas should be learned. He wanted Emile to learn to read, to write, to do geometry, geography, and history, etc., but these are abilities to be developed, not to be confused with specific knowledge to be acquired. Rousseau claimed that how much geometry and what specific elements of geometry are learned is unimportant, and what Emile knows should be tied to use and be an aspect of personal development. This is seen perhaps most succinctly in Rousseau's suggestions of teaching children to speak in public.

Teach him to speak plainly and clearly, to articulate well, to pronounce exactly and without affectation, to know and follow grammatical accent and prosody, always to employ enough voice to be heard but never to employ more than is required, a defect common in children raised in colleges. In all things, nothing superfluous.[254]

Rousseau recognized that one of the principle difficulties with the pedagogic processes he advocated (a difficulty that Bernstein points to in his discussion of competence based pedagogy—discussed beginning on page 243) is the problem of assessment. In brief, the problem is that in competence based pedagogy, which has no prescribed curriculum and does not seek displays or performances of learning, the teacher needs to be able to discern the student's learning through what-ever the student happens to show of that learning. Rousseau called mainstream assessment based on asking questions for which there are prescribed answers "vain and pedantic."[255] He believed that

> ...often a word caught in midflight depicts their [the students'] bent and their mind better than a long speech would. But care must be taken that this word is neither dictated nor fortuitous. One must have a great deal of judgement oneself to appreciate a child's.[256]

The reason that "care must be taken" is seen in Rousseau's criticism of "showy displays" discussed previously and his notions of knowledge. Rousseau believed that in mainstream education the emphasis on performance too frequently displays only

> the imitative spirit common to man and ape, which leads both mechanically to want to do everything they see done without quite knowing what it is good for.[257]

Rousseau believed that what is needed is astute observation of the child by the teacher in order to discern the student's talents, nature, disposition and understanding; as it is on the basis of these that the teacher can build. Rousseau claimed that, unfortunately, a person "is not seen in a moment"[258] except by very rare and perceptive observers, but the correct pedagogic practice requires this talent.

> I would want a judicious man to give us a treatise on the art of observing children. This art would be very important to know. Fathers and masters have not yet learned its elements.[259]

One of the difficulties that Rousseau believed teachers have in trying to study the student's "tastes, his inclinations, and his penchants and of seeing the first spark of his genius ignite"[260] is that the teacher confuses his own enthusiasm for that of the student's, which leaves the student looking on passively and uninvolved in the task at hand.[261]

Linking the question of teacher observation with the element of time discussed previously (see page 92, as well as page 236 in the sociological discussion): Teachers need to be able to see their students clearly to know through which stage of development a child is passing. Rousseau believed that teachers who ignore the child's stage of development, and focus instead on the stage they want the child to get to, end up cajoling and coercing what should come about naturally and, in the process, spoiling the very developments they wish to bring about.[262] Rousseau felt that lessons should resemble play: they should be appropriate to the student's development and interests, have as strong an experiential component as possible, and advance only as the student's interests progress (guided indirectly by the teacher).[263]

Obviously, a teacher must have one eye on the future and intended development if the previous discussion on Ultimacy is to make any sense. The other eye, however, must be firmly on what the child is in a position to learn at the time of the lesson,[264] and this depends not only on the specific developmental stage of the child, but the child's frame of mind as well.[265] If "time" (as an aspect determining what a child is in a position to learn) is ignored, then "with chains of truths we heap up only follies and errors in their heads"[266] and feel satisfied that we have given good instruction. This is what Rousseau felt normally occurs with the moralizing and sanctimonious preaching that passes for instruction for both young and old.[267] Rousseau was especially adamant about the element of time as it concerned moral instruction. Rousseau believed that attempts to instruct in morals before the correct time do more than "heap up follies and errors," they often corrupt the unprepared mind. Speaking about things that students can't properly understand serves only "to give them a desire to know those things,"[268] and the teacher ends up doing the work of the devil.

> On this earth, out of which nature has made man's first paradise, dread exercising the tempter's function in wanting to give innocence the knowledge of good and evil.[269]

It is hardly surprising, therefore, that with reference to time, Rousseau counseled delaying all acts that might trigger development which is not called for by the student's nature, situation or inclination. This does not ensure the greatest rate of advance, but it avoids most damage, which in the long run, is far more costly.

> Regard all delays as advantages; to advance toward the end without losing anything is to gain a lot. Let childhood ripen in children. And what if some lessons finally become necessary to them? Keep yourself from giving it today if you can without danger put it off until tomorrow.[270]

For Rousseau, the correct pedagogic processes must involve harnessing the inherent motivation mentioned previously. The teacher must understand that motivation is related to stages of development (i.e., a child is not inherently motivated to learn something that is beyond him or too easy for him), and related to *amour de soi*. Instruction should be "suitable to his [the student's] age" and "in forms which will make it loved."[271] This is as important for correct instruction in moral and emotional matters as it is for academic ones. Rousseau felt that if a love of something could be engendered as well as knowledge of how to learn, then the needed learning would always occur.[272] For moral, social and (what today might be called) "character" development, Rousseau felt that much is accomplished by engendering a love of beauty (the beauty of nature, of good relations, of acting rightly, etc.) and it is such a love that is the basis of real happiness.[273] Consequently, Rousseau insisted that "talent at instruction consists in making the disciple enjoy the instruction,"[274] to the extent that:

> They [students] should not be offered lessons; they should be the ones to ask for them. A reward ought not to be made into a chore; ...the first step toward success is to want to succeed.[275]

Rousseau felt the teacher should be wary of false or corrupted motivation, as would be the case if the motivation came from a per- verted *amour-propre*. Rousseau felt it was important to prevent this and gave careful instruction in several instances on how this can be avoided.[276] He was especially against comparisons and competition as motivation as these are particularly corrupting.

> I prefer a hundred times over that he not learn what he would only learn out of jealousy or vanity.[277]

Consequently, Rousseau felt it was necessary for the teacher to "pay less attention to the words [the student] pronounces than to the mo- tive which causes him to speak."[278] Seeing the student's motives, there- fore, is an important responsibility of the teacher in his care for the overall development of the student,[279] and an important part of the assessment a teacher is responsible for making. This makes sense if what needs to be learned is sagacious competence (see page 35), but it has little or no importance if performance is the goal of education.

Many of Rousseau's notions of correct pedagogic processes stem from his view that we have three sources of education—nature, men, and things.

> The internal development of our faculties and our organs is the education of nature. The use we are taught to make of this

development is the education of men. And what we acquire from our own experience about the objects which affect us is the education of things.[280]

The education coming from nature is beyond the control of people, "that coming from things is in our control only in certain respects,"[281] so it is only "the education of men" that can be entirely determined by the teacher. Rousseau felt these three sources of education must be in harmony for the student to grow in harmony. From this it follows that what is in the control of teachers must be directed so as to be in harmony with that over which there is no control. Consequently, Rousseau felt that education cannot succeed when it is prescriptive, as that is an activity removed from directly following nature as it exists in the student.

Teachers' Understanding of the Correct Pedagogic Relationship for Rousseau

With respect to Rousseau's views on what facilitates the necessary learning for Ultimacy, he also gave specific recommendations about the correct pedagogic relationship, as well as mistakes to avoid with respect to that relationship. Rousseau's notions of the correct pedagogic relationship that teachers must understand revolve around two issues, both of which have been discussed before and which are connected. The first of these issues is authority, and the second is Rousseau's notions of the law of necessity.

Rousseau's notions of authority are singular: for the most part, there shouldn't be any.

> Command him nothing, whatever in the world it might be, absolutely nothing. Do not even allow him to imagine that you might pretend to have any authority over him.[282]

This was his suggestion even for infants, and Rousseau felt there can be no compromise on the issue.

> ...there is no middle point here: nothing must be demanded from him at all, or he must be bent from the outset to the most perfect obedience.[283]

What Rousseau wanted instead is for the teacher to use the law of necessity which, in terms of the pedagogic relationship, means letting the child perceive that he is incapable of many things of which the teacher is capable, and for which the child needs the help of the adult. It is the exercise of capacity not authority that Rousseau sees as the precursor to the child learning the law of necessity. Preventing the child from doing things rather than forbidding it (and doing so through things, e.g., putting something the child should not play with out of reach rather than forbidding it) will help the child see that he must yield to "the heavy yoke of necessity" that exists in things rather than yielding to "the caprice of men."[284]

An aspect of authority that Rousseau frequently mentions is the authority of the child, which also has no place in the upbringing of a child. Rousseau would not allow the child to command and would especially not allow a power struggle to occur between the child and the adult, as this destroys the correct pedagogic relationship.[285]

There are other mistakes related to authority that can destroy the pedagogic relationship, which for Rousseau, must be based on affection and trust. Children automatically, and rightly (due to *amour de soi*) have a need to evade or reduce any authority that restricts their freedom, and this they do by looking for and exploiting the weaknesses of those who exercise authority.

> One of children's first efforts, as I have said, is to discover the weakness of those who govern them. This inclination leads to wickedness but does not come from it. It comes from the need to elude an authority which importunes them. Overburdened by the yoke imposed on them, they seek to shake it off, and the shortcomings they find in the masters furnish them with good means for that.[286]

This sets up a relationship of opposition where the teacher is trying to coerce the student and the student is trying to find and exploit the weaknesses of the teacher, with the result that the affection and trust Rousseau felt is necessary in education becomes impossible. When there is no authority and no attempt to coerce, Rousseau believed the student has no need to deceive or hide. With this transparency the teacher can engage in that vital activity of understanding the particular student and then "arrange all around him [the student] the lessons you want to give him without his ever thinking he is receiving any."[287]

In what Rousseau called "the Second Age" (placed between infancy and adolescence) the most obvious uses of the law of necessity to direct the child are, according to Rousseau, to be replaced by "chains…put around his heart. Reason, friendship, gratitude, countless affections speak to him in a tone he cannot fail to recognize."[288] Such complex emotions (which are all extensions of *amour de soi*, and so are "passions of nature"[289]) become possible at this age, and these should remain uncorrupted and the basis of the pedagogic relationship. Rousseau believed that if a student finds a teacher lying to him it "would ruin forever the whole fruit of the education,"[290] as would any deception on the part of the teacher that is perceived by the student.

A deception related to notions of authority, which Rousseau felt often occurred, was the teacher "affecting a magisterial dignity and wanting to pass for a perfect man in the mind of one's disciple."[291] This is a terrible mistake because the image is impossible to maintain, but even if it were to be, it would destroy the basis of a positive pedagogic relationship. In terms that adumbrate Rogers, Rousseau calls for authenticity, for being someone whose humanness generates empathy and, therefore, listening on the part of the students. Rousseau castigated teachers who "run down their pupils" in order to "play wise men," and implored teachers instead to "make them [the students] your equals in order that they may become your equals."[292] Of course, this isn't possible for a teacher who wants to maintain a power differential in order to control the student and, for Rousseau, such disempowering of the student is anti-educational.

Part of making a student "your equal" is to allow the student the freedom to make mistakes. Rousseau felt the teacher must "warn him [the student] of the perils to which he is exposed…clearly and sensibly, but without exaggeration, ill humor, pedantic display…" or advice disguised as an order.[293] If the student insists on doing what he is warned against, Rousseau advised the teacher to accompany him on his mistake, partly for protection and partly because Rousseau believed that the lesson for the child is reinforced by the child seeing the teacher also suffer the consequences of his mistake. What the teacher must never do is engage in rebukes and "I told you so" which can "only inflame [the student's] *amour-propre* and make it rebel."[294] There is another element to this accompanying the child in all things that Rousseau did not belabor but which is an interesting aspect of what he felt is the correct pedagogic relationship. It is learning with the student. Rousseau claimed of Emile, "I am convinced that he will only ever learn well what we learn together."[295] Rousseau often implies that even though the teacher may already know about a subject, he can always learn more, and the teacher's engaging in the learning process for himself is an important part of the student's learning to engage in the learning process.

Rousseau counseled a dramatic change in the pedagogic relationship when the student reaches young adulthood (which for Rousseau was determined by sexual development).

> When, by the signs of which I have spoken, you have a presentiment of the critical moment, instantly abandon your old tone with him forever. He is still your disciple, but he is no longer your pupil. He is your friend, he is a man. From now on treat him as such.[296]

The teacher's role now is to make himself wanted by the student by his charm, his worthy personality, and his wisdom. The student no longer feels he needs the teacher, but instead wants him as his confidant and his friend.[297]

Teachers' Self-Development for Rousseau

Rousseau believed that a teacher must first accomplish in himself the development he would wish in his student. He stated that he "cannot repeat often enough that to be the child's master one must be one's own master."[298] However, Rousseau didn't go further than seeing the value of this as residing in the importance of example.

> Remember that before daring to undertake the formation of a man, one must have made oneself a man. One must find within oneself the example the pupil ought to take for his own.[299]

As Rousseau believed that "being a man" lay in Ultimacy and that virtue was one of the prime characteristics of Ultimacy, Rousseau counseled the prospective teacher to gain mastery by developing virtue. This, Rousseau believed, would generate respect in other people who surround the student, which in turn would help the student have the correct respectful relationship with the teacher.[300]

CHAPTER 6

Johann Heinrich Pestalozzi

A BIOGRAPHICAL SKETCH
OF JOHANN HEINRICH PESTALOZZI
(12 JANUARY 1746 – 17 FEBRUARY 1827)

*P*estalozzi was born into an Italian merchant family which had immigrated to Switzerland in the middle of the 16th century. His family was only modestly prosperous, and trade kept his father away from home for the first five years of Pestalozzi's life. Some commentators have speculated that this early experience of having only a mother's influence in his life inspired the importance he placed on the role of mother in early childhood learning, but there seems little reason to suppose he could not have reached the same views had both his parents been present in his early life. He was an able student and progressed to the study of theology in order to become a clergyman at the prestigious Collegium Carolinum in Zurich. Once there, however, he became politically active and switched to the study of law with the intention of pursuing a political administration career. His political activism led him to join youthful idealists in promoting the Helvetic Society (a political movement proposing to overthrow the aristocratic cantonal governments of Switzerland), an activism which eventually caused him to be expelled from college. Before his expulsion, however, Pestalozzi read and was greatly inspired by the then newly published work of Rousseau, most notably *Emile*, and *The Social Contract*. Filled with idealism, he wanted to go 'back to nature'. Pestalozzi acknowledged the importance of Rousseau's influence right until the end of his life.

In 1769 Pestalozzi married Ana Schultess, daughter of a successful merchant and heiress. With her inheritance Pestalozzi and his wife bought their first of several farms, all of which were to fail for lack of agricultural skill and business acumen. A year after marriage, the Pestalozzis had a son who they named after Rousseau (Johann Jakob as the Swiss-German equivalent of Jean-Jacques), but for some reason and in some way now lost in history, this child was mentally challenged and remained his family's charge into adulthood.

By 1774 Pestalozzi was forced to abandon agriculture and tried to start a textile business on his property. His intention was to take in poor children, teach them to spin and weave, and at the same time give them lessons and moral instruction so that they could become self-supporting. He was, however, far more interested in not exploiting the children than in making money, and the costs of feeding, clothing, educating and housing these waifs caused this venture to lose money dramatically, and ended in financial failure.

In 1780 Pestalozzi wrote his first book, *The Evening Hour of the Hermit*, in which many of his lasting educational principles appear, e.g., education had to be according to nature, learning should proceed from the familiar to the new, emotional responses and the pace of learning of each individual child had to be respected, the security a child finds in the home is the foundation of morality and happiness, etc. His book was an immediate success, and Pestalozzi finally found an activity at which he wouldn't lose money, writing. The success of this book was followed by *Leonard and Gertrude* in 1787 which was an even greater success. In this novel, Gertrude saves her village by her morality and is an inspiration to all with her integrity and well ordered home, with which she clearly demonstrates the right foundation for early education. Ten years later Pestalozzi writes the non-fiction *My Inquiries into the Course of Nature in the Development of Mankind*. In this work, Pestalozzi claims to have studied from observation the nature of humans and to see the basis for helping people develop so that they can think for themselves.

By 1798 the French Revolution had spread to Switzerland, and Pestalozzi was asked by the new (French supported) central government in Stans to set up an orphanage and school for the children in that city whom the war had made destitute. Pestalozzi engaged in this project with all of his remaining resources and vigor, and despite what he claimed was the most exhausting time he ever knew, he often recalled this period as the happiest of his life. His building overflowed with more than four hundred children, and he would have taken more had space allowed. After only seven months, the orphanage had to close when the French army wanted Pestalozzi's buildings for a hospital after suffering reverses against the Austrians. The government of the Helvetic Republic then asked Pestalozzi to organize higher education in the devastated new republic, but Pestalozzi refused this offer as he felt his help was most urgently needed by the poor and usually orphaned children for whom no one else was caring.

Despite Pestalozzi's earnings from his writing and his wife's inheritance, Pestalozzi's care for poor children ruined him. All accounts of him remark on his appearance—tall, gangly, gaunt, often appearing underfed, and disheveled—yet they also remark on his obvious compassion, kindness, and selflessness. Throughout his career in education (which was almost always with poor children) he was known by his students as "Father Pestalozzi," a name of endearment which he seems to have repeatedly earned for always trying to create the loving family atmosphere (even for more than four hundred children at a time) that he felt children needed.

From 1800 to 1804 Pestalozzi ran another school, this time at Burgdorf, but again he spent on the children more money than he could find, and this too failed. During this time (1801) he published *How Gertrude Teaches Her Children* which served as an educational manual for mothers to teach their children. This was principally about intellectual education, which still had importance despite its secondary importance to moral education (or what today some call 'personal education'). Borrowing from Rousseau, he felt that humans have innate intellectual faculties, and these should evolve from observation to comprehension to the formation of "clear ideas."

In 1805 Pestalozzi started his most successful educational venture and the one that would make him most famous. For twenty years his school at Yverdon near Neuchâtel was visited by educators from all over Europe and America. It was the laboratory that proved the validity of his educational theories on intellectual, moral, and physical education. It was here that Froebel, Ritter, and other famous educators took their training and their inspiration. Yverdon had a combination of fee paying students and poor students, and Pestalozzi seems to have found a formula for a school that could make ends meet (when combined with his substantial publishing income). There was, however, to be no happy ending for Pestalozzi. Squabbles and infighting amongst the staff developed that Pestalozzi could do nothing to quell. Those who didn't leave, turned on Pestalozzi and soon the fee paying students started to leave. Pestalozzi left in 1825 hoping those who remained could make something of the place if he was gone, and he retreated to Neuhof with a few of his poor students, but Yverdon didn't last.

In 1826 Pestalozzi published *Swan Song*, a beautiful little book in which he presents what he felt life had taught him about education, and in which he insists that "life educates"—a phrase with which he would thereafter be associated.

A year later, after one of his many solitary evening walks on a cold rainy night, he contracted pneumonia and died.

PESTALOZZI'S NOTION OF ULTIMACY

Pestalozzi used language that is more conventionally religious than Rousseau, but not conventional enough to have prevented him from getting into trouble, like his hero, with the religious convictions of the governing authorities. He followed Rousseau in feeling that the best a person can aspire to is what is natural, but he tended to equate "nature" with "human nature" which he explicitly linked with the sacred: "[T]o elevate human nature to its highest, its noblest" requires developing "whatever of the divine and eternal lies within its nature."[301] This "elevation" was the goal of education, and is clearly a notion of Ultimacy.

While Rousseau had trouble with the governing authorities because of the religious views he espoused quite late in his career, Pestalozzi had similar trouble much earlier. During the early part of Pestalozzi's career, there was a great deal of political turmoil between monarchists and republicans, and between Catholic and Protestant movements that swept through the areas in which Pestalozzi was trying to start schools. Consequently, he avoided making statements that could be read as being against any religion, promoting only religiousness. Furthermore, he maintained that it is not through any church or dogma that the divine within is to be realized, rather "only in the holy power of love do I recognize the basis of the development of my [human] race to whatever of the divine and eternal lies within its nature."[302] As the "divine and eternal" was seen as within the nature of each child, the nature of each child has to be respected by education, and education itself must follow nature. Such statements many have avoided seeming to favor either Catholics or Protestants, but they succeeded in antagonizing both.

Ultimacy in Relation to Pestalozzi's View of Human Nature

In examining Pestalozzi's view of human nature, he didn't contradict the themes in Rousseau's work but often developed them. He, like Rousseau, described Ultimacy as "manhood" or "Man," but he is a bit more helpful in telling us what that means. He said, for example, that a "Man" is someone who "is developed in his innermost powers."[303] The reader is also told that "man will only become Man through his inner and spiritual life,"[304] and a spiritual life is not to be found by a person in any outward expression of religiosity, but only in "the innermost sanctuary of his being." It is only here that Pestalozzi believed that a person could "find a genuine foundation for future love and power."[305]

In the early part of his career, Pestalozzi felt that allowing a child to follow nature (as he saw it, and very much as Rousseau explained it) was enough to ensure Ultimacy, but he changed this view as he grew older.[306] Unlike Rousseau, Pestalozzi had the benefit of years of experimenting, and many of the lessons he learned were quite hard. He came to feel that "the education of nature" (i.e., a natural education or education according to divine nature) comes only from developing an awareness of one's inner life, which he called "the inner consciousness of thy powers."[307] These inner powers "are innate in every man"[308] and they include capacities of love and *Anschauung*.

Anschauung has no exact English equivalent, and Pestalozzi even used the word in an unorthodox way in German. This may be due to his being raised speaking Swiss German, or to his need to stretch the orthodox meaning to suit his purpose. *Anschauung* is variously translated as "sense impression," "perception," "intuition," and the *capacity* to see, hear or perceive, as well as other terms for subtle perception. Essentially, it refers to a person's direct, "natural," and unmediated contact with the world; "a face-to-face experience of the realities of the universe,"[309] a way of knowing that is non-conceptual or pre-conceptual.[310]

Capacities, Pestalozzi tells us, are in a child even before the child is born.[311] Children first learn of love from their mothers (if they are fortunate in having good mothers) even before they are old enough to realize they are learning. They do this through *Anschauung*. *Anschauung*, however, needs to be developed, and education, according to Pestalozzi, has a large responsibility in that development. *Anschauung*, Pestalozzi felt, is the first way we have of knowing as an infant, the primary way that we have of knowing new things, and the only way we have of knowing certain inner things. *Anschauung* also helps to explain Pestalozzi's version of listening or sensing within, and it is fundamental to Pestalozzi's view of the relationship between Ultimacy and human nature.[312] He frequently, and in many different ways, expressed the importance in his education of such sensing of the Ultimacy within.[313]

An important difference between holistic education and mainstream education follows from Pestalozzi's notions of the capacities of the child, capacities he described as "inner powers." Because of these inherent capacities, children ought not to be molded according to a model, or made into something that is alien to them. While this notion is mostly implied by Rousseau, Pestalozzi and all the Authors who historically succeed him wrote explicitly about this and that it marks one of their principal differences with mainstream education. Pestalozzi felt strongly enough about this that he not only wrote about it in his books, but often stated it to his students as though he felt he needed to frequently reassure them on this subject.[314]

Like Rousseau, Pestalozzi felt that forces of nature drive the "purposeful evolution" described above. Pestalozzi also—at first just hinting, but later more openly—wrote of another "unseen force in the human organism in the production of a Man, a being made in the image of God...."[315] We must understand "Man" as Pestalozzi used the word means both genders, and indicates a full maturity into Ultimacy, as it is the finest and most complete human development. This good, natural and "unseen force" is, in an unspecified way, related to the divine. In Pestalozzi's last book, it is implied that by a person becoming Man (which is his duty and his natural destiny) God manifests.

Ultimacy As an Aspect of Religiousness for Pestalozzi

In terms of Ultimacy as an aspect of religiousness, Pestalozzi felt that "nature forms the child as an indivisible whole," and that all of a child's capacities are linked.[316] Pestalozzi never said how or when children stop being whole, but by the time they are of school age, he claimed they are in need of an education that will give them the unification that forms part of his notion of Ultimacy. Pestalozzi implied that society (or parents, family, or bad education) creates this fragmentation or disharmony by over-emphasizing some of the faculties at the expense of others. This, he felt, is like a bud that only opens a few of its petals, with the result that the whole of the flower is ruined, for not only does the whole need each part, but each part needs the development of every other part for its full fruition.[317]

Pestalozzi repeated Rousseau's categories of head, heart, and hand, and saw these as an "important witness to the unity of man's nature"[318] because they represent man's moral, intellectual, and physical capacities. For Pestalozzi, "only that which affects man as an indissoluble unit is educative in our sense of the word," and warned: "'What God has joined [the wholeness of a human] let no man put asunder.'"[319]

WHAT NEEDS TO BE LEARNED FOR PESTALOZZI

Pestalozzi's View of Experiential Knowledge

Pestalozzi's doctrine of *Anschauung* forms the basis of his notions of experiential knowledge. Hayward sums up this doctrine as, "'Things before Words' and 'Concrete before Abstract'."[320] Pestalozzi stated his epistemology simply and frequently.

> The most essential point from which I start is this: Sense impression [*Anschauung*] of Nature is the only true foundation of human instruction, because it is the only true foundation of human knowledge.
> All that follows is the result of this sense impression [*Anschauung*], and the process of abstraction from it.[321]

Just as *Anschauung* meant the inner listening and seeing needed to know the divine within, for Pestalozzi, it also meant listening to the emotions and the mind.[322] Consequently, *Anschauung* also encompassed intuition for Pestalozzi,[323] reflecting what Rousseau called "the sixth sense."

For Pestalozzi, the notion of *Anschauung* reinforced Rousseau's contention that lessons should be found in the everyday experiences of the child and not imposed by some idea of curriculum. As mentioned, one of Pestalozzi's favorite maxims was, "life educates."[324] Lessons based on the immediate life of the child are able be contextualized by the child and are, therefore, more likely to be meaningful.

The most important mistake of present-day education is undoubtedly the following: Too much is expected of the child and too many of the topics only appear to be something [to the child] but are nothing.[325]

Pestalozzi felt that "the mode of doing this [ensuring lessons come from the child] is not by any means to talk much *to* a child, but to enter into conversation *with* a child;...."[326] This is one of many statements by Pestalozzi which indicate his sense that children deserve respect and that they have certain rights to determine their own education; a remarkable attitude towards children in eighteenth century Europe.

Such respect is also evident in Pestalozzi's notion of "spontaneous-activity" (which Froebel renamed "self-activity") whereby a child is left free to follow his impulses, generating activity that the teacher could then use for instruction. With children playing together, this same principle is applied to groups of children, becoming a group version of the doctrine of lessons following from experience.

Following impulses was also seen by Pestalozzi as a way for a child to learn about himself and what his vocation is. Watching such spontaneous-activity is, Pestalozzi felt, an important tool for the teacher in gaining insights into individual children, enabling the teacher to know how best to teach each child. Pestalozzi was firm in his commitment that education was meant to fit the child, not the reverse.

...education, instead of merely considering what is to be imparted to children, ought to consider first what they may be said to already possess, if not as a developed, at least as an involved faculty capable of development.[327]

The link between living and learning was extremely important for Pestalozzi. He claimed that knowledge disengaged from application is "a fearful gift from a fiendish spirit" because "knowing and doing are so closely connected, that if one ceases, the other [in any meaningful sense] ceases with it."[328]

For Pestalozzi, it is partly due to the emotions that "life educates." It is only in feeling things that, he believed, they really have meaning,[329] and this is as true for moral knowledge as for knowledge of objects.[330] Pestalozzi's notions of emotional development constituted an important aspect of *Anschauung*, and are the foundations of moral and social development. None of the other Authors wrote as frequently or as passionately about love. Pestalozzi felt that the natural love that children have for their mothers is "the first feeling of an higher nature"[331] (i.e., feeling of the Divine within), and he declared that it is this love that guided the development of his method of education. In an address to the students at his school in Yverdon he said,

> Children, that this love may increase, and be assured within you, is all that we propose for our object. Instruction, as such, and of itself, does not produce love, any more than it produces hate. Therefore it is that it is not the essence of education. Love is its essence.[332]

For Pestalozzi, "all human wisdom is based on a good heart,"[333] as is morality. Pestalozzi held that love gives rise to justice, justice to freedom, and "therefore freedom is also based upon love."[334] Moral development entails broadening the heart. It followed for Pestalozzi that "one of the most effective aids of moral education"[335] was music (with drawing following closely), because music and drawing can stir and extend the hearts of children.

Pestalozzi frequently demonstrated his belief in the primacy of experience, as he did in defining "clear ideas" as those "to which...experience can bring no more clearness."[336] However, Pestalozzi found more use for representational knowledge than Rousseau. While experience is the ultimate base of all knowledge, Pestalozzi believed that representations are often needed to enhance or extend experiential knowledge. More than Rousseau's summarizing of the child's experience into a maxim or drawing connections to similar knowledge, Pestalozzi held that words are needed after the experience for even simple things.[337] For example, Pestalozzi would have the mother (or infant teacher) give a child spheres of different sizes, roll them around on the floor, and indicate roundness with hand movements before saying the word "round." Saying the word, however, was important for Pestalozzi. To be presented with experience and representation in the reverse order was, for Pestalozzi, a violation of our nature (which develops senses before developing the capacity to understand representation). If such reversals become a habit, they make seeing truth more difficult because methods of learning become ingrained which are contrary to those of learning truth, which always conform to nature.[338]

Like Rousseau, Pestalozzi was scornful of representations substituting for experience, and Pestalozzi felt that "real knowledge" could not be derived from "word-teaching and mere talk."[339] However, unlike Rousseau, Pestalozzi addressed the issue of how things that have no physicality might be experienced and taught through experience.[340] It seems that, for Pestalozzi, there are, what can be called, levels of abstraction or representation. For example, the direct experience of a tree with no representation of any kind is the least abstracted. A painting of a tree is a representation of the tree but, as it has form and color which provide some sensory experience, it is less abstracted than a mere verbal description of the tree which would have no such experiences. As a consequence of this view of levels of abstraction, Pestalozzi encouraged teachers and others to give lessons about abstract notions (e.g., honesty, loyalty) with stories and songs which, he believed, give the child some level of experience. Pestalozzi's books for mothers and teachers are full of songs and stories he created for teaching such lessons. This is one of the few instances in which Pestalozzi is in direct opposition to Rousseau, who felt that the fables meant as moral lessons for children are useless because children do not have the necessary experiences to draw the intended inferences.

While Pestalozzi was not as disparaging as Rousseau about words being part of instruction, he did condemn as strongly as Rousseau the "baseless, wordy show" that passed for demonstrations of learning, likening such performance based pedagogy to toadstools growing on dung heaps of worthless learning.[341] Pestalozzi reinforced Rousseau's preference for competence based pedagogy over performance based pedagogy, and like Rousseau, identified the predominance of representations in education as what allowed, if not encouraged, the perversity of performance based pedagogy. Pestalozzi saw the mainstream preference for such pedagogy as responsible for both the failure of education in his society[342] and for the "civil, moral, and religious degradation" that, he felt, necessarily follows such failure.[343] In a statement that seems diametrically opposed to one of the goals often claimed for liberal education, Pestalozzi claimed that his approach to education demands that, "…knowledge be a product of the cultivated mind and not that the cultivated mind should be a product of knowledge."[344]

Pestalozzi claimed that his own knowledge of education was "real knowledge" because it came from his experiences of those who learned (children and adults)—not from books, but from life.

> In the matter of education I am usually very anxious to learn the ideas of people who have been brought up quite naturally and without restraint, who have been taught by life itself, and not by lessons. [345]

Competence for Pestalozzi

Pestalozzi, who had the benefit of actually running schools, was even more antagonistic to performance based pedagogy than Rousseau.

For Pestalozzi, the notion of competence is related to his notion of *Fertikgkeit*, which is variously translated as promptitude, readiness in skill or in performing (but not the skill or performance itself), habits of action, facility, capabilities, the ability to *do*, etc. Pestalozzi believed that *Fertikgkeit* comes from developing the "deeper faculties" which are common in everyone (as discussed on pages 110 to 111). In Pestalozzi's last book, he often explained the difference between his method of education (which he called "The Elementary Method") and other methods by describing his method's emphasis on competence.

> It is a psychological instrument for assisting Nature in the unfolding of our physical, intellectual, and moral powers. An intelligent visitor who had been watching a lesson in number remarked: *"C'est un pouvoir, ce n'est pas un savoir."* [It is an ability to 'do,' it is not a knowing.] His comment exactly and clearly expressed the position and the difference between the "elementary" method and all others.[346]

In that same book, Pestalozzi made a distinction between "unfolding man's natural capacities" and the "special branches of knowledge and special dexterities in which those powers are applied."[347] The development of these natural capacities (which, for Pestalozzi, are related to Ultimacy) must always take precedence over the "application and use of these powers…" which is a contrast between competence and performance.[348] Pestalozzi, in several places, acknowledged that performance based pedagogy can produce people who perform valued tasks (e.g., "tailors, shoemakers, tradesmen, and soldiers; …"[349]), but it fails to approach competence and so doesn't relate to Ultimacy, consequently failing in the principal task of education as he saw it. The mainstream emphasis on the application of capacities (rather than their unfolding) was the reason Pestalozzi gave for the failure of all the special educational systems he saw created for the poor; they only tried to train poor people for work "whereas human nature demands a whole education. A half education is worth nothing."[350] Pestalozzi felt that his method of education resulted in a person being as capable in "application" as performance based schools, but who would also be "a *man* in the highest sense of the word."[351]

Having criticized schools and teachers, as Rousseau had, for looking after their own interests ahead of the students', Pestalozzi reminded educators that "the ultimate end of education is, not the accomplishments of the school, but [the students'] fitness for life."[352] Pestalozzi believed that the inability in most schools to distinguish between competence based pedagogy and performance based pedagogy was responsible for "the waste of time and the deceptive exhibition of apparent knowledge" which he believed occupied most of the time and attention in schools.[353] He felt that this "artificial show of acquirement which ornaments over [the] lack of inner natural powers"[354] was peculiar to his century rather than as part of a trend, as it is still seen by many in holistic education today.

Reinforcing Pestalozzi's antagonism to performance based pedagogy was his aversion to children developing "virtuosity" (which today might be considered as "excellence") in any one discipline. He was suspicious of the motives (e.g., egotism) for developing virtuosity, and he felt it detracted from the demands of Ultimacy for balance. Ultimacy, for Pestalozzi, requires "that all the faculties implanted in human nature should be properly developed" which relates to meta-learning.[355]

Characteristics of Competence for Pestalozzi

Pestalozzi made no significant departure from Rousseau on questions of values or judgment. One small elaboration of the question of judgment is found in a letter he wrote to revise *How Gertrude Teaches Her Children* in which he describes the ideal man and why such a man would be so admired by his society. The qualities that rightly generate such esteem are "…judgment, kindness, and a sense of duty…"[356] with a further explanation that judgment always employs kindness and duty.

Pestalozzi frequently described social responsibility in relation to freedom from authority in a way which might initially seem paradoxical; only by being independent of society can one be truly useful to it. Pestalozzi sometimes seems to anticipate Jung's notion of differentiation.

> In relation to society, man should be qualified by education to be a useful member of it. In order to be truly useful, it is necessary that he be truly *independent*…. An individual whose actions bear the stamp of independence of mind cannot but be a useful as well as an esteemed member of society…. That such instances are but exceptions, and that these exceptions are so few, is owing to the system of education which generally prevails, and which is little calculated to promote independence of character.[357]

Consequently, Pestalozzi named one of the three ends of education as "to render him [the student] useful by rendering him independent with relation to society...."[358] Such independence must be practiced in school, and Pestalozzi believed a child should not be compelled to act against his will, or as Rousseau would have it "in spite of himself." This extended to not preventing a child from making mistakes (with due consideration to safety) if the child was determined. In his diary entry for 18th February 1774 Pestalozzi wrote, "If he often asks for something you do not think good, tell him what the consequences will be and leave him his liberty."[359]

Pestalozzi extended Rousseau's comments that judgment sometimes involves foresight to do something onerous in order to avoid something worse in the future. This judgment began, he felt, with learning deferred gratification. His belief that such judgment is an indicator of educational success has been borne out by some recent psychological studies.[360]

> Her [the mother's] first and almost infallible criterion [of whether she is educating her child well] will be, if she really succeeds in accustoming her child to the practice of self-denial.
> Of all the mental habits which may be formed by a judicious education, that of self-denial is the most difficult to acquire, and the most beneficial when adopted.[361]

Pestalozzi's educational method was widely adopted by the Prussians as a way of reconstructing their society after the devastation of the Napoleonic Wars,[362] partly because his approach was seen as a way of strengthening the culture of a country. Pestalozzi saw his Elementary Method as "...securing to their country her glory and her liberty by a moral elevation of her children."[363] Yet, he did not believe education should be for society or social adaptation (unlike Dewey); but rather, like Rousseau, he saw education as existing to help the individual approach Ultimacy, with the automatic consequence that such individuals contribute to their culture. Pestalozzi was as scathing as Rousseau about education for social intentions, and about state education "for the masses." One of the most interesting quotes from Pestalozzi on this issue is quoted by Jung.

> None of the institutions, measures, and means of education established for the masses and the needs of men in the aggregate, whatever shape or form they may take, serve to advance human culture. In the vast majority of cases they are completely worthless for that purpose and are directly opposed to it. Our race develops in human qualities in essence only from face to face, from heart to heart.

Essentially it develops only in little intimate circles which gradually grow in graciousness and love, in confidence and trust. All the means requisite for the education of man, which serve to make him truly humane and to bring him to mankindliness, are in their origin and essence the concern of the individual and of such institutions as are closely and intimately attached to his heart and mind. They never were nor will be the concern of the masses. They never were nor will be the concern of civilization.[364]

ASPECTS OF STUDENTS THAT FACILITATE THE NEEDED LEARNING FOR PESTALOZZI

Pestalozzi felt he was studying nature by his study of children because he believed he was studying what is natural in children. He was convinced that understanding the natural and, therefore, inherent learning processes would solve the problems of education, and he often described his educational method as a simple following of nature. He claimed that,

> All instruction of man is then only the Art of helping Nature to develop in her own way; and this Art rests essentially on the relation and harmony between the impressions received by the child and the exact degree of his developed powers.[365]

Like Rousseau, Pestalozzi felt that the "degree of…developed powers" progress in stages, although he was less specific than Rousseau in delineating these stages. He frequently repeated Rousseau's dictums that it is detrimental to reason with children too early[366] and that in pushing children to learn something before they are ready "the faculties of the mind are weakened, and lose their steadiness, and the equipoise of their structure."[367] Linking this topic with those of performance versus competence and learning through representations, Pestalozzi felt that such pushing is usually done with "the thousandfold confusions of word-learning and opinions."[368] Similarly, Pestalozzi felt that the stage in the inherent learning process that allows children to feel "faith and love in themselves" and to "think, feel, and act rightly" was prior to the stage which allows the student to understand theology. This prior stage of feeling, therefore, needs to be successfully completed before this second, more theoretical, study is started.[369]

For Pestalozzi, his doctrine of "free activity" or "spontaneous activity" (depending on the translator) helps the teacher determine when the successive stages are reached. This doctrine is linked to the topic of motivation and is discussed in greater detail below. However, it needs to be briefly mentioned here in its relation to the student's inherent learning processes. A child, in naturally trying to master and make sense of his world, takes on greater and more sophisticated challenges. These begin with the simple cries and movements of the infant and progress to the complex challenge of understanding the sacred. It is to approach this ultimate challenge (Ultimacy) that the child moves freely and spontaneously according to the child's stage of development and readiness to learn. Children ask (explicitly or implicitly) for the help they need in this process and, in so doing, indicate their stages of development. For Pestalozzi, following these indications is the only natural way of making progress in a child's education.[370]

All of the early Authors can be seen as part of the "naturalism" movement, and their views of the inherent learning process as an aspect of students that facilitates the needed learning must be seen in this light. "Naturalism" has been described as a nineteenth century conflation between the study of "natural events" and "substances" (today thought of as the physical sciences) and the religious extolling of nature (most famously practiced by the Romantics) that was a reaction against the industrial revolution and the supranaturalism of mainstream religions.[371] In this view "the world was conceived as a unified living organism of creatures, plants, stars and stones, all participating in the life of the universe."[372] This view has many correlations with modern Gaia theory. Pestalozzi, and later Froebel, explicitly indicated they felt they were on a religious quest in discovering the natural learning processes of students, and that by discovering and then becoming an ally of these natural processes the needed learning is most likely to occur. In Pestalozzi's last book, *Swan Song*, in a section entitled "Education Means the Development of the Whole of Man," Pestalozzi claimed that the whole of his educational endeavors had been to "conform to the order of Nature in the cultivation of man's capacities and powers."[373] As following the "order of Nature" is most important, Pestalozzi, like Rousseau, often expressed that what is learned is not nearly as important as how things are learned[374] since the needed learning comes not from knowledge but from engaging the inherent learning processes. Interestingly, before there was a recognized science of psychology, Pestalozzi claimed that in studying the natural learning processes in children and creating a system of education based on that, he was, "...trying to psychologize the instruction of mankind."[375] This is examined further in the discussion on Pestalozzi's notions of the teachers understanding of correct pedagogic practices (beginning on page 124).

One final element of the inherent learning process as seen by Pestalozzi is that this process develops gradually, methodically and somewhat mysteriously. It always builds at its own pace, on what already exists, and the exact outcome cannot be known ahead of time. To communicate this he often used plant metaphors, and often those of an acorn growing into a tree;[376] each part of the growing tree is an extension of existing parts, and the exact shape of the tree can never be anticipated. An anonymous author (who seems to be Greaves) writing of Pestalozzi's method after spending three years working with him at his school in Yverdon noted, "that development must be gentle, gradual; with progress imperceptible"[377] and "...any lessons...exceeding a child's capacity are utterly unprofitable, and will serve rather to confuse and tire, than to improve and amuse him."[378]

Pestalozzi's View of Inherent Motivation

Pestalozzi claimed that the schools of his time were onerous for most children so that children didn't want to be there and learned reluctantly and with difficulty. Not surprisingly, his contentions that learning is natural and naturally wanted by students were mocked by teachers in the mainstream education of his time. The fact that the students in his school *did* seem to want to be there caused his critics to dismiss his approach to education as not serious, and as nothing more than self-indulgent entertainment. Pestalozzi claimed that those who insisted that education was necessarily unpleasant and unwanted by students, were similar to those who contended that only medicine that tastes bad is good for you. To respond to his critics, he felt the need to reinforce Rousseau's point that learning must involve exertion. However, "a child should not be taught to look upon exertion as an unavoidable *evil*,"[379] which he felt was the result of the pushing of children which occurred in mainstream education. He felt that children naturally exert themselves when it is for something they enjoy or want, as children naturally exert themselves in games, and from such natural exertion students will come to see the value of exertion (which is needed for Ultimacy). If, however, children are pushed by someone else (e.g., a teacher or parent) this stops the very learning which needs to be engendered. Pestalozzi claimed that following the inherent learning process means fostering inherent motivation. To do this for each student is more difficult for the teacher as it demands more perspicacity on the teacher's part than the mechanical following of lesson plans.

One motivation that Pestalozzi was very insistent should never be used is fear. Pestalozzi believed that whenever fear is allowed to enter a child's learning process, it quickly destroys any interest that the child might have had for the topic and replaces it with dislike. In such instances, not only is the lesson lost, and perhaps even the future interest in the topic, but perhaps even an interest in education itself is lost.[380] Pestalozzi felt that children did not like school because it was made onerous by the teaching methods, not by the subjects themselves. The key to teaching, according to Pestalozzi, is generating interest, and nature herself will do the rest.

> This *interest* in study is the first thing which a teacher…should endeavour to excite and keep alive. There are scarcely any circumstances in which a want of application in children does not proceed from a want of interest; and there are, perhaps, none under which a want of interest does not originate in the mode of teaching adopted by the teacher. I would go so far as to lay it down for a rule, that whenever children are inattentive, and apparently take no interest in a lesson, the teacher should always first look to himself for the reason.[381]

ASPECTS OF TEACHERS THAT FACILITATE THE NEEDED LEARNING FOR PESTALOZZI

Teachers' Understanding of Students and their Needs for Pestalozzi

Unlike Rousseau, Pestalozzi was concerned with instructing classes rather than an individual tutee. However, Pestalozzi was as insistent as Rousseau that education is about the instruction of individual students even if they are in classes. In a series of local newspaper articles published in 1782, Pestalozzi tried to counter what he saw as the opposite tendency in mainstream education.

> …fixed attention to the particular situation of every child is one of the first and most essential of the rules of education, moreover, all more general educational principles which have in mind not a particular, definite individual but the entire [human] race, easily lead one astray.[382]

Pestalozzi felt that people easily understand a single object, and easily "abstract principles of education from the observation of their own children," but that understanding universal laws (which he insisted had to include Ultimacy) and then finding ways to apply them to the idiosyncratic individual was a rare talent.[383] Pestalozzi felt it is important to understand both the general and particular because educators have to understand what they are trying to achieve (both ultimately and in the short term), and they have to appreciate that the materials with which they have to work (i.e., students, including their contexts and circumstances) vary almost infinitely as each student needs to follow their unique path. An appropriate metaphor is that the same thermal laws form all snowflakes, yet each snowflake is different and has its own unique perfection. Pestalozzi discussed this in terms of distinguishing "the laws of Nature and her course; that is, her single workings..."[384] and insisted that education depends on harmony between the two.

Pestalozzi believed that humans are the most varied of all the species[385] and that the reason for this has religious roots.

> The idiosyncrasies of individuals are, in my opinion, the greatest blessing of human nature, and the one basis of its highest and essential blessings; therefore they should be respected in the highest degree.[386]

This "highest and essential blessing" is, of course, Ultimacy, which, according to Pestalozzi, is necessarily an individual accomplishment that must be uniquely achieved. Consequently, Pestalozzi felt that education which addresses amalgams of individuals, which he criticized mainstream education for doing, is a sacrilege because it ignores or inhibits the idiosyncratic. Any method of education that was to be considered positive for Pestalozzi, has to be concerned with the "blessing" of individuality.

> Inasmuch as the method [of education] is positive, it bases itself directly on the individual child whom it has in its care; indeed there is nothing positive in education and in teaching but the individual child and the individual talents he has.[387]

Teacher's Understanding of
the Correct Pedagogic Process for Pestalozzi

Pestalozzi came upon what he believed to be the correct pedagogic process from both conviction and experiment. As stated previously, he was greatly influenced by Rousseau who shaped many of his convictions. However, there is no record of Rousseau's trying to apply the method he advocated in *Emile* (although he might have tried aspects of it in some of his tutoring experiences early in his career). One of the earliest records of an attempt to apply Rousseau's method (very literally) is by an aristocratic English family,[388] whose daughter, so educated, eventually worked with Pestalozzi. It was Pestalozzi, however, who first tried to put Rousseau's insights into practice in classes (rather than a tutorial situation) and systematically experimented to find what worked.[389]

It has been claimed that it is with Pestalozzi that "scientific pedagogy can be said to begin"[390] (despite others claiming to have founded their educational initiatives on observations of children, including Rousseau[391]) because he not only based his pedagogy on observations of children, but on experiments of applying his hypotheses and then changing the hypotheses on the basis of his results and experimenting again. Pestalozzi certainly seems to have been quite honest in reporting his many failures and heartaches. Pestalozzi's process was 1) observing the nature of children in general, 2) observing the particular children in his care, 3) keeping in mind the goal of Ultimacy, 4) knowing the basic principles of pedagogy (e.g., the role of *anschauung*, "real" versus "unreal" knowledge, etc.), and 5) continually experimenting and changing on the basis of what was seen. Pestalozzi suggested this as the correct pedagogic process for all teachers.

Pestalozzi felt that part of the reason for observing the nature of children was in order to follow nature as it developed in children, and he frequently spoke of observing, respecting, and following nature in religious terms.[392] He claimed that his educational method was an endeavor

> to organize the several means of developing the individual powers and capacities in a psychological sequence corresponding to the course through which nature herself develops these powers.[393]

Consequently, Pestalozzi claimed that there "can be not *two good* methods of instruction" for only "the one that rests entirely upon the eternal laws of Nature"[394] can be good. Pestalozzi did not claim to have mastered that method, but such mastery was his aspiration, and had to be the aspiration of anyone interested in helping children acquire what needs to be learned.

Pestalozzi and Froebel often employed horticultural metaphors, and these metaphors clearly demonstrate what might be thought of as a paradox in their writing. In many instances the teacher is told that he must act as if he is nature, and at other times the teacher is simply to let nature act. As an example of the first, Pestalozzi told teachers,

> The mechanism of Nature as a whole is great and simple. Man! imitate it.[395]

The teacher is meant to act like nature in unfolding the capacities of each child, and Pestalozzi claimed that his method consisted of "various devices for developing"[396] these capacities.

As an example of letting nature act, Pestalozzi constantly reiterated that the child's surroundings did most of the work of stimulating the growth of the child's capacities ("life is the great educator"[397]), and the good teacher had to ensure the child's surroundings were rich in stimuli—very much like providing nutrients to plants. The teachers are encouraged to think of themselves as a gardener who "contributes nothing to their [the student's] growth" but "only sees to it that no external force should hinder or disturb the natural course of development...."[398] Pestalozzi's resolution of this paradox seems to be as follows: Man is endowed by nature with capacities that would unfold at the right time and in the right way and lead to each person's fullest development if only there were not so many powerfully corrupting forces that "are poisonous in their influence on man's primitive nature"[399] and which prevent nature from acting. The teacher's role is to both protect the natural forces, and at times to act for them, accomplishing what they would accomplish if they had not been thwarted. As such, the teacher can be thought of as contributing nothing to the child's development as the teacher is only an agent of nature.

Some of the difficulties in this seeming paradox may be resolved if the word "God" is substituted for "nature," which for both Pestalozzi and Froebel is often justifiable. It is presumptuous to believe that God needs a person to accomplish something, and yet a person may think their efforts are serving God's intentions and purposes (which both Pestalozzi and Froebel believed was true for them). It would be presumptuous for someone to think they saved another's soul as it is not within anyone's gift to grant salvation, yet people might think they are assisting another to be in a position to receive such a gift. The religious fervor with which the educational ideas of Pestalozzi and Froebel spread, and the terms that were used to describe these ideas make clear that such a transposition of the kind described above was not uncommon.[400]

In this way, part of Christianity was an anchoring idea for both Pestalozzi and Froebel.

Pestalozzi claimed that one of the pedagogic processes he came upon by chance

> worked with great force on the birth and growth of the conviction in me, that all true, all educative instruction must be drawn out of the children themselves, and be born within them.[401]

This process was of children teaching other children. Without a technique to rely on, and with the sensitivity to each individual that Pestalozzi felt is required, no teacher in his schools had enough time to do all of the teaching required. It fell quite naturally, according to Pestalozzi, to other children who had learned some lesson to help others who were in the process of learning it. Pestalozzi would ensure that these child-teachers understood certain basic premises (e.g., kindness, experiential knowledge, etc.) and claimed that he was often surprised by their creative and effective means. He claimed that, in this way, he would often learn better ways of teaching.

In a section entitled "Human Nature as a Whole Must be Educated" in Pestalozzi's last book, he describes the teacher's role as not only developing the different human capacities, but stresses that these capacities only have their meaning if they combine together in harmony to form the unity he felt was part of Ultimacy. Pestalozzi believed that mainstream education created imbalances by not seeing the importance of unity in students and by developing only some of their capacities in isolation.

> But in their isolation the cultivation of these faculties is not enough. There is always the danger of over-emphasis in one direction or another, which brings about internal disharmony.[402]

For Pestalozzi, disharmony (which precludes Ultimacy) was not a price worth paying for any worldly success, and he was against specialization or the early development of virtuosity as these, in his view, always generated imbalance and disharmony. However, trying to get the balance right for every student was not simple and could not be approached mechanically or by a formula. Pestalozzi felt that such harmony, such development of human nature as a whole "depends upon the successful establishment of the disposition of love and faith..."[403] in the student through these qualities being present in the teacher. The power of love and faith in the teacher would spread from the teacher to the students, ensuring the needed harmony.

Pestalozzi's view that there can be no technique or formula that is good for everyone went against the current of the mainstream education of his time. Pestalozzi felt that technique or formula-driven education always results in trying to fit the student to the system and leads to education that consists of a "series of admonitions and corrections, of rewards and punishments, of injunctions and directions, strung together without unity of purpose, or dignity of execution..."[404] and this is incompatible with education for Ultimacy, which has as its goal "the elevation of man to the true dignity of a spiritual being."[405] For Pestalozzi, education, like religion, had no single path to the truth.

> Moreover, a strict and stiff adherence to one order is not nature's way of teaching. If it were, she would train one-sided characters; and her truth would not accommodate itself easily and freely to the feelings of all men...
>
> The power of nature, although unquestionably leading to truth, leads with no stiffness.[406]

While, for Pestalozzi, the correct pedagogic process could not rely on any formula, it could rely on what has variously been translated as the sentiment or feeling of love or devotion. Pestalozzi believed this sentiment had its origin in the mother-child relationship and extends naturally to the feeling of man toward God. This feeling, Pestalozzi claimed, was the source of his educational method and what should lie at the root of all teachers' actions.[407] Teachers should love what they teach as well as who they teach. Pestalozzi claimed that students are very susceptible to a teacher's frame of mind and respond accordingly.[408] Consequently, Pestalozzi felt that teachers had to work on their own sentiments (discussed more fully beginning on page 129).

An aspect of what Pestalozzi feels is the correct pedagogic process is that students must feel that they are active participants in their education. Rousseau had wanted students to be able to say to themselves, "I conceive, I discern, I act, I learn"[409] and Rousseau felt that the *amour-propre* of teachers often prevented teachers from giving students such a feeling of freedom, self-mastery, and sovereignty. Pestalozzi agreed with Rousseau and added that students are often not given that sense of agency in their education because it is easier for adults to believe they know best and to conceive of the adult role as actor and the student role as recipient of action. Pestalozzi believed this approach is wrong due to all that has been previously discussed in relation to freedom, authority, and individual development. Pestalozzi gave more of an agent's role to the teacher than did Rousseau but still claimed that, even for very early education, "Let the child not only be *acted upon*, but let him be an *agent* in intellectual education."[410]

Teachers' Understanding of
the Correct Pedagogic Relationship for Pestalozzi

Pestalozzi and Froebel wrote a great deal about the importance of the correct pedagogic relationship, but added nothing to Rousseau's notions of affection, empathy and absence of authority.

Teachers' Self-Development for Pestalozzi

Pestalozzi had a more complex notion of the teachers' self-development than Rousseau. Part of his notion can be seen as professional self-development in that Pestalozzi encouraged teachers to continually seek out the "educating forces" in their students; to study the children and find the divine laws that express themselves in the children and that must be harnessed for education. Froebel extended this notion of Pestalozzi and claimed that "my teachers are the children themselves…and I follow them like a faithful, trustful scholar."[411] Yet, for both Pestalozzi and Froebel, such studying of the student could not occur without an equal self-study by the teacher. Pestalozzi advises,

> Man! Examine yourself and seek to find out in what ways you attain harmony within yourself and how you come to be at war with yourself and with your fellow-men. See in what ways you can come to be a friend of faith, of love, of truth, and justice, and, on the other hand, how you can come to be an enemy of all these. Examine yourself closely.[412]

Another part of his notion of teacher self-development stems from the religious nature of his view of Ultimacy and his notion of Ultimacy as the goal of education. Pestalozzi believed that a teacher could not help bring about in a child what the teacher is not bringing about in himself, and this is true even for the youngest infant. In answering the question of whether a mother will be able to "spiritualise the unfolding faculties" of the infant, Pestalozzi responds,

> Not unless she has first lent her own heart to the influence of a higher principle; not unless the germs of a spiritual love and faith, which she is to develop in her child, have first gained ground in the

better affections of her being.[413]

The reason the mother/teacher must first have the spirituality she would wish to develop in her child seems to be due to this needed learning being experiential. A child is able (through empathy) to experience the state of the mother/teacher, and through this to experience (in a childlike way) the spiritual experience of the mother/teacher. The spirituality of the mother/teacher is the only access the child has to that needed learning.

Pestalozzi presents much of his writing on education almost as a confessional, full of his errors, failures and shortcomings. He is never in doubt, however, about the nature of his endeavor or its importance, with a crucial role played in both by self-examination and self-knowledge.[414] Education for Pestalozzi is linked with Ultimacy, and without Ultimacy there can be no resolution to the problems of the individual or society. Pestalozzi does not present himself as an educational authority, but as a student of education which, for him, coincides with seeking religious truths.

CHAPTER 7

Friedrich Wilhelm August Froebel

A BIOGRAPHICAL SKETCH
OF FRIEDRICH WILHELM AUGUST FROEBEL
(21 APRIL 1782 – 21 JUNE 1852)

*F*roebel was the fifth child of a German clergyman. His mother died when he was nine months old, and by his accounts, he was neglected for all of his early years until he was old enough to attend school, at which time an uncle took him in. Some commentators have claimed that this neglected and wounded childhood was a source of his seeing the importance of early childhood education and his later claims about the effect of wounds suffered in youth.

In school, despite a facility for mathematics and languages, he seems to have had a natural affinity and a greater enthusiasm for the study of plants and natural phenomena. Upon leaving school, he apprenticed as a forester. This, however, did not last long, and he returned to school for some informal tertiary studies. This middle period of his life is only vaguely known. He tried his hand at a variety of jobs (with no apparent success) and spent time in debtors' prison. Eventually, he took up teaching, and as fortune would have it, it was in a Pestalozzi school in Frankfurt run by a progressive educator named Anton Guner. He claimed this was a turning point in his life because it was here he found his vocation.

After two years of working under Guner's instruction in the Pestalozzi method, Froebel felt he was ready to learn from the source, and he traveled to Yverdon. Froebel found himself enthralled with Pestalozzi's method of education and initially by Pestalozzi himself. However, after two years he became exasperated by Pestalozzi's lack of business acumen, and Froebel became one of the principal protagonists in the disputes at Yverdon that brought down that school. Froebel came to criticize Pestalozzi personally and bitterly.

Feeling the need to strike out on his own, and knowing a university degree would assist him in his aspirations, in 1811 Froebel left Yverdon to enter the University of Göttingen. His studies, however, were interrupted by military conscription against the Napoleonic campaigns. He seems to have been actively thinking and talking about education during his five years of service as he met two friends while in the service who became students of his in education and loyal supporters and co-workers.

In 1816, with his two service friends and their wives, Froebel set up his first school (very much along Pestalozzi's lines) at Griesheim in Thuringia (now in Germany). In 1818, political circumstance forced him to move his school to Keilhau. There it flourished, expanded greatly, and remained for the rest of his life.

In 1826 Froebel began his writing career with the publication of *The Education of Man*. This won him wide acclaim and recognition. Germany was looking for a national inspiration to rebuild its education after the devastation of the Napoleonic Wars, and Froebel's vague brand of nature-mysticism Christianity was able to be accepted by both the Catholic and Protestant population. With his book, Froebel distanced himself from Pestalozzi (who had been given honorary French citizenship and was therefore not as welcome in the German states), and although his views clearly owed a great deal to Pestalozzi, they were distinct enough for him to claim originality.

In 1831, Froebel left the school at Keilhau to his two friends and their wives in order to engage in what could be seen as a 'one-upmanship' on his old mentor. Froebel accepted the Swiss government's offer to train elementary school teachers (which Pestalozzi had turned down several years earlier) and to head the orphanage at Burgdorf (which Pestalozzi had started but gone bankrupt with twenty-seven years before). Froebel seems to have done both extremely well, and in 1837 he returned to Keilhau with his reputation greatly increased.

While living at Keilhau, Froebel started his first school for infants. It was in Blankenburg, Prussia, and has special significance as it is the first school he named Kindergarten (children's garden). His contention that early education lays the foundation for later education, and that education is the foundation for (the then much needed) social reform struck a popular chord. For the next fourteen years, Froebel's work flourished. The Kindergarten movement spread all over the German speaking world and, eventually, well beyond. He started a publishing firm for his educational work, and another firm which made educational materials (books, maps, and educational objects called "Froebel's gifts") for mothers and teachers to educate children.

In 1851, a year before his death, Froebel was to see almost all of his work collapse in his native land. Froebel had a nephew who was a socialist activist in the uprisings of that time, and either through a confusion of names, or fearing that Froebel was corrupting the youth with his nephew's views, the government closed and forbid the Kindergarten movement and closed the publishing works. This ban was not removed until eight years after Froebel's death. However, Froebel's work in other countries was not affected by this confusion or shortsightedness. Froebel's writing, his "gifts," and the Kindergarten movement thrived in Europe and America where they became standard.

FROEBEL'S NOTION OF ULTIMACY

Froebel was the most overtly theistic of all the Authors. For him Ultimacy is the "representation of the divine nature within"[415] achieved through unity which is "the goal of all human history, individual and collective...."[416] Froebel's use of conventional Christian language to convey his notions of Ultimacy ensured that his work was easily accepted by the populations of Europe and North America. A closer reading of his views, however, reveals that only his terminology was conventional, and that his religious views did not fit easily into any established church.

Ultimacy in Relation to Froebel's View of Human Nature

Like Pestalozzi, Froebel saw Ultimacy as man's unique destiny. Although he saw both nature and man as expressions of God, Froebel felt that man's unique mission was in representing the union of the two.[417] Such a mission is not to be approached at the end of one's development, according to Froebel, but to be engaged in throughout life.[418] This is Ultimacy as engagement, not an end state, and Froebel's educational program is based on fostering that engagement. Froebel saw such engagement as "...the realization of the divine principle in man..."[419] which could not be taught but accomplished only by inner listening or sensing.

Froebel (once he had returned to Germany after working with Pestalozzi in Switzerland) stridently reiterated what had been the principal cause of recrimination against Rousseau in Catholic France and Pestalozzi in Calvinist Western Switzerland. "Man is essentially good and it is the source of all evil to consider his nature to be evil or bad."[420] In several remarkable statements which foreshadow some later theories of neurosis, Froebel assured his readers that anything that appears to be bad is only a person's goodness "repressed, disturbed or misled," and that the proper cure is not to counter what is wrong (which is done by punishment) but to reinforce the natural goodness.[421] Since Froebel saw people as naturally good and as having an inherent "living principle of growth" within them that can manifest and direct development, "it follows...that the first condition of all education is the utmost freedom for the child."[422] He expanded on this principle by claiming

> ...the undisturbed operation of the Divine Unity is necessarily good—can not be otherwise than good. This necessity implies that the young human being—as it were, still in process of creation—would seek, although still unconsciously, as a product of nature, yet decidedly as surely, that which is in itself best; and, moreover, in a form wholly adapted to his condition, as well as to his disposition, his powers, and means.[423]

As one would expect, Froebel reiterated Pestalozzi's plea not to treat children as "a lump of clay" to be shaped but, instead, for each child to be appreciated for their uniqueness just as one appreciates other aspects of nature.[424]

Ultimacy As an Aspect of Religiousness for Froebel

In the one hundred years that passed between Rousseau's first work and Froebel's last, there seems to have been an increasing impetus in Germany for unification. Perhaps this can be explained by citing history—the Industrial Revolution and the Napoleonic Wars generated an increased sense of fragmentation, and the national aspirations to create a nation state became stronger at the beginning of Bismarck's era. This concern for unification in the common consciousness of Germany worked in Froebel's favor.

Froebel's notions of Ultimacy included unification with God, and he saw this as being approached by successive smaller unifications, including social unification.

> The goal of all human history, individual and collective, is unification; first, the unification of each individual's whole life within himself; the unification of his life with that of nature and his fellowmen; and finally his unification with God.[425] [underlines as in the original texts]

Froebel translated the nouns that Rousseau and Pestalozzi felt needed uniting (i.e., heart, hand, and head) into their actions (i.e., "feeling, acting and representing, thinking and perceiving"[426]), and he described this as the "tri-unity"[427] of human nature, claiming that all of human life is encompassed by these three. At the end of his life Froebel's categories had only slightly changed, but they became nouns again: "feeling," "intellect," and "will."[428] What is important is that Froebel saw the united development of all human capacities as necessary for full human development; and full human development as necessary for Ultimacy.

Like Rousseau and Pestalozzi, Froebel saw harmony and union with the divine as part of man's destiny because of man's inherent position between nature and God.

> Thus, too, the destiny of man as a child of God and of nature is to represent in harmony and unison the spirit of God and of nature, the natural and the divine, the terrestrial and the celestial, the finite and the infinite.[429]

Interestingly, and in opposition to Rousseau and Pestalozzi, Froebel saw union with the progressively larger wholes of family, community and nation as a way of growing toward the divine.[430] This, of course, gives divine sanction to political union, and gave Froebel many admirers. Rousseau saw the progression as going from family to humanity in general; a significant distinction. Froebel's religiousness seems to have consisted mostly of feeling oneness with nature and society, and perceiving the divine in these and in himself. He used Christian terminology, but has been described as more of a Christian Pantheist in the Romantic mold[431] than part of any mainstream Christianity. What Froebel described, however, were his own experiences of Ultimacy,[432] and such experiences were his stated goal in education.

WHAT NEEDS TO BE LEARNED FOR FROEBEL

Froebel's View of Experiential Knowledge

Froebel took Pestalozzi's notion of representations in relation to experiences one step further away from Rousseau. While still eschewing excessive verbal instruction for the young, he supported another form of representation. Froebel encouraged mothers to use hand signals (which he detailed in his books) to give an infant, what he believed to be, experiences that are unavailable from any physical object or other event. For instance, Froebel encouraged mothers to put their hands together as in prayer in front of a child to communicate an experience of piety. It is as if Froebel believed in something resembling a mixture of Platonic forms and Jungian archetypes. Froebel felt these hand gestures had inherent meaning for children, and stimulated some kind of pre-conscious recognition which gives children experiences of things they don't have words to recognize.

In addition to demonstrating a substantial shift from Rousseau's position on the role of representation (e.g., hand signals), Froebel also felt that at the age when words become viable tools for children, he placed greater importance on words and other forms of representation than did either Rousseau or Pestalozzi. Rousseau would give no lessons in words (at least for the young) although he might summarize a child's experience in maxims or use words to help the child see connections between various experiences. Pestalozzi encouraged more use of words than Rousseau (albeit after experiences), and wanted them used earlier in children's education. Finally, Froebel promoted "external, physical, productive activity interspersed in intellectual work...," and he wanted this principally because such activity refreshes and stimulates intellectual work.[433] So, while Froebel decried "merely extraneously communicated knowledge,"[434] the emphasis must be on his use of the word "merely." Experience, for Froebel, reinforces verbal lessons,[435] the reverse of Rousseau.

Competence for Froebel

Froebel added little in the way of theory to Rousseau or Pestalozzi on the subject of competence or competence based pedagogy versus performance based pedagogy. He did, however, make one interesting association. While Rousseau condemned swaddling clothes and all other physical constraints on infants for their deleterious effects on the child's physical growth, disposition and constitution,[436] Froebel associated such constraints with inhibiting freedom and Ultimacy. Froebel claimed that all physical constraints (as well as "being spoiled by too much assistance") prevent the "free all-sided use of his [the child's] powers,"[437] which hinders incipient freedom, competence and Ultimacy. Where Froebel did contribute to his predecessors' notions of competence came from his systematizing a competence based pedagogy, as discussed in the sections that follow.

ASPECTS OF STUDENTS THAT FACILITATE THE NEEDED LEARNING FOR FROEBEL

Froebel saw play in the early years of childhood as "the highest phase of child development"; "the purest, most spiritual activity of man at this stage..." and a child's playing "until physical fatigue forbids" as the foundation for becoming "a thorough, determined man, capable of self-sacrifice for the promotion of the welfare of himself and others."[438] Froebel fostered play by providing materials with which to play, and teachers to encourage play. Froebel's materials and teachers' efforts were to encourage the play to be directed toward the needed learning, but never cease to be play.

For Froebel (as for Pestalozzi), the "self-activity" of students was an expression of the child's nature, and, if allowed to follow its own course, would lead that child to unity with God and man, what Hamilton called "Rousseau with a Christian interpretation."[439] It amounts to an early understanding of homeostasis with implications for notions of freedom.

> Indeed, in its very essence, education should have these characteristics; for the undisturbed operation of the Divine Unity is necessarily good—can not be otherwise than good. This necessity implies that the young human being—as it were, still in process of

creation—would seek, although still unconsciously, as a product of nature, yet decidedly as surely, that which is in itself best; and, moreover, in a form wholly adapted to his condition, as well as to his disposition, his powers, and means.[440]

It is perhaps Dewey, in an article entitled "Fröbel's Educational Principles," who best expresses Froebel's notion of the inherent learning process that facilitates the needed learning.

> That the primary root of all educative activity is in the instinctive, impulsive attitudes and activities of the child, and not in the presentation and application of external material, whether through the ideas of others as through the senses: and that, accordingly, numberless spontaneous activities of children, plays, games, mimic efforts, even the apparently meaningless motion of infants— exhibitions previously ignored as trivial, futile, or even condemned as positively evil—are capable of educational use, nay, are the foundation stones of educational effort.[441]

Froebel agreed with Rousseau and Pestalozzi about the importance of "…the deepest possible search into the life of the child, and into what he must necessarily require according to his present stage of development,"[442] but he disagreed with the notion of distinct stages of development, feeling instead that maturing was a continuous series of transitions with a central core of humanness running throughout.[443]

Froebel's View of Inherent Motivation

Pestalozzi and Froebel shared the idea of "free activity" or "spontaneous-activity" (which Froebel called "self-activity") which was the basis of their notions of motivation. The idea of "spontaneous-activity" is essentially as follows: Every child is born with a capacity to receive impressions from the world and to react to them, as well as the capacity to generate movements that are not just a response to external stimuli. Such interior-stimulated movements are seen by Froebel as "free" or "spontaneous." These spontaneous movements can group to form tendencies or inclinations. After a certain age such grouped tendencies or inclinations become agents for specific forms of action (such as artistic, verbal, numerate, kinesthetic or dexterous operations), which favor a student's engagement in art, reading and writing, mathematics or logic, sports, or crafts. Any of these forms of action might absorb a child for a period, perhaps even a long period if they are nourished and supported, or they can be stifled by unfavorable circumstances. As a child satisfies its internal demands for these forms of actions, other forms of action seek to be satisfied until eventually the child exercises and develops all its capacities. For Froebel, it is by developing all of one's faculties that a person approaches Ultimacy. What is important, however, is that the impetus to engage in different forms of action comes from the child, because it is the burgeoning capacity calling out for its own flowering that needs to be developed, not another. Froebel held that only the child can know what form of action to move to and when to move. A teacher's role, however, is not just to passively watch and support the child's actions. As both Pestalozzi and Froebel (although especially Pestalozzi) worked with poor and often delinquent children, some of the "activity" that their charges engaged in was not very positive or educative. Both Pestalozzi and Froebel felt that the "wrong" kind of activity needed to be negatively reinforced, not through punishment, but through a kind of starving out with a lack of positive reinforcement.

ASPECTS OF TEACHERS THAT FACILITATE THE NEEDED LEARNING FOR FROEBEL

Froebel did not have anything significant to add to Rousseau or Pestalozzi in terms of how the teachers' understanding of students and their needs or of the correct pedagogic process, or even the teachers' own self-development could facilitate the needed learning. However, he did have some views of the correct pedagogic process that are worth noting.

Teachers' Understanding of the Correct Pedagogic Process for Froebel

Froebel's principal contribution to the notions of the correct pedagogic process that have significance for holistic education is his increased emphasis that education "originally and in its first principles, should necessarily be *passive, following* (only guarding and protecting), *not prescriptive, categorical, interfering,*" [italics in the original] [444] Froebel felt a non-prescriptive approach is especially important in early childhood, just when the mainstream education of his day was most prescriptive as young children were seen as most in need of being shaped. He also developed the educational materials mentioned earlier that came to be called "Froebel's gifts." These gifts were a series of educational manipulatives (often made of wood) meant to be given to children in a sequence that followed what he saw as the general progression of capacities in children's development (e.g., spheres, cubes, then rectangular blocks equivalent to two cubes, etc.).

For Froebel, humans are by nature reflections of divine will and, therefore, all their inherent capacities and tendencies are sacred.[445] Education must fit in with the child, and not the reverse, and all "prescriptive and categorical, interfering…instruction and training must, of necessity, annihilate, hinder, and destroy"[446] the very thing that education is meant for—Ultimacy. Froebel was more insistent than Rousseau or Pestalozzi that the only role of teachers is to understand the nature of each individual child and aid each child's unique and natural development.[447] He abhorred what he felt was the *tabula rasa* perception of children, and insisted that this was sacrilegious.[448] For the teacher to understand the nature of a child, the child should be encouraged to play. The nature of this play was to be closely followed by the teacher as play is actually "highly serious and of deep significance" because it "discloses the future inner life of the [person]" and so informs the teacher about the education appropriate for that child.[449]

As mentioned earlier, Froebel did not believe in the existence of evil, and was contemptuous of what he felt was the mainstream attitude which held that children, in much of their play, displayed inherent depravity (e.g., violence, dishonesty) confirming the presence of original sin. Froebel believed that only goodness exists, and that what appears evil is no more than perverted good. Froebel believed that "one of the highest functions of the educator is therefore to reveal the true source of the perverted impulse and to allow the original good to find a new direction,"[450] a process Froebel called "conversion."

CHAPTER 8

Carl Gustav Jung

A BIOGRAPHICAL SKETCH
OF CARL GUSTAV JUNG
(26 JULY 1875 – 6 JUNE 1961)

*J*ung claims that he had a lonely and unhappy youth. From a fairly early age, Jung is reported to have had little interest in relationships, seeming more content to observe people than to engage with them. He frequently feigned illness to avoid personal interaction, and would often faint if a social situation was even slightly stressful.

Jung's father was a brilliant pastor cum philosopher-scientist-scholar and materially successful. When Jung was only six, his father started teaching him Latin, which may have triggered his interest in languages, for as an adult Jung could speak several modern languages and a few ancient ones (including ancient Greek and Sanskrit). Jung's early relationship with his father soured when Jung reached adolescence, as his father went through a metaphysical crisis, lost his religious convictions, and seems to have become emotionally unavailable to his son. Jung's earnest youthful response was to try to "cure" his father's despondence by conveying to him the nature of his own religious experiences. This, however, didn't work, and Jung was left feeling that he and his deepest experiences were rejected and that he and his father couldn't communicate or understand one another any longer. This only increased his sense of isolation.

As Jung was clearly a bright student, it was assumed that he would join the clergy, which had been a tradition on both sides of the family. It has been assumed by some that his unhappy attempts at religion with his father and his distaste for social interaction encouraged him to resist the family pressure, and he took to studying philosophy and science instead. As he grew older he wanted to become an archeologist, but settled on medicine as more acceptable to his family, eventually specializing in the medicine of the mind, psychiatry. Jung's medical studies were in Zurich, where he worked under Eugen Bleuler (who systematically studied and named schizophrenia). While working there, Jung invented word-association as a form of diagnosis and discovered that the unconscious associations his patients had to words (which he called "complexes") revealed much about their illnesses which was otherwise hidden from view. This brought him extraordinary early acclaim.

Jung's word-association work seemed to confirm some of Freud's theories, and when they met, Jung was flattered to be welcomed by Freud as a brilliant young protégé. For five years Jung and Freud worked closely and Jung seemed to be Freud's intellectual heir, but in 1909 an estrangement began on a long ocean voyage to America. During that trip, Freud and Jung began to analyze each others' dreams as a form of amusement, but after several days, Freud abruptly broke off the game when he felt he was losing his authority. What finally drove a wedge between them was Jung's disagreement with Freud's insistence that sex lay at the basis of all neurosis and most other mental illnesses. This difference was made public and solid with Jung's publication in 1912 of *Psychology of the Unconscious*. For Freud the unconscious was the seat of suppressed, sublimated and often perverse psychic forces, whereas for Jung the unconscious was the locus of the universal and mystical.

One remarkable feature of Jung's work is the painstaking and systematic study Jung made of his own unconscious through his dreams, fantasies, and visions. He wrote, drew, painted, and sculpted what he could extract from his unconscious and then he analyzed it. From 1913 to 1928 his study was extremely laborious and tortured (to the point, some claim, of being neurotic). What began as a search for an understanding of his own psyche became an understanding of the human psyche in general and eventually transcended his science to become part of our present cultural understanding. That there are common universal experiences and perceptions (variously expressed) which lie at the base of all religions (eventually labeled "Perennial Philosophy" by Aldous Huxley) is widely accepted, as is the existence of a collective unconscious, archetypes, types of personality, and the equating of psychological development with spiritual development.

Jung popularized the notion that religions, religious texts and myths of other places and/or times can be stripped of their cultural aspects to reveal universal psychic and spiritual truths. This seemed to Jung to be easier to do with religions of simpler cultures, and to pursue this path to the universal, Jung visited the indigenous (and to his mind simpler) cultures of Africa, Asia, India, and the US. Contrary to much of the thinking of his time, which held such cultures as inferior to the more "developed" cultures, Jung found these less elaborated expressions of the universal laudable simply because they were less elaborated and culturally adulterated; a view that is now popular.

In 1955 Jung's wife of fifty-two years, Emma Rauschenbach, died and Jung retreated, secluding himself in his lakeside house, granting few interviews and even fewer public talks.

JUNG'S NOTION OF ULTIMACY

The Authors of the twentieth century lose the advantage of the shorthand of religious terms, but their notions of Ultimacy are no less religious.[451] Notions like "divine nature" need greater explication in the more pluralist and scientific modern world. Jung's *homo maximus*,[452] achieved through the arduous process of individuation,[453] attains what he calls "personality," which "means nothing less than the optimum development of the whole individual human being."[454] Jung used several words as synonyms for his understanding of Ultimacy (e.g., Tao, personality, Satori, Samadhi, liberation, Atman, etc.) as he struggled to convey a rich notion of perfection. Jung felt that terms from Eastern religions need to be employed partly because the East has a greater tradition that considers wholeness,[455] and partly because (except for a few Western mystics) there is nothing in Western terminology or thought forms which encompasses both release from the ego of consciousness and the consequent potential to "attain the inner (godlike) man."[456] Even if this goal is not (except in rare circumstances) achieved fully,[457] its existence establishes the nature of our perfectibility, what might be thought of as the trajectory of our intended development.

The Importance Given to Ultimacy by Jung

For the twentieth century Authors, living in perhaps a more cynical and jaded age, it was necessary to explain the importance of Ultimacy. Jung insisted that notions of Ultimacy have tremendous importance, whether or not there is any objective reality behind such notions.[458] Through most of his writing he insisted that, as an empiricist, he could not speculate beyond the processes and nature of the psyche, but he departed from this view late in his life, asserting the objective existence of Ultimacy.[459] All through his career Jung contended that we need notions of Ultimacy to protect us from the "powers of darkness—that is, of the unconscious."[460] Jung stated in several places that most of his clients (and certainly all of the ones over the age of thirty-five) suffered from inadequate notions of Ultimacy,[461] and adequate notions of Ultimacy are important for mental health. Ultimacy, for Jung, is important because without it a person "has failed to realize his life's meaning,"[462] and without meaning there is "psychic suffering" and sickness.[463] Ultimacy has this effect because "it leads in the end to that distant goal which may perhaps have been the first urge to life: the complete actualization of the whole human being...,"[464] and must, therefore, be considered the first and primary motivation of all humans.

Ultimacy in Relation to Jung's View of Human Nature

The Authors of the twentieth century worked from a psychological paradigm of human nature and, consequently, saw Ultimacy in relation to human nature in terms quite different from those of the earlier Authors. Their dichotomy of existence tended not to be between good and evil or salvation and damnation, but between fragmentation and wholeness or illness and wellness. An equation emerges that may have existed before Christianity was as moralized as it had become; when the *salv* in "salvation" connoted health, and physical healing was a sign of holiness; when "goodness" was not simply a moral position but equated with "wellness." All the twentieth century Authors cited existing pre-modernized cultures (i.e., Native American, African) where such connections of goodness and wellness still existed in their day, and in which shamans were a combination of healer, psychologist, and priest. The equation of the twentieth century Authors seems to be: 1) Well-being requires health (of at least the psyche), 2) health of the psyche requires some engagement with Ultimacy, 3) an engagement with Ultimacy necessarily involves what is "good" and of value.

Essentially, Jung argued that humans have a consciousness sophisticated enough to have a conscious and unconscious that can join to become a whole, and the resulting wholeness is "the highest good and the ultimate concern of life."[465] Jung, who frequently stated that he was an empiricist, claimed he was able to prove that, "our consciousness has, fundamentally, a tendency towards wholeness…,"[466] or Ultimacy. Jung used the name "Libido" (not to be confused with Freud's use of the same word) to describe the force, drive, or "energy concept" for wholeness (which Rousseau, Pestalozzi and Froebel held to be nature or some vague divine force) which is humanity's ultimate motivation. Libido should flow along a predetermined path (which Jung called "*rta*") and "this path is also fate… It is the path of our destiny and the law of our being."[467] The result of this energy flowing correctly is "personality" (one of Jung's terms for Ultimacy) and achieving this is humanity's "ultimate aim and strongest desire."[468] Therefore, there is, for Jung, a purposeful evolutionary force, but it is not one that most people can see through to its conclusion. Despite the universal availability of Ultimacy, the approach toward it is so arduous and requires such total commitment[469] that only those with a true calling or "vocation" for Ultimacy can endure it.[470]

In analytical psychology, the processes of listening or sensing within became very sophisticated when compared to the versions of such listening and sensing expounded by Rousseau, Pestalozzi and Froebel. The role of analytical psychologists "as physicians of the soul"[471] is to assist such inner listening and sensing—there really is no help to be sought from outside other than assistance in listening to that which is within. What Jung believed we are listening to or sensing is pre-existing potential wholeness and the innate forces that can bring about this wholeness; and he borrowed from Aristotle the word "entelechy" to designate the realization of an existent potential.[472]

Part of the listening and sensing within that analytical psychology developed is "being in the present" or "living in the present" first mentioned in reference to Rousseau. For Jung, being "aware of the immediate present" is extremely difficult because to accomplish it a person "must be conscious to a superlative degree," which "requires the most intensive and extensive consciousness, with a minimum of unconsciousness."[473] The resemblance between what Jung saw as necessary for Ultimacy and several forms of meditation fascinated Jung and has inspired some interesting research.[474]

Jung did not believe that only the good exists; but this has to be seen in the context of his overall worldview of necessary dichotomies, with progress being made through the reconciliation of these dichotomies. "Evil is the necessary opposite of good, without which there would be no good either."[475] He was, however, very optimistic in his view of human nature and its inherent spirituality, enough so that Browning classifies his approach to psychology (as well as humanistic psychology) as part of "the culture of joy."[476] Perhaps nowhere did Jung express more poetically what he felt was humanity's innate spirituality, mission and, meaning than in *The Development of Personality* in which he equated one of his terms for Ultimacy (personality) with Tao. He concludes this work with:

> To rest in Tao means fulfilment, wholeness, one's destination reached, one's mission done; the beginning, end, and perfect realization of the meaning of existence innate in all things. Personality is Tao.[477]

Ultimacy As an Aspect of Religiousness for Jung

Jung's contribution to religiousness not anchored to any religion—which might be called 'secular religiousness'—is probably unique, and he certainly addressed religious issues to a far greater extent than either of the other two modern Authors. Jung was not against religions. On the contrary, he saw religions as potentially performing a necessary function[478] but, unfortunately, one that they rarely performed adequately in modern times.[479] Many ordinary people and even theologians of different religions have claimed that their own faiths were reaffirmed, rediscovered, or reinforced by Jung's work in psychology.[480] It is interesting that, for Jung, the process of affirmation worked in the reverse direction; his reading of religious texts confirmed his psychological insights which he usually gained from exploring his own psyche.[481] Jung felt that if religions do not change with their constituencies, then their symbols and dogmas, instead of serving as a means of keeping people in touch with their higher selves, serve only to alienate the very people they were intended to serve. Jung held that people who are not alienated but who blindly follow dogma are also badly served by religions because this denies them necessary psychic growth.[482]

While a distinction is made here between religions and religiousness, Jung used "creed" to designate what we are calling religion, and frequently used "religion" to designate one aspect of what has been called religiousness in this book.

> ...the term "religion" designates the attitude peculiar to a

consciousness which has been changed by experience of the *numinosum*.

Creeds are codified and dogmatized forms of original religious experience. The contents of the experience have become sanctified and are usually congealed in a rigid, often elaborate, structure of ideas.[483]

Jung was concerned with religiousness throughout his career[484] (even his doctoral dissertation was on the psychology of occultism), and many excellent books have been written on the religious aspects of Jung's work. The subject is very complex, but fortunately only a brief outline of Jung's religiousness is needed to explore its importance for holistic education.

Among the most important influences on Jung (which he frequently acknowledged) were the Romantic, speculative, and metaphysical *Naturphilosophen*. These were inheritors of Rousseau (including Schelling and Goethe), and many became champions of an approach to medicine called *Naturphilosophie* (as opposed to the mechanical and reductionist *Naturwissenschaft*) that was practiced by many notable doctors, including Jung's father.[485] If, as the Romantics held, the divine is natural and to be found in nature (and nature includes the nature of man); and if the natural physical elements of man include both his body and his psyche (the psyche had previously been considered to be more ethereal and less physiological);[486] and if the psyche is seen as the locus of perception, experience, consciousness, and knowledge; then it follows that to study man's relationship to the divine means studying the human psyche—or so it seemed to Jung. For Jung, the psyche was the locus of religiousness and the bridge to the sacred.

> If one experiences himself and comes in the end to know more or less clearly who he is, then he has also experienced something of God and who he is.[487]

Jung's early contention was that an empiricist (which he considered himself to be) can only know human experiences as physiological and psychological processes without any view as to the objects of the processes. Consequently, someone's religious experience can only be studied as a kind of experience that the experiencer interprets as religious without any view as to the nature of the object being experienced, or the truth of the interpretation.[488] For example, what we experience when we physically see something is really just an inner experience—neurons firing in the brain making patterns which (for sane people) have a certain (though, ultimately, indefinable) correlation with objective reality. Eventually, Jung came to see that in observing psychic phenomena, those psychic phenomena themselves are altered. This led to a complex relationship between the observer and the observed, and as early as 1941 he noted some striking parallels between his studies of consciousness and the studies of microphysics, which he postulated might become more numerous.[489] This has certainly been borne out, many years later, by some esteemed physicists.[490]

Jung's views on what can be empirically studied in the psyche became more complex with the emergence of the importance he gave to the unconscious subsequent to his studies with Freud. Jung felt the unconscious has an importance equal to that of the conscious, and is also a seat of perception, knowledge, and experience, despite these being beyond the grasp of consciousness and, therefore, rationality. As the conscious cannot grasp the unconscious, the only tools for discovering something of the contents of the unconscious lie in noticing the symbolic representations that the unconscious projects (e.g., dreams, the contents of active imagination, etc.). Since there is a collective unconscious shared by groups of people with a similar psychic heritage, and a larger collective unconscious shared by humanity as a whole, there exist symbols that represent and are accessible to the members of those collectives. For this reason, Jung encouraged people to seek out the vitality and richness of the symbols in their cultural inheritance (e.g., Western people seeking out the Christian and western pre-Christian symbols) or the universal inheritance. Jung lamented some people's tendency to drop the richness of their own heritage for that of another group, which he saw in the often faddish adoption by Westerners of Eastern religions. If, on the other hand, exploring the symbology of others was helpful for discovering the symbols and therefore the unconscious of one's own psyche, then that was worthwhile, and Jung did a great deal of this himself.

Such use of many religions to discover universal truths is important for the intellectual precedents of holistic education. It also shows Jung to be an important contributor to the Western movement that began in the late nineteenth century of attempting to incorporate diverse religions into an all embracing metaphysics. In validating all religions; showing them to be only expressions (bound by the time and location of their foundation) of eternal truths; demonstrating that all religions express the same deep (perhaps ultimately ineffable) religiousness; and giving newer more inclusive and more appropriate expressions for the modern pluralist world; a new religion can be created. Such a new religion (and Jung's analytical psychology is said by some to be paramount to a new religion[491]) appears to be superior to all the old ones as it incorporates them and seems not bound by time or location, and is therefore closer to the eternal religiousness that lies at the origins of all religions. Theosophy, which Jung frequently mentions, was just such a movement, and was extremely popular and powerful during the formative years of Jung's life and work. It has been suggested that Theosophy was influential for Jung both through the books of Eastern religion it translated and published to which Jung referred, and through friends of his whom he often quotes and who were active Theosophical writers.[492]

One of Jung's contributions to this movement of creating an all inclusive religiousness, was his giving it a scientific and biological basis. This is important for holistic education as it allows the collective base of identity construction to be decentring, centring, and recentring, and allows identity constructions to be located in the past, and the present; an important consideration in the sociological analysis of the nature of holistic education. These aspects of identity construction are discussed in full in Section III; it is important here simply to indicate their relationship with Jung's work.

Fairly early in his career, Jung saw the necessity of both the conscious and unconscious working together. This is the notion of balance and harmony evident in Rousseau, Pestalozzi, and Froebel, but for Jung the notion is more complex. The conscious and unconscious have different and even contradictory functions, but the health of the individual depends on the struggle between them being "at least a fair fight, with equal rights on both sides."[493] This balancing of the conscious and unconscious working, perhaps in contention, but nevertheless in harmony was part of the process of psychological development that Jung called "individuation."

By paying careful attention to the contents of the conscious and (through its representations) the unconscious, there can be a union of them by what Jung called "the transcendent function."[494] This union was a "rounding out of the personality into a whole...."[495] Jung felt that his work empirically proved that "our consciousness has, fundamentally a tendency towards wholeness...."[496] Jung called the results of this wholeness the "self."[497] Jung proposed the self as a "psychological concept, a construct that serves to express an unknowable essence" which "might equally well be called 'God within us'."[498]

> What is meant by the self is not only in me but in all beings, like the Atman, like Tao. It is psychic totality.[499]

While Jung felt that he could empirically prove "the existence of a totality supraordinate to consciousness,"[500] it remains beyond the grasp of consciousness, hence rationality. It is not, however, beyond the combined and evolved forces of the conscious and unconscious —the self.

Jung also postulated the existence of the "ego." This is the conscious experience people have of themselves, and can be thought of as a personal and social construct. The ego is subordinate to the self, and "the experience of the self is always a defeat for the ego,"[501] as such an experience is one of non-ego or egolessness. This is one of the similarities between Jung's analytical psychology and mystical religions.[502] Both, Jung claimed, have as a result the emergence of a non-ego state that he felt is identical to experiencing the collective unconscious.[503] The reason for the similarity between experiencing the self and mystical experiences is that,

> the self can be distinguished only conceptually from what has always been referred to as "God," but not practically. Both concepts apparently rest on an identical numinous factor which is a condition of reality.[504]

Even though Jung felt that his discoveries were in many ways a rediscovery of the truths of religions and shamanism (which he studied directly and indirectly, and to which he appreciated being compared[505]), he felt that Ultimacy resulting from his analytical psychology is superior (especially for modern Western people) because with such Ultimacy, a person enters into an experience of self in a conscious state "without any diminution of moral responsibility which is one of the attainments of Western culture."[506]

Jung's claims of being an empirical scientist[507] and not "an atheist, a Gnostic, an agnostic, a mystic, a metaphysician, not a theologian," with no wish "to preempt the task of the philosopher or theologian"[508] rest on his notions of the truths that are accessible to science. He rejected the reductionist *Naturwissenschaft* view of science (which is the mainstream modern notion of science) and saw the limitations of Freud and Adler as being due to this limitation.[509] Jung felt that reductionist science created a division between religion and science that did not exist in antiquity, does not exist in the East, and is unhelpful for all the important questions of human existence.[510] Jung felt that "psychic truths" exist as well as physical ones, and that even though such truths are not derived by rationality, they are not beyond the bounds of psychology.[511] Without the speculative and metaphysical inclinations of the *Naturphilosophen*, Jung's scientific bias could well have left him as "Godless" as Freud described himself.

While most of the union in Jung's Ultimacy described so far can be considered a unification *of* (e.g., the conscious and unconscious, the fragments of the psyche, etc.) there remains one final form of union that would have to be considered to be a unification *with*, although, as with many things Jungian, it isn't entirely distinct. This is Jung's notion of *Unus Mundus*. At the end of a process Jung called "conjunction," he believed the psyche has

> a unison with the world—not with the world of multiplicity as we see it but with a potential world, the eternal Ground of all empirical Being...[512]

In this oneness with all of existence, the duality of spirit and matter disappear. This real, not imagined, event Jung saw as the union of "the personal with the suprapersonal Atman, and of the individual Tao with the universal Tao" and felt it was expressed by joining of the Ying and the Yang and by Satori in Zen Buddhism.[513] He claimed that, for Westerners, this event is so mysterious as to appear mystical.

Logically, such union must either be made by some magical or metaphysical power which transforms the nature of both matter and spirit, or there must be some common ground which allows the union to occur—something actual which exists in both spirit and matter that permits such a commingling so that they can form a oneness. For this Jung proposed the "psychoid unconscious"[514] and with this proposal all things have an animate aspect, even (so-called) inanimate objects. This allied him in yet another way to most archaic and shamanistic traditions.

Jung acknowledged that the notion of the psychoid unconscious "draws man more into the center of the picture as the measure of all things"[515] as no force, power, or entity external to man is needed to effect Ultimacy. It has been suggested that this notion of Jung's, more than any other, has given Jung his importance in New Age spirituality and neopaganism since the translation of his work on this in the 1960s.[516]

Jung insisted that he came to his insights from his own experience.

As the Ultimacy he discussed is (purportedly) the greatest that a human can experience, he has been considered by some to be as spiritually accomplished as any person in history—a view some of his critics have claimed he cultivated.[517] Although Jung insisted that a person needs to have the development of their psyche as a serious vocation to pursue it as far as he did,[518] he felt that "an experience of totality" or "becoming whole" was open to all those willing to commit themselves fully to it.[519] For holistic education such potential universality of acquisition is important. Jung was adamant that he was not creating a religion dressed as a science (something that he criticized Rudolf Steiner of doing with Anthroposophy, which Steiner called "spiritual science," and Mary Baker Eddy of doing with Christian Science).[520] Jung felt that religions don't suit modern man (though the truths of religions—called here *religiousness*—are available to modern man through a study of the psyche) because modern man needs to experience these truths and not just get them second hand.[521] Besides, religions (or "creeds" as Jung called them) are only expressions of eternal truths which are always expressing themselves anew; and Jung, with his new science of analytical psychology, searched for such expressions for the modern age—an endeavor viewed sympathetically by many holistic educators.

> The living spirit grows and even outgrows its earlier forms of expression; it freely chooses the men who proclaim it and in whom it lives. This living spirit is eternally renewed and pursues its goal in manifold and inconceivable ways throughout the history of mankind. Measured against it, the names and forms which men have given it mean very little; they are only the changing leaves and blossoms on the stem of the eternal tree.[522]

WHAT NEEDS TO BE LEARNED FOR JUNG

Jung's View of Experiential Knowledge

As Jung addressed issues in general education only slightly,[523] (feeling that conventional education was not within the purview of his science[524]) he did not elaborate his views on childhood acquisition of knowledge. He did have a great deal to say, however, about *knowing* that is needed in life which he sometimes referred to as knowledge and which at other times he counter-posed to knowledge (in which case he was referring to knowledge as intellectual knowledge). In general, Jung's view was that a major part of the non-cognitive or pre-cognitive knowledge needed for meaningful living (because of its relationship to Ultimacy) cannot be derived or even grasped cognitively as it lies in "a totality supraordinate to consciousness." For Jung, the unconscious can only be discovered through experience and such experience alters the nature of consciousness. A person must experience the truths of religion firsthand, and not get them secondhand; the latter being, for Jung, the nature of received beliefs.

Jung was interested in some epistemological questions and, in some regards, took a view not unlike Rousseau's in seeing knowledge as based on perception, with the relationships among perceptions, and the relationships between new perceptions and existing knowledge forming the basis of new knowledge. Both perception and knowledge are in the psyche. "'Knowing' therefore is based upon the perceived connection between psychic contents."[525] Apart from instrumental issues, such knowledge is important for modern individuals because "consciousness develops in civilized man by the acquisition of knowledge and by the withdrawal of projection"[526] which, Jung felt, get reintegrated into the psyche.

Perhaps one of the most interesting notions of experiential nonrational knowledge in Jung's work is exemplified by what he called "synchronicity." From 1929 onward,[527] Jung noted a relatively common kind of event in which psychic events (e.g., dreams, fantasies, etc.) correspond with material events, yet cannot be seen to have any causal connection (e.g., the dreams occur before the event they presage). Such phenomena are sometimes associated with parapsychology or telepathy. Even when the psychic event is presented only symbolically, it seems to have the same meaning for the experiencer as the physical event. This "phenomenon of synchronicity" indicated to Jung that psychic energy and physical energy are part of some larger reality. This being so, then at least on occasion, physical reality is in some way a mirror-image of psychic reality and indicates, therefore, a transcendent reality encompassing them both. The veracity of this, Jung felt, was borne out by some of the new discoveries in microphysics which was developing concepts he recognized as similar to some in depthpsychology.[528] What gives this relatively common phenomenon such importance is that it constitutes "the *empirical* indication of an ultimate unity of all existence...the *Unus Mundus.*"[529]

Synchronicity involves another distinct knowledge concept in Jung's work relevant to the present discussion: "absolute knowledge." This is "a self-subsistent 'unconscious' knowledge"[530] which forms part of the phenomenon of synchronicity. Through the "lowering of the threshold of consciousness"[531] (which can happen while asleep or in certain waking states) a person can gain access to the absolute knowledge evidenced in synchronicity. Jung believed this to be the same form of knowing that occurs in some Eastern mysticism, a sensing with "your inner eye, your inner ear."[532]

What emerges from Jung's work is that great swaths of essential knowledge are accessible only from experience. This brings the change in emphasis on the importance of experience as a form of knowing which occurred from Rousseau to Froebel, back to the emphasis that Rousseau expressed—experience is the only basis for most important knowledge.

Two other sources of experiential knowledge need to be briefly mentioned. One is "archetypes," which Jung described as "primordial images" and "the most ancient and the most universal 'thought-forms' of humanity" which "are as much feelings as thoughts."[533] The second source of experiential knowledge was alluded to earlier: transcendent reality, which can only be experienced and is always experienced as absolute. Jung felt these "intense inner experiences" lead to "lasting psychic growth" and should be the "unshakeable foundation...not of faith alone, but also of knowledge."[534]

> Religious experience is absolute; it is not to be disputed. ...No one can know what the ultimate things are. We must therefore take them as we experience them.[535]

Intellectual knowledge and rational understanding have an interesting role to play with non-conceptual knowing. Even though they add "nothing to the experience of wholeness," Jung claimed that they can facilitate the repetition of such experiences. Also, "intellectual representation...proves meaningful and helpful...when the road to original experience is blocked."[536] This does not mean Jung disparaged intellectual knowledge. Rather, he saw it as having a more limited place than he felt it was given by the modern Western culture of his time. "I believe strongly in the power and dignity of the intellect, but only if it does not violate the feeling-values."[537] Jung spoke of what is necessary for dream analysis (which for him is a form of education of the whole person) in a way that elucidates this approach to knowledge. He claimed that one needs an intellectual knowledge of the history of symbols, but that "mere intellect is not enough; one also needs feeling..."[538] cautioning that such feelings "must not give way to sentiment."[539]

In a reference to Rousseau that is interesting for this book, Jung wrote of the form of psychology he created as "a reaction against the exaggerated rationalization of consciousness"[540] and that unlike going "'back to nature' with Rousseau,"[541] Jung proposed that we need to contact the nature that is in our psyches.

The question arises as to what agency humans have for the experiences that form the basis of the needed learning. While Rousseau felt that, to a large extent, the experiences necessary for his student could be engineered, Jung felt that for the knowledge he valued,

> Experiences cannot be *made*. They happen—yet fortunately their independence of man's activity is not absolute but relative. We can draw closer to them—that much lies within our human reach. There are ways which bring us nearer to living experiences, yet we should beware of calling these ways "methods."[542]

Jung's analytical psychology, which gives attention to the unconscious, is one way to "draw closer" to such experiences. Another mechanism for such drawing closer is, according to Jung, intuition. Jung felt that intuition is not "an isolated gift but a regular function which is capable of being developed...with a specific range of knowledge based upon [it]."[543] He also felt that intuition is an activity "without which no realization is complete."[544]

Although Jung did not address the educational issues addressed by Rousseau, Pestalozzi and Froebel, like them, he identified words as a source of illusion. Jung felt the problem of being "deluded by words"[545] was especially acute with philosophers and theologians, and that words and concepts are too often substituted for and confused with reality. He felt that,

> ...our civilization is largely founded on a superstitious belief in words. One of the supreme religious assumptions is actually the "Word." Words can take the place of men and things.[546]

Like Rousseau and Pestalozzi, Jung seems to have been especially wary of words in making moral decisions.

> Since real moral problems all begin where the penal code leaves off, their solution can seldom or never depend on precedent, much less on precepts and commandments.[547]

Jung extended Rousseau's antipathy to representations to include thoughts as representations. Some of Jung's reasons for asserting that

nothing of importance could be captured by the intellect is that he felt
"…the mind [intellect or consciousness] cannot establish or assert anything beyond itself"[548] and that the conception of a thing cannot be
"identical with the nature of the thing itself, and this for very obvious
scientific reasons."[549] As the intellect cannot reach beyond itself, when
it tries to deal with things which are beyond intellect (such as all religious matters) it becomes "a great cheat and illusionist" by giving the
impression that the intellectual grasp is a real grasp, when in fact, "one
possesses nothing unless one has experienced it in reality…intellectual
insight is not enough."[550] The "intellectual one-sidedness of consciousness"[551] first makes a false dichotomy between matter and spirit—the
materialist perspective and the spiritual perspective[552]—and then attempts to rejoin them by trying sometimes to "spiritualize matter and
at other times materialize spirit."[553] This false dichotomy has left modern man fed up with this "warfare of opinions" and needing to "bring
meaning once more into life on the basis of fresh and unprejudiced
experience."[554] Jung contrasted this to the Eastern tradition in which,
he felt, such dichotomizing has not occurred.[555]

The importance Jung gave to self-knowledge is embedded in the
whole of his work. It is, in fact, impossible to discuss substantive parts
of his work without broaching the subject. However, Jung made a distinction between what he called self-knowledge and what he felt was
commonly thought of as self-knowledge.

> Most people confuse "self-knowledge" with knowledge of their
> conscious ego-personalities. Anyone who has any ego-consciousness
> at all takes it for granted that he knows himself. But the ego knows
> only its own contents, not the unconscious and its contents. People
> measure their self-knowledge by what the average person in their
> social environment knows of himself, but not by the real psychic
> facts which are for the most part hidden from them.[556]

In some of his work Jung uses the term "persona" to label the
person, personality, or socially-constructed-identity similar to the ego-
personalities or ego-consciousness named above which most people
think of as themselves. To know the persona is only to know a surrogate for the self and, while it may in many ways occupy the place of
the self, it does not resemble it very accurately.

In answering a question about the systematic preoccupation with
oneself in analytical psychology in relationship to egocentricity, Jung
made statements that would have found sympathy with Rousseau. He

claimed that,

> One *must* occupy oneself with oneself; otherwise one does not grow, otherwise one can not develop! …occupation with and meditation on one's own being is an absolutely legitimate, even necessary activity…[557]

Self-knowledge must include knowledge of one's emotions. For Jung this is much more complicated than knowledge of their existence or even of what generates them. It involves knowing the intensity and subtle nature of the emotions as these establish "feeling-value" which serve to contextualize the psychic landscape,[558] as it is heart or feeling which imparts an abiding value to what has been understood.

While Jung agreed that self-knowledge is necessary for all the reasons related to Ultimacy discussed in Chapter Two, Jung claimed that self-knowledge is also needed in order to understand other people, and understanding others is an important part of living.[559] Self-knowledge, therefore, is a foundation for the pragmatic as well as Ultimate aspects of living.

Jung's View of Competence

Jung did not discuss judgment, values, or freedom in education to any significant extent. He did write a great deal about independence in relation to the process of individuation and to 'the child' both as an actual person and as an archetype. For Jung, "'Child' means something evolving towards independence" which "requires detaching itself from its origins."[560] Jung equated freedom with self-mastery in this way.[561] Jung also stated that "there is no morality without freedom,"[562] claiming that the development humans need for Ultimacy requires at least enough freedom to be moral agents.

While Rousseau claimed that physical dominion and possessions necessarily infringe on liberty,[563] Jung felt psychic possession to be incompatible with freedom. In a discussion about the "psychic disposition that limits our freedom," Jung concluded that,

> Bondage and possession are synonymous. Always therefore there is something in the psyche that takes possession and limits or suppresses our moral freedom. In order to hide this undeniable but exceedingly unpleasant fact from ourselves and at the same time pay lip-service to freedom, we have got accustomed to saying apotropaically, " *I have*

such and such a desire or habit or feeling of resentment," instead of the more veracious "Such and such a desire or habit or feeling of resentment *has me*." The latter formulation robs us of the illusion of freedom.[564]

Social-ability for Jung

Another passage that Jung quoted from Pestalozzi highlights the distinction between culture and civilization, giving Pestalozzi's view that culture is based on individuals, and is fundamentally different from civilization; a distinction often made by holistic education which runs counter to many advocates of "citizenship education."

> More than a hundred years ago, in times not so unlike our own, Pestalozzi wrote (ibid., p. 186): "The race of men cannot remain socially united without some ordering power. Culture has the power to unite men as individuals, in independence and freedom, through law and art. But a cultureless civilization unites them as masses, without regard to independence, freedom, law or art, through the power of coercion". [N.B. Petalozzi evidently subscribes to the Germanic distinction between *Kulture* and *Zivilisation*, where the latter term is employed in a pejorative sense. The idea that culture, deriving ultimately from tillage and worship (*cultus*), is a natural organic growth, whereas civilization is an affair of the city (*civis*) and thus something artificial.][565]

Jung is clearly in agreement with Pestalozzi and Rousseau on many issues concerned with the relationship between the individual and society. As discussed earlier, Ultimacy for Jung is approached through the process of individuation, which is a singular engagement of a person discovering and uncovering himself. For Jung this has a social component, partly because everyone lives in social relationships, but also because everyone has a collective unconscious which lies beneath the personally acquired layer of the psyche. Part of the therapist's job is to reinforce the individual elements of the psyche when they are being smothered by the collective elements.

As the goal of individuation is the transformation of the psyche through uncovering and discovering it, alteration of the psyche in order to adapt to society was seen by Jung as counterproductive. Every individual is part of their society and indebted to it,[566] but for the transformation of the psyche to occur, the individual needs to separate himself from society. To accomplish this the individual, must offer a ransom in place of himself, that is, he must bring forth values which are an equivalent substitute for his absence in the collective personal sphere.[567]

Not only has society a right, it also has a duty to condemn the individuant if he fails to create equivalent values, for he is a deserter.[568]

Part of the reason for the divergence of interests between the individual and society is that they function according to different laws.

> The misfortune is that never under any circumstances are the laws of nations in such concord with those of nature that the civilized state is at the same time the natural state. If such concord is to be conceived as possible at all, it can be conceived only as a compromise in which neither state could attain its ideal but would remain far below it. Whoever wishes to attain one or other of the ideals will have to rest content with Rousseau's own formulations: "You must choose between making a man or a citizen, you cannot make both at once."[569]

While society is always hostile to individuation because of the desertion from the collective, according to Jung, society is even more hostile at some historical points than at others. Jung felt that "the tempo of the development of the consciousness through science and technology" has left modern man with an unconscious which has lagged behind and which reacts with "the frightful regressions of our time" (e.g., Nazism, Communism). In fact, Jung felt that all of the "social and political isms," no matter how ideal they claimed to be, had the effect of "inhibiting the possibilities of individual development."[570] In an interview about Nazism and Hitler, Jung pointed to the social pressure which made people "stupider and more suggestible"[571] and which worked against individuation. When asked how this could be cured, part of Jung's response was, "Education for fuller consciousness"[572]— education for Ultimacy.

Even though Jung emphasized the importance of maintaining society, he insisted that society is never "a carrier of life. The sole and natural carrier of life is the individual, and this is so throughout nature."[573] It is also the individual who is the carrier of the collective, "because the masses are not changed unless the individual changes."[574] Even though Jung, like the Authors before him, saw Ultimacy as "man's natural destiny," he, like they, saw this as part of being in the right relationship to the collective.

> ...the natural process of individuation brings to birth a
> consciousness of human community precisely because it makes us
> aware of the unconscious, which unites and is common to all mankind.
> Individuation is an at-one-ment with oneself and at the same time
> with humanity.[575]

Jung described only sketchily what an education that assisted individuation would look like. To do this he postulated three general kinds
of education, all of which a person should experience at different times
in their development: 1) "Education through example," which pro-
ceeds "wholly unconsciously and is therefore the oldest and perhaps
the most effective form of all."[576] 2) "Collective Education" by which
Jung did "not necessarily mean education *en masse* (as in schools), but
education according to rules, principles, and methods."[577] While Jung
did not feel this to be the best education for all individuals, he stated
that "we live in a collective world, and we need collective norms, just
like we need a common language,"[578] even if the cost of "the collective
mode of life" is a person's "wholeness."[579] 3) "Individual Education,"
in which all rules, principles, and systems must be subordinated to the
one purpose of bringing out the specific individuality of the pupil.
This aim is directly opposed to that of collective education, which
seeks to level out and make uniform.[580]

It seems that, just as individuation is "man's destiny," but suited
only for those who can withstand the arduous process, individual education is appropriate only for those who can withstand the difficulties
of separating themselves from the collective and pay the ransom described above. It is, however, an education that is in keeping with Jung's
notions of approaching Ultimacy.

ASPECTS OF STUDENTS THAT FACILITATE
THE NEEDED LEARNING FOR JUNG

A great deal has already been said about Jung's notions of the individuation process, the achievement of personality and *Unus Mundus*.
However, there remain to be discussed several elements of Jung's views
of the learning processes that facilitate such needed learning, especially those related to childhood.

Jung believed that "the unconsciousness is the matrix out of which
the conscious grows," however, the process of adding fragments from
the unconscious to the conscious slows down after puberty. In this

process of "the integration of consciousness," schools, as socializing agents, can play an important role.[581] It is generally only after consciousness has substantively developed that a new stage of development can occur; "…normally the psyche attains relative independence only after puberty. Up till then it has been largely the plaything of instinct and environment."[582] Childhood was seen by Jung as the time when contact with the unconscious needs to decrease because, for children

> …their problem lies mainly in adapting themselves to their surroundings. Indeed, their connection with the primordial unconsciousness must be severed, as its persistence would present a formidable obstacle to the development of consciousness, which is what they need more than anything else.[583]

During childhood, the child's psyche "is extremely susceptible and dependent, and is steeped for a long time in the atmosphere of the parental psychology,"[584] and this atmosphere is not generated mainly from the consciousness of the parents (which is within their means to manipulate) "but from their unconscious background."[585] In this, the most powerful influence comes from the "unlived life of the parents"[586] by which Jung meant "all the life which the parents could have lived, but of which they thwarted themselves for artificial motives."[587]

The process of growing out of childhood is partly, for Jung, the process of forming a separate identity (ego, in Jung's terms), a process he called "differentiation." This process, according to Jung, is never completed in some "primitive tribes" whose members don't develop a sense of separate selves and in many modern western adults who fail to tear themselves away from their familial identity and national prejudices.[588] Yet this process of differentiation is necessary for psychic growth. "In this battle for freedom the school plays a not unimportant part," as it should help a child construct a separate identity and loosen the grip of the parents' psychological influence.[589] For Jung,

> "Child" means something evolving towards independence. This it cannot do without detaching itself from its origins: …The symbol [child] anticipates a nascent state of consciousness. So long as this is not actually in being, the "child" remains a mythological projection which requires religious repetition and renewal by ritual. The Christ child, for instance, is a religious necessity only so long as the majority of men are incapable of giving psychological reality to the saying: "Except ye become as little children…"[590]

After the early stages of forming the conscious from the unconscious, this "evolving towards independence" is, for Jung, a crucial aspect of the inherent process that facilitates the needed learning. It is so
universally inherent that it lies behind the "child" archetype. As the
most subtle and complex forms of this "independence" are involved
in approaching Ultimacy, the "child" archetype has connections to "the
sacred." Jung believed that many adults engage in transference of the
sacredness of the archetype onto actual children,[591] and conflate their
enthusiasm for their own need for independence and psychic maturing
with their enthusiasm for children.[592]

However, Jung was quite insistent that the psychic development
that was possible for adults was not for children, and frequently warned
"that the high ideal of educating the personality is not for children…"[593]
as the very qualities required of personality, "definiteness, wholeness,
and ripeness…cannot and should not be expected of the child, as they
would rob it of childhood,"[594] a tendency that Jung felt was often present
in adults who know only a little about psychology. This amounts to a
form of coercion, and a person "should never be forced into a development that does not come naturally and spontaneously."[595]

Jung makes several references to the process of acquiring the needed
learning as being inherent or natural. He complained that the European (which today would be called the modern Western person) "has
become so far removed from his roots that his mind has finally split
into faith and knowledge…" and Jung felt that the modern Western
person's "task is to find the natural man again."[596] Jung claimed that he
means something slightly different than Rousseau by this expression,
but their different meanings are not in opposition to one another. One
of the possibilities of childhood is not to become "so far removed"
from one's roots of the collective unconscious and not to become too
immersed in "systems and methods" which "repress the natural man."[597]
For this, schools can again play a positive role by not confusing their
more important mission of personal growth with the lesser function
of conveying knowledge.[598]

The school can also play an important role in the development of
the child by ensuring that it maintains "a balanced education" which
avoids "over specialized fields" as this "is essential as a measure of
psychic hygiene" for all children but especially for gifted or highly-
strung children.[599] Jung would also include emotional development in
personal growth, and echoes Pestalozzi when he says that "there are,
besides the gifts of the head, also those of the heart, which are no whit

less important," and which often make a more valuable contribution to society.[600]

One aspect of conditioning in the West that Jung felt could be avoided in childhood is one that Jung also feels is particularly pernicious as it acts to block the very process necessary to acquiring the needed learning—dependency. Jung frequently states that the tradition that has emerged in the Western world of depending on outside agencies (e.g., God, Grace, priests, rituals, etc.) to achieve Ultimacy actually prevents Ultimacy by causing the psyche to be undervalued and preventing the individual from taking responsibility for their own "higher development."[601]

Jung's View of Inherent Motivation

We have already discussed Jung's claim that the quest for Ultimacy is a vocation, but it must again be touched on briefly here as it relates to his notions of motivation. Jung's use of the word "vocation" must be understood in the classical sense of a calling that is only ignored at one's peril. Hence, for one's well-being following one's vocation is a "prime necessity" and an "indispensable requirement."[602] This, for Jung, is the motivation a person has that facilitates the needed learning. However, unlike the classical Christian sense of "calling," for Jung it came from Nature (as present in the psyche) and not from any external agent.[603] Jung seems to claim that this vocation is in everyone, at least as a potential, but that most people's lives have so developed that by the time they are old enough to respond, they are incapable of hearing the call. The substance of this motivation is due to the libido, a concept of psychic energy (which Jung sometimes referred to as "inner Tao") which flows naturally and inexorably towards a harmonious and unified existence.

> The natural flow of the libido ... means complete obedience to the fundamental laws of human nature, and there can positively be no higher moral principle than harmony with natural laws that guide the libido in the direction of life's optimum.[604]

Jung felt that the libido is such a strong ordering principle that in people who have not been overly complicated and corrupted by civilization (as he believed some indigenous people to be), libido is even responsible for the natural creation of social laws and social order.

Jung felt that not only is the libido present as a motivating force, it is necessary, because without some form of compulsion the energy to bring about Ultimacy would never be expended.

> The only thing that moves nature is causal necessity, and that goes for human nature too. Without necessity nothing budges, the human personality least of all. It is tremendously conservative, not to say torpid. Only acute necessity is able to rouse it. The developing personality obeys no caprice, no command, no insight, only brute necessity; it needs the motivating force of inner or outer fatalities.[605]

ASPECTS OF TEACHERS THAT FACILITATE THE NEEDED LEARNING FOR JUNG

Teachers' Understanding of Students and their Needs for Jung

Jung seems to articulate Rousseau's and Pestalozzi's positions most fully for the modern Westerner, especially Pestalozzi's perhaps unclear claim that a teacher must have an understanding of students in both the general and the particular.

> There is and can be no self-knowledge based on theoretical assumptions, for the object of this knowledge is an individual—a relative exception and an irregular phenomenon. Hence it is not the universal and the regular that characterize the individual, but rather the unique. He is not to be understood as a recurrent unit but as something unique and singular which in the last analysis can be neither known nor compared with anything else. At the same time man, as member of a species, can and must be described as a statistical unit; otherwise nothing in general could be said about him. For this purpose he has to be regarded as a comparative unit. This results in a universally valid anthropology or psychology, as the case may be, with an abstract picture of man as an average unit from which all individual features have been removed. But it is precisely these features which are of paramount importance for *understanding* man. If I want to understand an individual human being, I must lay aside all scientific knowledge of the average man and discard all theories in order to adopt a completely new and unprejudiced attitude. I can only approach the task of *understanding* with a free and open mind, whereas *knowledge* of man, or insight into human character, presupposes all sorts of knowledge about mankind in general.[606]

This quotation reflects part of the previous discussion on knowledge and the way in which one kind of knowledge is seen as an inhibitor of another kind (in this case articulated as understanding).

Jung claimed that even though all humans share the same archetypes, psychic forces and psychic structures, and that the "universal Tao" or *Unus Mundus* for everyone is, of necessity, the same, yet "each person is a new and unique combination of psychic elements."[607] Jung claimed that the universal must be understood by the psychiatrist and educator because the universal is the psychic context in which to locate the individual, but it is only understanding the individual that facilitates the needed learning, as it is the individual psyche that "must nevertheless individuate itself if it is to become actualized…" and no two people do this identically.[608] Like Pestalozzi, Jung claimed that preventing or inhibiting the individual nature of a person prevented or inhibited Ultimacy.

Teachers' Understanding of the Correct Pedagogic Process for Jung

Jung contributes several important notions to what a teacher should understand about the correct pedagogic processes from the perspective of the development of the psyche. As stated previously, a child must begin the long process of individuation by breaking away from identification with the parents, a process in which schools can and should play a significant role; the classmates take much of the psychological place of siblings and teachers take the psychological place of parents. The classmates can not be expected to consciously take on their role as surrogate siblings. However, the correct pedagogic process requires that the teacher "be conscious of the role he is playing…and not be satisfied with merely pounding the curriculum into the child…."[609]

Part of what is required of teachers for the correct pedagogic process is to exercise "the delicate task of avoiding repressive authority…"[610] while simultaneously maintaining a minimum but appropriate authority. The teacher is mainly to direct and affect the child through the teacher's own personality, which must be done without artifice and through the teacher being "an upright and healthy man himself, for good example still remains the best pedagogic method."[611] This requires a personal approach to education and to relationship with the students, which is of such importance that "if the personal relationship of child to teacher is a good one, it matters very little…"[612] what method of teaching is used. Jung brings into the twentieth century the notion of the earlier Authors that the correct pedagogic process rests on the relationship of the teacher to the student, but Jung's basis for this is his understanding of psychological growth. As such growth is of the greatest importance, Jung also ends up agreeing with the earlier Authors that it is not important what "amount of specific information a child takes away with him from school...."[613]

Jung's analytic psychotherapy has been described by several commentators as a cure through increased knowledge and understanding and, therefore, as educative.[614] Consequently, it is appropriate to consider any part of the process Jung used with his patients that was not solely psychotherapeutic as also broadly educative. In this regard, a case can be made for examining Jung's technique of "active imagination" as there are several parallels between this and the "free activity" or "spontaneous activity" of Pestalozzi and the "self activity" of Froebel. This revealing of oneself to oneself and others through expressions of the unconscious[615] was used extensively by Jung. It was adapted and used for children more by Jung's friend and disciple Frances Wickes than by Jung himself.[616]

More interesting for this discussion on pedagogic process is an aspect of a technique Jung engaged in that emerged from a survey of his patients. This has been referred to as a "paradoxical technique,"[617] but is probably best described as "performative apophasis." Apophasis has been convincingly portrayed as an aspect of the discourse of Plotinus, John the Scot Eriugena, Meister Eckhart, Ibn Arabi, and others.[618] An example of apophasis is to say that the transcendent is beyond description; then to acknowledge that "beyond description" is in fact a description and so to add that the transcendent can't be thus described; then to acknowledge that "can't be thus described" is also a description, ad infinitum. It is in the necessary retraction of one proposition by the next that paradox is generated, and it is through this tension between the two propositions that meaning is conveyed rather than in the propositions themselves. It is "a propositionally unstable and dynamic discourse"[619] that defies conceptual construction and therefore eludes the conscious mind allowing the unconscious mind to operate. Such a technique by Jung "reflects his [Jung's] völkisch beliefs in the transformative effect of experiencing" the unconscious which for Jung was related to the "god within."[620] This is a pedagogic process based on experience of a very subtle nature.

Teachers' Understanding of
the Correct Pedagogic Relationship for Jung

For Jung, unlike Maslow or Rogers, it is questionable to what extent the psychotherapeutic relationship can be equated with the pedagogic one. That it can be equated to some extent seems fairly uncontentious, but for Jung the psychic structure of a child is so different from that of an adult that it would imply that a different relationship is necessary. Nevertheless, what Jung proposes for the correct therapeutic relationship has been taken by some holistic educators to be the correct pedagogic relationship, and, as such, is worth briefly noting.

> Psychotherapy is at bottom a dialectical relationship between doctor and patient. It is an encounter, a discussion between two psychic wholes, in which knowledge is used only as a tool. The goal is transformation—not one that is predetermined, but rather an indeterminable change, the only criterion of which is the disappearance of egohood. No efforts on the part of the doctor can compel this experience. The most he can do is to smooth the path for the patient and help him to attain an attitude which offers the least resistance to the decisive experience.[621]

Keeping in mind that "the disappearance of egohood" is part of Ultimacy for Jung, that experiential knowledge is what needs to be learned, and that the goal is not the shaping of people but their own discovering or uncovering of themselves; then an equation becomes possible of at least part of the correct therapeutic relationship and the correct pedagogic relationship of holistic education.

Jung claimed that "the attitude" of the therapist is more important than precepts, methods, or theories "which in any case never work properly unless they are applied with right understanding."[622] Jung equates such an attitude with both a religious attitude and with love, which are more important than any moral or social intervention.[623] Jung claims that this religious, empathetic attitude is, in fact, "unprejudiced objectivity," which is not to be "confused with a purely intellectual, abstract attitude of mind."[624]

> It is a human quality—a kind of deep respect for the facts, for the man who suffers from them, and for the riddle of such a man's

life. The truly religious person has this attitude. He knows that God
has brought all sorts of strange and inconceivable things to pass and
seeks in the most curious ways to enter a man's heart. He therefore
senses in everything the unseen presence of the divine will. This is
what I mean by "unprejudiced objectivity."[625]

Jung made several links between his notions of the correct therapeutic process and the correct pedagogic process in discussing the education of gifted children. He also showed his affinity with Rousseau,
Pestalozzi and Froebel with his emphasis on the role of affection in
pedagogy.

> ...I would say, in the light of my own experience, that an
> understanding heart is everything in a teacher, and cannot be esteemed
> highly enough. One looks back with appreciation to the brilliant
> teachers, but with gratitude to those who touched our human feelings.
> The curriculum is so much necessary raw material, but warmth is the
> vital element for the growing plant and for the soul of the child.[626]

Teachers' Self-Development for Jung

Given that a large part of Jung's analytical psychology derives from
his inspection of his own psyche, and that he felt this was an ongoing
and life-long endeavor, it is hardly surprising that he believed in the
benefits of continued self-development for all adults. He felt such self-
development was of special importance for the psychologist "if he is
not to be merely an unconscious fraud."[627]

> We could say, without too much exaggeration, that a good half
> of every treatment that probes at all deeply consists in the doctor
> examining himself, for only what he can put right in himself can he
> hope to put right in his patient.[628]

Jung felt that such self-development was equally important for teachers because "it is much better to educate oneself first before one educates others."[629] For Jung, "educating oneself" was not a matter of
acquiring more knowledge of the outside world; and he cites the social,
professional, and emotional disappointments in so many people's lives
as evidence of the lack of education and that "vast numbers of men
and women thus spend their entire lives in complete ignorance of the
most important things."[630] This marks an important shift in the study
of mind that is evident in all the modern Authors: what had been an

approach to treating an illness became an approach for all to healthy living. "What was formerly a method of medical treatment now becomes a method of self-education."[631]

In what may be a difficulty in the translation of the German *kulture* or a deliberate fusion on Jung's part, he conflates "culture" as social culture and as the noun form of "cultivating oneself."

> The teacher must not be a merely passive upholder of culture; he must actively promote that culture through his own self education. His culture must never remain at a standstill, otherwise he will start to correct in children those faults which he has neglected in himself. This is manifestly the antithesis of education.[632]

Even though Jung frequently emphasized that "the most important question next to the education of the child is the education of the educator,"[633] he never discussed this in terms of what could be called "teaching skills." In fact, Jung felt that "it is not knowledge, not technical skill" that achieves the wanted results in psychotherapy or in education, but the personality or quality of being of the doctor or teacher, and developing this "presupposes self-education."[634] Jung contended that "as a man is, so will be his ultimate truth, and so also his strongest effect on others."[635] Jung claimed that the flaws of the teacher will most likely be the source of things that go wrong with the students.[636] Consequently, Jung presented analytical psychology as a tool for the educator to develop himself. Such self-development is partly important because of the power of example. It is also important because a person who is undeveloped (in Jung's terms) can very easily act out unconscious forces that run counter to his intentions.[637] This is the damage often caused by the unlived lives of the parents mentioned previously, which applies to teachers as well as parents, and can take the form of the adult pushing the child instead of himself.

> ...when, as is unfortunately all too often the case, parents and teachers expect the child to make a better job of what they themselves do badly, the effect is positively devastating.[638]

Even though Jung was convinced that the teacher's use of analytical psychology for self-development "...will eventually rebound to the good of his pupils,"[639] to engage in such development, the teacher must first make the uncomfortable acknowledgement that he is in as much need of change and development as is the world around him;

echoing Rousseau's dictum of teachers needing humility, and Rogers's claim they need "realness." Unfortunately, such acceptance of "himself in all his wretchedness is the hardest of tasks."[640]

> ...the teacher has to be absolutely convinced that his personal attitude is in need of revision, even of actual change. Nobody will condescend to this unless he feels that there really is something wrong. In view of the actual condition of the world every intelligent person is ready to admit that there is something utterly wrong with our attitude. Yet this inclusive statement rarely ever includes the individual in question, namely, the would-be teacher. His attitude is surely right and only needs confirmation and support, but no change. It is a very long step from this conviction to the conclusion: the world is wrong and therefore I am wrong too. To pronounce such words is easy, but to feel their truth in the marrow of one's bones is a very different proposition, yet it is the *sine qua non* of the true teacher. In other words, it is a question of personalities, without which no method and no organization makes sense. *A man whose heart is not changed will not change any other's.* Unfortunately the world of today is inclined to belittle and to ridicule such a simple and evident truth as this and thereby proves its own psychological immaturity, which is one of the prime causes of the present state of affairs as well as of numberless neuroses and individual conflicts.[641]

Jung believed that such an attitude of including oneself with the world and of accepting one's wretchedness is a necessary part of the "unprejudiced objectivity" discussed previously.[642]

CHAPTER 9

Abraham Harold Maslow

A BIOGRAPHICAL SKETCH OF ABRAHAM HAROLD MASLOW (1 APRIL 1908 – 8 JUNE 1970)

*M*aslow was the eldest of seven children born to uneducated Russian Jewish immigrants who had settled in Brooklyn. Like many immigrants, his parents saw education as the means to success for their children and they pushed young Maslow very hard in his studies. He later stated that his childhood was poor, lonely and unhappy, and he was surprised that he hadn't gone insane.

At the instigation of his parents, Maslow went to City College in New York with a view of eventually studying law. After transferring to Cornell, and then returning to City College, he realized his heart was just not in the subject. To the chagrin of his parents, after a year and a half of pre-law studies, he went to the University of Wisconsin to study psychology and physiology. There he completed his graduate degree and did original research on the dominance and sexual behavior of Rhesus monkeys. What is significant in this research for his later work is that he began to see a hierarchy of needs in these monkeys (thirst before hunger, hunger before sex, etc.); an idea he was to refine and elaborate as part of his eventual theory of human psychology.

While at the University of Wisconsin, he married his first cousin Bertha Goodman against the express wishes of his parents. They would eventually have two daughters.

At the age of thirty-two Maslow completed his Ph.D., whereupon he went to Columbia to teach and do some research on human sexuality. Despite his training and research as a behavioral psychologist, while at Columbia, he met and had as a mentor Alfred Adler (an early follower and student of Freud). He also made acquaintance with several other intellectuals fleeing Nazi Europe such as Eric Fromm, and he was inspired to study Gestalt Psychology and other more "person centered" psychologies at the New School of Social Research in New York City.

While teaching at Brooklyn College from 1937 to 1951 Maslow found two other mentors who were to have a profound impact on his work, the anthropologist Ruth Benedict and the Gestalt psychologist Max Wertheimer. Not only did their thinking influence his, but he felt they were both "wonderful human beings" and he began to study them as subjects. This was the start of his study of highly developed people he would eventually describe as "self-actualized" (a term actually coined by his friend Kurt Goldstein).

Maslow felt that most of the psychology he had studied was concerned with abnormal mental states or illnesses, [643] whereas his study of these two mentors was concerned with extremely healthy mental states or perhaps even the fullest possible human development. He found this so important for understanding the human psyche that he continued to study "the finest, healthiest, people, the best specimens of mankind I could find."[644] This, he felt, was an important yet neglected part of psychology.

Maslow felt there was another important gap in the field of psychology of his time. He felt that behaviorism was too reductionist and mechanical, Freudian psychoanalysis was too negative and sordid about human nature, and Jungian analytical psychology was too abstract and theoretical. Maslow felt that something in between these mutually exclusive approaches to psychology was needed, and he proposed a third way or "third force" that he called humanistic psychology. Humanistic psychology is distinct from the mechanical approaches like behaviorism and the "high theory" of approaches like Freud and Jung. Maslow felt that humanistic psychology is accessible to the general public, brings meaning back to human nature, and puts normal healthy psyches to the forefront. It also seemed to offer hope to everyone that their fullest potential could be developed.

Maslow taught at Brandeis University from 1951 to 1969 where he was as much sought after by the students for personal advice as for his courses. He died soon after retiring.

MASLOW'S NOTION OF ULTIMACY

Maslow's initial investigation of what could be called Ultimacy was empirical—he recorded long lists of characteristics from subjective descriptions used by people and about people who seemed to have experienced Ultimacy. These people seemed generally to have been accepted as "the best specimens"[645] and included historical figures as well as some available for interview. His term for the ultimate state of development was "self-actualization" and his term for the ultimate engagement or experience was "peak-experience."

> The climax of self-actualization is the peak experience. "Peak experience" is a splendidly *naturalistic* idiom, hospitable to all the similar meanings in the vocabularies of religion and mysticism, yet confined to none of them. A peak experience is what you feel and perhaps "know" when you gain authentic elevation as a human being. We don't know how the peak experience is achieved; it has no simple one-to-one relation with any deliberate procedure; we know only that it is somehow *earned.* [646]

Maslow believed that "...sickness comes from the denial of human potential."[647] Maslow's notions of Ultimacy are at the center of his psychology; they are "the compass by which man gains a sense of the magnetic north of his existence,"[648] and without this a human is necessarily disoriented. Ultimacy was also important for Maslow as it provides the basis of all motivation. Maslow postulated a universal human "hierarchy of needs." In this scheme, the basic needs of survival (e.g., food, shelter, etc.) form the base level of the hierarchy, and these must first be met. When this first level is satisfied the next level in the hierarchy (e.g., belonging) is felt and cries out to be met. When this second level is met the needs move up to the next level of the hierarchy, etc. The final stage in the hierarchy is the need for self-actualization, the ultimate state for Maslow. In this scheme, however, the higher needs are not dormant until the lower ones are met. Instead, they are working in the background, so that the ultimate need (self-actualization) is seen as behind, and in a way, driving all the others. Consequently, Ultimacy, for Maslow as well as the previous Authors, has importance because it is our most fundamental and all pervading motivation.

Ultimacy in Relation to Maslow's View of Human Nature

For Maslow, Ultimacy defines what it means to be human to the extent that he often substituted phrases like "full humanness"[649] for his terms for Ultimacy (e.g., self-actualization, full Being, etc.). He goes so far as to say that those who are not actively engaged in the process of self-actualization "can be called 'human impersonators'."[650] Maslow felt that he had established an empirical base for his assertions about human nature claiming that, "man demonstrates *in his own nature* a pressure toward fuller and fuller Being."[651] As well as towards Ultimacy, this pressure is also a tendency toward the "sub-aspects of self-actualization," what we have called secondary values (see page 23), which for Maslow included "serenity, kindness, courage, knowledge, honesty, love, unselfishness, and goodness."[652] Maslow also frequently interchanged the term "self-actualization" with "psychological health"[653] reinforcing the notion that we are naturally approaching Ultimacy when we are in the best of health and fulfilling "our biological destiny."[654]

Maslow felt that in peak-experiences, which are the moments when we see most profoundly and clearly, "there is the realization that what 'ought to be' *is*"[655] which resembles Rousseau's principle of finding that "what is, is good." For Maslow this includes "the perception of evil"[656] which is no more than "a product of limited or selfish vision and understanding"[657] and which has its rightful place in the world. Maslow would agree with Jung that evil is a necessary part of a good universe, and therefore, paradoxically, is part of the good.

That "people at their best are far more admirable (godlike, heroic, great, divine, awe-inspiring, loveable, etc.) than ever before conceived, in their *own* proper nature..."[658] raised questions for Maslow, i.e. why were people ever considered to be otherwise? Maslow answered this by saying that if people are inherently bad yet need goodness (a need conceded by most cultures), then it follows that people are necessarily dependent on outside agents for goodness. Maslow felt that it is in the interests of some authorities and some social institutions (i.e., religious authorities and churches) to create and maintain such dependence. Therefore, the work in psychology that is "proving" man's inherent goodness reduces the authority of religions, and so helps liberate humans by contributing to the modern "decay in supernatural sanctions."[659]

Maslow claimed that being aware is more than an aspect of peak-experiences. He felt that a peak experience is a mental state that emotionally healthy people have frequently, and which positively influences a person's material success by fostering problem-centered thinking rather than ego-centered thinking. While he said that psychology experiments were proving this to be a better mind-set for all thinking and learning, he credited Krishnamurti for particular insights into the importance of "choiceless awareness," which he felt "contrasts to the abstracting, categorizing, and rubricating..."[660] in which people commonly engage.

Ultimacy As an Aspect of Religiousness for Maslow

While Jung came to the religiousness of his notions of Ultimacy by what seems to be inclination, and certainly an interest that he claimed went back to his childhood; Maslow came to it reluctantly. In studying the healthiest and finest people he could find, Maslow kept getting reports from them resembling mystical experiences.

> And, like most scientists, [he] had sniffed at them with disbelief and considered it all nonsense, maybe hallucinations, maybe hysteria— almost surely pathological.[661]

Maslow came only grudgingly to consider and finally accept the existence of a universal religiousness in human experience. He saw that what he was discovering in his studies of people was nothing new and could easily be found by "any reader of Zen, Taoistic, or mystical literature...."[662] Adding substantially to his popularity in the 1960s, he equated these religious experiences to those of many people taking psychedelic drugs (like Huxley). Part of religiousness, for Maslow, was "being lost in the present" which had "something to do with this ability to become timeless, selfless, outside of space, of society, of history," and which results in "transcendence."[663] Maslow advocated some common cultural activities that he felt encouraged this state, such as art and music.

Unlike Jung, but like the earlier Authors, Maslow saw religions as a corruption of religiousness. This corruption was partly perpetrated by special interests and partly by tendencies within consciousness, which he claimed to be the main thesis of his book *Religions, Values, and Peak-Experiences*.[664] Although Maslow had previously made such claims about religions, he used this book to summarize his notions and to correct what he had felt was a bias in his previous work on the subject. This book also shows one of his approaches to notions of balance between human feeling and thinking. Maslow named the tendency toward the experiential feelings and the mystical as "Dionysian," and the tendency towards the rational and formulaic as "Apollonian."[665] Maslow had previously been more critical of the generally dominant Apollonian tendency[666] in individuals which he felt (like Jung) was largely due to society's overemphasis on rationality. By the mid-1960s, however, he felt it necessary to emphasize that a balance of the two is what leads to Ultimacy.

While Maslow's notions of balance and harmony are not as complex as Jung's, they are just as all embracing. He claimed that the tendency to dichotomize, "is itself a pathological process,"[667] and when this stops there is the unity (which originally existed) of apparent opposites. Such notions of original unity, harmony and balance (or the unity, harmony, and balance in the universe) are Maslow's moral justification for developing all the faculties within the individual. It is this development that produces the unity, harmony, and balance within and consequently puts us in unity and harmony with the universe. Such ontological notions have led some of Maslow's critics (such as Browning) to claim that

> The images of harmony fuse at points in Maslow's writings with what must be called virtually monistic metaphysical metaphors... Monism is characterized by the idea that the sacred is a unified, motionless, timeless, unconditional, and self-caused perfection and, furthermore, that the human self in its depth is a manifestation of the divine life itself.[668]

Browning's contention that there are religious assertions in the work of Maslow and Rogers is well supported by statements which these psychologists both made, but Browning's contention that they should not stray into such areas as they are not theologians supports a fundamental claim made by Maslow, Rogers, and Jung. All three claimed that such dichotomizing of science and faith is one of the symptoms, as well as a cause, of many modern ills. All three also claimed that they had not sought to engage with the religious domain. They had sought to study the facts of human existence and in that pursuit found that they had to study people's notions of Ultimacy—religiousness forced itself into the picture. Jung, Maslow and Rogers all claimed that by keeping the study of the religious separate from everyday human experience, neither could be understood, and this separation was a source of human ills, not its cure.

Maslow felt that rejecting religiousness as part of what a scientist could consider was to establish preconditions of what could be found (a very unscientific position), which results in rejecting the very wholeness he had come to realize a scientist needs in order to understand the human condition. Maslow's Ultimacy involves integration of the person through "the recovery of aspects of the unconscious and preconscious,"[669] and for this the rational, analytical conscious intellect is completely inadequate. For Maslow, such integration leads to a "unitive consciousness."

> This is the ability to simultaneously perceive in the fact—the *is*—its particularity, *and* its universality; to see it simultaneously as here and now, and yet also as eternal, or rather to be able to see the universal in and through the particular and the eternal in and through the temporal and momentary. In my own phrasing, this is a fusion of the Being-realm and the Deficiency-realm: to be aware of the B-realm while immersed in the D-realm.[670]

Maslow's hierarchy of needs corresponds to states of being, and all of the activities engaged in while in a particular state are affected by that state. Hence, the nature of cognition in a lower state was seen by Maslow to be different from the nature of cognition in the highest state. Maslow's notion of Ultimacy or the highest state of being a person can aspire to, in which there are peak experiences, he described simply as 'Being'. Maslow attached 'Being' to activities or qualities characteristic of this state to distinguish them from their facsimile in other states. Maslow spoke, therefore, of Being-values (or B-values for short) and similarly of B-love, B-cognition, and B-knowledge.

While Maslow's notions of Being-realm and Deficiency-realm, and Being-values and Deficiency-values, etc. are discussed later, it is important to introduce the notions here because their fusion is an important aspect of the religiousness of Maslow's Ultimacy. For Maslow, as for Jung and Rogers, the mundane or everyday (the Deficiency-realm) is not negated or destroyed by the sacred (the Being-realm) but is subsumed by it. The first in Maslow's list of Being-values is "wholeness (unity; integration; tendency to one-ness; ...)"[671] and Being-cognition has no difficulty with the apparent paradox of seeing the whole world as a unity, or of seeing one small part, for a moment, as though it were all of the world.[672]

WHAT NEEDS TO BE LEARNED FOR MASLOW

Maslow's View of Experiential Knowledge

Like the preceding Authors, Maslow made a distinction between knowledge from experience and knowledge from abstraction, and, considering himself an empiricist, he gave precedence to experience.[673] Maslow's unique contributions to the question of what needs to be learned are his notions of the relationship between conceptual and non-conceptual knowledge. Unfortunately, Maslow's language complicates elucidating his thoughts on this as he used several terms to convey similar notions depending on what he was trying to emphasize.

Maslow asserted that some things can only be known experientially (e.g., colors) and other things can only be known if experiential knowledge is part of the knowing.

> Perhaps it is better to say that all of life must first be known experientially. There is no substitute for experience, none at all. All the other paraphernalia of communication and of knowledge—words, labels, concepts, symbols, theories, formulas, sciences—all are useful only because people already know experientially. The basic coin in the realm of knowing is direct, intimate, experiential knowing.[674]

Knowledge that can be thought of as logically compelled (which Maslow called "inductive knowledge"—giving mathematics as an example) is adequate for conceptual conviction, but this is a far cry from certainty. Maslow felt that certainty is more visceral and that "inductive knowledge can never bring certainty."[675] Echoing Jung's claims that a person's religious experience is a certainty for that person, Maslow claimed that experiential knowledge can bring certainty (perhaps the only certainty), and even when it doesn't, "in any case, it is real...."[676] In this statement and elsewhere, Maslow made the same simple distinction between "real" and "unreal" knowledge seen in the early Authors.

With this distinction, it is not surprising that, like his predecessors, Maslow was critical of an unbridled scientific perspective.

> It was primarily the physicists and the astronomers who created the *Weltanschauung* [or paradigm] and the subculture known as Science (including all its goals, methods, axiomatic values, concepts, languages, folkways, prejudices, selective blindnesses, hidden assumptions). This has been pointed out by so many as to amount to a truism by now.[677]

Maslow went on to say that it is only recently that this *Weltanschauung* has been shown to be inadequate for studying people as individuals. He felt that science as a form of nomothetic knowing must look for general laws in which each individual is necessarily treated as one of a group or class and "not unique, not sacred, not *sine quo non*."[678] However, Maslow felt that to know individuals, one needs to use what he called "The Holistic Approach,"[679] in which people are seen as a whole and reductionism has no role. Maslow further criticized classical science as knowing only how "to study people as objects"[680] when what had emerged from many of the insights of psychology was the importance of seeing them as subjects.

Like Jung, Maslow criticized nineteenth-century science for becoming "too exclusively mechanistic, too positivistic, too reductionistic, too desperately attempting to be value-free."[681] Science claimed to have nothing to say about ultimate or spiritual values, placing such issues outside of that which could be confirmed. As a consequence, in the scientific paradigm (which he felt was the dominant modern perspective) a person cannot feel they have objectively true knowledge about religious issues. Science and religion had become too narrowly conceived, and as a result, dichotomized, much to the detriment of modern man.

Maslow emphasized that, while experiential knowledge is primary,[682] "it is not enough."[683] Writing in the 'flower-power' 1960s, Maslow found it necessary to emphasize that accumulating and ordering objective facts is also necessary, an emphasis which none of the previous Authors found necessary. He described his approach as holistic, by which he meant making a place for "experientially-based concepts" and for "experientially filled words" which could generate an "experientially-based rationality in contrast to the a priori rationality that we have come almost to identify with rationality itself."[684]

Part of Maslow's approach to developing a language for discussing "experientially-based rationality" was his distinction between "extrinsic" knowledge and learning, and "intrinsic" knowledge and learning, a distinction he had in common with Rogers. They both felt that schools were mostly engaged with extrinsic knowledge.[685] Extrinsic learning is,

> ...learning of the outside, learning of the impersonal, or arbitrary associations, of arbitrary conditioning, that is, of arbitrary (or the best, culturally determined) meanings and responses. ...the learning is extrinsic to the learner, extrinsic to the personality, and is extrinsic also in the sense of *collecting* associations, conditionings, habits, or

modes of action. It is as if these were *possessions* which the learner accumulates...[686]

Maslow felt that extrinsic learning was promoted by the behaviorist paradigm which had come to dominate American education. Students were seen as needing to accumulate knowledge, skills, attitudes, and behaviors that could be measured.[687] Because such a paradigm cannot see and ally itself with the internal forces in every child which strive for self-actualization, the learning that it generates tends to be outside the meaning structures of the individual. Maslow felt that this was the principal cause for the failure of the American educational system.[688]

Intrinsic learning, on the other hand, requires the engagement of the person—the person's experiencing and consequent internalizing of events are fundamental. Maslow believed that intrinsic learning is the learning that occurs in the great eye-opening moments of our lives, when we learn significant things about the world and ourselves, and is part of "the process of growing into the best human being one can be."[689] Maslow claimed that, unlike the lessons we tend to have in schools, intrinsic learning experiences

> ...are apt to be unique moments, not a slow accumulation of reinforced bits. ...These are the experiences in which we discover identity.[690]

Maslow and Rogers both contended that even vocational training requires intrinsic knowledge in several ways, one of the most obvious of which is problem solving.[691] If a problem cannot be solved with prescribed procedures, then creativity is necessary. Creativity requires being able to approach B-cognition, to look at the situation afresh and to listen to and follow inner voices. Thus, creativity is necessary on pragmatic grounds alone, but creativity is also part of the hierarchy of needs[692] and necessary for self-actualization. Yet despite its obvious importance, Maslow and Rogers felt that creativity is usually (though perhaps unconsciously) punished in normal education where prescribed learning and conformity are wanted and rewarded.[693]

Maslow felt that if one saw the differences between intrinsic and extrinsic knowledge and learning, and one saw the relative importance of them in people's living, "then you *must* have a different picture of the good teacher and of his functions."[694]

For both Maslow and Rogers, it was not a matter of choosing intrinsic over extrinsic learning, but of integrating them and applying them in their proper domains. One of the ways in which this can be done is to ensure that extrinsic learning is motivated by intrinsic needs (e.g., personal needs of fulfillment, meaning, interest, etc.) and not from extrinsic stimuli (e.g., rewards or punishments).[695] These notions of intrinsic and extrinsic knowledge underlie most of Maslow's and Rogers' statements on education and also link several other notions such as self-knowledge, homeostasis, freedom, values and Ultimacy.

Before Maslow used the terms 'intrinsic' and 'extrinsic' he used 'concrete' and 'abstract' to convey similar meaning, and from early in his writing he was interested in the correct relationship between them.

> First comes "knowing" in the experiential sense; then come the checks on the fallibilities of the senses and of experiential knowledge; then come the abstractions, i.e., orthodox science.[696]

Maslow identified experiential knowledge as concrete knowledge, and wanted to stress that he was attacking "abstractness dichotomized from concreteness" and not "abstractness hierarchically-integrated with concreteness and experience"[697] which he felt "is a necessity for human life."[698]

Maslow was aware that his approach and many of the cultural trends he saw in the 1960s could veer over to "the anti-rational, the anti-empirical, the anti-scientific, the anti-verbal, the anti-conceptual,"[699] and such veering leaves a person with no way to check the experiential and so no protection from delusion. However, the integration of non-rational with the rational was difficult for most people and for education because non-rational knowing had been so little studied and was often conflated with anti-rationality. He described one form of non-rational knowing that was common as "experiential naïveté"[700] —a simple unmediated openness related to what is needed to appreciate art and music. Maslow believed this openness is often part of children's seeing and is retained by "the sages, in whom wisdom, goodness, perspicuity, and learning become a unity."[701] Experiential naïveté requires "not knowing" or the suspension of knowing, and this, Maslow felt, raises substantive questions about when and how rational knowledge blocks non-rational knowing. As such questions had not even been asked, much less resolved by mainstream education, Maslow felt that mainstream education too frequently generates knowledge that blocks experiential naïveté and, consequently, negatively affects the lives of its students.

Fundamental to the notions of intrinsic knowledge for both Maslow and Rogers was their conception "of the human being as having an essence"[702] which people are born with, and which, in many aspects, is different in everyone—"(anyone of you who has more than one child knows that)."[703] Maslow and Rogers saw people as having unique 'core selves' which must be discovered or uncovered so that people can be self-actualized. This is a rejection of the *tabula rasa* approach to education (which, they felt, implies that the same things can be learned by everyone regardless of their nature), and it pitted Maslow and Rogers against the popular existentialist philosophy of their time. While Maslow and Rogers both talked of "being" and "essence" they specifically and repeatedly negated the notion of being preceding essence popularized by Sartre (this, despite their support of existentialist psychology which also took a position on being and essence contrary to Sartre). Maslow and Rogers felt that *tabula rasa* notions support behaviorism with its promotion of operant conditioning and coping behavior. The dominance of the behaviorist paradigm in Western education, they felt, is tragic because "true learning is possible only when it is intrinsic, experiential, significant or meaningful"[704] which is always a response to inner needs as determined by the individual's "core self."

Maslow and Rogers held that both Ultimacy and discovering one's vocation are based on uncovering the self. Both require knowledge of what a person wants and doesn't want,[705] and the way in which each person is unique (with unique talents, abilities, capacities, and inclinations). Consequently, Maslow proposed what he felt would be a new kind of education, free from any prescribed learning that would allow the discovery of self, with the consequent discovery of vocation.[706]

> Another goal which our schools and teachers should be pursuing is the discovery of vocation, of one's fate and destiny. Part of learning who you are, part of being able to hear your inner voice, is discovering what it is that you want to do with your life. Finding one's identity is almost synonymous with finding one's career...[707]

While knowledge of vocation is related to self-knowledge, it is also related to Maslow's notions of homeostasis through what he called "intrinsic conscience," another form of non-rational knowledge.

> This is based upon the unconscious and preconscious perception of our own nature, of our own destiny, of our own capacities, of our "call" in life. It insists that we be true to our inner nature and that we do not deny it out of weakness or for advantage or for any other

reason.[708]

Maslow also described non-rational knowledge as Taoistic. In his book *The Psychology of Science* Maslow devoted one chapter to Taoistic Science which he described at length and in various ways. As Maslow considered such non-rational knowing, in certain instances, to be a path to more reliable and more veridical cognition, he considered it also to be suprarational. In general Taoistic knowing is,

> …laying aside all the characteristics of our most prideful rationality, our words, our analysis, our ability to dissect, to classify, to define, to be logical. All of these processes are postponed. To the extent that they intrude, to that extent is the experience less "full." Experiencing of this sort is much closer to Freud's primary process than to his secondary processes. It is in this sense nonrational—although it is by no means antirational.[709]

Suprarational is certainly the way he considered another form of non-rationality which he called either B-cognition or B-knowledge. Maslow spoke of B-knowledge as "veridical perception of hitherto unperceived truth."[710] The impact that "veridical perception" can have on very difficult pragmatic problems had been validated, in Maslow's view, by a fifty percent cure rate of chronic alcoholics through the use of LSD. These experiments were stopped for political reasons, but Maslow felt they demonstrated that knowledge from acute percep- tions (even artificially induced) can have life altering effects.

Maslow also referred to B-knowledge as "I-Thou knowledge" and "fusion knowledge,"[711] which has echoes of Jung's *Unus Mundus*. He claimed that such knowledge is related to love as it is "knowledge from within, by *being* what we are knowing" and asserted that this is a form of Ultimacy in knowledge.[712] Maslow postulated that love "seems likely to enhance experiential knowledge of the object" while its absence may "increase spectator knowledge of that same object."[713] For under- standing particular persons and even people in general, he was quite certain that B-knowledge is necessary. B-cognition for Maslow was cognition that sees "as a whole," in which there is "total attention," and no rubricizing,[714] which re-introduces Maslow's notions of abstract and concrete knowledge. Maslow felt that,

> There are substantial differences between the cognition that abstracts and categorizes and the fresh cognition of the concrete, the raw, and

the particular. …Most of our cognitions…are abstracted rather than concrete.[715]

One of the principal differences is that concrete cognition or B-cognition is "the purest and most efficient kind of perception of reality…"[716] mostly because it has not been corrupted by the "wishes, fears, and needs of the perceiver."[717] Maslow acknowledged that he had no evidence for making these claims which traditional science could accept as objective, nor could he imagine what such evidence would look like. Maslow could only have the subjective reports of people who claimed to have experienced what seemed to Maslow to be B-cognition, but this lends support to Maslow's call for an "experientially-based rationality."

One interesting aspect of B-cognition for the present purposes is Maslow's claim of its link to the normative. He reported that in B-cognition "the perception of the Being, the otherness, or the intrinsic nature of the person or thing" includes "the *oughtiness* of the object…."[718] "That is to say, oughtiness is an intrinsic aspect of deeply perceived facticity; it is itself a fact to be perceived."[719] Maslow felt that the relation of "oughtiness" to "isness" is especially important in matters of personal decisions as "…the best way to discover what [a person] ought to do is find out who or what he is…."[720] This is not an argument against Kant's conclusion that one can't move from an *is* to an *ought*; it is simply a denial of it.

Since a characteristic of B-cognition is non-intrusive receptivity—a perspicacity unpolluted by the observer's internal processes (e.g., wants, prejudices, etc.)[721]—it follows that Maslow would feel that meaning needs to be discovered and not constructed. This can be seen as a correlative to the non-constructivist view that Maslow and Rogers had of the nature of the "self," that it existed and was not a product of the mind.

> A reductionist tends to think that the human mind *puts* meaning into nature. He looks at the world critically, with pursed lips, confident of his own superiority to this hurrying, meaningless flow of events. Maslow was a true phenomenologist in the basic sense; he felt that the world *out there* was a damn sight more meaningful than anything *his* mind could add to it. There was a strong, clear sense of a 'central reality or essence' that he was only trying to observe and interpret.[722]

Maslow felt that if it is only humans who organize actuality into meaningful patterns, one must assume that "experience itself has no meaningfulness" and that as a consequence, meaning "is a gift from the knower to the known."[723] For Maslow, this makes no sense—meaning exists independently of humans and needs to be discovered by objective observation.[724] While Maslow felt this is true for knowledge about reality in general, it is even more true for knowledge about people.

> Any clinician knows that in getting to know another person it is best to keep your brain out of the way, to look and listen totally, to be completely absorbed, receptive, passive, patient, and waiting rather than eager, quick, and impatient. …Freud's term "free-floating attention" describes well this noninterfering, global, receptive, waiting kind of cognizing another person.[725]

One final note on Maslow's notions of needed knowledge is related to his notions of good and evil.

> Socrates taught that ultimately evil behavior can come only from ignorance. Here I am suggesting that good behavior needs as a precondition good knowledge and is perhaps a necessary consequence of good knowledge.[726]

Maslow didn't specify what "good knowledge" is, but we are left to presume that it is B-knowledge.

Competence for Maslow

While Maslow didn't have anything significant to add about the distinctions between competence based education versus performance based education, he is the first of the modern Authors to make a significant contribution to notions of judgment and values in the context of education. He did this principally through his notion of Being-values (or B-values) which he described as "characteristics of Being" and "perceived as ultimate"[727] by people in peak experiences or who are self-actualized. He preferred the term "choosing" to "judgment," and claimed that such values "guide one's choosing."[728] Maslow felt that the student's establishing of such values should be one of the major goals of education as this is necessary for generating positive social change.

Maslow stated that many of the social ills he saw as increasing were the result of a growing ethical relativism, meaninglessness, and loss of identity. "The churches are not much help"[729] in answering these problems because modern man needs

...a validated, useable system of human values, values that we can believe in and devote ourselves to because they are true rather than because we are *exhorted* to "believe and have faith."[730]

Humanistic psychology, Maslow believed, for the first time in history, was able to derive such a system of values from an empirically confirmed theory of human nature "without recourse to authority outside the human being himself...."[731] Issues that had been the exclusive jurisdiction of organized religion had become the "property" of scientists.[732] Maslow believed that the Humanistic theory and system of values were supracultural, and he likened them to "a religion—that can bind human beings together..."[733] and solve at least some of the growing social ills.

In several statements about culture, Maslow echoed the previous Authors in stating the importance of a person being as independent of cultural values as is possible. This is not the differentiation of Jung (although he doesn't seem to disagree with those notions) so much as the need for a non-culturally-bound perspective that might approach something universal. Maslow felt that the "clear impulse voices"[734] of self-actualizers do not speak in the language of cultural values but in that of universal values. Consequently, Maslow believed that education should not be for localized citizenship, but for world citizenship. In this, he was extremely anti-Deweyan, feeling that education is not for the inculcation of societal values, but for the discovery (by looking within[735]) of values that transcend the individual's society.

Maslow seems to have had very little to say about freedom that had not been stated by the previous Authors. He implied its importance in his many comments about the non-interference or Taoist approach to therapy. He also implied that humans can be trusted to be free, citing homeostasis in several books as support for humans (and animals in general) being able to intuitively find what is in their own best interests.[736] Linking freedom to values and homeostasis, Maslow felt that psychologically "healthy people," when left to choose freely, choose B-values[737] (extending the notions of 'own best interest' to include that which is pro-social and ethical); and that having the freedom to discover one's identity is part of becoming a psychologically healthy person.

Maslow's contribution to notions of meta-learning lies principally in his linking it directly to self-knowledge and Ultimacy. He felt that "the logically prior need, before knowing, [is] to be a good knower"[738] which is part of approaching self-knowledge and Ultimacy. Knowing oneself becomes, then, not a nice extra, but the basis for all other knowledge.

> In effect what I am implying is that honest knowing of oneself is logically and psychologically prior to knowing the extrapsychic world. Experiential knowledge is prior to spectator knowledge. ...The injunction might read, then: make yourself into a good instrument of knowledge. ...Become as fearless as you can, as honest, authentic and ego-transcending as you can.[739]

Social-ability for Maslow

Maslow presented an interesting perspective on Rousseau's old admonition of making a man rather than a citizen. Maslow believed that the interpersonal is simply a reflection of the intrapersonal.

> My general thesis is that many of the communication difficulties between persons are the by-product of communication barriers *within* the person; and that communication between the person and the world, to and fro, depends largely on their isomorphism (i.e., similarity of structure and form [to communication within])...[740]

As a consequence, Maslow was able to explain in simple terms that developing the intrapersonal (towards self-actualization) is the only way of making good social beings. He claimed that it is an "empirical fact" that "self-actualizing people" are the "most compassionate" and are the "great improvers and social reformers of society."[741] The old dichotomy of "the self" versus "the social" disappears with Maslow's hierarchy of values[742] but, in keeping with the previous Authors, the good citizen stems from the good individual.

Maslow saw the necessity of turning away from the social world in order to discover the inner world of the self in quite different terms from Jung. For Maslow, it was a matter of a person deriving their picture of reality from themselves rather than from the outside world. For example, he would question: Does a person think they have done something well because of the approbation they receive, or from seeing it as good themselves? This distinction was important for Maslow because,

> ...only by such differentiation can we leave a theoretical place for meditation, contemplation and for all other forms of going into the Self, of turning away from the outer world in order to listen to the

inner voices. This includes all the processes of all the insight therapies, in which turning away from the world is a *sine qua non*, in which the path to health is via turning into fantasies, the primary processes, that is, via the recovery of the intrapsychic in general.[743]

Maslow and Rogers placed less emphasis on sequencing these developments than the earlier Authors. While Rousseau has Emile develop first as a person in isolation from society, Maslow and Rogers claimed that social and personal developments can not occur separately.[744] This does not mean that the intrapersonal does not have primacy as the basic building block of the interpersonal, it simply means that the developments must take place simultaneously. Maslow quoted Rogers to illustrate his point.

> As Carl Rogers has phrased it: "How does it happen that the deeper we go into ourselves as particular and unique, seeking for our own individual identity, the more we find the whole human species?" Doesn't that remind you of Ralph Waldo Emerson and the New England Transcendentalists? Discovering your specieshood, at a deep enough level, merges with discovering your selfhood. Becoming (learning how to be) fully human means *both* enterprises carried on simultaneously.[745]

It is not surprising that the New England Transcendentalists who affected education (Ralph Waldo Emerson, Henry David Thoreau, William Ellery Channing, George Ripley, A. Bronson Alcott, and others) are frequently credited as founding thinkers in America of holistic education.[746]

ASPECTS OF STUDENTS THAT FACILITATE THE NEEDED LEARNING FOR MASLOW

For Maslow, the inherent learning process that facilitates the needed learning is related to his hierarchy of needs and his notions of homeostasis.

> The healthy spontaneous child, in his spontaneity, from within out, in response to his own inner Being, reaches out to the environment in wonder and interest, and expresses whatever skills he has…to the extent that he is not crippled by fear, to the extent that he feels safe enough to dare.[747]

Maslow believed that, in this process, a child encounters "the delight-experience"[748] in that something is pleasurable or it satisfies needs in the hierarchy. At the base of the hierarchy is the need for safety. If a child feels safe, this need no longer cries out to be satisfied and a child will naturally move to higher level needs, which are growth promoting. A child will naturally make choices that produce the "delight-experience" and growth.

> In order to be able to choose in accord with his own nature and to develop it, the child must be permitted to retain the subjective experiences of delight and boredom, as *the* criteria of the correct choice for him. The alternative criterion is making the choice in terms of the wishes of another person. The Self is lost when this happens. If the choice is really a free one, and if the child is not crippled, then we may expect him ordinarily to choose progression forward. In this way the psychology of Being and the psychology of Becoming can be reconciled, and the child, simply being himself, can yet move forward and grow.[749]

Maslow was especially concerned with what he believed occurred when choices are made according to "the wishes of another person" and "the Self is lost," as he felt that the very process necessary to acquire the needed learning is damaged. He felt that in such circumstances a person learns to distrust his delight-experience, and to ignore the inner voice; often out of fear of losing the love or approval of the person whose wishes the child feels compelled to accept. This results in a person being stuck in substantive ways at a low level on the hierarchy of needs—the belonging level—and the very processes that facilitate the needed learning cannot develop. Maslow, like Rogers, felt that human nature is inherently positive, pro-social, and not only could be trusted to determine its own development—it must be trusted. "They thought that only when the inner core of human nature was released from internal and external controls and allowed full expression would one become fully functioning and self-actualizing."[750]

As Maslow felt this process that facilitates the needed learning required listening to the inner voice, being spontaneous, etc, and that these same qualities seemed to be part of creativeness; he believed that

> ...the concept of creativeness and the concept of the healthy, self-actualizing, fully human person seem to be coming closer and closer together, and may perhaps turn out to be the same thing.
> Another conclusion I seem to be impelled toward, ...is that

creative art education, or better said, Education-Through-Art, may be especially important not so much for turning out artists or art products, as for turning out better people.[751]

Maslow's View of Inherent Motivation

Maslow's notions of motivation as a facilitator of the needed learning come from his notions of the hierarchy of needs and homeostasis. Maslow sounded, at times, like the early Authors who saw meaning in the earliest motions of infants, with Pestalozzi and Froebel developing this into their "spontaneous-activity" and "self-activity." For Maslow, all of the needs in the hierarchy are present at all times, but it is only as the lower ones become satisfied that the higher ones can move forward to dominate. However, even when the lower ones are predominating, the higher ones are exerting some form of latent force that still has some influence. Therefore, even though an infant must, of necessity, be primarily concerned with subsistence needs, Being (or higher level) needs can still make themselves felt and these should be allowed to act.[752] These higher level needs exist because they correspond with capacities, and all capacities, even incipient ones, are always "'wanting' to express and fulfill themselves."[753] Maslow felt his hierarchy of needs encompassed a motivational theory that could and should be used for all aspects of a child's development.

> The single holistic principle that binds together the multiplicity of human motives is the tendency for a new and higher need to emerge as the lower need fulfills itself by being sufficiently gratified. The child who is fortunate enough to grow normally and well gets satiated and *bored* with the delights that he has savored sufficiently, and *eagerly* (without pushing) goes on to higher more complex delights as they become available to him without danger or threat.
>
> This principle can be seen exemplified not only in the deeper motivational dynamics of the child but also in microcosm in the development of any of his more modest activities, e.g., in learning to read, or skate, or paint, or dance.[754]

As discussed previously, the very highest need in the hierarchy is for Ultimacy (self-actualization in Maslow's terms),[755] and this is because "man has a higher and transcendent nature, and this is part of his essence, i.e., his biological nature as a member of a species which has evolved."[756] For Maslow, who trained as and claimed to be an empirical psychologist, this was as evident and unarguable to anyone who cared to look at the evidence as describing people's faces as having two eyes as part of their biological nature. For Maslow, it follows that people who are responding to the higher needs, seek (and can therefore be said to be rewarded by or motivated by) "metagratifications," which is why he and Rogers felt that certain values can be said to be universal or biological, and one of the reasons they felt that the old dichotomy between "what is" and "what ought to be" is a false one.[757]

> People who are fully evolved tend to take as their greatest rewards the *metagratifications*, that is, the *B-values* or *intrinsic values*. Such men and women are most happy when they are advancing beauty, excellence, justice, or truth.[758]

This, as Maslow frequently pointed out, is in clear contradiction to the views of people such as Freud and Sartre who held that anything like benevolence or generosity, can only be sublimated self-defense or self-interest.

Maslow used his taxonomy to resolve the differences between his notions of man's higher motivation and the classical Eastern view that higher consciousness is "the transcendence of striving or desiring or wanting...."[759] Maslow claimed that only the lower level needs were traditionally recognized as needs (often labeled as instinctive), so that anything more subtle and refined was thought to be beyond need. According to Maslow, however, people naturally need self-transcendence, seeking the "far" rather than the "near," the "great" rather than the "small."

ASPECTS OF TEACHERS THAT FACILITATE THE NEEDED LEARNING FOR MASLOW

Teachers' Understanding of Students and their Needs for Maslow

Neither Maslow nor Rogers had much new to contribute to this issue other than to stress that education has as a central aim the development of identity, which must always be an individual matter. Maslow also emphasized that for human development, it "is the 'horticulture' rather than the 'sculpture' model"[760] that is most appropriate as each person has within themselves an inherent blueprint of their own unique design they will grow into if allowed. This is a sentiment that Pestalozzi and Froebel certainly agreed to as demonstrated by their frequent use of horticulture metaphors.

Teachers' Understanding of the Correct Pedagogic Process for Maslow

Maslow's approach to the correct pedagogical process stems principally from his notion of the hierarchy of needs and self-actualization. Like the other Authors, Maslow believed that humans are inherently good and each has a unique nature that needs to be discovered and actualized. Maslow's contribution is in employing language that is more currently accessible in saying that everyone needs

> to be true to his own nature, to trust himself, to be authentic, spontaneous, honestly expressive, to look for the sources of his actions in his own deep inner nature.[761]

Education should, Maslow believed, be based on this need and be part of a person's learning to meet this need. "Since this inner nature is good…it is best to bring it out…" because "if it is permitted to guide our life, we grow healthy, fruitful, and happy";[762] and, for Maslow, these are worthy secondary goals of education, second, of course, to his notion of Ultimacy.[763]

For a young person to learn to be "true to his own nature," Maslow believed that an educational system had to reflect the value of that fidelity. If schools reflect distrust of students (which Maslow felt most schools inadvertently do by wanting to change the students' natures or suppressing their spontaneity), then children learn to see themselves in the school's light. This can only bring about the opposite of the needed learning. Maslow believed that, "all this implies another *kind* of education…"[764] and not the same kind of education applied in new ways or with new subject matter, which is how Maslow saw the nature of most educational reform. He believed that what is needed is a pedagogic process that accepts students, and helps them learn what kind of people they are; what for each student are "his good raw materials, his good potentials"[765] that can be built upon. This requires, as mentioned in the discussion of experiential knowledge (beginning on page 160), what Maslow called a "Taoistic" approach; a non-interfering "letting-be"[766] which contradicts what Maslow variously described as the molding, lecturing, conditioning, reinforcing, intrusive, authoritative process in mainstream education.[767] Maslow insisted that "growth can emerge only from safety," and the correct pedagogic process must produce that first and foremost.[768] Maslow described the correct pedagogic process as "permissive, admiring, praising, accepting, safe, gratifying, reassuring, supporting, unthreatening, non-valuing, non-comparing...."[769]

> We would be nonthreatening and would supply an atmosphere of acceptance of the child's nature which reduces fear, anxiety, and defense to the minimum possible.[770]

One of the difficult but indispensable tasks in providing this safety and atmosphere of acceptance is for the teacher to understand "the naturalness of defensive and regressive forces"[771] and that "lesser delights, e.g., hostility, neurotic dependency"[772] must be expressed and worked out (rather than suppressed or denied) so that they can be "sufficiently catharted"[773] and the child can move on to higher and more socially approbated gratification.

It is worth noting that Maslow was not an advocate of laissez-faire child rearing. He claimed that

> Children, especially younger ones, essentially need, want, and desire external controls, decisiveness, discipline, and firmness. They seek firm limits in order to avoid the anxiety of being on their own and of being expected to be adultlike because they actually mistrust their own immature powers.[774]

This does not detract from his insistence that the child's nature be respected. On the contrary, it recognizes as part of the child's nature a need for safety that adults must provide and not confuse with lack of freedom.

Maslow believed he saw empirical evidence that the supportive pedagogy described above works partly by generating a feeling of safety that is necessary in order to experiment and explore (components he felt were part of learning). It also works by changing the student through changing the awareness children have of themselves as positive, good, and valued persons. It further works, Maslow felt, by allowing a person to be creative and aware of his inner nature and therefore to "become aware of the fact that peak-experiences go on inside himself."[775] As discussed previously, it is during conscious peak-experiences that a person experientially perceives Being-values and Being-knowledge.

Because of the link Maslow felt exists between creativeness and peak-experiences, he gave special attention to the nature of creativity and to teaching creativity. He claimed to agree with Freud that there is "primary creativeness" and "secondary creativeness"; by which he meant, "the inspiration phase of creativeness" and "the working-out phase of creativeness...."[776] Maslow claimed that mainstream schools (for reasons identifiable with performance based pedagogy) give far more attention to secondary creativeness. Yet, for Maslow (again claiming to agree with Freud), it is primary creativeness that is far more important for the development of the person and therefore should be far more important in education. Consequently, he claimed to "consider nonverbal education so important, e.g., through art, through music, through dancing..." as these can be a way of discovering primary creativeness and therefore to

> fostering the new kind of human being that we need, the process person, the creative person, the improvising person, the self-trusting, courageous person, the autonomous person.[777]

Maslow claimed to have slowly found himself using a form of communication in his most effective teaching that seems to resemble Rousseau's and Pestalozzi's wish to "make the language of the mind pass through the heart."[778] Maslow called it "rhapsodic communication" and defined it as "a kind of emotional contagion in isomorphic parallel" which "are often more apt to 'click,' to touch off an echoing experience, a parallel, isomorphic vibration, than are sober, cool, carefully descriptive phrases."[779] This amounts to giving someone else an experience rather than giving them information, and has an understandable importance for Holistic Education in view of its emphasis on experiential learning.

Teacher's Understanding of
the Correct Pedagogic Relationship for Maslow

Maslow and Rogers both saw relationships as pre-eminent in education[780] as they felt that in almost all

> professional work involving relationships with people...it is the *quality* of the interpersonal encounter...which is the most significant element in determining effectiveness.[781]

For Maslow this was most easily characterized as B-love, which he felt the teacher must have for the student,[782] while for Rogers the correct pedagogic relationship had the more complex elements of prizing, realness, and empathy.

Teachers' Self-Development for Maslow

It is clear from all that has been discussed that Maslow felt that until a person reached the pinnacle of the hierarchy of needs (self-actualization) he was still in need of development. At a certain point in becoming mature, a person takes direct responsibility for their continual growth and engages in deliberate self-development. For this, a mature person must study themselves. While Maslow believed that such conscious and deliberate self-development is needed by all mature adults, it is especially required of teachers who must understand themselves in order to understand others; "knowledge of one's own deep nature is also simultaneously knowledge of human nature in general."[783]

CHAPTER 10

Carl Ransom Rogers

A BIOGRAPHICAL SKETCH OF
CARL RANSOM ROGERS
(8 JANUARY 1902 – 4 FEBRUARY 1987)

B orn in Oak Park, Illinois, Carl Rogers was the fourth of six children. He could read before the age of five, and when he was finally old enough to go to school, he started in the second grade. His family moved to Chicago for awhile, but when Carl was twelve they moved to a farm thirty miles to the west. This was his home until he went away to university. By his own accounts, his upbringing was strict, even harsh, and certainly isolated. His parents were Christian fundamentalists and very demanding; they filled his days with farm chores, devotion, and study.

His first area of tertiary study was agriculture at the University of Wisconsin. This did not last very long, however, and he soon switched to become a theology student. In the course of that study he was selected for a prestigious six-month study program at The Christian Federation Conference in Beijing. Being in China opened his eyes to the cultural straightjacket in which he had been living, and opened his mind to new ways of thinking. This experience caused Rogers to question the certainties of his religious beliefs.

196

Immediately after graduating, and against his parents' wishes, he married Helen Elliot. They moved to New York City so that Rogers could continue his theological training at the Union Theological Seminary. For a short while Rogers was the pastor of a small church in rural Vermont. However, his metaphysical doubts only increased, and after two years he felt he could no longer continue that vocation. At the seminary he had been introduced to the study of clinical psychology, and he transferred to Columbia University's Teachers College where he eventually earned both an MA and a PhD. in psychology.

Early in his studies at Columbia he became inspired by the work of John Dewey through W.H. Kilpatrick, a former student of Dewey's. He was especially interested in the value Dewey placed on using experience as the basis of theorizing, on taking the human being as a whole, and on Dewey's optimistic view of humanity.

To support his doctoral studies, Rogers worked on a research project for the Society for the Prevention of Cruelty to Children in Rochester, New York. He was immensely committed to the Society's goals and became its director in 1930, before finishing his doctorate. During this time he came into contact with Otto Rank, whom he claimed greatly effected his own thinking about psychology.

Rogers continued to work and write about children's difficulties and lectured at the University of Rochester from 1935 to 1940. During this time he wrote *The Clinical Treatment of the Problem Child* which was highly acclaimed and brought him a full professorship at Ohio State University.

In the middle of his four years at OSU (in 1942) Rogers published *Counseling and Psychotherapy*, which enunciated his client-centered approach to therapy. He proposed that it is the relationship of the client to the therapist that is the key to a client's regaining mental health. This book solidified his reputation, and he was offered a professorship at The University of Chicago where he taught from 1945 to 1957. During this time Rogers set up a counseling center and became President of the American Psychologists Association. In the counseling center, Rogers developed the practice of transcribing verbatim his therapeutic sessions which he would subsequently analyze for indicators of possible later outcomes. This technique he pioneered has since become a standard practice. In 1951 Rogers published *Client-Centered Therapy* presenting studies confirming his theories and the efficacy of his treatments.

From 1957 to 1963 Rogers worked at the University of Wisconsin at Madison holding two professorships; psychology and psychiatry. He took this on because he wanted to integrate the study of both of these with social work, which he felt could have an enormous impact. However, the entrenched camps in all three fields frustrated his efforts, and he recalled this time as the "most painful and anguished" time in his career. Despite his difficulties he continued to write a great deal, publishing many papers as well as *On Becoming a Person* (1961).

Disillusioned with academia and its possibilities to have the impact he felt it should, he moved to La Jolla, California, to join The Western Behavioral Studies Institute founded by Richard Farson, a former student of his. After five years, however, Rogers could not resolve a difference he had with the structure of the organization which he felt had too many of the same limitations as universities.

In 1968 Rogers founded The Center for the Studies of the Person, which he claimed was a "nonorganization" run by a "non-director." There he was able to be more active in social work, concentrating on everything from racial to socio-economic difficulties. Rogers expanded his notion of psychological social work to include trying to resolve conflicts endemic in cultures. He brought together opponents in Northern Ireland, South Africa, and the Cold War.

Rogers's work in education and with many schools brought him to the conclusion that, like client-centered therapy, the best form of education was student-centered, and in this the student should determine the content, pacing, structure, and duration of learning. In 1969, at the height of the counter-culture movement in the United States, Rogers published *Freedom to Learn*. Like Maslow, Rogers became an icon for young intellectuals. As mentioned in the previous chapter, the Humanistic Psychology that he promoted with Maslow was often called "third force psychology"—behaviorism and neurosis/psychosis psychology being the first two. Rogers's work showed the value of emotional development, interpersonal skills, and goal-setting/goal-striving techniques. He eventually went on to become an early developer, along with Maslow, of Transpersonal Psychology.

Rogers's search for understanding of the most pressing issues of his day brought him into renowned discussions with many contemporary intellects including Paul Tillich, Gregory Bateson, Rollo May, Martin Buber, and of course his good friend Abraham Maslow.

In 1987, Rogers died from a heart attack after being hospitalized for a broken hip.

ROGERS'S NOTION OF ULTIMACY

As recognized pioneers of humanistic psychology, Rogers and Maslow broadly agreed and acknowledged each other's work,[784] yet they used different terminology, and pursued different aspects of their shared concerns. For Rogers, the ultimate state was the "fully functioning person,"[785] but he felt that "it is a process, a direction, not some static achievement."[786] He described this state in a number of different ways, depending on what he wished to emphasize, but the general thrust is that *all* of a person's capacities (which stretch to include what might be thought of as spiritual) are functioning in harmony and to their fullest extent.

The Importance Given to Ultimacy by Rogers

Rogers didn't differ from Maslow in his reasons for the importance of Ultimacy, but was more emphatic in enunciating that despite the universal human imperative of having a sense of Ultimacy, unfortunately

> traditional ethics have failed…because their validation, sought in supernatural concepts, sacred books, or a ruling class, was *a priori* authoritarian thinking. …Not surprisingly, the modern person questions whether there are universal or cross-cultural values.[787]

Rogers and Maslow felt that modern rootlessness and meaninglessness can only be solved by finding objective, universal and cross-cultural values "based squarely upon knowledge of the nature of man."[788]

Ultimacy in Relation to Rogers's View of Human Nature

Everything that has been said of Maslow in the previous chapter on this topic is also valid for Rogers. However, Rogers lay greater stress on the role of listening or sensing within. He felt that there is a wisdom in our total reacting organism, and that our distrust and underestimation of that wisdom "prevents us from living as unified, whole human beings."[789]

There is an interesting analysis of Rogers's work that deserves noting: Donald Walker demonstrated how Freud "inherits the tradition of Augustine in belief that man is basically and fundamentally hostile, anti-social, and carnal," whereas Rogers "in the same sense, is the successor to Rousseau."[790] Rogers, in answer to this comparison, agreed that his thinking is closer to Rousseau than most traditional Christian writers, yet insisted he was not influenced by Rousseau (curiously, despite admitting that he had read *Emile* as part of his doctoral work).[791]

Ultimacy as an Aspect of Religiousness for Rogers

Rogers added little explicitly to the other Authors' various notions of the religiousness of Ultimacy, preferring to eschew such terminology. His remarks on religion were almost purely negative; e.g., religions can no longer fill the one function they used to have, which was to act as a basis for a value system.

Rogers did, however, promote notions of balance, wholeness, and an esoteric but unreachable ideal. In answering his own question, "Can we permit ourselves to be whole men and women?"[792] Rogers stated that while we can be aware of what we think and feel, what is needed is a unification of these. Like Jung and Maslow, he saw the prevailing problem of our times as overemphasis on the rational with a corresponding under-valuation of the non-rational (not the irrational).[793] For Rogers, the non-rational includes feelings and wisdom, or insight, that comes from sensitivity to "our total reacting organism."[794]

Unlike Buddhist enlightenment, Christian sainthood or states of grace (which are at least reachable by a few), or Maslow's self-actualization (which is theoretically reachable by everyone); Rogers claimed that his model of Ultimacy had not been reached by anyone. Whether it is, in fact, unreachable is not clear. Rogers's model of the fully functioning, unified, whole human being only establishes the trajectory of intended development by showing what it is aiming toward; and this trajectory is best served by "the best of experiences of education, …therapy, …family and group relations."[795]

WHAT NEEDS TO BE LEARNED FOR ROGERS

Rogers's View of Experiential Knowledge

Carl Rogers made few pronouncements about knowledge itself that were not made by the previous Authors, other than that "…we will never have certain knowledge."[796] He said this in a way that goes beyond Jung's notion that the intellect can never know all of a thing. Rogers held that people cannot have complete non-intellectual knowledge either, which results in people never even being able to have certainty. Like Rousseau, Rogers felt that the value of knowledge is its usefulness (regardless of its partialness) and believed that, fundamentally, this is a sentiment shared by most educators.[797]

Rogers was, however, more vehement than any of the previous Authors (perhaps with the exception of Rousseau) in his attack on the meaningless learning that, he believed, occurred in most classrooms. Because, he believed, most of the material that children are compelled to learn is without any personal meaning to them (usually because their "background provides no context for the material"),[798] he likened it to some psychology tasks in which people are asked to memorize nonsense syllables.

> Such learning involves the mind only: It is learning that takes place "from the neck up." It does not involve feelings or personal meanings; it has no relevance for the whole person. In contrast, there is such a thing as significant, meaningful, experiential learning.[799]

What Rogers called "significant learning" necessarily involves: 1) personal involvement, 2) self-initiation, 3) an impact on behavior, and 4) meaning for the learner. "Significant learning combines the logical and the intuitive, the intellect and the feelings, the concept and the experience, the idea and the meaning."[800]

Competence for Rogers

As noted earlier, Rogers did not differ significantly from Maslow on questions of judgment and values, but he made unique contributions to considerations of freedom for holistic educators. Rogers had trained as a behavioral scientist,[801] and was acutely aware of the behaviorist position which claims that man is not free, and any views that he is free are only illusions. He thoroughly rejected this behaviorist position (as he felt many others in psychology had also done), but the behaviorist paradigm dominated education.

> While behaviorism has diminished in its importance for most psychologists, it continues to rule the educational system in this country. The examples are numerous. From the way students are

disciplined to the way teachers are evaluated, the method is one of control, reward, and punishment.[802]

Rogers believed that freedom is essential for development. It is only by giving a child freedom that the child can feel that he and his choices are respected, and through this he learns that he is worthy of respect. For Rogers, a system that seeks to control children teaches them that they can not be trusted; that they do not have the mechanisms, aptitudes or understanding to do what is right and must, therefore, depend on others to know and do what is right. Rogers felt that when many young people leave home and go to work or to university where they have a newfound freedom, they demonstrate just how well they have learned this lesson of being irresponsible. This is a clear example of education producing the opposite of what it intends.

Rogers also believed that, as experience is the best teacher, a person can only learn about freedom, and the responsibilities that are a necessary part of freedom, by experiencing them. Schools, which he felt resembled totalitarian regimes more than any other institution in the United States (matched only by prisons and the armed services), are therefore not environments in which a person can learn *of* democracy and freedom even though they might learn *about* them. It was not just the conformity and restriction of action that Rogers lamented, but the absence of freedom for attitudes and for thinking.

Like his predecessors, Rogers promoted a form of freedom that is "essentially an inner thing," which is not dependent on outward circumstances, and which he equates with the freedom "that Viktor Frankl vividly describes in his experience of the concentration camp."[803] Rogers wrote long descriptions of inner and outer freedom,[804] but for our purposes, two of the more interesting characteristics are "...the discovery of meaning from within oneself, meaning that comes from listening sensitively and openly to the complexities of what one is experiencing" and "...being responsible for the self one chooses to be."[805] These highlight one of the paradoxes in Rogers's work concerning freedom; freedom is needed for inner sensing and being who one wants to be, yet it is such sensing and being which generates freedom. The paradox seems to be resolved for Rogers by his contention that these are not sequential phenomena, but different aspects of a single process that he felt was "a central process or central aspect of psychotherapy."[806] This is freedom as Buddhist liberation; freedom as part of an approach to Ultimacy.

As Rogers felt that his approach to psychotherapy is conducive to

Ultimacy, and as the goal of education is Ultimacy (in the form of the "fully functioning person"), then, for Rogers, it followed that, "the *best* of education would produce a person very similar to one produced by the *best* of therapy."[807] Therefore, Rogers promoted educational programs and processes (from elementary to college levels) that reflect his discoveries in therapy, with due emphasis on freedom. "It seems at least a possibility that in our schools and colleges, in our professional schools and universities, individuals could learn to be free."[808]

Rogers felt educational institutions should have meta-learning as another primary goal, and not traditional knowledge. This seems to follow partly from his view of knowledge (i.e., that there is no absolute, final knowledge, or security in knowledge), and partly from his observations of the nature of the modern world in which an emphasis on "process" is a key to successful adaptation.

> We are, in my view, faced with an entirely new situation in education where the goal of education, if we are to survive, is the *facilitation of change and learning.* The only man who is educated is the man who has learned how to learn; the man who has learned how to adopt and change; the man who has realized that no knowledge is secure, that only the process of *seeking* knowledge gives a basis for security. Changingness, a reliance on *process* rather than upon static knowledge, is the only thing that makes sense as a goal for education in the modern world.[809]

Rogers went on to equate "the way in which we might develop the learner" (an educational goal) with "the way in which we can learn to live as individuals in process" (a life goal and a therapeutic goal), and in so doing he reiterated that education and psychotherapy have the same goal—Ultimacy. It is worth noting that there is now a substantial and growing body of research on the different consequences of process orientation and outcomes orientation that seems to support Rogers.[810]

ASPECTS OF STUDENTS THAT FACILITATE THE NEEDED LEARNING FOR ROGERS

Rogers frequently called the inherent process that facilitates the needed learning "organismic wisdom," as he felt that it is a facility of the entire human organism and not just consciousness. He felt that "conscious thought is full of fixed constructs" that interfere with per-

ception and that a person needs to use "*all* his avenues of knowing:
unconscious, intuitive, and conscious."[811] To access these avenues, a
person needs to "lay aside rigidly held preconceptions" and make use
of "the pregnant void, the fertile state of no-mind."[812] Rogers believed
that "all the capacities of the organism," some of which are "prelogi-
cal" and "intuitive" can sense a "gestalt: a hidden reality" long before
consciousness can formulate a pattern.[813] The more such an apprehen-
sion is "free from cultural values" and preconceptions, "the more adequate it is likely to be."[814] Rogers claimed that a child does this automatically (as consciousness has not developed fully enough to give the
impression that it can be trusted), but that also

> the psychologically mature adult trusts and uses the wisdom of her
> organism, with the difference that she is able to do so knowingly. She
> realizes that if she can trust all of herself, her feelings and intuitions
> may be wiser than her mind, that as a total person she can be more
> sensitive and accurate than her thoughts alone. Hence she is not afraid
> to say, "I feel that this experience (or this thing, or this direction) is
> good. Later I will probably know *why* I feel it is good." She trusts the
> totality of herself.[815]

For Rogers, the human organism as a whole also provides the basis
for discovering universal values. It is important to see this as forming
part of a process that facilitates the needed learning and not as a form
of knowledge or ethical construction as these are normally understood.
Rogers called it "the valuing process" and although it operates as an
ethical structure, it is seen as part of the same inherent process that
tends towards becoming a "fully functioning human" and, therefore,
Ultimacy. Maslow and Rogers both argued that the choices made by
people approaching Ultimacy "embody the species-wide intrinsic values of human nature conducive to psychological health" which "ought
to be the basis for a universal and naturalistic system of ethics."[816] However, the "organismic base for an organized valuing process within the
human individual" is only effective "to the degree that the individual is
open to the experiencing that is going on within,"[817] which means that
if a person is not sensitive to inner experiences, he cannot act ethically.
For Rogers the process of "becoming" (which was often his shorthand expression for becoming a fully functioning person) and the "valuing process" frequently seem to be synonymous; the natural, the normative, and the ultimate all seem to merge.[818] In a section of his book
Freedom to Learn he lists at length some of the value directions he felt
people universally move towards,[819] and these value directions are strik-

ingly similar to the qualities he described, more than thirty years previously, in people who were "becoming."[820] At the end of this second list Rogers stated that the most important question a person can ask themselves is: "Am I living in a way which is deeply satisfying to me, and which truly expresses me?"[821] Since people are naturally good, and inherently pursue values that are pro-social, Rogers felt a person can safely ask himself this question if they are sensitive to inner listening, without the risk of being selfish.

Rogers' notion of "significant learning" allowed him to juxtapose the processes he felt facilitated needed learning with what he believed normally passes for learning. He decried "the lifeless, sterile, futile, quickly forgotten stuff that is crammed into the mind of the poor helpless individual tied into his seat by ironclad bonds of conformity,"[822] and insisted that, unlike the learning in mainstream education, "significant learning" was "more than the accumulation of facts" and the "accretion of knowledge, but [learning] which interpenetrates every portion of [the learner's] existence."[823] "Significant learning" was seen by Rogers as having "the quality of personal involvement, being self initiated...pervasive...evaluated by the learner"[824] and therefore affecting behavior, attitudes and personality, because it increased the sense of meaning and consequently the person's relationship with reality. Rogers felt that "significant learning" involved the whole of the person as well as making that person whole.

> Significant learning combines the logical *and* the intuitive, the intellect *and* the feelings, the concept *and* the experience, the idea *and* the meaning. When we learn in that way, we are *whole*, utilizing all our masculine and feminine capacities.[825] [Italics in the original]

As a consequence, Rogers felt that schools in which students are compelled to learn specified subjects that are not meaningful to the student are not just a waste of the student's time, they inculcate a false learning that usually involves ignoring or silencing the "organismic wisdom" to which people should be learning to pay attention. In fact, the very relationship between teaching and learning was one that Rogers questioned.

> It seems to me that anything that can be taught to another is relatively inconsequential, and has little or no significant influence on behavior.
> ...I have come to feel that the only learning which significantly

influences behavior is self-discovered, self-appropriated learning. Such self-discovered learning, truth that has been personally appropriated and assimilated in experience, cannot be directly communicated to another.

...Hence I have come to feel that the outcomes of teaching are either unimportant or hurtful.[826]

Hence, Rogers referred to what some of the Authors called "teaching" as "facilitating," and it is in the Rogerian sense that the term has been used throughout this book. The distinctions of facilitating versus teaching are discussed further in the next section.

ASPECTS OF TEACHERS THAT FACILITATE THE NEEDED LEARNING FOR ROGERS

Teachers' Understanding of the Correct Pedagogic Process for Rogers

Rogers held that people 1) are innately good, 2) have an inherent capacity to penetrate their own complexities and arrive at their core nature (given the right conditions), 3) can release an inner wisdom through contact with their core nature, 4) have the ability to understand and reorganize their psyches, 5) have an inherent tendency towards Ultimacy, and 6) naturally want to become more expert at dealing with their world (i.e., want to learn). This led Rogers to establish what he called "client centered therapy" which held that clients are the greatest expert in their own inner lives and outer circumstances, and that (given the right psychological conditions) patients have the capacity to explore and know their own inner natures thus becoming more fully functioning human beings. The therapist's role is merely to become an ally with these inherent capacities and help the patients remove the inner and outer barriers to their natural growth. The therapist does not generate the growth, does not determine how the patient should be at the end of development, and has no plan through which the patient is to progress. This is essentially also Rogers's notion of the correct pedagogic process.

Rogers and Maslow (and several commentators) credit the principal difference between humanistic education and mainstream education to the latter being a captive of behaviorist psychology, while the humanistic psychology model of education is a total rejection of behaviorism. This was examined in the previous discussions on intrinsic and extrinsic learning. With a behaviorist paradigm (in which every-thing that a person learns comes in from the outside and what he becomes is determined by external positive or negative reinforcement), the educator feels "the need to control, to shape the educated," whereas with a paradigm like that of humanistic psychology, the educator is "to give to the educated the care and responsibility of his own education."[827]

The conclusion for Rogers was that

> ...it is most unfortunate that educators and the public think about, and focus on, *teaching*. It leads them into a host of questions that are either irrelevant or absurd so far as real education is concerned.
>
> I have said that if we focused on the facilitation of *learning*—how, why, and when the student learns, and how learning seems and feels from the inside—we might be on a much more profitable track.[828]

Rogers therefore called for the adults in schools to be "facilitators" and not "teachers." This is not just a change of name. Rogers felt that even with a very good teacher (in the traditional sense) the correct pedagogic process can not be engaged in because the problems the teacher is trying to solve are fundamentally different to those a facilitator is trying to solve. Essentially, for Rogers, the good traditional teacher wants to know what the student needs to learn at a particular stage in life, discover the best way to encourage the student to learn it, and finally evaluate what has been learned. However, the facilitator wants to discover the students' own questions or the problems the students want to solve, thinks of what resources can be brought in to assist the students, and finally helps the students assess their own progress.[829]

Rogers claimed alliance with Heidegger in seeing the teaching role as facilitating as well as insisting that education had to be concerned with meta-learning.

> The primary task of the teacher is to *permit* the student to learn, to feel his or her own curiosity. Merely to absorb facts is of only slight value in the present, and usually of even less value in the future. Learning *how* to learn is the element that is always of value, now and in the future.[830]

As a result Rogers would frequently insist that the primary focus of the correct pedagogic process must be "on fostering the continuing process of learning...," on the individual's relationship with learning per se, and could not be on "the content of learning."[831] Rogers felt that a course could be said to be satisfactorily concluded not when an amount of knowledge is acquired, but when the student "has made significant progress in learning *how to learn* what she wants to know."[832]

The facilitation or "permission" to learn that Rogers spoke of has several aspects which mirror the correct pedagogic processes of the preceding Authors. Rogers felt that what students learn must be concerned with issues that "have meaning and relevance for them,"[833] echoing Rousseau's insistence on the "utility" of what students learn. Also like Rousseau, Rogers encouraged educators to create situations in which students are confronted with problems they then need to solve, and in this way guide learning. Also like the previous Authors, Rogers felt that students must not only be involved in the direction of their learning, they must feel they are involved. One contribution of Rogers to this issue is that he tied the students' being an active agent in determining their own learning to satisfying the inherent wish to be in control of as many facets of life as possible (which, for Rogers, is related to notions of freedom). He also tied such active involvement to engendering responsibility in students, especially responsibility for life-long learning. Rogers felt that mainstream education (which he believed deprives students of responsibility for what is learned, when it is learned, and evaluation of learning) acts as a disincentive to developing life-long learning which he saw as indispensable in the modern world.

The problems of evaluation in mainstream education, for Rogers, are especially insidious.

> I believe that the testing of the student's achievements in order to see if he meets some criterion held by the teacher, is directly contrary to the implications of…significant learning.[834]

Rogers felt that it is the learner who should decide what criteria are valid for the learning that is meaningful and what goals should be achieved. Such "self-evaluation may be influenced and enriched by caring feedback from other members of the group and from the facilitator,"[835] but essentially remains the responsibility of the learner. For this reason Rogers recommended to "do away with examinations" as "they measure only the inconsequential type of learning," and it followed for him that grades, credits and degrees "as a measure of competence"[836] should also be dispensed with.

One of the human aspects that Rogers believed was ignored by mainstream education (and as a consequence, underdeveloped) was the "feeling life." Rogers claimed that people "must develop a feeling life as well as a cognitive life," and supports his contention by citing Thomas Hanna who spoke of the value of *"soma*—body *and* mind, feelings *and* intellect."[837]

Rogers insisted that he was not "talking about a method or a technique," but rather "a way of being in an educational situation." [838] This does not preclude a facilitator developing his own methodology or expertise, because personal methodology reflects the personality of the facilitator, the context, and the students. Rogers seemed to feel that received methodology is like received truth or received meaning— it is, at best, second hand, and a far cry from 'revealed' truth and meaning.

Rogers felt that his approach places "emphasis on the dignity of the individual, the importance of personal choice, the significance of responsibility, the joy of creativity" and that the results were the "empowering [of] each individual."[839] Rogers believed that his success with therapy proved the importance of such empowerment for psychological health, and he was convinced that such empowerment was crucial to the social and common weal.

Rogers was able to see his educational ideas put into practice in several cities, at different educational levels, in different contexts and in different countries. He was able to examine some of the empirical studies conducted on these practices. It was only after his death that a full review of the research was published in the third edition of *Freedom to Learn,* which was co-authored by H. Jerome Freiberg. In the third edition the research is shown to support the case that, not only is the approach to education Rogers advocated psychologically more healthy than mainstream education, but also that students learn conventional subjects more quickly and thoroughly.

Teachers' Understanding of
the Correct Pedagogic Relationship for Rogers

What Rogers called both "prizing" and "unconditional positive regard," he described as a non-judgmental, non-possessive caring of the other person's individuality, feelings, and opinions; "an acceptance of the other individual as a separate person who has worth in her own right."[840] Rogers claimed that his empirical experience is that such prizing, or "acceptance of the most complete sort…is the strongest factor making for change that I know."[841] Rogers believed that when a person found himself prized, the normal defensive barriers that the person uses are no longer needed and "then what takes over are the forward moving processes of life itself" with the result that a person "can't help but change."[842]

"Realness" was a quality that Rogers felt the facilitator has to have. Rogers also called this quality "congruence" and described it as the facilitator (or therapist) being

> ...unified, or integrated, ...What is meant is that within the relationship he is exactly what he *is*—not a façade, or a role, or a pretence. ...It is when the therapist [or facilitator] is fully and accurately aware of what he is experiencing at this moment in the relationship, that he is fully congruent. Unless this congruence is present to a considerable degree it is unlikely that significant learning can occur.[843]

When a facilitator is "real" he is aware of his feelings and has a "willingness to be and to express" in words and behavior "the various feelings and attitudes which exist," and "it is only in this way that the relationship can have *reality*...."[844] A relationship which has *"reality"* was felt by Rogers to have its own effect. Rogers believed that such "realness" in relationship

> is sharply in contrast with the tendency of most teachers to show themselves to their pupils simply as roles. It is quite customary for teachers rather consciously to put on the mask, the role, the façade of being a teacher and to wear this façade all day removing it only when they have left the school at night.[845]

For Rogers, the "quality of being" of the facilitator has an effect on the "quality of being" of the student, and a recognition of this is fundamental in the correct pedagogic relationship.

The third characteristic of the correct pedagogic relationship for Rogers is "empathy." He described this as understanding the other person's "world as seen from the inside," of feeling the other person's "anger, fear, or confusion as if it were your own, yet without your own anger, fear, or confusion getting bound up in it...."[846] Rogers felt such empathy is important in many spheres in life, but in education it is critical since the facilitator must have "a sensitive awareness of the way the process of education and learning seems *to the student*...."[847]

Rogers felt that the pedagogic relationship is one of the raw materials that the facilitator presents for each student's possible use. Like all educational materials, the pedagogic relationship is not to be interjected into the student's life to create a specific predetermined effect. Rogers believed that the good facilitator asks, "How can I provide a relationship which [the student] may use for his own personal growth?"[848] feeling confident that "the other person will discover within himself the capacity to use that relationship for growth, change, and personal development...."[849] At the same time, there is something of a calculated effect (though perhaps not specific) that Rogers sought and which he felt the correct pedagogic relationship helps generate. Rogers believed that there is a "reciprocal"[850] mechanism by which the correct relationship with a person alters that person's relationship with himself. Altering the way a person looks at and, consequently, sees himself can contribute to the process of becoming a "fully functioning person."

> If I can create a relationship characterized on my part:
> by genuineness and transparency, in which I am my real feelings;
> by a warm acceptance of and prizing of the other person as a separate individual;
> by a sensitivity to see his world and himself as he sees them.
> Then the other individual in the relationship:
> will experience and understand aspects of himself which previously he has repressed;
> will find himself becoming better integrated, more able to function effectively;
> will become more similar to the person he would like to be;
> will be more self-directing and self-confident;
> will become more of a person, more unique and more self-expressive;
> will be more understanding, more accepting of others;
> will be able to cope with the problems of life more adequately and more comfortably.[851]

In its most subtle form, Rogers believed that such a correct relationship resembles Martin Buber's 'I-Thou' relationship.[852] In its simplest form, Rogers believed such a correct relationship resembles the best of the parent-child relationships as studied by Baldwin and others[853] in which the "acceptant-democratic" relationships were seen as increasing the intellectual, social, and emotional development of the child while, on the other end of the spectrum, the "actively rejectant" relationship had the opposite effect. Rogers believed the research of parent-child relationships reflects his findings for the correct pedagogic relationship. This picture fits nicely with Maslow's notion of hierarchy of needs in which the lower needs of safety and belonging need to be satisfied to liberate higher order activities. Rogers also quoted Paulo Freire and drew parallels between the correct pedagogic relationship he proposed and Freire's transformation of the teacher-of-students and students-of-teachers into teacher-students and student-teachers respectively.[854]

Rogers said that prizing, realness, and empathy are an "operational expression" of trust in the inherent goodness of human nature,[855] and he felt that a distrust of human nature is built into mainstream schooling.

> ...[no] one can hold the three attitudes I have described [realness, prizing, empathy], or could commit herself to being a facilitator of learning unless she has come to have a profound trust in the human organism and its potentialities. If I distrust the human being, then I *must* cram her with information of my own choosing lest she go her own mistaken way. But if I trust the capacity of the human individual for developing her own potentiality, then I can provide her with many opportunities and permit her to choose her own way and her own direction in her learning. ...The teacher is attempting to develop a quality of climate in the classroom and a quality of personal relationship with students that will permit these natural tendencies to come to their fruition.[856]

Teachers' Self-Development for Rogers

For Rogers the question of the need for self-development is largely bound up with his notions of the correct pedagogic relationship.

> ...the optimal helping relationship is the kind of relationship created by a person who is psychologically mature. Or to put it another way, the degree to which I can create relationships which facilitate the growth of others as separate persons is a measure of the growth I have achieved myself.[857]

What Holistic Education Does: A Sociological Analysis

CHAPTER 11

Competence Based Models of Pedagogy

*T*he task of this section is to describe what holistic education *does* with a view to showing this as a reflection of what it *thinks*, which has been elaborated in the previous two sections. It is also the task of this section to locate holistic education within the entire field of education. It is worth reiterating that identifying holistic education requires distinguishing what Wittgenstein called "family resemblances" with their "complicated network of similarities overlapping and crisscrossing...."[858]

It would be possible to use many categorizations, dimensions or polarities to describe what holistic education does. Some people, for instance, may think of it as 'progressive' as opposed to 'formal' or 'traditional'. Other people think of holistic education as concerned with the education of 'persons' rather than the teaching of 'subjects'; etc. Having considered some possible categories and models, I have found that the last work of Basil Bernstein offers the most sophisticated tool for examining holistic education, and I shall use this as the starting-point.

In *Pedagogy, Symbolic Control and Identity: Theory, Research, Critique* [859] and a subsequent lecture Bernstein compares what he calls 'competence based pedagogic models' and 'performance based pedagogic models,' analyses the different modes contained in each of the two models, and describes the identities projected by each mode. Bernstein feels that competence as a "...knowledge concept...traveled across the major social sciences in one form or another..."[860] in the 1960s and 1970s and can be found in linguistics, psychology, social anthropology, sociology, and socio-linguistics. Bernstein's analysis is valuable as a framework for examining the whole field of pedagogy and, hence, for describing the nature of holistic education and locating it within that whole field.

I shall make the case that holistic education fits within Bernstein's analysis of competence based pedagogy by going through the major categories which Bernstein uses to distinguish competence based pedagogy from performance based pedagogy, and showing how holistic education fits into Bernstein's competence model. However, holistic education is differentiated from other forms of competence based pedagogy as it does not belong to any of Bernstein's three modes of competence based pedagogy. The case will be made that holistic education should be considered as a fourth mode.

Bernstein also details the identity constructions inherent in different modes of performance based and competence based pedagogy. In its identity constructions, holistic education again shows itself to be a distinct form of competence based pedagogy, further meriting its description as a fourth mode.

Bernstein's use of the word 'competence' is undoubtedly confusing for some people as he uses it in a way that is not common. The reader of this book (or Bernstein's later work) needs to abandon the common notions of 'competence'. What is commonly seen as 'competence' is, for Bernstein, merely "generic performance," (performance based knowledge of a generic form). [861]

Bernstein claims that the concept of 'competence' as a kind of knowledge has its origin in the work of Chomsky, Piaget, Lévi-Strauss, Garfinkle, Dell Hymes, and Wittgenstein.

> The concept refers to procedures for engaging with, and constructing, the world. Competences are intrinsically creative and tacitly acquired in informal interactions. They are practical accomplishments. The acquisition of these procedures are [sic] beyond the reach of power relations and their differential unequal positionings, although the form the realizations may take are clearly not beyond power relations. From this point of view the procedures which constitute a given competence may be regarded as social: the negotiation of social order as a practice, cognitive structuring, language acquisition and new cultural assemblies on the basis of the old. These procedures are not the gift of any one culture, in the sense they are culture free.[862]

By contrast, Bernstein discusses performance models of pedagogy as follows:

> Briefly, a performance model of pedagogic practice and context places the emphasis upon a specific output of the acquirer, upon a particular text the acquirer is expected to construct, and upon the specialized skills necessary to the production of this specific output, text or product.[863]

It is worth noting the difference between Bernstein's 'procedures' and 'performance'. He says that competences may require mastering several procedures (e.g., one may have to know how to form sentences as part of a competence in human relations), while performances are seen as a final product or at least a goal in themselves.

The two pedagogic models do not necessarily promote mastery of different procedures (both a competence based pedagogy and a performance based pedagogy may want students to know how to form sentences), but they engage in different pedagogic approaches. The performance model has performance as a goal, even if this goal is acknowledged as only a way station towards some larger goal. Few, if any, mathematics teachers feel that learning to do algebraic equations is a goal in and of itself. It is seen as developing a larger understanding of mathematics. However, performing the numeric manipulations taught is an accomplishment that can be taught, learned, and examined apart from any other considerations, and it is this disconnection that distinguishes performance based pedagogy.

Bernstein contrasts the school activity of woodworking (an "imaginary discourse") which is "inside pedagogy" with what he calls the "real discourse" of carpentry, which is "outside pedagogy." This recalls the discussions in previous chapters on 'real' and 'unreal' knowledge. Clearly the Authors felt that knowledge cannot be extracted from the lives the students live and the genuine questions they have if the knowledge is to be 'real' or meaningful. In Bernstein's terms, even if a student can perform excellently the procedures of school woodworking, it is not the equivalent of acquiring those same procedures in the "real discourse" of carpentry. A discussion of whether, and if so, how an imaginary discourse can become a real discourse is one that many in holistic education would feel is close to their concerns.

That the procedures in a competence are not the gift of any one culture makes them at least multi-cultural if not pan-cultural or even supra-cultural. It would probably make most sense to think of them as supra-cultural if they do not have their origin or impetus in culture but in an inherent meaning-making capacity that humans and possibly other mammals possess. For the Authors and holistic education the procedures in what we have called sagacious competence have their origin in the nature of humans, most specifically in the inherent learning processes and the development that is seen as approaching Ultimacy. As such, the procedures are supra-cultural. This is important for holistic education which is very concerned with the pluralism of modern existence, and which sees being culturally bound as a hindrance to development. Any competence that is culture or era bound is as useful as proficiency in mediaeval chivalric courtly conduct—it may still be used in some rarefied social strata, but in most others it is just strange behavior.

Remembering Rousseau's notions of 'natural man', Pestalozzi's promotion of people "who have been brought up by life itself, and not by lessons"[864] and therefore not ruined by *civis*, and both Jung's and Maslow's fascination with indigenous cultures, it is not surprising there is also substantial interest in indigenous cultures amongst supporters of holistic education. Many people have a sense that less complicated cultures have simpler and more authentic procedures that have relevance because they are more universal. Discovering such procedures is valued as a key to understanding other people, to liberation from the confines of one's own culture, and possibly to understanding something inherent and essential about ourselves. (The appearance of this in holistic education is discussed in more detail on page 261.)

THE SOCIAL LOGIC OF COMPETENCE MODELS

Bernstein claims that there is a social logic for the concept of competence which has five parts. What would strike anyone familiar with different approaches to holistic education is how closely Bernstein's social logic of competence mirrors the reasons many people give for some aspects of holistic education. Bernstein's five-part social logic and its applications to holistic education are as follows:

The first social logic:

> ...an announcement of a universal democracy of acquisition. All are inherently competent and all possess common procedures... There are no deficits.[865]

In holistic education (as with the Authors), students are usually seen as possessing inherent learning processes and motivation and even latent wisdom. Without performances that children are expected to accomplish, schools can allow children to naturally 'flower', each in his own equally valid way. This contrasts with many of the development theories based on presumptions of deficits (e.g., personality deficit,[866] motivational deficit,[867] intellectual deficit,[868] moral deficit,[869] social skills deficit,[870] socio-cognitive deficit[871]). If there are no deficits, only differences, then the principles of evaluation in mainstream education lose coherence.

The second social logic:

> …the subject [here read student] is active and creative in the construction of a valid world of meaning and practice…. Consider creativity in language production (Chomsky), creativity in the process of accommodation (Piaget), the *bricoleur* in Lévi-Strauss, a member's practical accomplishments (Garfinkle).[872]

This fits with a tendency towards heuristic learning present in most approaches to holistic education, and runs counter to the convention of pedagogic authorities deciding what and when learning occurs.[873] Some holistic education advocates seek support for heuristic learning in some post-modern philosophers (like Richard Rorty), but the distinction between individually constructing meaning and finding meaning often gets lost. There is little in holistic education writing to suggest the relativism in much post-modernism; recalling instead Maslow's criticism of relativism (see page 185). Much holistic education is concerned with finding meaning (or 'truth') or constructing individual *approaches* to meaning, but this is not the same as inventing meaning or arbitrarily deciding on things being true. Some would have it that 'truth' exists but we cannot do more than see aspects of it. Others feel that what is true can be perceived, but the limitations of language prevent it from ever being fully expressed.[874] What does seem frequent in holistic education is the view that meaning has to be found or discovered by each person; meaning cannot be 'meaningfully' received. People can receive the meaning of another—and in fact it is important for many reasons that we do in order to live with others (the communitarians have much to say on this point that would be in sympathy with much in holistic education)—but received meaning is not 'meaningful' until we see it as meaningful for ourselves.[875]

Some of the problems with found and accepted meaning may be

elucidated by the following example. Suppose we have the task of deciding which of several lights is brightest if we have no scientific instruments. A person can look at the lights and see that one is brighter than the others, and that person may try to confirm the assessment by asking several other people. If other people feel that some light other than the one our subject chose is the brightest, then our subject can re-evaluate his judgment or conclude that 1) the viewing angles that he and other people used effected the perception of brightness (therefore both 'meanings' can be correct), 2) there is something wrong with the other people (only his 'meaning' is correct), or 3) something is wrong with him (received 'meaning' is more reliable). However, we would find the character, integrity, or at least the judgment of our subject suspect if he consistently went along with the assessment of the others, denying the evidence of his own eyes. We would also find it suspect if our subject stridently dismissed the evaluations of others and insisted that he was invariably right. We are uncomfortable with the view that a collection of subjectivities constitutes objectivity, and we are equally uncomfortable with ignoring or dismissing the subjectivity of others when subjectivity is all there is.

Holistic education usually acknowledges and tries to address these issues in both governance and group meaning-finding. Sometimes it is addressed through notions of consensus building[876] (related to regulative discourse criteria—see page 246), at other times through notions of tolerance and accommodation, and at still other times by constructing convergent meaning through dialogue.[877] What is central to our discussion is that holistic education emphasizes the importance of each student having an individual network of meaning, and yet, because of its very subjective nature, this network cannot be discovered in isolation. Rather, the meaning should be shared and scrutinized by others, and revisions should be made as necessary in the light of this process. The importance of this in holistic education has usually generated an equal importance given to the capacity to work co-operatively as a primary skill in itself.

The importance that holistic education usually gives to finding meaning (as opposed to accepting meaning) follows the epistemology of Rousseau and Pestalozzi. Seeing the relations or connections between things is how ideas are formed, and it is the forming of ideas rather than the holding of ideas that is important. Although 'meaning' was not part of the language most of the Authors used, they used related terminology (e.g., 'real' and 'unreal' knowledge) to indicate similar or identical concepts. Consequently, Rousseau and Pestalozzi were interested in developing this ability. The later Authors were also interested in this phenomenon as they saw the finding of 'meaning' as the agent that transforms consciousness, and their work is rich in terms that point to this process (e.g., insight, B-cognition, veridical perception, significant-learning processes, etc). At the extreme of such meaning-finding are terms that describe epiphanies or transcendence of a religious nature; a seeing of connections that reveals the greatest possible unity. (This topic is discussed in more detail beginning on page 259.) While the connections that people make are necessarily unique (following from everyone's unique experiences and perceptions), there is the sense that these connections or meaning structures should be at least partly communicable to others; and if they are not, then they may be delusional or, at worst, psychotic.

Finding meaning is often equated in holistic education with understanding, and simply having knowledge is equated with received meaning; echoing the arguments in the previous chapters distinguishing knowledge from experience and knowledge from representations. Holistic education sometimes speaks of 'book bright and life dumb', which underscores many of their criticisms of mainstream education.

The third social logic:

> ...an emphasis on the subject [student] as self-regulating, a benign development. Further this development or expansion is not advanced by formal instruction. Official socializers are suspect, for acquisition of these procedures is a tacit, invisible act not subject to public regulation.[878]

If finding meaning is equated with understanding, and finding meaning is an individual endeavor, it follows that finding meaning cannot be regulated. With this view of understanding, holistic education advocates often claim that since understanding cannot be regulated, to be primarily concerned with learning that can be regulated is to be primarily concerned with learning that, by its very nature, cannot be based on the individual making his own meaning. At best, regulation must be concerned with seeing validity in received meaning. Such seeing of the validity of received meaning may be the necessary goal of some disciplines (like those typified by Maslow's 'inductive knowledge,' e.g., abstract mathematics). However, a distinction is made between a thing being meaningful within a socially accepted system and meaningful in the student's life. One might liken this to the fantasy games which are popular today—games with very developed characters, histories, terrain, and time frames—where things are said to be 'virtually real', to have a reality within a fiction. Knowledge that is without connections or meaning is similar; it has an 'abstracted-from-the-life-lived' quality even if it is coherent and connected with other things within the same domain. It is frequently suggested that sex education, AIDS education and drugs education have this 'abstracted-from-the-life-lived' quality so students are able to pass exams on the subjects, yet fail to make any connection to their life as it is lived. Perhaps this is related to Plato's *espisteme*—knowledge that is real knowledge is knowledge that affects behavior.

For many advocates of holistic education this marks a central difference between the ways in which they see the nature of what it means to be human and the way they feel it is seen in mainstream education. As stated by the Authors, children are not seen as needing to be shaped by older, more knowing adults into forms that the adults feel are right. Consequently, the child's meaning structures do not need shaping, which is seen as the main purpose of the regulation that Bernstein describes. 'Public regulation' is a hindrance to the correct developmental process as all public regulation implies a predetermined outcome fixed by the public (otherwise how could it be regulated), and so violates the central tenets of self-regulation, individual meaning finding, and being true to one's nature.

In holistic education, self-regulation is often seen both as a means and an end.[879] It is felt that one can't learn to be self-regulating through being regulated by others. Self-regulation needs practice if it is to be learned and, although certain guidance is needed for the safety of infants, such guidance should be withdrawn as soon as physical safety is not imperiled. Not all danger should be removed, as a certain amount of physical peril provides a healthy arena in which to grow. In this the arguments of Rousseau and Pestalozzi to allow children to make mistakes is heard. Such self-regulation is seen as possible because of all that was previously discussed about the nature of humans being basically good, and the notion of homeostasis. This is not just seen as a moral virtue, but as the only way to learn about the kind of regulation that is needed in subtle circumstances that are part of life. Imagine the example of riding a bicycle: even the most skilled bicyclist could not give instruction fast enough, subtle enough, or complete enough to keep another person they were instructing from falling off their bicycle. New riders must be able to regulate their own balance, not for some moral reason, but because that is the only way in which it can work. Similarly, the regulations that one needs in one's own life are too complex, too fast, and too subtle to rely on regulation from outside. Consequently, while some regulation from the outside may be necessary in some circumstances or for some initial limited period (like holding a person up when they first get on a bicycle) there must be an early release from such support as a tendency to rely on outside regulation is counter-developmental.

The fourth social logic:

> ...a critical, sceptical view of hierarchical relations. This follows from (3) as in some theories the socializer's [here read teacher's] function should not go beyond facilitation, accommodation, and context management. Competence theories have an emancipatory flavour. Indeed in Chomsky and Piaget creativity is placed outside culture.[880]

This enunciates one of the most obvious characteristics of holistic education, the relationships between the teachers and students, and reflects much in the previous sections on authority and the correct pedagogic relationship. To avoid what is commonly seen as the danger of hierarchy and the implication that one group (the teachers) is in some way deliberately and formatively acting upon another group (those being taught), many holistic schools have different names for the adults in the learning environment, such as facilitators, guardians or staff members. In many holistic schools the wish to avoid what is seen as the damage of positional power has resulted in students having a determining role in the hiring and firing of the adults who work in the school. It is interesting to see that this is now being used in at least two British state-run secondary schools.[881] Some of the activities of the adults in the holistic school are discussed in the section on the economic implications of competence models that begins on page 254, so it will suffice for our present purposes to say that the adult's role is to support the individual learning processes of the students and not to determine them. In some holistic schools this may involve doing nothing until the student asks for something (even then possibly refusing if it doesn't interest the adult, thus reinforcing everyone's rights), while in less radical holistic models the role of adults is to ensure that certain intellectual skills (like numeracy and literacy) and certain non-intellectual skills (like social and emotional skills) are acquired, but the adult is not there to determine the way in which such learning occurs.[882]

Bernstein points to one interesting implication for the teachers of the two models.

The explicitness of the transmission makes such modes [in performance models] less dependent upon personal attributes of the teacher and so their supply is less restricted [than competence models].[883]

In previous chapters it was shown that the aspects of teachers (or Bernstein's "personal attributes") which the Authors feel facilitate the needed learning are primarily concerned with understanding (the students and their needs, the correct pedagogic process, the correct pedagogic relationship, and the importance of their own development). Such understanding is resonant with the understanding advocated for the students (i.e., the understanding has to do with meaning and self, either alone or in relationship). The meaningful understanding of the teachers is, therefore, also not subject to public regulation and is also hindered by hierarchical relations. Teachers in holistic education must also be "active and creative in the construction of a valid world of meaning and practice" just like students. This militates against performance based pedagogic models for holistic teacher training, which in turn makes it impossible to have publicly regulated and mass produced holistic education teachers. Hence, their restricted supply.

Keeping in mind the importance of experiential learning, many holistic educators would want to include objects, events, and even environments that are experienced as part of what facilitate the needed learning, thus reinforcing Bernstein's description of the teachers' role as "facilitation" and "context management." In many traditional cultures there are formative events like rituals, rites of passage or ceremonies of transition, and formative places. These have varying degrees of deliberate construction, but they often do not have a determined content. A person undergoing such an event or experiencing such a place may be expected, for example, to know more about themselves at the end, but just what the content of that knowledge is can not be known or regulated by another. There are several groups who construct modern rites of passage because of the importance they feel such 'instructorless instruction' has for development.[884] Similar views are held by many who are involved in presenting 'formative experiences', such as Outward Bound or various schools that involve extended periods of travel. In some indigenous cultures (and the holistic educational approaches that take a lead from them) there is also learning from animals, and time is spent observing animals for this purpose. Advocates of this claim the traditional role of animals in fables shows how common such learning from animals was in all cultures. When the environment is the instructor it may appear that there is 'instructorless instruction', but such a view dis-animates nature and runs counter to Jung's notion of the psychoid unconscious and most of the Author's views of unity, both of which are held (in some form) by most holistic educators.

The fifth social logic:

> a shift in temporal perspective to the present tense. The relevant time arises out of the point of realization of the competence, for it is this point which reveals the past and adumbrates the future.[885]

'Realizations' arising out of 'the now' has become such a common theme as to have become a cliché, but it is not necessarily any less true because of that. 'The now' is perceived as when the connections that lie at the heart of finding meaning are made, and when the connections always need to be remade if something is to remain meaningful. Remembered connections have a second-hand feeling to them. They are like remembering a good meal; there is recollection of a pleasure that was once present, and there is a pleasure in the remembering. However, both pleasures (the recollected one and the one in recollecting) are different from the first hand pleasure of eating the good meal, which can only be experienced in any way resembling the original pleasure by eating a similar meal again. The remembered connections that one has made in the past are better than the recalled connections that one has acquired from someone else, but they are still not as full or meaningful as those that are present during the actual act of making the connections, and these can only exist in the present.

The present tense is also emphasized in the therapeutic uses which Bernstein claims are often made of competence based pedagogic models. In working with students who are characterized as having behavioral difficulties, the therapist often works to help the student attend to what that student is actively doing, or actively thinking when that student is doing or thinking it—'in the present tense'.

I would suggest a sixth social logic to competence models, at least as it applies to holistic education. It is that 'being' precedes 'doing' which, in the simplest sense, would support the culturally accepted view that what a person 'is' is of greater importance than what a person 'does'. However, from this it follows that education (seen from the perspective of preparing young people for adulthood) should primarily be about developing the nature of a young person's 'being'. This echoes the notion of the greater encompassing the lesser discussed in

Chapter Two, with 'doing' holding the lesser position. In this thinking, 'doing' either comes of its own consequent to the development of 'being', or doing is acquired more easily subsequent to the development of 'being'. At the very least, 'being' gives 'doing' its necessary context without which learning how to 'do' certain things can be meaningless or even dangerous (e.g., learning how to handle a gun without first developing judgment or maturity). This logic also has it that the future is unknowable, and preparing for that future primarily by learning to 'do' things which, at the time of learning, are seen as needed is often learning things which will be obsolete by the time they will supposedly be needed. Learning 'to be' fully (which entails certain qualities dependent on the nature of the competence proposed) is the safest way to prepare for a world which cannot be anticipated.

Philip Wexler claims that the culture emerging in the modern Western world supports this sixth logic. He claims that it is becoming a given that "cultural and social transformation occurs first evidently as the 'transformation from within', at the site of the self'" and is concerned with what he variously calls "optimal being," "delineated being," etc.[886]

Another aspect of this sixth logic has to do with avoiding what could be called the 'becoming trap'. This is a complex topic which deserves much more attention than is needed in this book, especially as it has long and respected traditions attached to it. Briefly put, the dangers of living in the future rather than in the present, of engaging with life on the basis of what one *hopes will be* instead of on the basis of *that which is*, of focusing on an imagined good in some future condition rather than focusing on the perception of good in the present, has been the subject of many writings in religion and psychology. In this sense, 'becoming' is a form of 'doing', and the primacy of 'being' avoids the trap.

A final aspect of the sixth logic holds that when 'doing' is seen as preceding 'being' they often become conflated. Very often, in a person's thinking of who they are there is a response concerned with what they do. From this it often follows that the value of what people are is determined by the value of what they do. Despite this being clearly contradicted in all the world's major religions (e.g., Christianity holds that charity is not determined by what is given but by the quality of 'being' in the giving), this conflation seems to continue in all the world's major cultures based on these religions.

For holistic education, a seventh social logic of competence models is that everyone engaged in the learning process must be actively learning; the adults do not stand outside the learning process to effect the process for others. All the students and adults (and the parents in their interaction with the school) are learning even if they focus on different contents or with different sophistication. In the practices of holistic education, the correct pedagogic relationship implies reciprocity in the activities of both students and adults. Often in holistic schools, even adults who give most of their time to cooking or cleaning are thought of as engaged in the learning process; not just in terms of learning to do their jobs better, but in terms of learning how their presence, their interaction with the students and staff, and the way they engage in their activities can have an effect on the learning of everyone else. Usually in holistic schools there is a great deal of discussion amongst the adults about their learning and constant analysis of it.[887]

ISSUES OF SOCIAL POWER IN COMPETENCE MODELS

Bernstein's long-standing interest in the distribution of social power and the mechanisms for this inherent in different educational models has him conclude that "this idealism of competence" [888] does not take into consideration the structure of social power and what an individual needs to learn in order to engage as an active agent in the struggle with that structure. While this statement may be correct for many instances of competence based pedagogy (e.g., some therapeutic schools where the intent is simply to produce more or less normal socially acceptable behavior—on which Bernstein based much of his thinking of competence based pedagogy) and even some instances of the holistic education mode, Bernstein's analysis is not correct for all or even most instances of holistic education. This indicates one of the ways in which holistic education differs from other examples of competence based pedagogy.

In holistic education there is "a celebration of what we are," but it is not in contrast to what a person has become so much as in contrast to what a person *will* become: a rejection of the future as a focal point as indicated in the discussion of the 'becoming trap'. The present, as expressed by what a person has become, is embraced for its indications of what that person *essentially is*, echoing the Authors' notions of self-discovery.

Holistic education also does not necessarily pay the price that Bernstein indicates, which is to remove the person from specialized

learning required for some high-power careers. Holistic education often prepares people to enter universities, and so it sends people into
"selective specializations" even though it does not have such preparation as its goal. Holistic education does not preclude student engagement in procedures which are similar to those of performance based
pedagogy, it only precludes the dominance of procedures (their acquisition and performance) which is the hallmark of performance based
pedagogy. Hence, for holistic education procedures fit within and are a
subset of the characteristics of competence. Just as many mainstream
schools see music, art, religious, social or personal education as 'add-
ons' beyond the necessary curriculum, so many holistic educators see
the procedures of performance based education as 'add-ons'. Thus,
mastering the knowledge to do well on the college entrance mathematics exam can be acceptable in holistic education, but is not seen as
central to sagacious competence. Hence, the ideal of competence need
not necessarily "point away from such selective specialisations"[889] so
much as change the place these specializations have in the life of a
student and the school.

There is support for the perspective that "such selective
specialisations" are given more importance in education than they have
in real life, supporting the notion that education points too insistently
toward them. In *The London Sunday Times* on 5th January 1997, James
Tooley wrote, "Numerous recent surveys reveal that employers are not
necessarily particularly interested in the skills and knowledge that A-
levels and GCSEs bring..." and said that other reports show that for
university graduates "60% were 'underemployed' in their work, with
employers not utilizing the skills and knowledge learnt in their degrees."

The relationship of students to the distributions of power in holistic education merits discussion as a distinguishing element of such
education. In most approaches to holistic education (due to notions
of hierarchy discussed earlier) power in the school and in society is
candidly discussed and analyzed. Often, the students are given a great
deal of power and encouraged to be politically active (on at least a local
level). There may indeed be elements of control that are invisible to
the students, but usually they are invisible to the adults as well. Societal
power exists, as do principles of control within the different academic
disciplines, as Bernstein so eloquently shows. But it is the learner's relationship to that power and control that is essential. In this there are
echoes of the Authors' notions of being *in* society but not *of* it, and
differentiation. A student needs to learn about the nature of power,
when it is right to go along with it and when it is right to engage in civil

disobedience. Consequently, holistic schools are often hot beds of breaking the social codes, if not legal ones; confronting power structures within the school and outside it often makes the schools difficult to manage. Some holistic education modeling itself on 'the pedagogy of liberation' of Paulo Freire[890] and others[891] have local power structures as a prime focus. Contrary to Bernstein, the problem is usually not a 'macro blot' because it is frequently made explicit in holistic education, not obfuscated.

FEATURES OF EDUCATION USED BY BERNSTEIN FOR ANALYSIS

Bernstein's work is usually described as brilliant but difficult. His conceptualisations of the elements and processes of education, his analysis, and his methodology (e.g., his coding) are generally seen as ingenious but almost inaccessible. His writing style is seen as extremely dense, which some of his critics claim is an unnecessary difficulty. In Bernstein's defence, it needs to be understood that he often relates (sometimes only implicitly) the elements he is examining to larger theoretical social concerns. For instance, Bernstein calls that which is studied in any form of education the "pedagogic discourse" rather than 'the curriculum'. He does this partly to distance himself from some of the narrower discussions of curriculum, but largely because he is relating his thoughts to social science and philosophical work on the nature of 'discourse'. Consequently, while it would simplify this discussion to translate his terminology, too much would be lost of the deeper implications of his analysis if his terminology were ignored. Therefore, in what follows, Bernstein's language will be mostly used but explained.

Bernstein has eight features of education which he uses as a basis for showing differences between performance based pedagogy and competence based pedagogy. For holistic education, these eight features serve not only to show ways in which holistic education is distinct from performance based pedagogy, but also to distinguish holistic education from other forms of competence based pedagogy.

Bernstein's eight features are:

1) *Pedagogic discourse.* This is Bernstein's term for that which is studied in schools—what some people have called the explicit curriculum. While Bernstein is also concerned with implicit curricula (what has been called 'hidden curricula'), with this term Bernstein only includes what is explicit.

2) *Space*. With this term Bernstein refers to the areas either designated for or requisitioned by education, as well as the way in which those areas are controlled and/or constructed.

3) *Time*. This is a complex feature for Bernstein. He includes the following: A) the time in a person's life in which education occurs, B) the way time is used (e.g., time regulated by punctuated intervals or not), and C) the temporal sense. This last aspect of time is more difficult than the first two but is related to them. Bernstein sees some activities as emphasising (by deliberately constructing and therefore drawing attention to) a future and others as emphasising the present, or the past.

4) *Pedagogic Text*. This is what Bernstein calls the work which students produce in the course of their education. He includes non-work which is produced (such as play) as well as work which deliberately isn't produced by a student.

5) *Evaluation*. Bernstein uses this term to indicate the way in which the teacher relates to the students' work. It is closely tied to the following feature.

6) *Control*. For Bernstein 'control' indicates the ways in which order in the pedagogic space is generated, by whom and on what basis.

7) *Autonomy*. Bernstein uses this term to refer to the autonomy each teacher has in the classroom as well as the autonomy each institution has. Both have implications for accountability.

8) *Economy*. Bernstein uses this term to refer to costs of both material and time. He also considers the time costs in training teachers for both competence based pedagogy and performance based pedagogy.

I. Pedagogic Discourse

Comparing what students study (which Bernstein calls the 'pedagogic discourse') in the two pedagogic models highlights a significant difference between holistic and mainstream education. Bernstein claims that in competence based pedagogy, there are no explicit rules for deciding what is a legitimate text to study. Any text that brings out the competences which the students "already possess, or are thought to possess" is legitimate. The differences between students in dealing with text are thought of as simply differences and not a basis for hierarchical ranking.[892] In performance based pedagogy, on the other hand, the rules for deciding what is a legitimate text, as well as the rules for showing that the text has been mastered are explicit. Students have much less control over what is studied, and it is easy to rank hierarchically students according to their mastery of a text. [893]

It is difficult for holistic education advocates to talk about 'legitimate texts' in isolation from the learning processes. Texts are seen as not more than elements in a process, and it is the process that can be said to have independent legitimacy. The extent to which a text contributes to that process is its measure of legitimacy, with the measuring necessarily done by each learner and his teacher. Here the role of the teacher may simply be to try to incorporate the texts chosen by the student or to assemble texts appropriate to each student or to the class.

> The pedagogic resources required by competence models are less likely to be pre-packaged as textbooks or teaching routines. The resources are likely to be constructed by teachers and autonomy is required for such construction.[894]

There may be an element of communitarian legitimizing, with an implicit understanding that something like *The Rights of Man* is more likely to contribute to a student's development than *Mein Kampf,* but a case could be made in holistic education for any text being legitimate depending on the circumstances of the learner.

Texts being legitimate in isolation from the learning process is problematic for advocates of holistic education partly because of principle (e.g., surrendering self-regulation, the relationship to hierarchy, etc.), but also because legitimate texts can be a hindrance to developing the learning process or other qualities such advocates aspire to for their students.[895] This reflects the discussion in the previous sections on inherent motivation, and the importance given by the Authors to what Maslow called 'intrinsic motivation' rather than secondary motivation. Every teacher knows that it is easier for students to learn things that interest them. If, as holistic education advocates claim, it is the learning process itself that needs to be developed so that students can, in principle, learn more easily, quickly, and enjoyably in any domain they choose, then a particular text has no objective importance, only a subjective one inasmuch as it is part of a student's construction of meaning. In this view, learning does not derive its value by what that learning is *about.* Learning about mathematics, football, one's cultural past (history), one's cultural present ('street-smarts'), cooking or chemistry is essentially the same. Different skills are certainly needed for acquiring different kinds of text, but those skills *per se* have no objective value. As discussed previously, for holistic education, knowledge and skills derive their value from their relationship to Ultimacy and sagacious competence.

Some critics of this perspective claim that it ignores social values and that, by ignoring these values and the power implications of different kinds of knowledge, students can be disempowered (e.g. knowing car mechanics has different social values and generates different power than knowing chemistry because different kinds of knowledge lead to different opportunities in life). They also claim that students choose different kinds of knowledge because of their social background and that if they are to be able to move beyond the limitations of their background, they must be able to acquire the cultural capital that will give them the greatest opportunities in life.

The counter argument from holistic education is that this is simply selling out to a set of values that are wrong and destructive to both the individual and society. Cultural capital may indeed be the way to financial capital, but it is not the way to Ultimacy or the psychological and social changes needed. Social values are seen as needing to be challenged, not perpetuated. In this there are perceptions of cultural imperialism or corrupt cultural power: authorities who decide what is a legitimate text also decide the potential goals of learning and the valid steps toward their attainment. While the validity of this is suspect enough in intellectual areas (Einstein failing mathematics in school is a favorite example), it becomes more dubious in less objective academic subjects like art or history, and positively pernicious in areas like moral education or anything that presumes to deal with the development of 'persons'.

Strong objections are usually raised by holistic educators to those who claim to know what, as persons, students 'should become' and to know how students will become that. The implication is that those who don't become 'that' are less than those who do; from which it follows that those who have not yet become 'that' are less than those who have. This disparity in value justifies disparities in rights, power, and privileges. Hence, children (who have not yet become fully developed persons) are seen as not deserving the rights given to adults. It may be relevant to note in relation to this that in Britain, a fully developed dog has more rights than an early term human fetus, and that certain people (e.g., Down's syndrome people who are often perceived as unable to develop fully) have fewer rights (in practice if not in theory) to national health services.

Other objections to the notions of 'legitimate texts' stem from views about socializing students to questionable social norms which have destructive, though often indirect, consequences. This may take the rather simple form of studying the history of the country in which the student lives (rather than another country) with the implication that the culture of that country is more important than other countries, or it may be more indirect such as valuing Shakespeare which indirectly supports one set of cultural values and implicitly demeans another set. Every educator knows that no education is 'value free', and even if a student chooses to study another history or another author, values are still being perpetuated. What is important for holistic education is that these values are transparent and open to question, while accepting a text determined by others as legitimate obscures and closes those questions and perpetuates values that might be objectionable.

Bernstein's comments that students in competence models are not stratified may imply to some that there is no assessment possible in competence based pedagogic models. This is not the case as will be seen in the section on assessment beginning on page 243.

II. Space

One of the aspects that immediately strikes an observer of holistic education who is not used to such approaches to education is the pedagogic space. There often does not appear to be anything recognizable as a classroom. Bernstein anticipates this, and says that for competence based pedagogic models,

> There are few specially defined pedagogic spaces, although facilitating sites (e.g. sandpits) may be clearly bounded. Acquirers [students] have considerable control over the construction of spaces as pedagogic sites and circulations are facilitated by the absence of regulatory boundaries limiting access and movements.[896]

This contrasts to the use of space in performance models where,

> Space and specific pedagogic practices are clearly marked and explicitly regulated...[897]

Consequently, holistic schools easily speak of classes or schools without walls, and that all of life is an arena for learning, both of which are seen to encourage attitudes of life-long learning. With no delineation of the spaces for learning, time boundaries for learning are more difficult to construct on the basis of space; i.e., delineation of time according to when one is in a learning space. Therefore, as learning cannot be seen as the provenance of any particular place, all places and consequently all times have pedagogic potential. This would certainly be in accord with Rousseau's view that education must come from the life of the child and Pestalozzi's view that "life educates."

As there is no particular learning space, it follows that the space in which learning occurs does not have to be configured in any particular way. Consequently, the space can be altered by the participants in whatever way they feel is appropriate to the content of what is being learned. This can, and frequently does, extend to not using a classroom at all, but using the students' homes or other environments. Dewey was an eloquent proponent of this and schools that he helped found [898] and many holistic schools claim Dewey's ideas on this as their inspiration. Taking the class out of the classroom may be a common idea in mainstream education with field trips to study nature, museums, etc. All too often, however, these opportunities to go outside of the classroom are simply exercises in turning outside environments into pseudo-classrooms, where the students' lives are dominated by worksheets, walking in lines, staying in small groups or otherwise tightly regulated by teachers.

Many holistic educators reject the effects on what is learned as well as the learning process which follow from pedagogic spaces that are "clearly marked and explicitly regulated." They would also often claim there is a hidden agenda (or "invisible pedagogy" in Bernstein's terms) in training people to live with a relationship to space in which their activities and movements are bound, restricted, and ordered by others; and in which it is normal to submit to authority in just about everything from tasks to bodily functions. For many holistic educators the idea that a child needs to get permission or even an institution-granted pass to go to the toilet is very strange. Many holistic educators would point to the difference between a person being a feature of the space in which they exist, or the space as a resource for the people who live in it, an arena of their choosing for their construction of meaning.[899]

It is probably significant in a discussion of space in holistic education to note that many holistic schools (especially day schools, but some boarding schools as well) spend a great deal of time educating the parents in the educational process. If the pedagogic space is not limited to the confines of the school premises, then what goes on in a child's home can be (and some would say should be) part of the educational process with which the adults running the school are necessarily concerned.

III. Time

The concept of time in pedagogy involves the time in a person's life for pedagogy and the use of time in pedagogy. Bernstein indicates many differences between competence and performance models in their relationship to time. He says that competence models,

> ...select the present tense as the temporal modality. Time is not explicitly or finely punctuated as a marker of different activities, as a consequence the punctuation of time does not construct a future. The present tense is thus emphasized. Further, the weak and implicit sequencing of different activities (no apparent progression) combines with weak pacing to emphasize the present tense. Inasmuch as the emphasis is upon what each acquirer [student] is revealing *at a particular moment* (known only to the teacher), and that this is a signifier of what should be made available by the teacher, then the time dimension of the pedagogic practice is the present tense from the point of view of the acquirer.[900]

Most holistic education advocates would insist that when pacing and sequencing are determined by the student and/or the contents of the subject studied, pacing and sequencing are strengthened in their contributions to the learning process.

There is no generalizable pacing or sequencing across all individuals in competence models of education, but this is also somewhat accepted in mainstream education. Very few, if any, teachers believe that all students, regardless of their inclinations, backgrounds, capacities, or psychologies should progress in the same tasks at the same pace. What is believed is that there are sufficient similarities amongst the members of groups of students (e.g., highly motivated, white, upper middle class, from a stable family, bright, etc.) with the consequence that each member of that group should progress through certain learning procedures at a similar pace. This, however, does not take into account that even if there are identical students (which some suggest is impossible) the life experiences of the students (e.g., family stress, personal trauma. etc.) has a marked effect on the temporary academic ability of a student, and these experiences reduce any previous affinity. Most teachers will have experienced the destructive effects on students who are bored with a class because they learn much more quickly than their peers, and the equally destructive effects on someone who can't keep up with the class. In both cases there are often behavioral problems which follow such inappropriate pacing. With increased use of optional subjects and the use of tracking or other devices to delineate inclination and ability in many schools, the groups that comprise a class may have substantial affinity. Nonetheless, in performance based pedagogic models, it is thought possible and preferable for someone other than the students to determine the pacing and sequencing, and to fit this sequencing and pacing into the larger scheme of aspirations of the educational authorities. Holistic educators carry the tracking of mainstream education further by claiming it is to the advantage of every learner to have sequencing and pacing specific to the individual learner in each subject and appropriate for that moment, and probably determined at least partly by each learner. This has implications for assessment, as discussed beginning on page 243.

Holistic educators speak of following the pacing and sequencing inherent in the student's relationship to what is being learned. Any teacher will know that when a student or group of students is interested in a topic, there is not enough time for it; and when the topic is not working well, there is too much time. An externally determined pace dictates the depth of study for a topic, whereas a student-determined pace follows the depth of study. Bernstein seems to use generalizability as the criteria for indicating weakness or strength, but generalizability may be misleading. Holistic educators would want to use the criteria of what allows a student to learn most or best and, as there is no legitimate text or performance goals to dictate what has to be learned, they would suggest that the strongest pacing and sequencing is that which allows the learning process to move with the fewest obstacles or constraints towards that which needs to be learned.

There is the non-holistic view that pacing and sequencing are important to drive the learning process along, because without it the student would do little that constitutes valid learning. Holistic educators reject this view, as seen by all that has been discussed in previous chapters about inherent learning processes and inherent motivation.

In previous discussions about learning for holistic education not being bound by space and the consequences that this has for time and regulation, it is not surprising that time is not "finely punctuated as a marker of different activities" within specific learning activities. There is not a fixed time determined by someone other than the learner for moving from one learning activity to another, any more than there is a time to move out of learning. We can call such time concerns the micro-pacing in pedagogy—the time periods (within a day) given to acquiring a discourse and the frequency of those time periods (within a week or year). If micro-pacing and micro-sequencing restrict the discourse, then they can be said to be weak, and if they support the desired range and depth of learning, they can be said to be strong. Consider the example of a student learning botany and studying the growing cycle of a plant. If the sequencing of the approach is determined by society or the institutions of education at large (e.g., having the course start in September—at the end of the seasonal growing cycle) and is to be approached in forty-five minute periods because of the institutional requirements (which isn't enough time to get out tools, work a piece of land and replace the tools), and has to be done three times a week regardless of the season or the weather; then clearly the student can only study the growing cycle academically with not more than periodic reference to the real life phenomena (or the "real discourse" as Bernstein calls it). Likewise in studying cookery, the micro-pacing inherent in the discourse may permit short periods (like forty-five minutes) for initially learning some minor procedures, but learning to cook a complicated dish or meal has an inherent micro-pacing that cannot be confined to forty-five minutes. While this is obviously true for botany and cooking, it is less obviously true (but, holistic educators would insist, just as true) for more traditional academic discourses. In these cases, the micro-pacing of mainstream education, as it does not support the desired range and depth of study, can be said to be weak.

Even if it is generally accepted that forty-five minutes is the *average* attention span, most teachers will have experienced students with much shorter attention spans and those with longer ones, and they will have seen attention spans of individual students vary substantially according to mood or the imperatives in the students' lives. They will also know that students who are able to take an occasional *attention-break* (appropriate to them) from a subject that interests them, are able to work at that subject for many hours. Some activities that are used by most schools, like project work, benefit from sustained application beyond forty-five minutes. When such activities must be artificially truncated to fit into a typical class period, a student confined to that micro-pacing not only cannot engage fully in that activity, he cannot discover what that activity really is any more than he can discover what it means to cook a full meal if he only ever cooks for forty-five minutes at a time. Pacing and sequencing determined by the relationship of the student to a discourse and by the dynamics of the discourse are seen as strong by a criterion of learning as an open-ended activity, and externally determined pacing and sequencing are seen as strong by a criterion of learning as the acquisition of the contents of predetermined procedures.

Bernstein's point that "the punctuation of time does not construct a future" is most appropriate for holistic education because for holistic education the outcome of the learning process is unknown (at least partly if not wholly). In general, the punctuation of time can be preset for a task only when one knows (at least approximately) the conclusion of the task and when that conclusion must be reached. The time a task takes may be punctuated for purely subjective reasons (like attention span, or muscles getting tired), but this is more the student's engagement with the task being punctuated for subjective reasons of relationship (always in the present tense and idiosyncratically) rather than time punctuating a task. The focus in time punctuation is on a future state or goal, while the focus for the student-in-the-relationship-to-the-task punctuation is on the relationship to the task, in which one can be absorbed or "lost" in time.

Time, especially toward predetermined conclusions, is also related to the 'becoming trap' previously discussed (see page 226). Being in the 'becoming trap' is what holistic educators feel is the position of mainstream education. Activities that are onerous or at least boring are engaged in for some ability that is theoretically to accrue in the future. This future ability is then supposed to open the doors (still further in the future) for an opportunity (e.g., higher education or a job); and this opportunity is an important prerequisite for a hypothetical end condition still further ahead in the future which has labels like 'success', 'security' or 'happiness'. Holistic education advocates are concerned that from first entering school, children are too often taught to focus on a future goal toward which there are clearly delineated and ordered steps with only X amount of time to get through those steps. This is not to say that holistic education eschews deferred gratification. On the contrary, there is a great deal of talk by holistic educators about how modern society and our environment suffer from a lack of deferred gratification. Holistic education advocates speak of much mainstream education as deferred meaningful living, and echo Dewey's much quoted phrase, "Education is a process of living, not a preparation," or Krishnamurti,

> Our education from childhood is built round this idea of *becoming* somebody, achieving success, and very few of us have ever learnt to love what we are doing.[901]

Holistic education advocates feel that to learn for some future meaningful existence is to learn to live with present meaninglessness, and that this lesson is usually too well learnt; a sentiment that echoes several of the Authors' views about living in the present. That the processes of planning or projecting are necessary and valid for some things in life (like planting a crop, or constructing a building) is beyond question. However, it is not beyond question that these processes occasionally need to be mediated by reference to the present reality, or that the original goal may need to be changed. What is more difficult to determine are the areas of life for which these are not appropriate processes (such as developing a loving relationship, or understanding oneself), and the possible approaches to learning in those areas. Holistic education feels that such areas in life (for which planning and projecting are not appropriate) far outnumber and are far more important than those for which these processes have relevance.

Avoiding the 'becoming trap' does not mean denying that a person changes, and in some sense goes from being one thing to being another. Nor does it deny that these changes may in some sense be progressive towards some end state. Ultimacy would make little sense without such a notion. What it does claim is that whatever a person is, they are fully; people are not partial or incipient versions of something else, thereby denying the deficit theories of development referred to earlier and supporting some of the current psychological theories that eschew development models.[902]

IV. Pedagogic Text

Bernstein calls a student's work (or that which a student produces in the course of his learning) "the pedagogic text." Part of his analysis of the pedagogic text for both the competence and performance model elaborates the topic of time.

> Here [in the performance model] the pedagogic text is essentially the text the acquirer produces, that is, the pedagogic text is the acquirer's performance...I have stated previously that performance models relative to competence models emphasize the future. However, with reference to the production of the pedagogic text it can be said that performance models signify the past. The pedagogic practice which produces the text positions the acquirer, *invisibly*, in the past and its rituals which have produced the instructional discourse. Thus in the case of performance models, the future is made visible, but that which has constructed this future is a past invisible to the acquirer. In the case of the competence models it is the *future* which is invisible to the acquirer (only known to the teacher) and the present which is continuously visible.[903]

An important question for holistic educators is: What is the most desirable relationship to the past, present and future for young people to have as they are growing? This may have been a simpler question in previous eras. Consider first the past. It may indeed be advisable or even necessary to "position(s) the acquirer [student]...in the past and its rituals" for cultural transference, but in today's pluralist world holistic educators ask, 'whose past'? In most modern societies there are now too many cultural pasts to include; and if, for example, the answer in America is, 'the American past' then too many students will be positioned in a foreign and alienating arena. To say that only one cultural past is legitimate or can be a source of legitimate texts is to make a politically unacceptable and educationally alienating statement, yet because this positioning is *"invisibly"* accomplished, this statement is silently, though nonetheless emphatically, made.

Most holistic educators would feel that a statement that legitimizes one cultural past over another is inaccurate, and if it is done *"invisibly"* it is probably suspect. This is partly from a general distrust of nationalism *per se* (discussed in more detail in the sections on modes and identity construction) and partly from being wary of vested interests. If the past of one group is the source of the pedagogic discourse, the members of that group have an obvious advantage in producing the pedagogic text. There are also the perceived vested interests of those who are the guardians of the discourse. A statement about one cultural past being the only source for legitimate texts may be invisibly made because those making it don't want it challenged—an excellent reason for many holistic educators to openly challenge it. If no single culture is to be automatically valued above others, then if anything cultural is to be valued, it must be elements in different cultures or aspects found in all cultures (like art, music, myths, ritual, or kinship groups). The criteria for whether a particular expression of a cultural aspect should be valued must be (in keeping with our previous discussion) the role of that particular expression in the student's finding of meaning. As such, the history of black female slaves can be as important as the history of white male political leaders of the same period. The street poetry of today can be as important as the poetry of World War I. Holistic education does not deny a past, but claims there are a variety of pasts, not the least of which is the student's own personal past; and that if a student's learning is to be positioned in any past, it should be done explicitly and that past should be one that has the richest potential for each student in finding meaning.

If "in the case of performance models, the future is made visible," then one needs to ask to what extent this visible future is real or illusory. The future can be said to be real within the context of a pedagogic discourse; one may know that after learning addition one learns subtraction, or after studying World War I there is the study of World War II, etc. There may even be procedural futures or future stages that can be known; one will go to secondary education after primary, etc. But as Bernstein correctly points out, the pedagogic discourse is abstracted from the "real discourse"; the activities of pedagogic physics only very loosely resemble the activities of real life physicists. To what extent then is the future made visible in performance models, not just a future that exists only within the pedagogic discourse and divorced from real life? Life in 'the ivory tower' has long been lampooned. The divergence of the real world from the world of school and the dichotomies produced have been noticed by many educators and have recently produced fascinating studies in street mathematics versus school mathematics.[904] In these studies, child street vendors are able to do complex mathematical problems in their heads as they relate to the activities that are actual to these children, yet they are unable to do the very same problems on paper when asked to do them in the way these children are learning to do them in school.

Bernstein's comment that in competence models it is "the present which is continuously visible" has significance with reference to all that has been said previously about living in the present. Holistic educators (and the Authors) would naturally support an approach to pedagogic texts that assists in making the present "continuously visible" because of its effect on being present and therefore on self-knowledge, both of which are seen as related to Ultimacy.

Bernstein's point at the end of the previous quote about the future in competence models being visible to the teacher alone is only partly true, but this is covered at length in the discussion on assessment.

What Bernstein says of the pedagogic text for competence based pedagogy is largely accurate, but it needs some elaboration to fit holistic education more exactly. Although such elaboration touches on assessment (the following discussion), Bernstein's concepts of what is visible to the learner and the teacher in the pedagogic text needs discussion here.

> Here [in a competence model] the text is less the product of an acquirer for this product indicates something other than itself. It reveals the acquirer's competence development, be this cognitively affective as social, and these are the foci. The teacher operates with a theory

of reading through the product the acquirer offers (or does not offer) to the teacher. This theory of reading marks the professionalism of the teacher and is recontexualized from the social and psychological sciences which legitimize this pedagogic mode. The consequence is that the meaning of an acquirer's signs is not available to the acquirer, only the teacher.[905]

For holistic education, the teacher, as an outside evaluator with different experiences, reads (potentially) different things into the pedagogic text, not better things. Everyone learns to read indications of their developing competence from infancy, from the time we first try to put something in our mouths or crawl—we can find our mouths or hold ourselves up on our hands and knees, etc. The "meaning" of the student's (or infant's) signs may have a significance to a teacher or caregiver that is different to the student (or infant) because such an adult has perhaps seen such signs before and is able to relate such signs to other signs that make a pattern which is invisible to the student (or infant). However, as the nature of the competence in holistic education concerns meeting the challenges of life in the deepest and broadest sense, and this is based partly on the students' finding of meaning, it is necessarily mistaken to assume that the signs have no meaning or less meaning to the students than they do to the teachers. This could even be argued for performance based pedagogy, though for other reasons. A teacher in mainstream education may, for example, see signs that a student has grasped the essential concepts of fractions and that the student has done this with less or more difficulty than his peers and at a younger or older age than is usual. This may mean something to the teacher about the student's over-all mathematics ability and probable progress, all of which would be invisible to the student. The student in this example, however, may feel that a whole new world has opened up before them and that suddenly so many things that were mysterious before now make sense. The point is that the meaning visible in the pedagogic text is different for the teacher and the student even in performance based pedagogy; and which is better, greater, or more authentic would be a difficult question.

As the holistic education student's ability to see meaningful signs in their own pedagogic text is important, and as some of the meaning will remain beyond the scrutiny of all but the student, part of the skill of the educator is in helping the student learn to read more deeply "through the product" to understand the development of their competence. In fact, developing self-knowledge can imply developing such ability to read more deeply into one's own text. This is also important in view of the student as self-regulating and the correct pedagogic relationship as non-hierarchical. A holistic educator may even suggest producing pedagogic texts which can only have significance to the student but which the educator feels may be especially revealing. Much of the education that is felt to occur from Outward Bound and other educational programs started by Kurt Hahn is of this nature as are various educational initiatives based on rites of passage.[906]

Even though such "reading through the product" is "recontextualized from the social and psychological sciences which legitimize this [competence based] pedagogic mode," it is a process much older than these disciplines as evidenced in traditions of religious education and child rearing, and as seen in the early Authors.

V. Evaluation

Bernstein uses the term 'evaluation' but holistic education has a distinctly different understanding of this topic, so that another term emphasizing this difference is merited. 'Evaluation' will be taken to mean a judgment to which it is possible to attach a value, which makes stratification possible. 'Assessment' will be taken to mean a judgment that distinguishes the nature of what is assessed, but which implies no value and, therefore, does not generate stratification. Bernstein claimed that there can be no education without evaluation (although he used the term in the way 'assessment' will be used in this discussion).[907] I take Bernstein to mean that intentional learning (i.e., education) cannot occur unless there is something assessed as not yet learned, and cannot consciously be built upon unless such learning is assessed as having occurred. In similar terms, it can be argued that life is impossible without assessment; e.g., a person can't walk home without a myriad of assessments concerned with when it is correct to turn, or safe to cross a street, etc. Consequently, for holistic education assessment is necessary; but holistic education has claimed that what, why, how, and by whom assessments are made require different answers to those found in mainstream education.[908] Assessment for holistic education is not simple. Keeping in mind that for holistic education (as for the Authors) the response to the question, 'what needs to be learned' involves experiential learning, self-knowledge, and sagacious competence, it is not surprising that holistic educators claim that their task is to learn how to assess what is valued rather than the mainstream solution which they feel is simply to value what is easily assessed.

In distinguishing major differences between evaluation for competence and performance based pedagogic models, Bernstein identifies aspects of how assessment is seen by holistic education.

> Here [in the competence based pedagogy model] the emphasis is upon what is *present* in the acquirer's product... Criteria of evaluation of instructional discourse are likely to be implicit and diffuse.[909]

Whereas in the performance model:

> the emphasis is upon what is *missing* in the product...then criteria will be explicit and specific, and the acquirer will be made aware of how to recognize and realize the legitimate text.[910]

Part of the reason assessment for holistic education is "likely to be implicit and diffuse" is that it cannot be meaningfully abstracted from the overall competence that gives the procedure meaning. This could be seen as analogous to assessing whether one is balanced when riding a bicycle; assessing the procedure of staying balanced is necessary for not falling off, but it cannot sensibly be abstracted from the general activity of bicycle riding and judged on its own merits even though the procedure of balancing needs to be learned (to some extent) prior to riding a bicycle. Being "implicit and diffuse" does not imply the criteria are not discernible. What makes them "implicit and diffuse" yet discernible is that they are inherent in the discourse. We can take art as an example of such a discourse. The criteria for what makes a good picture may be "implicit and diffuse" yet they are discernible, and there may even be some aspects for which the assessment criteria are explicit. To say otherwise is to deny technique and a general consensus on aesthetics.

As the assessment criteria are inherent in the discourse, we can say that it is the experience of what is learned (or 'acquired' in Bernstein's words) that creates the basis for assessing, which is an aspect of experiential learning. Consider again the analogy of riding a bicycle (which is not a competence, but is still useful as an analogy). The initial criterion for assessing what is learned is simply not falling off. This may be implicit, but it is very discernible. The experiential criteria for assessing further learning may be getting from point A to B with speed, safety, ease, or gracefulness. As a discourse becomes regulated, and a competence is transformed into a performance (e.g., Chomsky's language production versus the skill of public speaking), criteria for assessing elements (like pronunciation) may become "explicit and specific" (as in public speaking), at which time assessment can be turned into evaluation and follows Bernstein's description for performance based pedagogy.

Some criteria for assessment may be inherent in the everyday understandings of a particular discourse (rather than the discourse itself), and so can be said to be implicit and diffuse even though they are socially constructed and, therefore, externally determined (e.g., 'this meal tastes good', 'he is nicely dressed', or 'she is behaving well'). In such cases the extent to which a person has been socialized determines the availability of criteria for assessment.

Many holistic educators feel that communitarianism can contribute to understanding socially derived values, social expectations, boundaries, learning norms, and the social role of a discourse. As the Authors affirmed, and holistic education would agree, none of us are autonomous agents existing outside of social contexts. Consequently, an external assessor (or externally determined assessment) can act as a normative response of the community to a student's pedagogic text, helping to socialize the student. Critics of this idea wonder how such a process can foster the innovation or creativity that our rapidly changing world requires. Such critics also question the consequences of using the norm as a criterion in a pluralist world, where the norm may disadvantage minority groups.

The nature of assessment or evaluation reflects its purpose. If the purpose of evaluation is to establish the extent to which a text seen as legitimate has been acquired, then that evaluation can be said to be summative—it computes "the aggregate value of conditions, qualities, etc." (Oxford English Dictionary for *summation*). If the purpose of assessment is to provide feedback that is a necessary part of the learning process, then it can be said to be formative—and, as mentioned earlier, learning cannot occur without it.

For holistic education, the potential formative nature of assessment indicates an important role for external assessors. The role of an external assessor (one role of the teacher) is to aid the student in receiving needed feedback. In cases where the feedback may not have been received by students on their own, the reasons may be:

1) It was simply not noticed (e.g., "You have forgotten to carry the two in that multiplication.").

2) The student has not yet learned to receive such information (e.g., "Have you noticed the rhythm scheme of that poem?").

3) The student has dismissed such feedback as being unimportant

(e.g., "If you don't keep track of your references now you'll have a terrible time finding them later.").

The educator who engages in formative assessment acts as an extension of the student's ability to assess, with the intention of extending the student's own self-assessment capacity and, therefore, also extending the student's experience of what is being learned.

VI. Control

Bernstein's analysis of the differences in control between performance based pedagogy and competence based pedagogy explains why so many observers have labeled the latter as anarchic.

> As space, time and discourse do not give rise to explicit structures and classifications [in competence based pedagogy] these cannot serve both to constitute and relay order. The absence of explicit structures and classification makes both the possibility and use of positional control a low priority strategy.
>
> Further, such control [positional control] militates against the concept of the transmitter, as a facilitator and acquirer, as self-regulating.[911]

For holistic schools, this usually translates as a relatively low level of control (or none at all) that is automatically conferred on holders of positions or roles, which means there must be other ways to create the necessary order. While all social organizations necessarily have mechanisms (visible or invisible) which act as controls to maintain a needed order, Bernstein indicates the attention given to create (and often continuously re-create) the necessary order usually found in holistic education. Because the basis for creating and maintaining order (which Bernstein calls the "regulative discourse criteria") in competence based pedagogy is not implicit in the structure (i.e., not automatically conferred on holders of positions or roles), it needs to be explicit. [912] These processes of making explicit the "regulative discourse criteria" often involve flexible groups of staff and students as well as ad hoc committees. The process of selecting a temporary 'controller' through chance (e.g., picking the short straw) usually occurs in activities where everyone is recognized as equally capable of leading, but where a leader is nonetheless needed. This is often the case in mountain climbing teams: the activity requires a leader, but it doesn't matter (amongst equally qualified climbers) who the leader is. The leader can be chosen by the other climbers, selected by chance, or the position can rotate through the group. That there is a controller is important; who that controller is, is not important.

For holistic education (and also for the Authors), what is important is unlinking social position, role, and classification from authority. Most control is seen as rightly belonging to each individual (self-control, discipline) or the group (the ideal of democracy) and should not be abdicated even though it can be temporarily lent to another for utilitarian reasons. Knowing when to accept external controls (e.g., following the instructions of a traffic officer) and when not to accept them (e.g., civil disobedience), as well as knowing when to take control of another (e.g., preventing a child from running into a busy street) and when to refuse to do so (when someone wants to put you on a pedestal to follow) are seen as requirements for living a life of integrity. Holistic educators often say (or imply) that these important lessons, which are subtle and complex, are not likely to be learned in an environment where the opposite is practiced any more than one is likely to learn how to be kind from being brutalized. They further claim that the typical mainstream classroom resembles no political structure so much as a totalitarian regime, while simultaneously wanting the children to grow up into responsible democratic citizens.[913] Reducing positional control is important in holistic education for all that has been previously discussed in relation to authority and freedom. Holistic education would recognize Bernstein's claim that in performance models of pedagogy "structures and classifications are resources for positional control which in turn legitimizes the structures and classifications"[914] and, for many holistic education advocates, this smacks of corruption.

The mechanisms by which holistic schools fulfill Bernstein's point that "regulative discourse criteria...are likely to be more explicit"[915] are as varied as the number of schools. What is significant for our purposes is that most holistic educators would say the competence which holistic education aims to achieve includes learning to see 1) what 'regulative discourse criteria' are appropriate, 2) how to agree on them, 3) the reasons for acting in accord with them, and 4) how to support them in the community (even if the community is just the school).

VII. Autonomy

Bernstein's claims about autonomy for competence based pedagogic models would be partly accepted by most holistic educators, but these claims need further elaboration to describe holistic education more completely. He claims that competence models, require a relatively wide area and range of autonomy, although teachers in any one institution are likely to have reduced autonomy over their pedagogic practice as this mode requires homogeneity of practice.[916]

There are limits to autonomy in any social grouping; individuals cannot arbitrarily decide to have very different meanings for the same words if they want to communicate, or use different chronologies if they want to coordinate their movements. Holistic schools also require a sacrifice of autonomy for some homogeneity of practice if the school is not to send confusing messages to the students (and parents) about the nature of their education. To what extent such homogeneity is greater or lesser than that found in mainstream schools is not clear. There is a de facto homogeneity generated when people of one perspective consciously or unconsciously hire others for having a similar perspective, and the hiring practice of most holistic schools involves the deliberation of most, if not all, of the staff and often of the students. In holistic education there also tends to be a great deal of discussion amongst the adults (as mentioned earlier) about the nature of the school and its activities as there are few procedures or structures that are considered givens, and such discussion tends to generate homogeneity. However, a case can also be made for there being less homogeneity in holistic education than mainstream education as there is rarely a coordinated curriculum with its consequent sequencing, usually no standard teaching technique, nor a standardized method of evaluation. Also, because holistic education usually gives great importance to students as individuals, homogeneity in pedagogic practice is hampered. As Bernstein says of competence models in general,

> ...any particular context and practice will also be dependent upon the particular features of the acquirers [read students] and their contexts.[917]

This may be analogous to parents raising several children. The parents presumably have perspectives that are at least compatible, if not identical, and have compatible if not identical aspirations and child-rearing techniques for all of their children. Nevertheless, because of "the particular features of acquirers [read each child] and their contexts" the particular aspects of each child's rearing will inevitably be different. In this regard it is worth recalling that on page 231 Bernstein is quoted as saying that in the competence model pre-packaged materials such as textbooks or teaching routines are less likely to be used and that resources are usually constructed by the teacher. Teachers need a high degree of autonomy in order to do this, again militating against homogeneity.

Almost all mainstream education understands that pedagogy must make some accommodation of the individuality of the student—in most mainstream schools a student can now choose amongst subjects (after a certain age), will sometimes be tracked or otherwise grouped according to perceived ability, and may even go to different kinds of secondary schooling according to their anticipated futures. Holistic education asks the question, "How much accommodation is needed?" It is a question of getting the right fit, analogous in some ways to fitting men's suits. Suits can simply come in sizes small, medium, and large. However, a person is likely to get a better fit if the suits come in 38, 40, 42, etc.; an even better fit if they come in sizes 38, 39, 40, 41, etc.; and an even better fit still if they come in 38 short, 38 regular, 38 long, 39 short, etc. Yet, generally, nothing will fit as well as a properly made bespoke suit. The general rule being: the more variations there are, the closer one gets to fitting the particular individual (unless a person happens to have exactly the same measurements as one of the categories, like medium). To think anything different is to claim that people only come with three or six, etc. different combinations of dimensions to their bodies, and we know that people's bodies have tremendous variation. There is no reason to assume that their minds and psyches (interests, capacities, informally acquired knowledge bases) are any less variable than their bodies. Of course one could argue that tailor-made suits are a luxury, perhaps even an immoral opulence; but how much accommodation to the "particular features of acquirers and their contexts" is required before it can be considered a luxury; or, from a holistic education perspective, how much fitting of a student into a pedagogic content that doesn't fit the student is moral? Holistic educators ask to what extent education authorities (not teachers who generally work hard to do the opposite) are saying, "Only those who are like us (mediums, for instance) can wear the mantle of education. For all of you who are too big or too small or shaped differently, we're sorry but, you'll have to wear something else."

The autonomy of competence models (including holistic education) has implications for accountability and therefore for the protection of students' welfare. As Bernstein explains,

> Competence models are less susceptible to public scrutiny and accountability, relative to performance models, as their products are

more difficult to evaluate objectively. Finally, competence models are not geared to specialized futures and are therefore less dependent and less regulated.[918]

The lack of public scrutiny must be conceded by holistic education, but the reason for this often mirrors the differences previously discussed between evaluation and assessment. Applying the performance criteria of mainstream education to evaluate a holistic school would make as much sense to holistic educators as judging a painting by its weight. Some of the important questions involved for holistic educators would be:

1) Which aspects of a child's development are able to be reliably scrutinised by the public? Performances certainly can be scrutinized by the public, but what is there in the development of competences which lends itself to such scrutiny?

2) How appropriate are the various means of public scrutiny for presenting an over-all picture of any particular child's development? Can one develop a picture of the whole child from an assemblage of snapshots (even if they are completely reliable, which they clearly are not) of different aspects, and if one can't, just what does such an assemblage represent?

3) What is 'scrutinisable' by others who are not the public (parents, teachers, school administrators, students' peers, the student themselves) and what are the merits of such scrutinies in relation to public scrutiny?

4) What is the effect on pedagogy if it is dominated or restricted to that which can be publicly scrutinised? This is often a very strong point of complaint from students or their parents who are coming from a mainstream school and entering a holistic school. A pedagogic system that seems 'evaluation-driven' is often felt to be serving bureaucratic needs more than the students' needs.

5) To whom do different forms of scrutiny make different parties accountable? (e.g., are the teachers accountable to the school administrators, government bureaucracies, or to the students and parents)? This question goes quite far within some holistic schools where students evaluate the teachers and school administrators; in some schools the students can even fire adults whom they feel are not performing adequately. In other schools, the parents have this authority; in others it is the teaching staff as a whole who scrutinize their peers and administrators; while in still others, members of a school (students, teachers, or administrators) are determined by everyone involved in the school

(students, teachers, parents, and administrators). In some pedagogic systems there is talk of 'clients' and 'providers'. For holistic educators, it is interesting that many state-run schools that use this terminology and that see the students and parents as 'clients' and the teachers and administrators as 'providers', rarely give the power to their clients that a market economy is supposed to confer.

6) What is used to calculate the accounts of the different parties who are accountable, i.e., what is the role of that which can be publicly scrutinised in the accountability of teachers, school administrators, and students; and what is the role of that which cannot be publicly scrutinised in this accountability? In Britain today there is the notion of 'value added' benefits. This refers to what has been added to each child's education which is not visible from an evaluation of a schools performance. For example: Child X is socially advantaged and comes from excellent elementary school A and goes to secondary school B. Child Y is socially disadvantaged and comes from a terrible elementary school C and goes to secondary school D. At the end of a school year both children (X and Y) get the same score on comprehensive tests. Can one say that both schools have performed equally well? 'Value added' is not easily measured, and there do not seem to be very clear ways of weighing these factors into an overall balance for public scrutiny.

Most of these questions are recurrent for holistic educators because they revolve around notions of control, authority and the relationship of the individual to society and its different institutions, all of which are central concerns in holistic education.

As holistic education sees the experience of learning as invariably different for everyone, and as it is the experience of learning and the effect it has on the development of each student's competence (rather than the demonstration of learning through performance of some legitimate task) that is most important, the most important elements for accountability are directly available only to the students. Indications of these elements may be available to parents, teachers, a student's peers, and (to a lesser extent) school administrators, but such indications must necessarily be like tracks in the snow—traces of the thing rather than the thing itself. Holistic educators will often say that without knowing the individual student and their context, it is not possible to see even vaguely whether a particular teacher, course or school is really helping a child develop. Furthermore, different indications of development are available to different people or groups of people (a student's peers, teachers, parents, and school administrator), all of whom may see different indications of the development of a student. All those perspectives need to be assembled in order to give a reasonable account of that child's learning experience. A student's performance in certain academic tasks relative to others of the same age may have something interesting to say, but given the different socio-economic backgrounds, sub-cultural background, innate capacities, life experiences, informal learning, and environments, such measures have little significance in themselves. Holistic educators would say that accountability based on a narrow band of indicators (which is necessarily the case with performance as indicators) must, of necessity, be very partial and therefore makes only a fraction of a student's educational experience susceptible to accountability; a fraction that leaves out almost all that the Authors felt needs to be learned.

What must be acknowledged is that in the holistic model, the student is not publicly protected from a school's indifference, incompetence, or exploitation. If the parents, teachers, and/or school administrators are indifferent, incompetent, or exploitative, then there is no protection for the student. No outside agency is in a position to rescue the child's educational experience, and historically there certainly have been, and no doubt continue to be, cases of this. Holistic educators and the parents of the students attending holistic schools must recognize this and realize that they must assume the responsibility of accountability.

It must be further recognized that the associated responsibilities cannot be imposed on those unwilling or unable to carry them, and that the model does not work on its own. The parents of holistic school students who are unsure of their capacities to assume this responsibility often still prefer this vulnerability to what they see as public scrutiny distorting education to suit the needs of the system of scrutiny. Such parents would also often claim that there is no protection for the child in mainstream education from system-wide indifference and exploitation by those in power, with indifference evidenced by such things as reduced funding, ignoring the long term effects of mainstream teaching on many teachers, and political parties manipulating educational policy for political purposes. What holistic educators might point to about public scrutiny, especially the increasing public scrutiny of mainstream education, is the implication that teachers, school administrators, and parents can't be trusted with the educational welfare of the students in their charge; they would ask for evidence of anyone or any group as being more trustworthy.

To what extent holistic educators would agree with Bernstein's claim that competence models are not geared to specialized futures depends on what is meant by "geared." If "geared" means 'focused on' and 'determined by' a future, then Bernstein is correct. As previously stated, holistic schools are more firmly rooted in the present time frame as a consequence of having Ultimacy as a goal. If, however, "geared" means that they cannot prepare students for specialized futures, then this is clearly wrong. Students do go from holistic schools to become doctors, lawyers, engineers, professional musicians, etc., but there are a number of hurdles put in their way by the tertiary educational establishments that in many countries have performance criteria for entrance. This problem has been overcome in a variety of ways, depending on the country.

Another indication that holistic schools do not preclude their students being "geared to specialized futures" is evidenced by the frequent occurrence of students in such schools finding a special interest which absorbs them for long periods of time (weeks, months, years) encouraged by the frequent use of project work and the importance given to students pursuing their own interests. By allowing students to pursue their interests, and with the notion that education should help students find their vocation (both of which are part of self-discovery as discussed in previous chapters), holistic education could be seen as exceptionally good at gearing students to specialized futures.

VIII. Economy

The costs of holistic education are higher than mainstream education, although those higher costs are often not passed on to the students. This disparity between cost and price is usually accomplished by not paying the adults of holistic schools at the same levels paid to corresponding adults in mainstream schools. Bernstein gives several reasons for the costs of competence models in general being greater than performance models, and these hold true for holistic education.

> The transmission costs of these [competence] models are likely to be higher than the costs of performance models. The costs of training the teachers are likely to be high because of the theoretical base of the competency models... Further, there is a range of hidden costs if the competence model is to be successful in its own terms. The hidden costs are time based. The teacher often has to construct the pedagogic resources; evaluation requires time in establishing the profile of each acquirer [student]; and in discussing projects with groups, socializing parents into the practice is another requirement; establishing feedback on the acquirer's development (or lack of it) is

a further time cost. Within the institution extensive interaction between teachers over the practice is required for purposes of planning and of monitoring, as the structure is constructed rather than received.[919]

These higher costs are often given as a reason for the holistic model being impractical for wider implementation. Many holistic education advocates argue that while there may be good reasons for not implementing holistic education more widely (like people simply not wanting it), the argument cannot be made on the basis of costs. It may be true that politicians would not want to spend what is required for publicly funded holistic education, but neither do they appear overly keen on spending the money necessary for the upkeep of the current system or even the maintenance of its buildings—and this is not an argument against having mainstream education.

Holistic educators also point to the way costs are calculated and they use environmental issues as analogies. It is cheaper to pollute the environment than to keep it clean, but the long-term costs (from increased health care costs to people moving away to more pleasant areas) of pollution actually make it more cost effective to not pollute. Similarly, a calculation of the true costs of mainstream education should include:

1) All development costs (e.g., curriculum, text materials).

2) Enforcement costs (e.g., inspection, examination, enforcement of education laws such as truancy).

3) Remedial education costs (i.e., recovery in adulthood of failing to educate people at school age).

4) Under-skilled manpower costs (i.e., of a workforce that learned early to shun learning).

5) Social costs (e.g., delinquency, or criminal incarceration which currently costs more per annum per prisoner than is earned by a middle class family with two significant wage earners).

Holistic education advocates often see the lack of full human development of a student as a failure of education, because that is what they see education is for. They will claim that no society can afford not to have its population as fully developed as the individual potentials will allow, and this is just on material grounds. The moral grounds for such an aspiration do not need arguing.

Support for some of these extended cost ideas comes from unexpected quarters. Those interested in the nature of successful groups have begun to recognize the importance of paying for some of the group processes that holistic education has long felt to be necessary, but which are very labor intensive. Peter Senge from MIT was one of the first to demonstrate that group success depended on the group learning together and that this involves individuals flourishing.[920] Taking some of this to heart, the US military now gives time to group consultation and more autonomy to lower levels of command although the initial dollar costs are much greater. Many of these practices in business and the military (with names like, 'group vision building' or 'owning the mission') are recognized as indirectly linked to performance and, in the long run, are cost effective.

While the eight features (pedagogic discourse, space, time, pedagogic text, evaluation, control, autonomy, and costs) that Bernstein uses to distinguish competence based pedagogy from performance based pedagogy demonstrate, in the same process, how holistic education differs from mainstream education, another purpose is also served. These same features distinguish different approaches to holistic education. For pedagogic discourse, approaches vary from some things being deemed worthy of study (e.g., ecology) even if there is no 'legitimate text', to nothing being worthy of study unless the student deems it to be so. The "competences that acquirers already possess or are thought to possess" might be spiritual, psychological or an amalgam of the two (resonating with the emphases of the Authors). Notions of pedagogic spaces vary from thinking that wherever a child is (even if only virtually) is his classroom, to thinking that the pedagogic space must be specially constructed to nourish the child and ensure a feeling of security and respect which learning requires. Approaches to pacing, sequence and development (as a feature of time) range from being entirely determined by the individual student to structures resembling mainstream education with classes and courses that follow a timetable and progress through the years of schooling. Pedagogic text in holistic education varies from specific challenges to be met (e.g., a portfolio) to no expectation of any kind. Assessment varies from explicit (e.g., a portfolio or project demonstrating that criteria have been met) to the view that the learner must assess himself. For control, there are very political structures (e.g. committees and voting), therapeutic structures (e.g. rap groups, counseling), and communitarian structures (e.g., dialogue, consensus building, etc.). The variation in understandings of autonomy is enormous and reflects very different understandings of human nature, society, and actualization. Financial costs differ from almost nothing (e.g., online classes or parent co-operatives) to those of maintaining very expensive private grounds. Consequently, while these features are valuable for the present purposes of examining the nature of holistic education, they are also useful for distinguishing the different modalities of holistic education.

Holistic Education As a Fourth Mode of Competence Model

MODES OF COMPETENCE MODELS

*B*ernstein claims that there are three modes or kinds of both the performance based pedagogic model and the competence based pedagogic model. It is not relevant to our purposes to discuss Bernstein's three modes of the performance model. We shall, however, examine in detail the three modes Bernstein feels exist for the competence model, as this will further distinguish the nature of holistic education. Bernstein claims that all competence models focus on commonalities shared within a group. These commonalities may be shared with other groups within a population (e.g., an ethnic, social or gender group), and represent a "similar to" relation that is seen by the group as fundamental to who the individuals are. Differences between individuals are not as significant as the similarities and are not a basis for stratification or ranking. Instead, differences in "similar to" groups are seen as complimentary to the "similar to" relation in that such differences can be an aid to "the actualization of the common potential."[921] This fundamental insight can serve as an organizing principle for what appear to be very diverse educational endeavors in different forms of holistic education. Bernstein goes on to distinguish his three modes by their location of the "similar to" relations.

It is important to understand all three modes suggested by Bernstein in order to understand the case made here: that holistic education represents a distinct or fourth mode. Holistic education (the fourth mode) uniquely shares some aspects with the other three to an extent that are sufficient to put it into a category of its own; but it also contains elements which are essential to its nature and that do not appear in the other three modes. It is necessary, therefore, to understand Bernstein's three modes and the location of their "similar to" relations in order to make a case for a fourth location, and so a case for holistic education as a distinct mode of the competence model of education.

> In the first mode (first historically), 'similar to' relations are located *within* the individual and refer to common procedures that all individuals share. This mode was opposed to what it considered were repressive forms of authority (usually male) in the family and school, and industry, and was emancipatory with respect to the new concept of child to be actualized by appropriate pedagogic practices and controls... Essentially and briefly the focus of this mode was upon intra-individual potential which could be revealed by appropriate pedagogic practice and contexts. The mode could be called liberal/progressive...
>
> The second mode locates 'similar to' relations not within the individual but within a local culture (class, ethnic, region). The reference here is to the validity of communicative competences intrinsic to a local, usually dominated, culture. This second mode presupposes an opposition between a dominating official pedagogic practice and local pedagogic practices and contexts.... The sponsors of this mode show or attempt to show that a group of competences...are generated by local communicative practices, but are ignored, unseen or repressed by members of official pedagogic fields....
>
> The third mode follows from the second in locating competence within a local dominated group or class, but does not focus upon indigenous competences as does the second mode... The third mode focuses upon inter-class/group opportunities, material and symbolic, to redress its objective dominated positioning. The pedagogic practice and contexts created by this mode presuppose an emancipatory potential common to all members of the group. This can be actualized by the members' own exploration of the source of their imposed powerlessness under conditions of pedagogic renewal.[922]

The "similar to" relation for holistic education is located in a multifaceted process that we have called 'approaching Ultimacy'. In modern times such 'approaching Ultimacy' is most often seen as an activity of consciousness, as ever since Jung consciousness is often understood as incorporating 'soul', 'spirit', '*karma*', and other numina. In this view, consciousness is rarely seen as being confined to the skull or even the body of an individual, not just because its effects are outside, but because it has an operative existence outside the physical person. This may resemble modern depth psychologists who postulate a higher self which extends and acts beyond the individual. The exact nature of the process of approaching Ultimacy as well as the exact nature of the Ultimacy that is approached are described differently by different (what Bernstein calls) modalities of the fourth mode, and may even be disputed amongst them; but there are enough elements which are held in common by a sufficient number of fourth mode advocates to create some coherence.[923]

'Approaching Ultimacy' is seen as a process that lies at least partly within the individual, and often it is seen as mostly within the individual. In this it is like Bernstein's first mode with its emphasis "upon the intra-individual potential," but it is very unlike Bernstein's first mode in what it opposes. Bernstein's first mode "was opposed to what it considered were repressive forms of authority," while the fourth mode is opposed only to not approaching Ultimacy.

By locating the "similar to" relation in the potential for Ultimacy, or even more concretely, in that-which-makes-Ultimacy-possible (TWMUP) which is similar in everyone, important implications are made about 1) the nature of human beings, 2) the purposes of learning (in the largest sense and education in the smallest), 3) an overarching value if not a hierarchy of values, and 4) the relation between the individual and society. Enough has been said about the various understandings of TWMUP in the Authors, and the differences today in holistic education reflect those differences and have multiplied. However, in general it is felt that if or when contact with TWMUP is lost, then people lose touch with something of their essence, and with their profoundest link with others. Consequently, they lose their most fundamental "similar to" relation, a "similar to" relation which is much more fundamental than anything of culture, time, or peer group.

A clear distinction between Bernstein's three modes and the fourth mode is that all three of Bernstein's modes postulate dominance by 'others'—either gender and role (as in his first mode), another culture (as in his second mode), or other classes or groups within the culture (as in his third mode)—with the intention of the competence focusing on emancipation from those others. The "similar to" relations of the fourth mode tend not to have such 'them and us' constructions, although that kind of language is sometimes used. Part of the reason for the lack of 'them and us' constructions lies in the nature of the "similar to" relation itself: the only individual or group that could possibly not be 'one of us' would have to be those who do not have available TWMUP; which usually turns into an unacceptable 'chosen people' syndrome. For the fourth mode, emancipation is not from another person or group of persons, it is from states of being that are in themselves 'non-liberated'. In this they echo enlightenment philosophies, or the emancipatory elements in many religions which feel the common state is one shackled to lower elements (often of forces, desires, or nature), and that transformation to a higher state of being is a freedom from such shackles. Emancipation is not gained from opposition to others who are in fact "similar to" us, and is not a consequence of any social restructuring such as the redressing of power arrangements in a culture.

The fourth mode is not, however, indifferent to political and cultural circumstances. On the contrary, there is often a view that the 'outer' situation both reflects and influences the 'inner', and the line between the two is blurred in many approaches to holistic education. This reflects some social representation theory in which an 'outer' cultural perspective can be "ontogenic"[924] in shaping the nature of a person's being, as the 'outer' becomes part of the fabric of a person's inner world. Fourth mode advocates are often politically active in order to redress imbalances that are perceived as affecting people's consciousness (it is hard to talk to a starving man about Ultimacy) or to affect some other social aspect that is seen as adversely impinging on the nature of consciousness (e.g., protecting the environment or reducing the amount of violence in the media), but these concerns are usually of a second order. The *raison d'être* of social action for fourth mode advocates is affecting contact with TWMUP, not to counter injustice or power imbalances in and of themselves.

All major cultures (though not all subcultures) postulate, and often formalize, a means of contacting TWMUP; so that, as members of at least one culture, we are all similar in having such postulations and formalizations (e.g., dogma, rituals, symbols, etc.) as part of our cultural understandings (even if we have rejected their verity). Paradoxically, as the exact postulations and formalizations of different cultures differ from one another and are even mutually exclusive, this very prominent potential "similar to" basis destroys the feeling of itself and creates a 'different from' sense. Fourth mode advocates are uncomfortable with such sources of 'different from' feelings, especially as they stem from what should produce its opposite. They tend, therefore, to

be more eclectic in their relationship to TWMUP and view exact postulations and formalizations as expressions of the time and place of
their origin. Furthermore, as the time of origin of these postulations
and formalizations becomes increasingly distant and the place of their
origin is often foreign (and usually increasingly so through the cultural
changes that occur over time), fourth mode advocates usually view the
particularities of postulations as increasingly removed from modern
expressions of the experiences of Ultimacy—those very experiences
which originally gave rise to such postulations. There is also the alteration and elaboration that seems unavoidable in any transmission over
time, especially over a long time and many languages—like some ex-
traordinarily complex and lengthy child's game of Telephone (the
American name) or Chinese Whispers (the British name for the same
child's game). Just as Bernstein's claim that pedagogic physics is removed from the real discourse of physics, so the particularities of the
postulations about TWMUP become removed from the real experience of Ultimacy that gave rise to them.

Many holistic education initiatives explicitly reject what they see as
the narrowness of exclusively endorsing any particular cultural postulations about TWMUP, what we shall call 'exclusive-truth-claims'. Exclusive-truth-claims effectively set a person apart from others who make
opposing exclusive-truth-claims, working against the holistic education
'similar to' notion. Instead, holistic educators tend to look for similarities between cultural postulations, trying to construct meaning from
understanding what is common to different postulations. In this, the
work of Aldous Huxley with his book *The Perennial Philosophy*[925] and
Joseph Campbell's *The Hero of a Thousand Faces*[926] found wide appeal, as
have many subsequent authors similarly seeking to celebrate the commonalities of humanity with pan-cultural postulations. The tendency
of holistic educators has been to remain with the general (described by
Bohm as "that which generates the particular"[927]) partly because it is
felt to be closer to the original truth (before alteration by a particular
time and place) but also because it is inclusive rather than exclusive—
something seen as essential in a pluralist world. For this reason postulations from indigenous cultures (cultures seen as less complicated and
devolved from their original impetuses than modern cultures) are valued as providing insights into TWMUP which existed prior to sophisticated postulations.

Critics have called such attempts to extract the pan-cultural 'cultural strip-mining' and claim that decontextualizing the postulations
distorts or removes their meaning. Advocates of pan-culturalism feel

that it is the human experience of what is being postulated and the perception of what lies behind the postulations that gives them meaning. These human experiences are each individual's finding of their own meaning, and as such these individuals feel they are acknowledging an authentic less-culturally-tainted approach to Ultimacy. These advocates claim that it is experiencing Ultimacy, no matter how partially, that validates postulations, not history, cultural or social authority. They claim that if postulations cease to assist contacting TWMUP, or another postulation is better at assisting this contact, then the old postulation loses validity and the new one replaces it. Holistic education advocates claim that this is not religious relativism, as some critics assert, any more than switching from one translation of the Bible to another or changing the language or form of religious ceremonies is religious relativism. They claim that it is recognizing that what is transcendent cannot be culturally bound or encapsulated by any single human expression or formalization. The fundamental "similar to" relation of the fourth mode allows any postulation that is authentic for one individual to be authentic for another, for new ones to be generated from experience, and for these new postulations to be authentic for others.

The major difference between Bernstein's second and third mode is that in the second mode indigenous competences struggle against those of the dominating groups or cultures, while in the third mode a group or culture struggles to find parity not through promoting indigenous competences but through exploiting "inter-class/group opportunities, material and symbolic, to redress its objective dominated position."[928]

The fourth mode is similar to the second mode in that adherents of the fourth mode "attempt to show that a group of competences" which are *indigenous in nature* are repressed by the dominating culture (typically modern and western, although this same movement is appearing in an increasing number of third world countries and former second world countries), and that exercising these competences can liberate a person from this dominant culture. 'Indigenous in nature' is used here as a deliberate replacement for Bernstein's 'indigenous', as this is one way in which the fourth mode differs from Bernstein's second mode. Competences that are 'indigenous in nature' are often not native to the particular location in which they are advocated, but they do have an origin that is indigenous (e.g., Native American, Druidic, Aboriginal, African, early Christian, Sufi), or they spring from a frame of mind that is 'indigenous-like' in that it is dominated by a strong sense of place which includes nature and pre-industrial traditions. The pluralist world we inhabit, and which often inhabits us (e.g., mixed culture or mixed race parentage, multi-cultural upbringing, etc.), is seen as making us indigenes of multiple locations. Some of these locations where people feel an 'at-homeness' or where they find meaningful 'roots' may not even be locations they have visited. Witness the number of people who find meaning in the myths or other aspects of Native American cultures, have no Native American blood and have never even been to America. There are a large number of films and books that promote finding the 'indigenous in nature'[929] and which borrow from such promotions models for education.[930] Perhaps Wexler best summarizes this tendency.

> This new age builds on the core civilizations, submerged by modernism, in order to counter the deadening "mechanical petrification" by life-affirming practices. These practices are not morally induced, but are inductive artefacts of the self at work within the polarized apparatus. In Fromm's terms, they are "experienced values." …The creation of individuated practices necessarily draws cultural resources from outside the West European history of the last two centuries…[931]

While this may be dismissed and ridiculed by its critics, for those who find meaning in such non-native cultures it is no less authentic or sensible than someone else finding meaning in events that occurred in the Middle East two thousand years ago. Again, importance is given to finding meaning. Indigenousness indicates perspective rather than location, and the fourth mode differs from the second in focusing on indigenousness rather than what is literally indigenous, i.e., located within a local culture. Principle aspects of indigenousness in which fourth mode advocates locate the "similar to" relation are those concerned with TWMUP and consequently, one can say that the "similar to" relation is located in a particular aspect of culture rather than a particular culture.

Bernstein's third mode has the "similar to" relation located within a dominated group or class that "focuses upon inter-class/group opportunities, material and symbolic, to redress its objective dominated positioning." In this the fourth mode is similar in seeing itself struggling for what advocates often call 'a paradigm shift' away from the dominant paradigm of the conventional modern industrial world (also labeled as materialism, Cartesian, atomistic, Western capitalism, etc.) which is seen as destroying the world morally, physically, and spiritually.

These advocates claim that another paradigm, a holistic paradigm, is struggling to gain dominance. The battle is within the 'hearts and minds' of individuals as ecological perspectives struggle against perspectives of progress, and systems thinking struggles against atomistic thinking.[932] Some groups are felt to be representatives of perspectives and are frequently defined by their perspectives (e.g., the road construction protesters or road expansion advocates), but the members of any such perspective-defined group may be in union with members of the opposite perspective-defined group on another issue (e.g., gender or race issues). What is most significant is that this battle of paradigms takes place invisibly within most members of the culture. People's perspectives on paradigm-defining issues slide gradually as the result of changing cultural understandings, and dominated paradigms see changes "material and symbolic" which affect the social order. In this way, fourth mode advocates struggle for a paradigm shift on matters concerned with Ultimacy (amongst other matters as explained earlier) against paradigms that are felt to suppress, inhibit or prevent Ultimacy; and while this struggle often has the appearance of opposing groups (like road protesters and local planners), no way exists of defining members other than on an issue-by-issue basis.

We need to return to the rejection of exclusive-truth-claims by fourth mode advocates in order to look at one more comparison between the fourth mode and Bernstein's third mode. Exclusive-truth-claims are seen not only as creating 'different from' relations by fourth mode advocates, they are also seen as serving the interests of groups or individuals (religious or secular/religious amalgams like religiously anointed leaders) who claim authority on the basis of the particularities of postulations and/or from their role in the formalizations of TWMUP. Such groups or individuals are seen placing themselves as mediators between individuals and TWMUP in order to maintain their position. By rejecting exclusive-truth-claims, it is felt that the foundations of such power bases are also rejected, thereby promoting and effecting fundamental social change through the paradigm shift. In this attempt to "redress its objective dominated position," the fourth mode is like the third mode, but as before, the *raison d'être* is Ultimacy and not social change for any other reason.

Bernstein claims that, "competence modes are generally found regulating the early life of acquirers or in repair sections,"[933] expressing part of the attraction for the fourth mode. Many advocates of holistic education speak of society and the human condition as needing repair. They point to evidence of increasing dysfunction in society, in social or ethnic groups within society, in families, and within individuals. The perspective that societies and individuals in general are in need of repair is supported by long-standing traditions including 'fallen man' traditions, needing to find unity to repair fragmentation, returning to nature to repair the damage of civilization, and by much psychology which sees neuroses as pandemic. If the notion of repair is extended to include developing the capacity for self-reparation, then it can include theories of life-span psychology,[934] psychological resistance building,[935] and character building.

Bernstein recognizes that competence modes are seen as "'empowering' by their sponsors"[936] and this is certainly true for the fourth mode. With the "similar to" relation located in approaching Ultimacy for the fourth mode, it is seen by its advocates as concerned with what is most empowering in human experience. The first mode is seen as the "basis of cognitive empowerment," the second mode as "the basis for cultural empowerment," and the third mode as "the basis for political empowerment."[937] Bernstein also describes the relationships of his three modes to consciousness.

> All competence modes, despite oppositions, share a preoccupation with the development (liberal/progressive) [first mode], the recognition (populist) [second mode] and change (radical) [third mode] of consciousness.[938]

Fourth mode advocates would claim a similarity to the third mode in the above, in that they are concerned with the radical change (i.e., transformation) of consciousness, both individually and collectively.

IDENTITY CONSTRUCTION

Concerns with "similar to" relations obviously imply identity, and Bernstein's analysis of identity constructions in competence based pedagogy also helps distinguish the nature of holistic education. Holistic education is unusual in that it usually intends explicitly to create or to foster the development of identities, and these identities are different from those commonly held in the modern world. The discovery of new identities usually entail new relationships to one or more of the following: to the earth, to other humans, to other cultures, to one's own nation, or to the problems of living that are believed to follow these new views of what it means to be human. Such new identities are often seen by advocates of holistic education to be the most complete and lasting way of solving the world's problems (e.g., seeing one's identity as part of nature changes environmental behavior). The perceived loss of identity in the modern world as well as attempts to sustain incoherent identities (with the loss or warping of relationships that follow) are seen as a major source of current problems. Holistic education advocates often claim that the current cultural paradigm offers a unique opportunity for people to find new identities, echoing sentiments of many who work in field of life span identity:

> Our unique selves…are a matter of our own crafting, and particularly in the modern world where traditional constraints of time and space exert far less control over who we *can* be.[939]

Bernstein makes a similar statement.

> Much has been written about postmodernism, late modernism, and the localizing of identities…. However, it does seem clear that, in the old speak, those identities which were given a biological focus (age, gender, age relation), 'ascribed' identities, have been considerably weakened, are ambiguous and to some extent can be achieved. These cultural punctuations and specializations (age, gender, age relation) are now weak resources for the construction of identities with a stable and collective base. Further, again in old speak, locational 'achieved' identities of class and occupation have become weak resources for stable unambiguous identities. This weakening of stable, unambiguous, collective resources for the construction of identities consequent upon this new period of transitional capitalism, has brought about a disturbance and disembedding of identities and so created the possibility of new identity constructions.[940]

Bernstein speaks of constructing identities, while holistic education (in accord with the Authors) might prefer to speak of finding identities to indicate its relation to self-discovery and to avoid postmodern relativism with its consequent denial of a core self. However, a distinction between identity and self can be made (as with Jung's *persona* and *ego* mentioned earlier) that would solve this difference. The Authors speak of 'self' as unique and inherent and needing to be discovered or uncovered, and not as anything having to do with occupation or role in society. Bernstein and other modern social psychologists and sociologists speak of self as role, so that, "a self, then, virtually awaits the individual entering a position…" and a person has as many selves as they have roles.[941] Bernstein uses 'identity' in this second sense, and like Jung's *persona*, it makes sense to see the social and cultural role in constructing identity.

As well as distinguishing two pedagogic models (competence and performance) and three modes within each (while I have made a case for a fourth competence mode), Bernstein also distinguishes different identities that he feels are constructed by the different modes of each model. It is not necessary to repeat what Bernstein says about the relationship of the various identity constructions to the modes within the performance model. It is, however, important to relay briefly some of his views on the different identity constructions for the three modes of his competence model, as well as the nature of identity construction itself. Bernstein's categories, while tremendously helpful as a base, do not completely cover the needs of holistic education, and I shall propose extending his framework in order to accommodate the identity construction of holistic education.

Bernstein originally proposed three "launching pads for the construction of identities,"[942] which he later extended to four.[943] These launching pads are the resources for the construction of identities. Rather than detailing the characteristics of Bernstein's four identity construction "launching pads," I shall discuss only those aspects that apply to the identity construction of holistic education. As in the discussion on modes, holistic education shows itself to be a distinct pedagogy on the basis that it crosses the boundaries that distinguish the other approaches to pedagogy (according to Bernstein) as well as containing elements that are unique.

Part of the "launching pads" that Bernstein proposes are three kinds of relationships that identities can create: decentering, centering, or recentering. The identity of holistic education is very strongly all three.

Holistic education is distinctly *decentering* in Bernstein's terms in that it proposes an identity which removes the individual from the "collective base" of what is perceived as the 'old paradigm'. Holistic education is also decentering in that it does not generally have any social organ that holds the center of the identity and, in fact, eschews such centering. Instead, like nature, the identity is seen as needing to be self-organizing and self-regulating. The holistic education identity is *centering* in Bernstein's terms in that it invites people to resonate with (and in that sense join) older, time-honored groups (e.g., indigenous groups). It is also centering in that people with this identity seek to co-operate with others of like mind, and yet does not divorce them from the rest of humanity. A holistic education identity is *recentering* in Bernstein's terms in that it claims to be a world-wide and grassroots movement "giving the identity a new collective base."[944]

Bernstein also proposes that the resources for identity construction are generally located in one of three time frames: past, present, or future. Again, holistic education is distinctive with reference to these locations, because it crosses the boundaries between them and also because of the distinctive ways in which it uses these time frames as resources. One of Bernstein's identity constructions is what he calls "retrospective"—it uses a grand narrative from the past as a resource. This is the construction of fundamentalist and old conservative movements which look at visions of their (real or imagined) history in order to see what they are and should be. For holistic education this would also apply, but in a different way, based on the trans-culturalism and indigenousness as discussed previously. The "narratives of the past which provide exemplars and criteria"[945] for holistic education do not make exclusive-culture-virtue-claims any more than their postulations about TWMUP make exclusive-truth-claims. The exemplars and criteria elucidate characteristics of what is seen as noblest in humans (and which forms part of the 'similar to' relation) regardless of their culture, place or time. Narratives from Africa, North America, Japan and chivalric Europe easily mix to provide resources for constructing an identity of a non-time-located and non-place-located human, a tendency identified by Wexler as unique.[946]

In this, forth mode narratives (even if they are as historically accurate as any narrative can be) take on a mythical quality: they are told only to convey timeless truths about the nature of things, and the receiver of the narrative is not expected to relate to its time or place which are relevant only to the internal coherence of the narrative. Unlike Bernstein's retrospective identity constructions, which project the past into the future more or less as a cultural whole with only a few concessions to the passage of time, the holistic education identity construction seeks, from the many pasts, meaning about the condition and the potential of both the collective and the individual. The assemblage of the many possible narratives makes the grand narrative of the unfolding of the human story.

Another element that is common between Bernstein's retrospective identity construction and holistic education construction is what Bernstein says of the fundamentalist retrospective identity.

> … [this identity construction] gives it a site outside current and future instabilities… It produces a strong insulation between the sacred and the profane such that it is possible to enter the profane world without being either appropriated or colonized by it.[947]

These could be the words of many parents describing why they send their children to holistic schools at what is often, for them, a very great cost.

Bernstein claims that there are other identities which draw on the present. He feels that both the market-oriented and therapeutic identity constructions do this, but in different ways and for different purposes. The holistic education mode shares this resource but, again, for different reasons. The process of approaching Ultimacy is generally seen as requiring 'being in the present' (as previously discussed). Being 'present' has become a favored topic amongst many people looking at the nature of consciousness and has become a focus for extremely interesting scientific research.[948] The many slogans in the holistic education movement that echo 'Be here now', and which try to help people be aware of what they are doing as they are doing it, testify to this. Unlike Bernstein's market-oriented identities, which are seeking to meet the contingencies of ever changing markets, or his therapeutic identities, which are "produced by introjection"[949] and which are "personal project(s)" and are only "a truly symbolic construction…[with] internal linearity,"[950] the holistic education identity seeks to make sense of the ever-changing contingencies as a reflection of the inner state. This is more like a 'circumjection' in which the outer world is scrutinized for indications of and reflections on the 'inner'. This is not just a personal project; in keeping with the Authors' indications of the self extending to become social, it is one that is engaged in for others as well.

Bernstein also characterizes some identity constructions as launching themselves from projections of the future, and he does so in a way in which many in holistic education would see themselves described.

> …prospective identities point to a new basis for solidarity for those entitled to be recognized. …They change the basis for a collective recognition and relation. Prospective identities are launched by social movements, for example those of gender, race or region. They are, in their take-off stage, evangelist and confrontational. …Prospective identities, as with fundamentalists, are engaged in conversion, and as

with fundamentalist identities engage in economic and political activity to provide for the development of their new potential.[951]

Those who look to the future often engage positively with change. They are the technophiles, the ones embracing most new technologies with all of the implications, which often involve new life styles and new relationship structures. Holistic educators have often been very active in the use of computers in primary and secondary education, and have an inordinate number of homepages and websites. This is an identity that feels its day has not yet come.

While the identity construction of the holistic education mode may share elements with the other modes by drawing on the past, present and future, there is one temporal notion that Bernstein does not mention but which is important to holistic education and which was alluded to before in the discussion on the use of narrative. By drawing on the mythical qualities of many narratives, and mythologizing historical accounts, holistic education advocates draw on what can be called 'mythological time'. This kind of time has been discussed by writers like Mircea Eliade who identify this non-chronological temporal sense as "sacred time."[952] Sacred time is evoked during religious ceremonies when a sacred event is re-enacted, and people are thought of as transcending time and participating in the original event. The sacred event, like the Last Supper for Christians, is not located in irreversible chronological time; it is in reversible time, time that can be made present again so that the sacredness of that event is present.

As a result of 1) the eclecticism advocated by much of holistic education, 2) a notion that timelessness exists (partly supported by some popular understandings of modern physics, partly by religious traditions, and partly by the sense that some things like 'truths' are perennial), and 3) so many traditional, cultural, and religious elements being recontextualized and mixed; there is a sense that sacred or mythological time is available in a variety of ways. Entering this mythological or sacred time through some deliberate act (like ceremony, ritual or meditation) or through something beyond one's will (e.g., epiphany) is an important part of a person's discovery of self. By locating the self outside the present time, one becomes contemporary with that which is timeless and that which has ultimate meaning. While such self-location has existed in many religions, Jung legitimized secular and transcultural versions.

Such a dispersal of the time in which the sacred is located conforms to Bernstein's analysis of the present sense of the location of
the sacred.

> What appears to be happening at the end of the 20th century is a
> weakening of the location of the sacred. In the beginning of this
> century the sacred was centrally located and informed the collective
> base of society through the inter-relation of state, religion and
> education. Today this collective base has been considerably weakened
> as a resource for a centralized sacred. The sacred now reveals itself
> in dispersed sites, movements and discourses. It is less the
> fragmentation of the sacred but more its dispersal, localization and
> specialization.[953]

CONCLUSION TO A SOCIOLOGICAL ANALYSIS OF HOLISTIC EDUCATION

Distinguishing what holistic education *does*, is particularly well served
by Bernstein's competence based pedagogic model. It demonstrates
that holistic education tries to accomplish different ends to those of
performance based pedagogy, and as such treats the various aspects of
pedagogy (i.e., the pedagogic discourse, space, time, pedagogic text,
evaluation, control, autonomy, and costs) very differently from those
in performance based pedagogy. These aspects, in general, show competence based pedagogy to be more of a 'bottom up' approach than
the 'top down' approach of performance based pedagogy, and less of
a predetermined-outcomes form of pedagogy. These same aspects also
serve to show that holistic education is unique as a form of competence based pedagogy.

Holistic education also shows itself to be unique in that it doesn't
fit within Bernstein's three modes of competence based pedagogy.
Holistic education is a fourth mode, partly because its "similar to" relation is located in approaching Ultimacy. In this it is supra-culturally
(non-spatially and non-temporally) located. Many advocates of holistic education would even claim that because of this "similar to" relation, which sees Ultimacy as having religious qualities (as discussed previously), the "similar to" relation extends beyond the human. The opposition which Bernstein claims is part of all "similar to" relations is

against the non-ultimate or non-actualized, which many holistic education advocates would feel is part of the age-old struggle of man with himself.

As a consequence, the "similar to" relation does more for the fourth mode to determine its identity construction than is found in the other modes. The universality of such a construction is felt, by its advocates to best prepare people from any world for any world they might find themselves in during this period of pluralism and rapid change.

CHAPTER 13

Summary

*T*he task of this book has been to answer the question, 'What is holistic education?' As much of the foregoing has necessarily been detailed, a brief summary would be useful. Such a summary also serves as part of a concluding answer to this complex question. It has been argued that holistic education stems from notions of Ultimacy, perceives experiential knowledge and sagacious competence as what needs to be learned, and perceives certain personal attributes of the students and teachers as most facilitative of the needed learning.

As indicated in the introduction, holistic education has no core text spelling out what it is and what it isn't, so this task involves making sense of disparate elements in the different approaches to holistic education. This book has sought a coherence that most holistic educators could say approximates at least a large part of their concerns, and which at the same time distinguishes holistic education from other approaches to education.

CRITIQUE OF METHOD ADOPTED

There is an inherent limitation in this kind of work. One of the two criteria of success for this task, as stated in the introduction, would be (like that of psychological or literary interpretation) that its adherents acknowledge the interpretations as being a fair representation of their experience or views. This is reinforced by Lincoln who feels that the subjects of research on marginalized groups must feel that the work accurately reflects them if it is to be authentic. This presumes that the group members or adherents are identifiable, which is greatly facilitated if they are from a gender, race, ethnicity, sexual preference group, etc. But when the identifier is a philosophical perspective or worldview, it is the perspective or world-view that must first be delineated in order to identify a group. Without a clear meaning as to what that group is, simply claiming to be a member of it is insufficient. Recently a U.S. Marine Sergeant claimed in a television interview to be making the basic training for Marines more holistic, by which he meant he would instruct his charges so as to avoid trouble with the locals when they are overseas. Can he be considered a holistic educator simply because that is how he describes his activity?

To ascertain whether the views expressed in this book do represent those of the adherents of holistic education, I have consulted some of those who work in the field. However, I have only consulted those in the field with whom I have a friendship (to ask someone to read this work as it has developed required a friendship that can bear some taxing), and such a friendship indicates some affinity. Therefore, this has not been a random sampling of people in the field, but again, the field itself has not previously been delineated so no random sampling was possible.

A combination of disciplines has necessarily been drawn upon for this book so that it resembles *Allgemeine Pedagogic* (as practiced in Germany and Holland), which holds that the activity of education is too complex and multifaceted for any large view of it to be approached from one discipline alone. This certainly seems to be the case in trying to understand the nature of holistic education. This task has been approached as a philosophical one in the sense that Isaiah Berlin engaged in philosophy. It has also partially been an examination of the history of ideas, but not a straight history as it is not the progression of evolving ideas that has been of interest, so much as a delineation of the notions as they first appeared historically which have been woven into the presently held notions. Holistic education does not exist as a set of studied historical texts, but as a tapestry of transformed and conflated notions each of which has a historic origin. It has also been necessary to draw upon the Sociology of Education as elucidated by Basil Bernstein. Such a mixture of disciplines may seem simply undisciplined at first glance, but holistic education does not have a single starting point or rationale. Instead it has gradually emerged from a variety of disciplines and perspectives. In sum, the intellectual precedents of holistic education reveals such a mixture of disciplines involving philosophy, pedagogy, psychology, and (with Jung at least) something of a history of theological ideas.

NOTIONS OF ULTIMACY

Rousseau is generally accepted as one of the earliest proponents of holistic education notions, though many holistic educators would claim that going back to the origins of human religiosity is the real starting point. This is because holistic education is rooted in notions of Ultimacy. It claims to be interested in the fullest possible development of "persons," and feels that this puts it in opposition to education for functions, roles, or enculturation. For holistic education, the nature of "persons" has its essence inextricably linked with Ultimacy and, as such, is fundamentally a religious notion without necessarily being part of any religion. Holistic educators often question the view of human nature implied by many other approaches to education— views of human nature are necessarily embedded in all approaches of education. Holistic education has felt that notions of what it means to be human must be explicit, taken to their logical ends, and educational systems should be clearly designed in keeping with such notions.

The notions of Ultimacy for the Authors led them and lead holistic educators to their views of human nature and meaningful living. Holistic educators claim their view of original goodness stands in opposition to that of original sin, and that different views concerning the need (or lack of need) to control and shape children necessarily follow. Hence, holistic educators feel they have a different view of development which holds that people will naturally go towards the good, and that progress consists largely of unfolding, uncovering, or discovering what is natural or inherent in the child. As there is usually thought to be an inherent link between each individual and Ultimacy (as at least a latency), such unfolding, uncovering, or discovering is seen as related to something that could be called religiousness or wisdom. This is not self-knowledge as narcissistic obsession, but as an approach to Ultimacy.

The link between Ultimacy and both human nature and a human's meaningful living means that approaching Ultimacy is linked with a person's well-being. In the Authors and in many holistic education texts, the outer world derives its meaning from its relation to the inner world. Approaching Ultimacy is even seen as pragmatic due to the understanding that the greater encompasses the lesser; i.e., without understanding the greater, and having one's actions informed by the greater, actions on the lesser will be inefficient or even counter-productive. Further supporting such a worldview are ideas like Gaia and Systems Theory which are popular amongst holistic educators and almost have quasi-religious status. Consequently, a holistic education criterion for what needs to be learned is the relation of such learning to Ultimacy. A question for the Authors and for many holistic education advocates is: If Ultimacy refers to something actual (rather than just an idea or aspiration), and has such consequences for well-being and pragmatic success, what value could education have that is not directed toward and by Ultimacy? For many holistic educators, education for a career or for socialization seems inadequate.

One of the consequences of having Ultimacy as the goal of education is that there is no logical intermediate stopping point. This invites life-long learning and affects the identity of teachers. The teacher is not someone who has accomplished the goal of education and is therefore an expert (unless they have achieved Ultimacy which, by most accounts, would be a risible claim to make), but is instead a fellow learner with the student, albeit at a different stage of the journey. This has led some holistic educators (like Pestalozzi) to encourage slightly more advanced students to help those less advanced, and forms the basis of the therapeutic relationship for humanistic psychology and others. The students' (or patients') experiences of the teachers' (or therapists') own learning are seen as fundamental to the students' learning to learn. Consequently, the onus is on teachers to continue their learning as that is fundamental to the students' learning. It is teaching as an exercise in learning rather than as an exercising of what has been learned.

Similarly, part of what is seen as meaningful living is helping others to find meaning. This relates to both the topics of social development and teaching as a vocation rather than as a career. In the Authors there is often a sense of the missionary, and in the writings of many of the disciples of Pestalozzi, Froebel, and Jung, there is a evangelical tone that far exceeds even that of the Authors themselves. Unfortunately, claims of heresy, schism, and "the infidel" have often accompanied this zeal.

Ultimacy is seen as fundamental to the "similar to" relation of the identity construction (in Bernstein's terms) for holistic education. Such a "similar to" relation is supra-cultural, supra-temporal, and (for some) supra-human. This has allowed some (including Campbell and Huxley[954]) to postulate new grand narratives which many feel are necessary in our pluralist and rapidly changing world.

WHAT NEEDS TO BE LEARNED

In examining what holistic education feels needs to be learned, experience has special significance. It indicates both a kind of knowledge and a form of learning. Rather than the classic division of forms of knowledge according to content, this division is based on the manner of acquisition. Experiential knowledge derives its importance from notions of Ultimacy. Knowledge from experience is seen as better partly because such learning involves more than just the head of the learner, so that more of the whole person is involved in knowing. It is also thought that more of the object of knowledge can be known when it is known experientially (e.g., sensations can not be known except through experience). Consequently, educators like Howard Gardner,[955] whose theory of multiple intelligences results in proposing that all learning be more experiential, are applauded by holistic educators.

Experiential knowledge has another important relation to Ultimacy for holistic educators. Clearly, not all experience generates learning, and not all experiential learning is applauded by holistic education (e.g., learning how to steal). The experiences promoted are those experiences which sparks insight or perception. Developing the capacity to have insights is thought of as developing the capacity to see truths and is therefore related to Ultimacy. A truth seen is thought to be of an entirely different order than a truth believed, so that learning to know things through experience is thought of as learning to know in a way that is part of approaching Ultimacy.

Experiential knowledge is also related to Ultimacy through the nature of heuristic learning. What is known from experience depends partly on the questions that the learner asks. As such, learning how to ask and shape questions is seen as very important, often more important than finding answers. The questions a person asks of the universe are seen as determining the relationship the person has with the universe, and related to the activity of finding meaning. Hence, anything that enhances the capacity to ask questions is seen as positive. Performance based pedagogy, which is seen as preoccupied with answers, is not felt to do this.

The only content of knowledge that holistic education would generally consider essential is knowledge of the self. However, self-knowledge cannot solely be approached as content or the object of knowing, as it is also the subject, i.e., the self is the knower who has self-knowledge. In this the implication (found in all the Authors, systems of psychoanalysis and meditation, and many religions) is that the self is altered by what it sees of itself. For those who hold that Ultimacy partially exists in a core-self, this transformative process mirrors the myths of people being transformed by seeing the sacred. Regardless of the object, the self is at least the subject of all experiential knowledge, and is what develops or changes with each insight. In this there can be a confusion in the use of "self" that is often apparent in holistic education writing, but to which the modern Authors (particularly Jung) gave clarity. For Jung, there is the "self" that is "the inner guiding principle tending towards wholeness," "an integrating factor which is not of the individual's own making but which tends toward achieving unity," and that is "equivalent to the God within."[956] There is also, for Jung, two other things which are commonly called "self": 1) a core of inherent characteristics or attributes which must be discovered or uncovered, and 2) an entity which is socially constructed and changes from insights or seeing "truth." Jung labeled these *ego* and *persona* respectively, and it is a distinction that could well serve writers in holistic education.

Some of what are thought of as core elements of the *ego* are individual while others are universal. The individual elements are what make each person naturally idiosyncratic, with all that follows from such idiosyncrasy for educational pacing and content in holistic education. The universal elements of the *ego* are part of the basis for the "similar to" relation and are usually thought of as related to that-which-makes-Ultimacy-possible. The *persona* is the acquired self, the product of conditioning (e.g., culture, environment, training, etc.) and, as such, is accidental. As the *ego* has the universal elements, it is the extent to which *persona* approximates or comes into harmony with *ego* that is seen as the extent to which a person is true to himself (his "real" self), or is seen as self-actualized, individuated, or has sagacious competence.

For the early Authors and for many holistic educators, self-knowledge begins with a young person learning about what might be thought of as their outer capacities (e.g., the capacities to move, talk, make, etc.). With development, a young person moves inward, to learn about the inner capacities (e.g., empathy, compassion, mastering emotions, etc.). This is often put in terms of *doing* and *being* with *being* seen as the greater of the two, and (with the greater encompassing the lesser) it is felt that *doing* always expresses *being*. Such dependence of *doing* on *being* is seen in many religions (e.g., the Christian criterion of charity rests not on what is given, but the quality of being that is in the act). This issue emphasizes the importance that holistic educators feel should be placed on *being* over *doing* in education. This favors competence based pedagogy over performance based pedagogy and, for holistic education, sagacious competence would describe the nature of the *being* they favor.

For holistic education, self-knowledge is also the basis for social renewal. Contrary to much that seems to have influenced mainstream education (which holds that society is renewed through initiation of the young into the social or cultural discourse), holistic education holds that society is renewed through the psychological and spiritual development of individuals. Holistic education usually sees the need to challenge the status quo (as in Bernstein's notions of competence identity constructions always being in opposition) rather than maintaining it. Holistic educators claim that society is not renewed by maintaining the status quo, but by changing it. Holistic education holds that loosening of cultural and social certainties, cultural and social "not knowing" (like the naïveté promoted by Maslow) when coupled with self-knowledgeable individuals generates genuine commonweal.

WHAT FACILITATES THE NEEDED LEARNING

What holistic educators feel facilitates the needed learning cannot be prescriptive as there is no sense in which it is seen as being caused to occur. What does facilitate the needed learning are principally elements that are in both the students and teachers, giving them both agency in the learning process, with the students' agency being inherent while that of the teachers is acquired. The students' agency is mostly in-herent learning processes and inherent motivation, with students learning about their agency (e.g., learning about their learning processes as part of meta-learning, and learning of their inherent motivation to avoid the seduction of secondary motivation, etc.) being part of sagacious competence. The teachers' agency is an acquired understanding of humanity in general and their students as individuals in particular.

Teachers must also understand the correct pedagogic process, which consists largely of understanding the inherent learning processes in students and protecting that. In this, the students' and teachers' tasks are similar even if they are approached from different perspectives. Teachers must also understand the correct pedagogic relationship, and this relationship is not very different from what is promoted as social development for students (e.g., having compassion and empathy while simultaneously keeping differentiated, and having a profound sense of responsibility for others while simultaneously according them freedom, etc.). Many holistic educators quote Goethe who maintained that "we only learn from those we love." This does not mean that we can't acquire information (e.g., how to get from A to B) from those we don't love, but the acquisition of information is not learning for holistic education or Goethe.

Teachers also have to be responsible for their own development, which means developing their self-knowledge, sagacious competence and approach to Ultimacy, all of which facilitate the correct pedagogic relationship and understanding of humanity at large and individuals in particular. The teachers have a non-reciprocal responsibility to provide materials and experiences that students don't have, and to protect the students. This fits with the view, expressed above, of teaching as an exercise of learning, and notions of experiential learning. A large part of what every student experiences in schooling is the teacher. If the students experience someone who is learning and developing sagacious competence, then the students have experiences (vicariously, empathetically, or through some non-conscious communication) of such learning. Consequently, teaching is a *doing* that is seen as very much stemming from the doer's *being*.

Unlike the shaping or prescriptive model, being a teacher in holistic education mirrors the Buddhist notions of being a Buddha; a person does not become a teacher by virtue of teaching but by virtue of the student's learning. A person becomes a teacher only when a student of that teacher learns. In this sense, being a teacher is a gift from the student (not the reverse). While an idea can be acquired from and with others, discovering that an idea is true (the "real" learning called by the Authors and holistic educators by various names, e.g., "significant learning," insight, etc.) is always done alone, and no one can claim credit for that insight other than the person who has it. A person making a significant contribution to the insights of another is seen as what distinguishes that person as a teacher. Often in holistic education, as in many indigenous cultures, animals, objects and events can be spoken of as "teachers."

HOLISTIC EDUCATION AS DISTINCT

Many writers have proposed two incompatible developmental or educational approaches, some of which help elucidate the nature of holistic education. Bernstein proposes performance based pedagogy and competence based pedagogy. Kieran Egan proposes the Platonic and Rousseauian views of development.[957] In this distinction Egan claims that the Platonic model views the mind as an epistemological organ which develops, to a significant degree, according to the knowledge it acquires. Consequently, development occurs by mastering various forms of knowledge which bring the mind from ignorance to understanding the truth about reality. In this, emphasis is necessarily placed on the construction of curriculum as it is that which constructs the mind. Rousseau's model of the mind is more biological; the mind has its own inherent process of development and knowledge acquired does not really affect that development. For Rousseau, the inherent process is encouraged by giving it an appropriate environment. Several writers have contrasted views of education that could be labeled "constructivist" (just providing bricks and mortar to a site will not construct a wall) and "horticultural" (an acorn need only be provided with light, soil and water and will develop into an oak tree on its own). Even Rousseau had a contrasting view of development for education, i.e., education for becoming a "man" or for becoming a "citizen." What all of these views have in common is that they claim their contrasting models are incompatible, with no approach to education able to do both.

The incompatibility of non-holistic education with holistic education has led advocates of each to view the other with suspicion and often as misguided. It may be more accurate to conclude that they have different views of development, different views of human nature, and are trying to accomplish different ends. The views of development, human nature, and educational ends in holistic education do not have any significant educational sponsors. As has been seen, holistic education does have its champions; Rousseau, Jung, Maslow and Rogers, are generally seen as worthy of respect. Yet, these champions' views of development, human nature and educational ends have had very little, if any, impact on the organizations which shape mainstream education. Holistic education claims that its increasing popularity is a grassroots movement that, like the counter culture of the 1960s, has not had a institutional organization to promote it. Holistic education advocates claim that the general public's views of development, human nature, and the needed goals for education are increasingly those held by holistic education, and that the dissonance many students and parents feel towards their schools stems from their views on these things differing from those embedded in mainstream schools. This is not to the discredit of the teachers or administrators in those schools; it is a systemic problem and not easily solved. This is why so many teachers and parents have simply turned their backs on mainstream education to start or join holistic schools, or to homeschool with holistic approaches.

Insofar as any conclusion can be reached from this book, it is that holistic education is a true alternative to mainstream education with a carefully thought out philosophical foundation. With innumerable schools and programs claiming to be holistic now existing, it is certainly time that holistic education became clearly recognized for what it is attempting and why it is attempting it. With such clarity the various kinds of holistic schools might better reflect and refine what they are doing, and non-holistic schools might benefit from the years of effort and insights of holistic education. Perhaps this book is a step toward that progress.

Notes

1. (Mintz 1994).
2. (Miller 1992).
3. (Dudty and Dudty 1994; Miller 1993; Miller, Bruce Cassie, and Drake 1990; Pathfinder 1997).
4. (Wittgenstein 1953) p. 32 § 66–67.
5. e.g, (Miller 1992).
6. From (Heafford 1967) p. 43.
7. (Darling 1994) p. 17.
8. e.g., (Berlin 1999).
9. (Lincoln 1993) p. 29.
10. (Lincoln 1993) p. 29.
11. (Lincoln 1993) p. 44.
12. (Winch 1990) p. 88.
13. (Purpel 1989).
14. (Tillich 1957).
15. (Maslow 1968) p. 24. See Appendix note 1.
16. e.g., (Maslow 1993) p. 45 & (Smith 1990) p. 22. See Appendix note 2.
17. (Maslow 1968) p. 5. See Appendix note 3.
18. (von Franz 1975) p. 115.
19. (Rousseau 1979) pp. 41–42.
20. (Maslow 1966) p. 45.
21. (Hayward 1904) pp. 24–25. See Appendix note 4.
22. (Krishnamurti 1970) p. 113.
23. (Bernstein 1996a) p. 55.
24. (Rousseau 1979) p. 83.
25. (Bernstein 1996a) p. 67.
26. (Bernstein 1996a) p. 55.
27. (Bernstein 1996a) p. 55.
28. (Bernstein 1996a) p. 55.
29. (Bernstein 1996a) p. 55.
30. (Froebel 1890) p. 329.
31. (Taylor 1989).
32. (Rousseau 1979) p. 41.
33. (Rousseau 1979) p. 205. See Appendix note 5.
34. e.g., (Rousseau 1979) p. 445. See Appendix note 6.
35. (Rousseau 1979) p. 194.
36. (Rousseau 1979) pp. 41–42. See Appendix note 7.
37. (Rousseau 1979) p. 201.
38. (Rousseau 1979) p. 92. See Appendix note 8.
39. (Rousseau 1979) p. 37. Jung quotes this statement as being typical of Rousseau as well as of the whole romantic movement. (Jung 1971c) p. 81 § 121.
40. (Rousseau 1979) p. 37. See Appendix note 9.
41. (Rousseau 1979) p. 383.
42. (Rousseau 1979) p. 83.
43. (Rousseau 1979) pp. 117–118. See Appendix note 10.
44. (Rousseau 1979) p. 79. See Appendix note 11.
45. (Rousseau 1979) pp. 82–83. See Appendix note 301.
46. (Rousseau 1979) p. 83.
47. (d'Entrevèves 1963).
48. (Rousseau 1979) pp. 313–314. See Appendix note 12.
49. (Rousseau 1979) p. 260. See Appendix note 13.
50. (Grimsley 1968) p. 69. See Appendix note 14.
51. (Rousseau 1979) p. 381. See Appendix note 15.
52. (Rousseau 1979) p. 38. See Appendix note 16.
53. (Rousseau 1790).
54. (Rousseau 1979) p. 126. See Appendix note 17.

[55] (Rousseau 1979) p. 118.

[56] (Rousseau 1979) p. 202.

[57] (Rousseau 1967) letter no.743; my translation only.

[58] (Rousseau 1979) p. 158.

[59] (Rousseau 1979) p. 165. See Appendix note 18.

[60] (Rousseau 1979) p. 107. See Appendix note 19.

[61] (Rousseau 1979) p. 158.

[62] (Rousseau 1979) p. 203.

[63] (Rousseau 1979) p. 168. See Appendix note 20.

[64] (Rousseau 1979) pp. 157–158.

[65] (Rousseau 1979) p. 203. See Appendix note 21.

[66] (Rousseau 1979) p. 166. See Appendix note 22.

[67] (Rousseau 1979) p. 52.

[68] (Rousseau 1979) p. 125. See Appendix note 23.

[69] (Rousseau 1979) p. 125.

[70] (Rousseau 1979) p. 112. See Appendix note 24.

[71] (Rousseau 1979) p. 168. See Appendix note 25.

[72] (Rousseau 1979) p. 157.

[73] (Rousseau 1979) p. 157.

[74] (Rousseau 1979) pp. 99–100. See Appendix note 26.

[75] (Rousseau 1979) pp. 109–110. See Appendix note 27.

[76] (Rousseau 1979) p. 248.

[77] (Rousseau 1979) p. 125.

[78] (Rousseau 1790) p. 295. See Appendix note 28.

[79] (Rousseau 1979) p. 92.

[80] (Rousseau 1979) p. 245. See Appendix note 29.

[81] (Rousseau 1979) p. 184.

[82] (Rousseau 1979) pp. 450–451. See Appendix note 30.

[83] (Rousseau 1979) p. 98. See Appendix note 31.

[84] (Rousseau 1979) p. 180. See Appendix note 32.

[85] (Rousseau 1979) p. 168. See Appendix note 33.

[86] (Rousseau 1979) p. 178.

[87] (Rousseau 1979) p. 323. See Appendix 34.

[88] (Rousseau 1979) p. 321. See Appendix note 35.

[89] (Rousseau 1979) pp. 168–169. See Appendix note 36.

[90] (Rousseau 1979) p. 78.

[91] (Rousseau 1979) p. 445. See Appendix note 37.

[92] (Rousseau 1979) p. 446. See Appendix note 38.

[93] (Grimsley 1969).

[94] (Rousseau 1979) p. 213.

[95] (Rousseau 1979) p. 213.

[96] (Rousseau 1979) p. 214.

[97] (Rousseau 1979) p. 235.

[98] (Rousseau 1979) p. 92.

[99] (Rousseau 1979) p. 244.

[100] (Rousseau 1979) pp. 212–213. See Appendix note 39.

[101] (Rousseau 1979) p. 212.

[102] (Rousseau 1979) p. 215.

[103] (Rousseau 1979) p. 214. See Appendix note 40.

[104] (Rousseau 1979) p. 212.

[105] (Rousseau 1979) p. 445. See Appendix note 41.

[106] (Rousseau 1979) p. 212.

[107] (Rousseau 1979) p. 219. See Appendix note 42.

[108] (Rousseau 1979) p. 444. See Appendix note 43.

[109] (Rousseau 1979) p. 444.

[110] (Rousseau 1979) p. 222. See Appendix note 44.

[111] (Rousseau 1979) pp. 222–223. See Appendix note 45.

[112] (Rousseau 1979) p. 226. See Appendix note 46.

[113] (Rousseau 1979) p. 451. See Appendix note 47.

[114] (Rousseau 1979) p. 108. See Appendix note 48.

[115] (Rousseau 1979) p. 119.

[116] (Rousseau 1979) p. 160.

[117] (Rousseau 1979) p. 126.

[118] (Rousseau 1979) p. 162.

[119] (Rousseau 1979) p. 171. See Appendix note 49.

[120] (Rousseau 1979) p. 161 & p. 169. See Appendix note 50.

[121] (Rousseau 1979) pp. 143–144. See Appendix note 51.

[122] (Rousseau 1979) p. 187.

[123] (Rousseau 1979) p. 232.

[124] (Rousseau 1979) p. 139.

[125] (Rousseau 1979) p. 444.

[126] (Rousseau 1979) p. 444.
[127] (Rousseau 1979) p. 241. See Appendix note 52.
[128] (Rousseau 1979) p. 339.
[129] (Rousseau 1979) p. 327.
[130] (Rousseau 1979) p. 242.
[131] (Rousseau 1979) p. 244.
[132] e.g., (Rousseau 1979) p. 335.
[133] (Rousseau 1979) p. 160. See Appendix note 53.
[134] (Rousseau 1979) p. 472.
[135] (Rousseau 1979) p. 120.
[136] (Rousseau 1979) p. 116.
[137] (Rousseau 1979) p. 172.
[138] (Rousseau 1979) p. 84. See Appendix note 54.
[139] (Rousseau 1979) pp. 472–473.
[140] (Rousseau 1979) p. 177.
[141] (Rousseau 1979) p. 432. See Appendix note 55.
[142] (Rousseau 1979) p. 92.
[143] (Rousseau 1979) p. 85.
[144] (Rousseau 1979) pp. 471–472.
[145] (Rousseau 1979) p 473.
[146] (Rousseau 1979) p. 425.
[147] (Rousseau 1979) p. 176.
[148] (Rousseau 1979) pp. 207 & 176. See Appendix note 56.
[149] (Rousseau 1979) p. 171. See Appendix note 57.
[150] (Rousseau 1979) p. 205.
[151] (Rousseau 1979) p. 207. See Appendix note 58.
[152] (Rousseau 1979) p. 205.
[153] (Rousseau 1979) p. 119.
[154] (Rousseau 1979) p. 119. See Appendix note 59.
[155] (Rousseau 1979) p. 418.
[156] (Rousseau 1979) p. 39.
[157] (Rousseau 1979) p. 92.
[158] (Rousseau 1979) p. 187.
[159] (Rousseau 1979) p. 249.
[160] (Rousseau 1979) p. 255.
[161] (Rousseau 1979) p. 205. See Appendix note 60.
[162] (Rousseau 1979) p. 39.
[163] (Rousseau 1979) p. 41. See Appendix note 61.
[164] (Rousseau 1979) p. 195. See Appendix note 62.
[165] (Boyd 1963) p. 236.
[166] (Rousseau 1979) p. 112.
[167] (Rousseau 1979) p. 473.
[168] (Rousseau 1979) p. 97. See Appendix note 63.
[169] (Rousseau 1979) pp. 244–245. See Appendix note 64.
[170] (Rousseau 1979) pp. 89–90. See Appendix note 65.
[171] (Rousseau 1979) p. 148.
[172] (Rousseau 1979) p. 148.
[173] (Rousseau 1979) p. 316. See Appendix note 66.
[174] (Rousseau 1979) p. 416.
[175] (Rousseau 1979) pp. 139–143.
[176] (Rousseau 1979) p. 442.
[177] (Rousseau 1979) p132.
[178] (Rousseau 1979) p178.
[179] (Rousseau 1979) p. 182.
[180] (Rousseau 1979) p. 328. See Appendix note 67.
[181] (Rousseau 1979) p. 350.
[182] (Rousseau 1979) pp. 33–34.
[183] (Rousseau 1979) p. 126.
[184] (Rousseau 1979) pp. 33–34. See Appendix note 68.
[185] (Rousseau 1979) p. 158.
[186] (Rousseau 1979) p. 79.
[187] (Rousseau 1979) p. 90.
[188] (Rousseau 1979) p. 182.
[189] (Rousseau 1979) p. 257. See Appendix note 69.
[190] (Rousseau 1979) p. 259.
[191] (Rousseau 1979) p. 257.
[192] (Rousseau 1979) p. 314.
[193] (Rousseau 1979) p. 212.
[194] (Rousseau 1979) p. 167.
[195] (Rousseau 1979) p. 92.
[196] (Rousseau 1979) p. 116.
[197] (Rousseau 1979) p. 178.
[198] (Rousseau 1979) p. 178. See Appendix note 70.
[199] (Rousseau 1979) p. 92.
[200] (Rousseau 1979) p. 179.
[201] (Rousseau 1979) p. 116. See Appendix note 71.
[202] (Rousseau 1979) p. 94. See Appendix note 72.
[203] (Rousseau 1979) p. 192.
[204] (Rousseau 1979) p. 179.
[205] (Rousseau 1979) p. 35. See Appendix note 73.
[206] (Rousseau 1979) p. 219. See Appendix note 74.
[207] (Rousseau 1979) p. 100.
[208] (Rousseau 1979) p. 115.

[209] (Rousseau 1979) p. 317.
[210] (Rousseau 1979) p. 107.
[211] (Rousseau 1979) p. 41.
[212] (Rousseau 1979) p. 119. See Appendix note 75.
[213] (Rousseau 1979) pp. 93–94. See Appendix note 76.
[214] (Rousseau 1979) p. 117. See Appendix note 77.
[215] (Rousseau 1979) p. 93. See Appendix note 78.
[216] (Rousseau 1979) p. 107.
[217] (Rousseau 1979) p. 104. See Appendix note 79.
[218] (Rousseau 1979) p. 104.
[219] (Rousseau 1790) pp. 295–296; my translation only.
[220] (Rousseau 1979) p. 206.
[221] (Rousseau 1979) p. 187.
[222] (Rousseau 1979) p. 101. See Appendix note 80.
[223] (Rousseau 1979) p. 85.
[224] (Rousseau 1979) pp. 86–87. See Appendix note 81.
[225] (Rousseau 1979) p. 120.
[226] (Rousseau 1979) p. 92.
[227] (Rousseau 1979) p. 185. See Appendix note 82.
[228] (Rousseau 1979) p. 167.
[229] (Rousseau 1979) p. 63.
[230] (Rousseau 1979) p. 323.
[231] e.g., (Rousseau 1979) p. 145. See Appendix note 83.
[232] (Rousseau 1979) p. 177.
[233] (Rousseau 1979) p. 111–112. See Appendix note 84.
[234] (Rousseau 1979) p. 97.
[235] (Rousseau 1979) p. 237. See Appendix note 85.
[236] (Rousseau 1979) p. 240.
[237] (Rousseau 1979) p. 250. See Appendix note 86.
[238] (Rousseau 1979) p. 231. See Appendix note 87.
[239] (Rousseau 1979) p. 223.
[240] (Rousseau 1979) p. 223. See Appendix note 308.
[241] (Rousseau 1979) p. 224.
[242] (Rousseau 1979) p. 224.
[243] (Rousseau 1979) p. 224.
[244] (Rousseau 1979) p. 205.
[245] (Rousseau 1979) p. 239.
[246] (Rousseau 1979) p. 187.

[247] (Rousseau 1979) p. 187.
[248] (Rousseau 1979) p. 241.
[249] (Rousseau 1979) p. 217.
[250] (Rousseau 1979) p. 327. See Appendix note 88.
[251] (Rousseau 1979) p. 327.
[252] (Rousseau 1979) p. 327.
[253] (Rousseau 1979) p. 327. See Appendix note 89.
[254] (Rousseau 1979) p. 149.
[255] (Rousseau 1979) p. 162.
[256] (Rousseau 1979) p. 162.
[257] (Rousseau 1979) p. 198.
[258] (Rousseau 1979) p. 162. See Appendix note 90.
[259] (Rousseau 1979) p. 199.
[260] (Rousseau 1979) p. 198.
[261] (Rousseau 1979) p. 189. See Appendix note 91.
[262] (Rousseau 1979) p. 94. See Appendix note 92.
[263] (Rousseau 1979) p. 170. See Appendix note 93.
[264] (Rousseau 1979) pp. 183–184. See Appendix note 94.
[265] (Rousseau 1979) p. 319. See Appendix note 95.
[266] (Rousseau 1979) p. 170.
[267] (Rousseau 1979) p. 319. See Appendix note 96.
[268] (Rousseau 1979) p. 217. See Appendix note 97.
[269] (Rousseau 1979) p. 96.
[270] (Rousseau 1979) p. 94.
[271] (Rousseau 1979) p. 325. See Appendix note 98.
[272] (Rousseau 1979) p. 172. See Appendix note 99.
[273] (Rousseau 1979) p. 344. See Appendix note 100.
[274] (Rousseau 1979) p. 248.
[275] (Rousseau 1979) p. 375.
[276] e.g., (Rousseau 1979) p. 202. See Appendix note 101.
[277] (Rousseau 1979) p. 184. See Appendix note 102.
[278] (Rousseau 1979) p. 172.
[279] (Rousseau 1979) footnote on p. 89. See Appendix note 103.
[280] (Rousseau 1979) p. 38.
[281] (Rousseau 1979) p. 38.
[282] (Rousseau 1979) p. 91. See Appendix note 104.

283 (Rousseau 1979) p. 91.
284 (Rousseau 1979) p. 91.
285 (Rousseau 1979) p. 91. See Appendix note 105.
286 (Rousseau 1979) p. 121.
287 (Rousseau 1979) p. 120. See Appendix note 106.
288 (Rousseau 1979) p. 316.
289 (Rousseau 1979) p. 316.
290 (Rousseau 1979) p. 216. See Appendix note 107.
291 (Rousseau 1979) p. 334. See Appendix note 108.
292 (Rousseau 1979) p. 246. See Appendix note 109.
293 (Rousseau 1979) pp. 246–247. See Appendix note 110.
294 (Rousseau 1979) p. 247.
295 (Rousseau 1979) p. 201.
296 (Rousseau 1979) p. 316.
297 (Rousseau 1979) p. 325.
298 (Rousseau 1979) p. 97.
299 (Rousseau 1979) p. 95.
300 (Rousseau 1979) p. 95. See Appendix note 111.
301 (Pestalozzi 1859b) p. 176. See Appendix note 112.
302 (Pestalozzi 1859b) p. 176. See Appendix note 112.
303 (Pestalozzi 1859a) p. 156.
304 (Pestalozzi 1907) p. 160. See Appendix note 113.
305 (Pestalozzi 1912b) p. 178.
306 (Pestalozzi 1912c) p. 271. See Appendix note 114.
307 (Pestalozzi 1859a) p. 156.
308 (Pestalozzi 1931e) p. 99.
309 (Hayward 1904) p. 37.
310 This may seem like a philosophical contradiction, but it is increasingly examined in some literature concerned with states of consciousness and mind, e.g., (Claxton 1998). Non-conceptual insight or understanding (*Prajna*) has been part of the Buddhist tradition for more than two thousand years.
311 From (Green 1912) p. 189. See Appendix note 115.
312 (Pestalozzi 1907) pp. 202–203. See Appendix note 116.
313 e.g., (Heafford 1967) p. 60. See Appendix note 117.
314 e.g., (Biber 1859) p. 176. See Appendix note 118.
315 From (Anderson 1931) p. 127.
316 From (Heafford 1967) pp. 47–48. See Appendix note 119.
317 (Pestalozzi 1827a) p. 7. See Appendix note 120.
318 From (Green 1912) p. 281.
319 (Pestalozzi 1912c) pp. 268–269. See Appendix note 121.
320 (Hayward 1904) p. 39.
321 (Pestalozzi 1907) p. 200.
322 (Anderson 1931) p. 7.
323 (Diesterweg) p. 25.
324 From (Green 1912) p. 290.
325 From (Heafford 1967) p. 40.
326 From (Anderson 1931) p. 200. See Appendix note 122.
327 (Pestalozzi 1827c) p. 87.
328 (Pestalozzi 1907) p. 173. See Appendix note 123.
329 From (Green 1912) p. 293. See Appendix note 124.
330 From (Green 1912) p. 290. See Appendix note 125.
331 (Pestalozzi 1827h) p. 147.
332 (Pestalozzi 1859b) p. 177.
333 (Pestalozzi 1859a) p. 158.
334 From (Raumer 1859) p. 60.
335 (Pestalozzi 1827d) p. 95.
336 (Pestalozzi 1907) p. 157.
337 (Pestalozzi 1827f) p. 123. See Appendix note 126.
338 (Russell 1926) p. 17. See Appendix note 127.
339 From (Raumer 1859) p. 60. Raumer worked with Pestalozzi, and he translated this excerpt from Pestalozzi's first book, The Evening Hour of a Hermit published 1781.
340 (Pestalozzi 1827f) pp. 195–197. See Appendix note 128.
341 (Pestalozzi 1907) p. 58. See Appendix note 129.
342 (Pestalozzi 1827f) p. 195. See Appendix note 130.
343 (Russell 1926) p. 100. See Appendix note 131.
344 (Pestalozzi 1931d) p. 133.
345 (Pestalozzi, 1907) pp. 18–19. See Appendix note 132.
346 From (Green 1912) p. 315.
347 (Green 1912) p. 284. See Appendix note

133.

[348] (Pestalozzi 1859a) p. 156. See Appendix note 134.

[349] (Pestalozzi 1907) pp. 156–157. See Appendix note 135.

[350] From (Heafford 1967) p. 81.

[351] (Pestalozzi 1907) p. 157.

[352] (Pestalozzi 1827c) p. 85. See Appendix note 136.

[353] (Pestalozzi 1827f) p. 195. See Appendix note 130.

[354] (Pestalozzi 1859a) p. 157.

[355] From (Anderson 1931) p. 211. See Appendix note 137.

[356] (Pestalozzi 1912a) p. 157.

[357] (Pestalozzi 1931b) pp. 209–210.

[358] (Pestalozzi 1931c) pp. 212–213.

[359] From (Russell 1926) p. 20.

[360] (Goleman 1995) pp. 80–83.

[361] (Pestalozzi 1827b) pp. 66–67.

[362] (Diesterweg 1859) p. 27.

[363] From (Russell 1926) p. 2.

[364] From (Jung 1954k) footnote on p. 106.

[365] (Pestalozzi 1907) p. 26.

[366] e.g. (Pestalozzi 1907) p. 32.

[367] (Pestalozzi 1859a) p. 157. See Appendix note 138.

[368] (Pestalozzi 1859a) p. 157.

[369] (Pestalozzi 1907) p. 50–51.

[370] From (Green 1912) p. 312. See Appendix note 139.

[371] (Furst and Skrine 1971).

[372] (Furst and Skrine 1971) p. 3.

[373] From (Green 1912) p. 267.

[374] e.g. (Pestalozzi 1827f).

[375] (Pestalozzi 1907) p. 199.

[376] (Pestalozzi 1907) pp. 202–203. See Appendix note 140.

[377] (A Foreigner 1823) p. 38.

[378] (A Foreigner 1823) pp. 6–7.

[379] (Pestalozzi 1827g) p. 130. See Appendix note 141.

[380] (Pestalozzi 1827g).

[381] From (Green 1912) p. 253.

[382] (Pestalozzi 1931a) p. 39.

[383] (Pestalozzi 1931a) pp. 39–40. See Appendix note 142.

[384] (Pestalozzi 1907) pp. 159–160. See Appendix note 143.

[385] (Pestalozzi 1931a) p. 37. See Appendix note 144.

[386] (Pestalozzi 1907) pp. 6–7.

[387] From (Heafford 1967) p. 47.

[388] (Paterson 1914).

[389] (Barnard 1859).

[390] (Anderson 1931) p. 6.

[391] (Rousseau 1979) p. 254. See Appendix note 145.

[392] (Pestalozzi 1859a) p. 155 & (Pestalozzi 1818) pp. 3–4. See Appendix note 146.

[393] (Pestalozzi 1931d) pp. 131–132. See Appendix note 147.

[394] (Pestalozzi 1907) p. 156.

[395] (Pestalozzi 1907) p. 202. See Appendix note 140.

[396] From (Green 1912) p. 319.

[397] From (Green 1912) p. 289.

[398] (Pestalozzi 1931d) pp. 127–128. See Appendix note 148.

[399] From (Green 1912) p. 289.

[400] (Ullich 1935; Woodham-Smith 1952a).

[401] (Pestalozzi 1907) p. 17.

[402] From (Green 1912) p. 319.

[403] From (Green 1912) p. 320.

[404] (Pestalozzi 1827b) p. 65.

[405] (Pestalozzi 1827b) p. 65.

[406] (Pestalozzi 1859a) p. 157.

[407] (Pestalozzi 1907) p. 191. See Appendix note 149.

[408] (Pestalozzi 1827g).

[409] (Rousseau 1979) p. 248.

[410] (Pestalozzi 1827e) p. 125.

[411] (Woodham-Smith 1952b) p. 23.

[412] (Pestalozzi 1931d) p. 127.

[413] (Pestalozzi 1827b) p. 66.

[414] (Pestalozzi 1907) p. 196. See Appendix note 150.

[415] (Froebel 1890) p. 332. See Appendix note 151.

[416] From (Lawrence 1952) p. 188.

[417] (Froebel 1890) p. 19 .

[418] (Froebel 1890) p. 332. See Appendix note 151.

[419] (Lawrence 1952) p. 190. See Appendix note 152.

[420] (Froebel 1890) p. 120.

[421] (Priestman 1952) p. 157. See Appendix note 153.

[422] (Lawrence 1952) p. 191.

[423] (Froebel 1890) p. 8.

[424] (Froebel 1890) pp. 8–9. See Appendix note 154.

[425] From (Lawrence 1952) p. 188.

[426] From (Murray 1914) p. 14.

[427] From (Murray 1914) p. 14.

428 From (Murray 1914) pp. 15–16. See Appendix note 155.

429 (Froebel) p. 19.

430 (Lawrence 1952) p. 188. See Appendix note 156.

431 (Hayward 1904) p. 29. See Appendix note 157.

432 (Hamilton 1952) p. 166.

433 (Froebel 1890) p. 237. See Appendix note 158.

434 (Froebel 1890) p. 231.

435 (Froebel 1890) p. 279.

436 (Rousseau 1979) pp. 42–44.

437 (Froebel 1890) p. 21.

438 (Froebel 1890) pp. 54–55. See Appendix note 159.

439 (Hamilton 1952) p. 174.

440 (Froebel 1890) p. 8.

441 From (Murray 1914) pp. 6–7.

442 From (Murray 1914) p. 3.

443 (Froebel 1890) p. 28. See Appendix note 160.

444 (Froebel 1890) p. 7.

445 (Froebel 1890) p. 137. See Appendix note 305.

446 (Froebel 1890) p. 9.

447 (Froebel 1890) p. 21. See Appendix note 161.

448 (Froebel 1890) p. 328. See Appendix note 162.

449 (Froebel 1890) pp. 54–55.

450 (Hamilton 1952) p. 175.

451 (Browning 1987) p. 8. See Appendix note 163.

452 (Jung 1959d) p. 314 § 557.

453 (Jung 1959b) p. 288 § 522–523. See Appendix note 302.

454 (Jung 1954c) p. 171 § 289. See Appendix note 164.

455 (Jung 1958b) pp. 554–555 § 905. See Appendix note 165.

456 (Jung 1958b) p. 545 § 890. See Appendix note 166.

457 (Jung 1954c) p. 172 § 291. See Appendix note 167.

458 (Jung 1953a) p. 70.

459 (Sands 1961) & (Jung 1957) p. 4. See Appendix note 168.

460 (Jung 1958e) p. 344 § 531. See Appendix note 169.

461 (Jung 1958e) p. 334 § 509 & (Jung 1958e) p. 331 § 497. See Appendix note 170.

462 (Jung 1954c) p. 183 § 314. See Appendix note 171.

463 (Jung 1958e) pp. 330–331 § 496–497. See Appendix note 172.

464 (Jung 1954h) p. 160 § 352. See Appendix note 173.

465 (Smith 1990) p. 89. See Appendix note 174.

466 (Jung 1977g) p. 655 § 1485.

467 (Jung 1971b) p. 212 § 355.

468 (Jung 1954c) p. 167 § 284.

469 (Jung 1958b) p. 556 § 906. See Appendix note 175.

470 (Jung 1954c) pp. 175–177 § 299–302.

471 (Jung 1954b) p. 62 § 125.

472 (Jung 1959c) pp. 164–165 §278. See Appendix note 176.

473 (Jung 1964b) pp. 74–75 § 149–150.

474 e.g. (Ergardt 1983).

475 (Jung 1959d) pp. 322–323 §567.

476 (Browning 1987) p. 5. See Appendix note 177.

477 (Jung 1954c) p. 186 § 323.

478 (Heisig 1979) p. 78n. See Appendix note 178.

479 (Jung 1964b) p. 83 § 168. See Appendix note 179.

480 e.g., (White 1952), (White 1960) & (Ergardt 1983).

481 (Coward 1985).

482 Jung sums up all of his past comments on this in (Jung 1959a).

483 (Jung 1958d) pp. 8–9 § 9–10. See Appendix note 180.

484 The Dominican Friar, Victor White claimed, "While it is difficult to divest Freud of the professor's gown, it is quite impossible to divest Jung of his surplice." (White 1952) p. 71.

485 (Noll 1996) pp. 41–42.

486 (Ellenberger 1970).

487 from (Heisig 1979) p. 94.

488 (Jung 1958a) p. 363 § 558. See Appendix note 181.

489 (Jung 1963) p. 538 § 768. He worked on this manuscript from 1941 to 1954.

490 e.g., (Bohm 1980).

491 (Noll 1996).

492 e.g., (von Franz 1975).

493 (Jung 1959b) p. 288 §522–523.

494 (Jung 1960f).

495 (Jung 1959b) p. 289 §524.

496 (Jung 1977g) p. 655 § 1485.

497 (Jung 1959c) pp. 164–165 § 278. See Appendix note 176.

498 (Jung 1953b) p. 236 § 399.

499 (Jung 1964a) p. 463 §873.

500 (Jung 1964a) p. 463 §874. See Appendix note 182.

501 (Jung 1963) p. 546 § 778.

502 (Jung 1963) p. 547 § 779. See Appendix note 183.

503 (Jung 1958c) p. 490 § 782 & (Jung 1959b) pp. 287–288 §520. See Appendix note 184.

504 (Jung 1963) p. 546 § 778.

505 (von Franz 1975) pp. 13–14. See Appendix note 185.

506 (von Franz 1975) pp. 116–117. See Appendix note 186.

507 Jung's claims of acting only as a scientist have been criticised, e.g.; (Browning 1987) p. 164. See Appendix note 187.

508 (Heisig 1979) pp. 89–90.

509 (Jung 1958e) p. 330 § 496. See Appendix note 188.

510 For a summary Jung's frequent comments on this see (Jung 1958c) pp. 477–480 § 763–768.

511 e.g., (Jung 1958a) pp. 359–361§ 553–555. See Appendix note 189.

512 (Jung 1963) p. 534 § 760.

513 (Jung 1963) pp. 533–540 § 760–771.

514 (Jung 1958e) pp. 552–553 § 788.

515 (Jung 1958e) p. 553 § 789.

516 (Noll 1996) p. 6.

517 e.g, (Noll 1996) & (Browning 1987).

518 (Jung 1954c) pp. 175–179 §299–305.

519 (Jung 1958b) p. 556 § 906.

520 (Jung 1964b) pp. 83–84 § 170.

521 (Jung 1964b) pp. 83–84 § 171. See Appendix note 190.

522 (Jung 1958e) p. 347 § 538.

523 (Jung 1954a; Jung 1954b; Jung 1954e; Jung 1954l).

524 (Jung 1954a) p. 131 § 228.

525 (Jung 1960d) p. 390 § 753.

526 (Jung 1967) p. 92 § 122.

527 (von Franz 1975) p. 236.

528 (Jung 1963) p. 538 § 768. See Appendix note 191.

529 (von Franz 1975) p. 247.

530 (Jung 1960e) p. 493 § 931.

531 (Jung 1960e) p. 481 § 912.

532 (Jung 1960e) p. 489 § 923. See Appendix note 192.

533 (Jung 1953a) pp. 65–66 § 104.

534 (Jung 1959d) p. 315 § 619.

535 (Jung 1958d) pp. 104–105 § 167. See Appendix note 193.

536 (Jung 1963) p. 545 § 777.

537 (Jung 1954a) pp. 99–100 § 183.

538 (Jung 1954a) pp. 106–107 § 198. See Appendix note 194.

539 (Jung 1954a) pp. 106–107 § 198.

540 (Jung 1960a) pp. 380–381 § 739. See Appendix note 195.

541 (Jung 1960a) pp. 380–381 § 739.

542 (Jung 1958e) pp. 331–332 § 500–501. See Appendix note 196.

543 (Jung 1977e) p. 821 § 1820.

544 (Jung 1954j) p. 279 § 492.

545 (Jung 1964a) p. 456 § 858.

546 (Jung 1977i) p. 625 § 1428.

547 (Jung 1959a) p. 25 § 48.

548 (Jung 1958c) p. 476 § 760.

549 (Jung 1977h) p. 664 § 1504.

550 (Jung 1959a) pp. 31–33 § 60–61. See Appendix note 197.

551 (Jung 1959d) p. 313 § 555.

552 (Jung 1958c) pp. 477–478 § 763.

553 (Jung 1959d) p. 313 § 555.

554 (Jung 1958e) p. 343 §529. See Appendix note 198.

555 (Jung 1958c) p. 480 § 768. See Appendix note 199.

556 (Jung 1964d) p. 249 § 491.

557 (Jung 1977d) p. 817 § 1813.

558 (Jung 1959a) p. 28 § 53.

559 (Jung 1977c) p. 611 § 1398.

560 (Jung 1959c) pp. 168–169 § 287.

561 (Jung 1953b) p. 227 § 380. See Appendix note 200.

562 (Jung 1971b) p. 213 § 357.

563 (Rousseau 1979) p. 472. See Appendix note 201.

564 (Jung 1958d) pp. 86–87 § 143.

565 From (Jung 1954k) footnote on p. 108.

566 (Jung 1977a) p. 452 § 1098.

567 (Jung 1977a) p. 451 § 1095. See Appendix note 202.

568 (Jung 1977a) p. 451–452 § 1096.

569 (Jung 1971c) pp. 87–88 § 134.

570 (Jung 1959d) p. 349 § 617.

571 (Jung 1977b) p. 605 § 1386.

572 (Jung 1977b) p. 605 § 1387.

573 (Jung 1954k) p. 106 § 224.

574 (Jung 1959d) p. 349 § 618. See Appendix note 203.

575 (Jung 1954k) p. 108 § 227. See Appendix note 204.

576 (Jung 1954l) p. 149 § 253.

577 (Jung 1954l) p. 150 § 254.

578 (Jung 1954l) p. 151 § 256.

579 (Jung 1954c) p. 174 § 296. See Appendix note 205.

580 (Jung 1954l) p. 151 § 257.

581 (Jung 1954b) p. 52 § 104. See Appendix note 206.

582 (Jung 1954b) p. 54 § 107.

583 (Jung 1954a) p. 119 § 211.

584 (Jung 1954b) p. 50 § 99. See Appendix note 207.

585 (Jung 1954f) p. 42 § 84. See Appendix note 208.

586 (Jung 1954a) p. 78–79 § 154. See Appendix note 209.

587 (Jung 1954g) p. 191 § 328. See Appendix notes 210 and 211.

588 (Jung 1964c) pp. 486–487 § 921.

589 (Jung 1954b) p. 55–56 § 107. See Appendix note 212.

590 (Jung 1959c) pp. 168–169 § 287.

591 (Jung 1959c) pp. 168–169 § 287.

592 (Jung 1954c) p. 169 § 286. See Appendix note 213.

593 (Jung 1954c) p. 169 § 286. See Appendix note 214 and 215.

594 (Jung 1954c) p. 171 § 288.

595 (Jung 1959d) p. 351 § 621.

596 (Jung 1958f) p. 534 § 868. See Appendix note 216.

597 (Jung 1958f) p. 534 § 868.

598 (Jung 1954b) pp. 55–56 § 107.

599 (Jung 1954e) p. 144 § 250.

600 (Jung 1954e) p. 140 § 242. See Appendix note 217.

601 (Jung 1958c) pp. 481–482 § 770–771. See Appendix note 307.

602 (Jung 1960b) p. 60 § 112.

603 (Jung 1959c) pp. 170 171 § 289. See Appendix note 218.

604 (Jung 1971b) pp. 212–213 § 356.

605 (Jung 1954c) p. 173 § 293.

606 (Jung 1964d) p. 250 § 495.

607 (Jung 1954a) p. 93 § 173. See Appendix note 219.

608 (Jung 1954c) p. 179 § 307.

609 (Jung 1954b) p. 55–56 § 107. See Appendix note 212.

610 (Jung 1954b) p. 55–56 § 107.

611 (Jung 1954b) p. 55–56 § 107.

612 (Jung 1954b) p. 55–56 § 107.

613 (Jung 1954b) p. 55–56 § 107.

614 e.g., (Smith 1990).

615 (Jung 1960c).

616 (Wickes 1977).

617 (Noll 1996) p. 282.

618 (Sells 1994).

619 (Sells 1994) p. 3.

620 (Noll 1996) p. 282.

621 (Jung 1958b) p. 554 § 904.

622 (Jung 1958e) p. 346 § 537.

623 (Jung 1958e) p. 347 § 537.

624 (Jung 1958e) pp. 338–339 §519.

625 (Jung 1958e) pp. 338–339 §519.

626 (Jung 1954e) p. 144 § 249.

627 (Jung 1958e) pp. 339–340 §521.

628 (Jung 1954d) p116 § 239.

629 (Jung 1977d) p. 817 § 1813.

630 (Jung 1954b) p. 57 § 109.

631 (Jung 1954i) p. 75 § 174.

632 (Jung 1954b) p. 58 § 110.

633 (Jung 1977f) p. 822 § 1824.

634 (Jung 1954e) p. 140 § 240. See Appendix note 220.

635 (Jung 1954a) pp. 119–120 § 211.

636 (Jung 1954a) pp. 119–120 § 211. See Appendix note 221.

637 (Jung 1954a) p. 132 § 229.

638 (Jung 1954a) pp. 131–132 § 228.

639 (Jung 1954b) p. 57 § 108.

640 (Jung 1958e) pp. 339–340 § 521.

641 (Jung 1977c) pp. 610–611 § 1396.

642 (Jung 1958e) pp. 339–340 § 521.

643 (Thorsen 1983) p. 20. See Appendix note 222.

644 (Wilson 1972) p. 15.

645 See the appendices of (Maslow 1968; Maslow 1993; Maslow 1994). For a short form of such a list of the characteristics of self-actualised people see Appendix note 223.

646 (Geiger 1993) pp. xvi–xvii. See Appendix note 224.

647 (Maslow 1996e) p. 117. See Appendix note 225.

648 (Wilson 1972) p. 189.

649 e.g., (Maslow 1993) p. xvi.

650 (Maslow 1993) p. 126.

651 (Maslow 1959b) p. 130. See Appendix note 226.

652 (Maslow 1959b) pp. 125–126. See Ap-

pendix note 227.

[653] e.g., (Maslow 1993) p. xvi.

[654] For example, (Maslow 1968) p. vi. See Appendix note 228.

[655] (Geiger 1993) p. xvii.

[656] (Maslow 1994) p. 64.

[657] (Maslow 1994) p. 64.

[658] (Maslow 1994) footnote p. 37.

[659] (Maslow 1994) pp. 36–37. See Appendix note 229.

[660] (Maslow 1996a) pp. 36–37.

[661] From (Wilson 1972) pp. 15–16. See Appendix note 230.

[662] (Maslow 1993) p. 111.

[663] (Maslow 1993) pp. 59–60. See Appendix note 231.

[664] (Maslow 1994) p. viii. See Appendix note 232.

[665] These terms had previously been used by Jung (Jung 1971a) and Jung gives credit to Nietzsche their coinage.

[666] (Maslow 1994) p. viii. See Appendix note 303.

[667] (Maslow 1993) p. 88. See Appendix note 233.

[668] (Browning 1987) p. 81. See Appendix note 234.

[669] (Maslow 1993) p. 66.

[670] (Maslow 1993) p. 111.

[671] (Maslow 1968) p. 83.

[672] (Maslow 1968) pp. 88–89.

[673] (Maslow 1966) p. 69. See Appendix note 235.

[674] (Maslow 1966) p. 45. See Appendix note 236.

[675] (Maslow 1966) p. 58.

[676] (Maslow 1966) p. 58.

[677] (Maslow 1966) p. xiii.

[678] (Maslow 1966) p. 9. See Appendix note 237.

[679] (Maslow 1966) p. 11. See Appendix note 238.

[680] (Maslow 1966) p. 54.

[681] (Maslow 1994) p. 11.

[682] (Maslow 1966) p. 46. See Appendix note 239.

[683] (Maslow 1966) p. 48. See Appendix note 240.

[684] (Maslow 1994) pp. xi–xii.

[685] (Maslow 1993) pp. 49–50.

[686] (Maslow 1959a) p. 309.

[687] (De Carvalho 1991) pp. 101–102. See Appendix note 241.

[688] (Maslow 1993; Maslow 1994).

[689] (Maslow 1993) pp. 49–50.

[690] (Maslow 1959a) p. 310.

[691] (Maslow 1993) pp. 94–95. See Appendix note 242.

[692] (Maslow 1993) p. 79.

[693] (Maslow 1993) p. 173. See Appendix note 243.

[694] (Maslow 1993) p. 173.

[695] (De Carvalho 1991) p. 104. See Appendix note 244.

[696] (Maslow 1966) p. 70.

[697] (Maslow 1966) p. 67.

[698] (Maslow 1966) p. 66.

[699] (Maslow 1994) p. ix. See Appendix note 245.

[700] (Maslow 1966) pp. 62–63. See Appendix note 246.

[701] (Maslow 1966) p. 64.

[702] (Maslow 1959a) pp. 306–307. See Appendix note 247.

[703] (Maslow 1959a) p. 307.

[704] (De Carvalho 1991) pp. 100–101. See Appendix note 248.

[705] (Maslow 1993) p. 176.

[706] (Maslow 1993) p. 176.

[707] (Maslow 1993) p. 177.

[708] (Maslow 1968) p. 7.

[709] (Maslow 1966) pp. 53–54.

[710] (Maslow 1993) p. 103.

[711] (Maslow 1966) p. 52.

[712] (Maslow 1966) p. 112. See Appendix note 249.

[713] (Maslow 1966) p. 51.

[714] (Maslow 1968) pp. 74–75. See Appendix note 250.

[715] (Maslow 1968) pp. 88–89. See Appendix note 251.

[716] (Maslow 1993) p. 160.

[717] (Maslow 1993) p. 160.

[718] (Maslow 1993) p. 118.

[719] (Maslow 1993) p. 118.

[720] (Maslow 1993) pp. 106–107. See Appendix note 252.

[721] (Maslow 1966) p. 101. See Appendix note 253.

[722] (Wilson 1972) p. 165.

[723] (Maslow 1966) p. 84. See Appendix note 254.

[724] (Thorsen 1983) p. 63. See Appendix note 255.

[725] (Maslow 1966) p. 10.

[726] (Maslow 1966) p. 59.

727 (Maslow 1994) p. 91. See Appendix note 256.

728 (Maslow 1993) pp. 187–188. See Appendix note 257.

729 From (Thorsen 1983) p. 14.

730 (Maslow 1959a) p. viii.

731 (Maslow 1959b) pp. 119–120. See Appendix note 258.

732 (Maslow 1994) p. 12. See Appendix note 259.

733 From (Thorsen 1983) p. 14.

734 (Maslow 1993) p. 177. See Appendix note 260.

735 (Maslow 1993) p. 178. See Appendix note 261.

736 (Maslow 1959b) p. 120 & (Maslow 1968) pp. 150–151. See Appendix note 262.

737 (Maslow 1968) pp. 168–170. See Appendix note 263.

738 (Maslow 1966) p. 48. See Appendix note 264.

739 (Maslow 1966) p. 48.

740 (Maslow 1993) pp. 149–150. See Appendix note 265.

741 (Maslow 1994) p. xii. See Appendix note 266.

742 (Wilson 1972) pp. 188–189. See Appendix note 267.

743 (Maslow 1968) p. 182.

744 (Maslow 1996b) pp. 31–32. See Appendix note 268.

745 (Maslow 1993) p. 180.

746 (Miller 1992) pp. 81–94.

747 (Maslow 1968) p. 57.

748 (Maslow 1968) p. 57.

749 (Maslow 1968) pp. 57–58.

750 (De Carvalho 1991) p. 3.

751 (Maslow 1993) p. 55.

752 (Maslow 1968) p. 45. See Appendix note 269.

753 (Maslow 1996b) p. 27.

754 (Maslow 1968) pp. 55–56.

755 (Maslow 1968) p. 25. See Appendix note 270.

756 (Maslow 1993) p. 337.

757 (Maslow 1968) p. 167. See Appendix note 271.

758 (Maslow 1996c) p. 71.

759 (Maslow 1993) p. 289.

760 (Maslow 1996b) p. 27.

761 (Maslow 1959b) p. 131.

762 (Maslow 1968) p. 4.

763 (Maslow 1993) p. 162. See Appendix note 272.

764 (Maslow 1994) p. 89.

765 (Maslow 1993) p. 182.

766 (Maslow 1993) p. 50.

767 (Maslow 1993) p. 181.

768 (Maslow 1968) pp. 53–54.

769 (Maslow 1968) p. 53.

770 (Maslow 1993) p. 182.

771 (Maslow 1968) p. 54.

772 (Maslow 1968) p. 53.

773 (Maslow 1968) p. 53.

774 (Maslow 1996d) p. 45.

775 (Maslow 1994) p. 89.

776 (Maslow 1993) p. 95.

777 (Maslow 1993) p. 96.

778 (Rousseau 1979) p. 323.

779 (Maslow 1994) pp. 84–85.

780 (Rogers 1983) p. 121. See Appendix note 273.

781 (Rogers and Stevens 1973) p. 89.

782 (Maslow 1994) pp. 16–17.

783 (Maslow 1993) p. xv.

784 For a list of such acknowledgements and instances of their referring to each others work see (De Carvalho 1991) p. 15.

785 (Rogers 1983) p. 290. See Appendix note 274.

786 (Rogers 1983) p. 39.

787 (De Carvalho 1991) p. 78.

788 (Maslow 1959a) p. viii.

789 (Rogers 1990a) p. 369.

790 (Walker 1956) p. 89. See Appendix note 275.

791 (Rogers 1990b) p. 402.

792 (Rogers 1990a) p. 368.

793 (Rogers 1990a) p. 369. See Appendix note 304.

794 (Rogers 1990a) p. 369.

795 (Rogers 1983) pp. 295–296. See Appendix note 276.

796 (Rogers 1990c) p. 284. See Appendix note 306.

797 (Rogers 1961) p. 281.

798 (Rogers and Freiberg 1994) p. 35.

799 (Rogers and Freiberg 1994) p. 35.

800 (Rogers and Freiberg 1994) p. 37.

801 (Rogers and Freiberg 1994) p. 296.

802 (Rogers and Freiberg 1994) p. 296.

803 (Rogers 1983) p. 276.

804 (Rogers and Freiberg 1994) p. 304.

805 (Rogers and Freiberg 1994) p. 304.

806 (Rogers and Stevens 1973) pp. 47–48. See Appendix note 277.

807 (Rogers 1983) p. 283.

808 (Rogers and Stevens 1973) p. 56. See Appendix note 278.

809 (Rogers 1983) p. 120.

810 (Langer 1989).

811 (Rogers 1990c) p. 270.

812 (Rogers 1990c) p. 270.

813 (Rogers 1990c) pp. 271–272.

814 (Rogers 1990c) p. 272.

815 (Rogers 1983) p. 264.

816 (De Carvalho 1991) p. 90.

817 (Rogers 1983) pp. 264–265.

818 (Rogers 1983) p. 268. See Appendix note 279.

819 (Rogers and Freiberg 1994) pp. 288–291. See Appendix note 280.

820 (Rogers 1961) pp. 115–119. See Appendix note 281.

821 (Rogers 1961) pp. 115–119.

822 (Rogers 1983) p. 18. See Appendix note 282.

823 (Rogers 1961) p. 280.

824 (Rogers 1983) p. 20. See Appendix note 283.

825 (Rogers 1983) p. 20.

826 (Rogers 1961) p. 276.

827 (Boutin 1976) pp. 18–20; my translation only.

828 (Rogers 1983) p. 133.

829 (Rogers 1983) pp. 135–136. See Appendix note 284.

830 (Rogers 1983) p. 18.

831 (Rogers and Freiberg 1994) p. 213.

832 (Rogers and Freiberg 1994) p. 213.

833 (Rogers 1983) p. 148.

834 (Rogers 1961) p. 290.

835 (Rogers and Freiberg 1994) p. 213.

836 (Rogers 1961) p. 277.

837 (Rogers 1983) p. 142.

838 (Rogers 1983) p. 95.

839 (Rogers 1983) p. 95.

840 (Rogers and Freiberg 1994) p. 156.

841 From (Anderson and Cissna 1997) p. 94.

842 From (Anderson and Cissna 1997) p. 94.

843 (Rogers 1961) p. 282.

844 (Rogers 1961) p. 33.

845 (Rogers 1983) p. 122.

846 (Rogers 1961) p. 282.

847 (Rogers 1983) p. 124.

848 (Rogers 1961) p. 32.

849 (Rogers 1961) p. 33.

850 (Rogers and Stevens 1973) p. 55.

851 (Rogers 1961) pp. 37–38.

852 (Anderson and Cissna 1997).

853 (Baldwin, Kalhorn, and Breese 1945).

854 (Rogers 1983) p. 81 & (Freire 1995a) p. 61.

855 (Rogers 1983) p. 124.

856 (Rogers 1983) p. 127.

857 (Rogers 1961) p. 56.

858 (Wittgenstein 1953) p. 32 § 66–67.

859 (Bernstein 1996a).

860 (Bernstein 1996a) p. 55.

861 (Bernstein 1996a) p. 67. See Appendix note 285.

862 (Bernstein 1996a) p. 55.

863 (Bernstein 1996a) p. 57.

864 From (Russell 1926) p. 18.

865 (Bernstein 1996a) p. 56.

866 (Eysenck 1964).

867 (Kaplan 1980).

868 (Hirschi and Hindelang 1977).

869 (Jennings, Kilkenny, and Kohlberg 1983; Smetana 1990).

870 (Freedman et al. 1978; Spence 1981).

871 (Dodge 1986).

872 (Bernstein 1996a) p. 56.

873 See Appendix note 286.

874 (Krishnamurti 1953; Krishnamurti 1974; Krishnamurti 1994).

875 See Appendix note 287.

876 (Mitchell 1994).

877 (Bohm 1993).

878 (Bernstein 1996a) p. 56.

879 See Appendix note 288.

880 (Bernstein 1996a) p. 56.

881 Abbeydale Grange School in Sheffield, and Akland Burley School in Tuffnal Park, North London.

882 See Appendix note 289.

883 (Bernstein 1996a) p. 63.

884 (Luvmour and Luvmour 1997).

885 (Bernstein 1996a) p. 56.

886 (Wexler 1997) p. 76.

887 See Appendix note 290.

888 (Bernstein 1996a) p. 56. See Appendix 291.

889 (Bernstein 1996a) p. 56. See Appendix 291.

890 (Freire 1995a; Friere 1995b).

891 e.g., (Hooks 1994).

892 (Bernstein 1996a) p. 58. See Appendix

note 292.

893 (Bernstein 1996a) pp. 58–59. See Appendix note 293.

894 (Bernstein 1996a) p. 62.

895 See Appendix note 294.

896 (Bernstein 1996a) p. 59.

897 (Bernstein 1996a) p. 59.

898 e.g., The City and Country School in New York, see (City 1997).

899 See Appendix note 295.

900 (Bernstein 1996a) p. 59.

901 (Krishnamurti 1962)

902 e.g., (Burman 1994; Morss 1992).

903 (Bernstein 1996a) p. 61.

904 (Nunes, Schliemann, and Carraher 1993).

905 (Bernstein 1996a) p. 61.

906 e.g., (Luvmour and Luvmour 1997).

907 (Bernstein 1997).

908 See Appendix note 296.

909 (Bernstein 1996a) pp. 59–60.

910 (Bernstein 1996a) p. 60.

911 (Bernstein 1996a) p. 60.

912 (Bernstein 1996a) p. 60.

913 See Appendix note 298.

914 (Bernstein 1996a) p. 60.

915 See Appendix note 297.

916 (Bernstein 1996a) p. 61.

917 (Bernstein 1996a) p. 61.

918 (Bernstein 1996a) p. 62.

919 (Bernstein 1996a) pp. 62–63.

920 (Senge 1990).

921 (Bernstein 1996a) p. 64. See Appendix note 299.

922 (Bernstein 1996a) p. 64.

923 See Appendix note 300.

924 (Duveen and Lloyd 1990).

925 (Huxley 1946).

926 (Campbell 1949).

927 (Bohm 1980; Bohm 1994).

928 (Bernstein 1996a) p. 64.

929 e.g., *Dances with Wolves,* (Carter 1976), (Elk 1988), (Liedloff 1989) etc.

930 e.g., (Cajete 1994), (Egan 1989), etc.

931 (Wexler 1997) p. 88.

932 (Hanson 1995).

933 (Bernstein 1996a) p. 65.

934 e.g., (Sugarman 1986).

935 (Grotberg 1995).

936 (Bernstein 1996a) p. 67.

937 (Bernstein 1996a) p. 71.

938 (Bernstein 1996a) p. 68.

939 (Coupland and Nussbaum 1993) p. xxi.

940 (Bernstein 1996a) p. 76.

941 (Goffman 1997) p. 35.

942 (Bernstein 1996a).

943 (Bernstein 1996b).

944 (Bernstein 1996a) p. 76.

945 (Bernstein 1996a) p. 78.

946 (Wexler 1997) p. 113.

947 (Bernstein 1996a) p. 78.

948 (Langer 1989; Langer 1997; Nunn 1996).

949 (Bernstein 1996a) p. 77.

950 (Bernstein 1996a) p. 77.

951 (Bernstein 1996a) p. 79.

952 (Eliade 1959).

953 (Bernstein 1996a) p. 81.

954 (Campbell 1949; Huxley 1946).

955 (Gardner 1983; Gardner 1993; Gardner 1987).

956 (Storr 1999).

957 (Egan 1998).

Appendix

1. For the writers…. Fromm, Horney, Jung, C. Buhler, Angyal, Rogers, G. Allport, Schachtel, and Lynd, and recently some Catholic psychologists, [M. Arnold, J. Gasson, J.Nuttin], growth, individuation, autonomy, self-actualization, self-development, pro- ductiveness, self-realization, are all crudely synonymous, designating a vaguely per- ceived area rather than a sharply defined concept. In my opinion, it is *not* possible to define this area sharply at the present time. Nor is this desirable either, since a defi- nition which does not emerge easily and naturally from well known facts is apt to be inhibiting and distorting rather than helpful, since it is quite likely to be wrong or mistaken if made by an act of the will, on a priori grounds. Its meaning can be *indicated* rather than defined, partly by positive pointing, partly by negative contrast, i.e., what it is *not*. (Maslow 1968) p.24.

2. …self-actualization is not only an end state but also the process of actualiz- ing one's potentialities at any time, in any amount. (Maslow 1993) p.45.

According to Jung's use of the term, individuation designates both a process and a goal. As a goal it refers to the realization of the self (*Selbstverwirklichung*), while as a process it refers to the stages or "way" leading to that goal (*der Weg der Individu- ation*). (Smith 1990) p.22.

3. Every age but ours has had its model, its ideal. All of these have been given up by our culture; the saint, the hero, the gentleman, the knight, the mystic. About all we have left is the well-adjusted man without problems, a very pale and doubtful substitute. Perhaps we shall soon be able to use as our guide and model the fully growing and self-fulfilling human being, the one whose inner nature expresses itself freely, rather than being warped, suppressed, or denied. (Maslow 1968) p.5.

4. Both Pestalozzi and Froebel, like Rousseau (who, in the long run, was their inspirer), were in revolt against the traditions of the Renaissance or Revival of Learning … {which}… had led to the enthronement, in all schools, of *book knowledge*. The men of the Renaissance had rediscovered the treasures of ancient learning, and they were so entranced by the discovery—especially as the printing press seemed provi- dentially designed to help on the dissemination of books—that they set to work to transform every school into an institution where the classical languages, and practi- cally nothing else, could be taught and acquired. Henceforth "scholar" meant "book- reader"—reader of Latin and Greek books…

The "bookishness" of schools continued for two or three centuries, despite the protest of "Realists," that is, of men who regarded a knowledge of external nature as possessing a higher value than any knowledge or culture that could be derived from books. The most violent of all these protests came from Rousseau; ...(Hayward 1904) pp.24-25.

5. I will be told that I abandon nature. I do not believe that at all. It chooses its instruments and regulates them according to need, not to opinion. Now, needs change according to the situation of men. There is a great difference between the natural man living in the state of nature and the natural man living in the state of society. Emile is not a savage to be relegated to the desert. He is a savage made to inhabit cities. He has to know how to find his necessities in them, to take advantage of their inhabitants, and to live, if not like them, at least with them. (Rousseau 1979) p.205.

6. Do not expect lengthy precepts of morality from me. I have only one precept to give you, and it comprehends all the others. Be a man. Restrain your heart within the limits of your condition. Study and know these limits. (Rousseau 1979) p.445.

7. In the natural order, since men are all equal, their common calling is man's estate and whoever is well raised for that calling cannot fail to fulfill those callings related to it. Let my students be destined for the sword, the church, the bar. I do not care. Prior to the calling of his parents is nature's call to human life. Living is the job I want to teach him. On leaving my hands, he will, I admit, be neither magistrate nor soldier nor priest. He will, in the first place, be a man. All that a man should be, he will in case of need know how to be as well as anyone; and fortune may try as it may to make him change place, he will always be in his own place. (Rousseau 1979) pp.41-42.

8. Let us set down as an incontestable maxim that the first movements of nature are always right. There is no original perversity in the human heart. There is not a single vice to be found in it of which it cannot be said how and whence it entered. (Rousseau 1979) p.92.

9. Everything is good as it leaves the hands of the Author of things; everything degenerates in the hands of man. ...[Man] wants nothing as nature made it, not even man; for him, man must be trained like a school horse; man must be fashioned in keeping with his fancy like a tree in his garden.

Were he not to do this, however, everything would go even worse, and our species does not admit of being formed halfway. In the present state of things a man abandoned to himself in the midst of other men from birth would be the most disfigured of all. Prejudices, authority, necessity, example, all the social institutions in which we find ourselves submerged would stifle nature in him and put nothing in its place. (Rousseau 1979) p.37.

10. If, according to the plan I have begun to outline, you follow rules directly contrary to the established ones; if instead of taking your pupil's mind far away; if instead of constantly leading it astray in other places, other climates, other times, at the extremities of the earth and up to the heavens, you apply yourself to keeping him always within himself and attentive to what touches him immediately, then you will find him capable of perception, memory, and even reasoning. This is nature's order. (Rousseau 1979) pp.117-118.

11. What, then, must be thought of that barbarous education which sacrifices the present to an uncertain future, which burdens a child with chains of every sort and begins by making him miserable in order to prepare him from afar for I know not what pretended happiness which it is to be believed he will enjoy? Even if I were to suppose this education reasonable in its object, how can one without indignation see poor unfortunates submitted to an unbearable yoke and condemned to continual labor like galley slaves, without any assurance that so many efforts will ever be useful

to them? The age of gaiety passes amidst tears, punishments, threats, and slavery. The unlucky fellow is tormented for his own good; ... (Rousseau 1979) p.79.

12. So long as one concedes nothing to the authority of men or to the preju-dices of the country in which one was born, the light of reason alone cannot, in the education founded by nature, lead us any farther than natural religion. This is what I limit myself to with my Emile. If he must have another religion, I no longer have the right to be his guide in that. It is up to him alone to choose it. (Rousseau 1979) pp.313-314.

13. It is especially in matters of religion that opinion triumphs. But we who pretend to shake off the yoke of opinion in everything, we who want to grant noth-ing to authority, we who want to teach nothing to our Emile which he could not learn by himself in every country, in what religion shall we raise him? To what sect shall we join the man of nature? The answer is quite simple, it seems to me. We shall join him to neither this one nor that one, but we shall put him in a position to choose the one to which the best use of his reason ought to lead him. (Rousseau 1979) p.260.

14. To find God man has only to make 'good use of his faculties.' The authority of other men, with their claim to privileged knowledge, is a serious hindrance to the experience of genuine religion, which every man must and can discover for himself in the simplicity of his own heart and 'in the silence of his passions.' (Grimsley 1968) p.69.

15. Therefore, neglect all these mysterious dogmas which are only words with-out ideas for us—all these bizarre doctrines whose vain study takes the place of virtues in those who indulge in it and serves to make them mad rather than good. Always keep your children within the narrow circle of the dogmas connected with morality. Persuade them that there is nothing useful for us to know except that which teaches us to do good. Do not make your daughters theologians and reasoners; teach them regarding heaven only those things that serve human wisdom. Accustom them always to feel themselves under the eyes of God; to have Him as witness of their actions, their thoughts, their virtue, and their pleasures; to do good without ostentation because He loves it; to suffer evil without a murmur because He will compensate them for it; finally, to be all the days of their lives as they will be glad to have been when they appear before Him. This is the true religion; this is the only one which is susceptible of neither abuse nor impiety nor fanaticism. Let them preach more sublime religions as much as they want; I recognize none other than this. (Rousseau 1979) p.381.

16. This education comes to us from nature or from men or from things. The internal development of our faculties and our organs is the education of nature. The use we are taught to make of this development is the education of men. And what we acquire from our own experience about the objects which affect us is the education of things.

Each of us is thus formed by three kinds of masters. The disciple in whom their various lessons are at odds with one another is badly raised and will never be in agreement with himself. He alone in whom they all coincide at the same points and tend to the same ends reaches his goal and lives consistently. He alone is well raised. (Rousseau 1979) p.38.

17. All those who have reflected on the way of life of the ancients attribute to gymnastic exercises that vigor of body and soul which distinguishes them most palpably from the moderns. The way in which Montaigne supports this sentiment

shows that he was powerfully impressed by it. He returns to it endlessly and in countless ways in speaking of a child's education. To stiffen his soul, he says, his muscles must be hardened; by becoming accustomed to work, he becomes accustomed to pain; one must break him to the harshness of exercise in order to train him in the harshness of dislocations, colics, and all illness. The wise Locke, the good Rollin, the learned Fleury, the pedant Crousaz—so different among themselves in everything else—all agree on this single point that there should be much exercise for children's bodies. It is the most judicious of their precepts; it is the one which is and always will be the most neglected. (Rousseau 1979) p.126.

18. From where does man's weakness come? From the inequality between his strength and his desires. It is our passions that make us weak, because to satisfy them we would need more strength than nature gives us. Therefore, diminish desires, and you will increase strength. He who is capable of more than he desires has strength left over; he is certainly a very strong being. (Rousseau 1979) p.165.

19. Although memory and reasoning are two essentially different faculties, nevertheless the one develops truly only with the other. Before the age of reason the child receives not ideas but images; and the difference between the two is that images are only absolute depictions of sensible objects, while ideas are notions of objects determined by relations. An image can stand all alone in the mind which represents it, but every idea supposes other ideas. When one imagines, one does nothing but see; when one conceives, one is comparing. Our sensations are purely passive, while all our perceptions or ideas are born out of an active principle which judges. (Rousseau 1979) p.107.

20. Let us transform our sensations into ideas but not leap all of a sudden from objects of sense to intellectual objects. It is by way of the former that we ought to get to the latter. In the first operations of the mind let the senses always be its guides. No book other than the world, no instruction other than the facts. The child who reads does not think, he only reads; he is not informing himself, he learns words. (Rousseau 1979) p.168.

21. The manner of forming ideas is what gives a character to the human mind. The mind which forms its ideas only on the basis of real relations is a solid mind. The one satisfied with apparent relations is a superficial mind. The one which sees relations such as they are is a precise mind. The one which evaluates them poorly is a defective mind. The one which makes up imaginary relations that have neither reality nor appearance is mad. The one which does not compare at all is imbecillic. The greater or lesser aptitude at comparing ideas and at finding relations is what constitutes in men greater or lesser intelligence, etc. (Rousseau 1979) p.203.

22. Human intelligence has its limits; and not only is it impossible for a man to know everything, he cannot even know completely the little that other men know. Since the contradictory of each false proposition is a truth, the number of truths is as inexhaustible as that of errors. A choice must, therefore, be made of the things that ought to be taught as well as of the proper time for learning them. Of the fields of learning that are available to us, some are false, others are useless, others serve to feed the pride of the man who possesses them. The small number of those which really contribute to our well-being is alone worthy of the researches of a wise man and, consequently, of a child whom one wants to make wise. It is a question not of knowing what is but only of knowing what is useful. (Rousseau 1979) p.166.

23. Since man's first natural movements are, therefore, to measure himself against everything surrounding him and to experience in each object he perceives all the

qualities which can be sensed and relate to him, his first study is a sort of experimental physics relative to his own preservation, from which he is diverted by speculative studies before he has recognised his place here on earth. While his delicate and flexible organs can adjust themselves to the bodies on which they must act, while his still pure senses are exempt from illusion, it is the time to exercise both in their proper functions, it is the time to teach the knowledge of the sensible relations which things have with us. (Rousseau 1979) p.125.

24. The kind of memory a child can have does not, without his studying books, for this reason remain idle. Everything he sees, everything he hears strikes him, and he remembers it. He keeps in himself a record of the actions and the speeches of men, and all that surrounds him is the book in which, without thinking about it, he continually enriches his memory while waiting for his judgement to be able to profit from it. It is in the choice of these objects, it is in the care with which one constantly presents him the objects he can know, and hides from him those he ought not to know, that the true art of cultivating in him this first faculty consists; and it is in this way that one must try to form in him a storehouse of knowledge which serves his education during his youth and his conduct at all times. This method, it is true, does not form little prodigies and does not make governors and preceptors shine. But it forms men who are judicious, robust, healthy of body and understanding, men who, without having made themselves admired when young, make themselves honored when grown. (Rousseau 1979) p.112.

25. Make your pupil attentive to the phenomena of nature. Soon you will make him curious. But to feed his curiosity, never hurry to satisfy it. Put the questions within his reach and leave them to him to resolve. Let him know something not because you told it to him but because he has understood it himself. Let him not learn science but discover it. If ever you substitute in his mind authority for reason, he will no longer reason. He will be nothing more than the plaything of others' opinion.

Be satisfied, therefore, with presenting him with objects opportunely. Then, when you see his curiosity sufficiently involved, put to him some laconic question which sets him on the way to answering it. (Rousseau 1979) pp.168-169.

26. Young masters, think, I beg you, about this example, and remember that in everything your lessons ought to be more in actions than in speeches; for children easily forget what they have said and what has been said to them, but not what they have done and what has been done to them. (Rousseau 1979) pp.99-100.

I do not tire of repeating it: put all the lessons of young people in actions rather than in speeches. Let them learn nothing in books which experience can teach them. (Rousseau 1979) p.251.

Do not give your pupil any kind of verbal lessons; he ought to receive them only from experience. (Rousseau 1979) p.92.

One must speak as much as one can by deeds and say only what one does not know how to do. (Rousseau 1979) p.182.

Master! Make few speeches! But learn to choose places, times, and persons. Then give all your lessons in examples, and be sure of their effect. (Rousseau 1979) p.232.

27. In any study whatsoever, unless one has the ideas of the things represented, the representative signs are nothing. However, one always limits the child to these signs without ever being able to make him understand any of the things which they represent. Thinking he is being taught a description of the earth, he learns only to

know some maps. He is taught the names of cities, of countries, of rivers which he does not conceive as existing anywhere else but on the paper where he is showed them. I remember having seen somewhere a geography text which began thus: "What is the world? It is a cardboard globe." Such precisely is the geography of children. I set down as a fact that after two years of globe and cosmography there is not a single child of ten who, following the rules he has been given, knows how to get from Paris to Saint-Denis. I set down as a fact that there is not one who, on the basis of a map of his father's garden, is able to follow its winding paths without getting lost. These are the doctors who know on the spur of the moment where Peking, Ispahan, Mexico, and all the countries of the earth are. (Rousseau 1979) pp.109-110.

28. In all schools gyms or places of corporeal exercise should be established for the young. This is so neglected and, from my perspective, is the most important part of education. This is so not only for forming robust and healthy temperaments, but even more for moral education purposes which are neglected and which we now meet with so many vain and pedantic precepts, which amount to nothing more than lost words. {*my translation only*}(Rousseau 1790) p.295.

29. The sole folly of which one cannot disabuse a man who is not mad is vanity. For this there is no cure other than experience—if, indeed, anything can cure it. At its birth, at least, one can prevent its growth. Do not get lost in fine reasonings intended to prove to the adolescent that he is a man like others and subject to the same weaknesses. Make him feel it, or he will never know it. (Rousseau 1979) p.245.

30. The abuse of books kills science: Believing that we know what we have read, we believe that we can dispense with learning it. Too much reading only serves to produce presumptuous ignoramuses. Among all literary ages there has been none in which men read so much as in this one, and none in which men are less knowledgeable. (Rousseau 1979) pp.450-451.

In general, never substitute the sign for the thing except when it is impossible for you to show the latter, for the sign absorbs the child's attention and makes him forget the thing represented. (Rousseau 1979) p.170.

31. Readers, in this example and in a hundred thousand others, I beg you to note how we stuff children's heads with words which have no meaning within their reach and then believe we have instructed them very well. (Rousseau 1979) p.98.

32. I do not like explanations in speeches. Young people pay little attention to them and hardly retain them. Things, things! I shall never repeat enough that we attribute too much power to words. With our babbling education we produce only babblers. (Rousseau 1979) p.180.

33. You want to teach geography to this child, and you go and get globes, cosmic spheres, and maps for him. So many devices! Why all these representations? Why do you not begin by showing him the object itself, so that he will at least know what you are talking to him about? (Rousseau 1979) p.168.

34. Never reason in a dry manner with youth. Clothe reason in a body if you want to make youth able to grasp it. Make the language of the mind pass through the heart, so that it may make itself understood. I repeat, cold arguments can determine our opinions, but not our actions. They make us believe and not act. They demonstrate what must be thought, not what must be done. If that is true for all men, it is a fortiori true for young people, who are still enveloped in their senses and think only insofar as they imagine. (Rousseau 1979) p.323.

35. One of the errors of our age is to use reason in too unadorned a form, as if men were all mind. In neglecting the language of signs that speak to the imagination,

the most energetic of languages has been lost. The impression of the word is always weak, and one speaks to the heart far better through the eyes than through the ears. In wanting to turn everything over to reasoning, we have reduced our precepts to words; we have made no use of actions. Reason alone is not active. It sometimes restrains, it arouses rarely, and it has never done anything great. Always to reason is the mania of small minds. Strong souls have quite another language. It is with this language that one persuades and makes others act. (Rousseau 1979) p.321.

36. Full of the enthusiasm he feels, the master wants to communicate it to the child. He believes he moves the child by making him attentive to the sensations by which he, the master, is himself moved. Pure stupidity! It is in man's heart that the life of nature's spectacle exists. To see it, one must feel it. The child perceives the objects, but he cannot perceive the relations linking them; he cannot hear the sweet harmony of their concord. For that is needed experience he has not acquired; in order to sense the complex impression that results all at once from all these sensations, he needs sentiments he has not had. (Rousseau 1979) pp.168-169.

37. Restrain your heart within the limits of your condition. Study and know these limits. However narrow they may be, a man is not unhappy as long as he closes himself up within them. He is unhappy only when he wants to go out beyond them. He is unhappy only when, in his senseless desires, he puts in the rank of the possible what is not possible. He is unhappy when he forgets his human estate in order to forge for himself imaginary estates from which he always falls back into his own. The only goods that it is costly to be deprived of are those one believes one has a right to. (Rousseau 1979) p.445.

38. Do you want, then, to live happily and wisely? Attach your heart only to imperishable beauty. Let your condition limit your desires; let your duties come before your inclinations; extend the law of necessity to moral things. Learn to lose what can be taken from you; learn to abandon everything when virtue decrees it, to put yourself above events and to detach your heart lest it be lacerated by them; to be courageous in adversity, so as never to be miserable; to be firm in your duty, so as never to be criminal. Then you will be happy in spite of fortune and wise in spite of the passions. Then you will find in the possession even of fragile goods a voluptuousness that nothing will be able to disturb. You will possess them without their possessing you; and you will feel that man, who can keep nothing, enjoys only what he knows how to lose. You will not, it is true, have the illusion of imaginary pleasures, but you will also not have the pains which are their fruit. You will gain much in this exchange, for these pains are frequent and real, and these pleasures are rare and vain. As the conqueror of so many deceptive opinions, you will also be the conqueror of the opinion that places so great a value on life. You will pass your life without disturbance and terminate it without fright. You will detach yourself from it as from many things. How many others are horror-stricken because they think that, in departing from life, they cease to be? Since you are informed about life's nothingness, you will believe that it is then that you begin to be. Death is the end of the wicked man's life and the beginning of the just man's. (Rousseau 1979) p.446.

39. The source of our passions, the origin and the principle of all the others, the only one born with man and which never leaves him so long as he lives is self-love [*amour de soi*]—a primitive, innate passion, which is anterior to every other, and of which all others are in a sense only modifications. In this sense, if you wish, all passions are natural. But most of these modifications have alien causes without which they would never have come to pass; and these same modifications, far from

being advantageous for us, are harmful. They alter the primary goal and are at odds with their own principle. It is then that man finds himself outside of nature and sets himself in contradiction with himself. (Rousseau 1979) pp.212-213.

40. Thus what makes man essentially good is to have few needs and to compare himself little to others; what makes him essentially wicked is to have many needs and to depend very much on opinion. On the basis of this principle it is easy to see how all the passions of children and men can be directed to good or bad. (Rousseau 1979) p.214.

41. It is an error to distinguish permitted passions from forbidden ones in order to yield to the former and deny oneself the latter. All passions are good when one remains their master; all are bad when one lets oneself be subjected to them. What is forbidden to us by nature is to extend our attachments further than our strength; what is forbidden to us by reason is to want what we cannot obtain; what is forbidden to us by conscience is not temptations but rather letting ourselves be conquered by temptations. It is not within our control to have or not to have passions. But it is within our control to reign over them. All the sentiments we dominate are legitimate; all those which dominate us are criminal. A man is not guilty for loving another's wife if he keep this unhappy passion enslaved of the law of duty. He is guilty for loving his own wife to the point of sacrificing everything to that love. (Rousseau 1979) p.445.

42. This is, then, the summary of the whole of human wisdom in the use of the passions: (1) To have a sense of the true relations of man, with respect to the species as well as the individual. (2) To order all the affections of the soul according to these relations.

But is man the master of ordering his affections according to this or that relation? Without a doubt, if he is master of directing his imagination toward this or that object or of giving it this or that habit. (Rousseau 1979) p.219.

43. Who, then, is the virtuous man? It is he who knows how to conquer his affections; for then he follows his reason and his conscience; he does his duty; he keeps himself in order, and nothing can make him deviate from it. Up to now you were only apparently free. You had only the precarious freedom of a slave to whom nothing has been commanded. Now be really free. Learn to become your own master. Command your heart, Emile, and you will be virtuous. (Rousseau 1979) p.444.

44. At sixteen the adolescent knows what it is to suffer, for he has himself suffered. But he hardly knows that other beings suffer too. To see it without feeling it is not to know it; and as I have said a hundred times, the child, not imagining what others feel, knows only his own ills. But when the first development of his senses lights the fire of imagination, he begins to feel himself in his fellows, to be moved by their complaints and to suffer from their pains. It is then that the sad picture of suffering humanity ought to bring to his heart the first tenderness it has ever experienced. (Rousseau 1979) p.222.

45. Thus is born pity, the first relative sentiment which touches the human heart according to the order of nature.

Thus, no one becomes sensitive until his imagination is animated and begins to transport him out of himself. (Rousseau 1979) pp.222-223.

46. In a word, teach your pupil to love all men, even those who despise men. Do things in such a way that he puts himself in no class but finds his bearings in all. Speak before him of humankind with tenderness, even with pity, but never with contempt. Man, do not dishonor man!

It is by these roads and other similar ones—quite contrary to those commonly taken—that it is fitting to penetrate the heart of a young adolescent in order to arouse the first emotions of nature and to develop his heart and extend it to his fellows. (Rousseau 1979) p.226.

47. Let us then leave the vaunted resource of books to those who are so constituted as to be satisfied by books. Like Raymond Lulle's art, they are good for learning to babble about what one does not know. They are good for training fifteen-year-old Platos to philosophize in polite society and for informing a gathering about the practices of Egypt and India on the testimony of Paul Lucas or Tavernier. (Rousseau 1979) p.451.

48. The pedagogues who present such a showy display of the instruction they give their disciples are paid for using other language than mine. However, one sees by their very conduct that they think exactly as I do, for what do they teach them after all? Words, more words, always words. Among the various sciences that they boast of teaching their pupils, they are quite careful not to include those which would be truly useful to them, because they would be sciences of things, and with these they would not succeed. Rather they choose those sciences one appears to know when one knows their terminology: heraldry, geography, chronology, languages, etc.—all studies so far from man, and especially from the child, that it would be a wonder if anything at all in them were of use to him a single time in his life. (Rousseau 1979) p.108.

49. Remember always that the spirit of my education consists not in teaching the child many things, but in never letting anything but accurate and clear ideas enter his brain. Were he to know nothing, it would be of little importance to me provided he made no mistakes. I put truths into his head only to guarantee him against the errors he would learn in their place. Reason and judgement come slowly; prejudices come in crowds; it is from them that he must be preserved. But if you look at science in itself, you enter into a bottomless sea, without shores, full of reefs. You will never get away. When I see a man, enamoured of the various kinds of knowledge, let himself be seduced by their charm and run from one to the other without knowing how to stop himself, I believe I am seeing a child on the shore gathering shells and beginning by loading himself up with them; then, tempted by those he sees next, he throws some away and picks up others, until, overwhelmed by their multitude and not knowing anymore which to choose, he ends by throwing them all away and returning empty-handed. (Rousseau 1979) p.171.

50. He will not stupidly question others about everything he sees, but he will examine it himself and will tire himself out to discover what he wants to learn before asking. (Rousseau 1979) p.161.

Raised in the spirit of our maxims, accustomed to draw all his instruments out of himself and never to have recourse to another person before he has himself recognised his insufficiency, he examines each new object he sees for a long time without saying anything. He is pensive, and not a questioner. Be satisfied, therefore, with presenting him with objects opportunely. Then, when you see his curiosity sufficiently involved, put to him some laconic question which sets him on the way to answering it. (Rousseau 1979) p.169.

51. Children, who are great imitators, all try to draw. I would want my child to cultivate this art, not precisely for the art itself but for making his eye exact and his hand flexible. And in general it is of very little importance that he knows this or that exercise, provided that his senses acquire the perspicacity and his body the good

habits one gains by this exercise. I will, therefore, carefully avoid giving him a drawing master who would give him only imitations to imitate and would make him draw only from drawings. I want him to have no other master than nature and no other model than objects. I want him to have before his eyes the original itself and not the paper representing it, to sketch a house from a house, a tree from a tree, a man from a man, so that he gets accustomed to observing bodies and their appearances well and not to taking false and conventional imitations for true imitations. I will even divert him from drawing from memory in the absence of the objects until their exact shapes are well imprinted on his imagination by frequent observations, for fear that, by substituting bizarre and fantastic shapes for the truth of things, he will lose the knowledge of proportions and the taste for the beauties of nature. (Rousseau 1979) pp.143-144.

52. Eighteen years of assiduous care have had as their only object the preservation of a sound judgement and a healthy heart. (Rousseau 1979) p.241.

53. He does not know what routine, custom, or habit is. What he did yesterday does not influence what he does today. He never follows a formula, does not give way before authority or example, and acts and speaks only as it suits him. So do not expect from him dictated speeches or studied manners, but always the faithful expression of his ideas and the conduct born of his inclinations. (Rousseau 1979) p.160.

54. Nature has, for strengthening the body and making it grow, means that ought never be opposed. A child must not be constrained to stay when he wants to go nor to go when he wants to stay. When children's wills are not spoiled by our fault, children want nothing uselessly. They have to jump, run, and shout when they wish. All their movements are needs of their constitution seeking to strengthen itself. But one should distrust what they desire but are unable to do for themselves and others have to do for them. Then true need, natural need, must be carefully distinguished from the need which stems from nascent whim or from the need which comes only from the superabundance of life of which I have spoken. (Rousseau 1979) p.84.

55. Most of the habits you believe you give to children and young people are not true habits. Because children only adopt such habits by force and stick to them grudgingly, they are only waiting for the occasion to be rid of them. One does not get the taste for being in prison by dint of staying there. Far from diminishing the aversion, the habit then increases it. (Rousseau 1979) p.432.

56. Forced to learn by himself, he uses his reason and not another's; for to give nothing to opinion, one must given nothing to authority, and most of our errors come to us far less from ourselves than from others. From this constant exercise there ought to result a vigor of mind similar to the vigor given to bodies by work and fatigue. Another advantage is that one advances only in proportion to one's strength. The mind, no less than the body, bears only what it can bear. When understanding appropriates things before depositing them in memory, what it draws from memory later belongs to it; whereas, by overburdening memory without the participation of understanding, one runs the risk of never withdrawing anything from memory suitable for understanding. (Rousseau 1979) p.207.

Without question, one gets far clearer and far surer notions of the things one learns in this way by oneself than of those one gets from another's teachings. One's reason does not get accustomed to a servile submission to authority; furthermore, we make ourselves more ingenious at finding relations, connecting ideas, and inventing instruments than we do when, accepting all of these things as they are given to us, we let our minds slump into indifference—like the body of a man, who, always clothed, shod, and waited on by his servants and drawn by his horses, finally loses the strength and use of his limbs. (Rousseau 1979) p.176.

57. …the goal is not that he know exactly the topography of the region, but that he know the means of learning about it. It is of little importance that he have maps in his head, provided that he is able to get a good conception of what they represent, and that he has a distinct idea of the art which serves to draw them. See the difference there already is between your pupils' knowledge and mine's ignorance! They know maps, and he makes them. Here are new ornaments for his room. (Rousseau 1979) p.171.

58. Emile has little knowledge, but what he has is truly his own. He knows nothing halfway. Among the small number of things he knows and knows well, the most important is that there are many things of which he is ignorant and which he can know one day; there are many more that other men know that he will never know in his life; and there are an infinite number of others that no man will ever know. Emile has a mind that is universal not by its learning but by its faculty to acquire learning: a mind that is open, intelligent, ready for everything, and, as Montaigne says, if not instructed, at least able to be instructed. It is enough for me that he knows how to find the "what's it good for?" in everything he does and the "why?" in everything he believes. Once again, my object is not to give him science but to teach him to acquire science when needed, to make him estimate it for exactly what it is worth, and to make him love the truth above all. With this method one advances little, but one never takes a useless step, and one is not forced to go backward. (Rousseau 1979) p.207.

59. As for my pupil, or rather nature's, trained early to be as self-sufficient as possible, he is not accustomed to turning constantly to others; still less is he accustomed to displaying his great learning for them. On the other hand, he judges, he foresees, he reasons in everything immediately related to him. He does not chatter; he acts. He does not know a word of what is going on in society, but he knows very well how to do what suits him. Since he is constantly in motion, he is forced to observe many things, to know many effects. He acquires a large experience early. He gets his lessons from nature and not from men. He instructs himself so much the better because he sees nowhere the intention to instruct him. Thus his body and his mind are exercised together. Acting always according to his own thought and not someone else's, he continually unites two operations: the more he makes himself strong and robust, the more he becomes sensible and judicious. This is the way one day to have what are believed incompatible and what are united in almost all great men: strength of body and strength of soul; a wise man's reason and an athlete's vigor. (Rousseau 1979) p.119.

60. Now, needs change according to the situation of men. There is a great difference between the natural man living in the state of nature and the natural man living in the state of society. Emile is not a savage to be relegated to the desert. He is a savage made to inhabit cities. He has to know how to find his necessities in them, to take advantage of their inhabitants, and to live, if not like them, at least with them. (Rousseau 1979) p.205.

61. He who in the civil order wants to preserve the primacy of the sentiments of nature does not know what he wants. Always in contradiction with himself, always floating between his inclinations and his duties, he will never be either a man or

a citizen. He will be good neither for himself nor for others. He will be one of these men of our days: a Frenchman, an Englishman, a bourgeois. He will be nothing. (Rousseau 1979) p.41.

62. You owe others more than if you were born without property, since you were favored at birth. It is not just that what one man has done for society should relieve another from what he owes it; for each, owning himself wholly, can pay only for himself and no father can transmit to his son the right to be useless to his fellows. (Rousseau 1979) p.195.

63. Our first duties are to ourselves; our primary sentiments are centered on ourselves; all our natural movements relate in the first instance to our preservation and our well-being. Thus, the first sentiment of justice does not come to us from the justice we owe but from that which is owed us; and it is again one of the mistakes of ordinary educations that, speaking at first to children of their duties, never of their rights, one begins by telling them the opposite of what is necessary, what they cannot understand, and what cannot interest them. (Rousseau 1979) p.97.

64. Emile, in considering his rank in the human species and seeing himself so happily placed there, will be tempted to honor his reason for the work of yours and to attribute his happiness to his own merit. He will say to himself, "I am wise, and men are mad." In pitying them, he will despise them; in congratulating himself, he will esteem himself more, and in feeling himself to be happier than them, he will believe himself worthier to be so. This is the error most to be feared, because it is the most difficult to destroy. If he remained in this condition, he would have gained little from all our care; and if one had to choose, I do not know whether I would not prefer the illusion of the prejudices to that of pride. (Rousseau 1979) pp.244-245.

65. To reason with children was Locke's great maxim. It is the one most in vogue today. Its success, however, does not appear to me such as to establish its reputation; and, as for me, I see nothing more stupid than these children who have been reasoned with so much. Of all the faculties of man, reason, which is, so to speak, only a composite of all the others, is the one that develops with the most difficulty and latest. And it is this one which they want to use in order to develop the first faculties! The masterpiece of a good education is to make a reasonable man, and they claim they raise a child by reason! This is to begin with the end, to want to make the product the instrument. If children understood reason, they would not need to be raised. But by speaking to them from an early age a language which they do not understand, one accustoms them to show off with words, to control all that is said to them, to believe themselves as wise as their masters, to become disputatious and rebellious; and everything that is thought to be gotten from them out of reasonable motives is never obtained other than out of motives of covetousness or fear or vanity which are always perforce joined to the others. (Rousseau 1979) pp.89-90.

66. On the other hand, how could your young people, who are bored and exasperated by your insipid lessons, your long-winded moralizing, and your eternal catechisms, fail to refuse to apply their minds to what has been made a gloomy business for them—the heavy precepts with which they have constantly been burdened, and the meditations on the Author of their being, Who has been made the enemy of their pleasures? They have conceived only aversion, disgust, and distaste for all that; constraint has repelled them. What means is left to make them devoted to such things when they begin to decide for themselves? They have to have novelty to be pleased; they no longer can stand anything children are told. (Rousseau 1979) p.316.

67. Each sort of instruction has its proper time, which must be known, and its dangers, which must be avoided. (Rousseau 1979) p.328.

68. This is the study to which I have most applied myself, so that even though my entire method were chimerical and false, my observations could still be of profit. My vision of what must be done may have been poor, but I believe I have seen clearly the subject on which one must work. (Rousseau 1979) pp.33-34.

69. If I had to depict sorry stupidity, I would depict a pedant teaching the ·catechism to children. If I wanted to make a child go mad, I would oblige him to explain what he says in saying his catechism. Someone will object to me that since most of the dogmas of Christianity are mysteries, to wait for the human mind to be capable of having a conception of them is not to wait for the child to be a man but to wait for the man to exist no more. To that I answer, in the first place, that there are mysteries it is impossible for man not only to conceive but to believe, and that I do not see what is gained by teaching them to children, unless it be that they learn how to lie early. I say, moreover, that, to accept the mysteries, one must at least comprehend that they are incomprehensible, and children are not even capable of this conception. At the age when everything is mystery, there are no mysteries strictly speaking. (Rousseau 1979) p.257.

70. Let the child do nothing on anybody's word. Nothing is good for him unless he feels it to be so. In always pushing him ahead of his understanding, you believe you are using foresight, and you lack it. To arm him with some vain instruments which he will perhaps never use, you take away from him man's most universal instrument, which is good sense. You accustom him to let himself always be led, never to be anything but a machine in others' hands. You want him to be docile when little: that is to want him to be credulous and a dupe when he is grown up. You constantly tell him, "All that I ask of you is for your own advantage. But you are not in a condition to know it. What difference does it make to me whether you do what I demand? It is only for you yourself that you are working." With all these fine speeches that you make to him now in order to get him to be obedient, you are preparing the success of those speeches which will be made to him one day by a visionary, an alchemist, a charlatan, a cheat, or any kind of madman in order to catch your pupil in his trap or to get him to adopt his madness. (Rousseau 1979) p.178.

71. The art of speaking to and hearing from absent people, the art of communicating our feelings, our wills, our desires to them at a distance without a mediator is an art whose utility can be rendered palpable to all ages. What wonderful means were used to turn so useful and so agreeable an art into a torment for childhood? Because the young are constrained to apply themselves to it in spite of themselves, it is put to uses of which they understand nothing. A child is not very eager to perfect the instrument with which he is tormented. But arrange things so that this instrument serves his pleasures, and soon he will apply himself to it in spite of you.

A great business is made of seeking the best methods of teaching reading. Desks and cards are invented; a child's room is made into a printing shop. Locke wants him to learn to read with dice. Now is that not a clever invention? What a pity! A means surer than all these, and the one always forgotten, is the desire to learn. Give the child this desire; then let your desks and your dice go. Any method will be good for him. (Rousseau 1979) pp.116-117.

72. Another consideration confirms the utility of this method. One must know well the particular genius of the child in order to know what moral diet suits him. Each mind has its own form, according to which it needs to be governed; the suc-

cess of one's care depends on governing it by this form and not by another. Prudent man, spy out nature for a long time; observe your pupil well before saying the first word to him. To start with, let the germ of his character reveal itself freely; constrain it in no way whatsoever in order better to see the whole of it. Do you think this time of freedom is lost for him? Not at all. This is the best way to use it, for you are learning now not to lose a single moment in a more valuable time; while if you begin to act before knowing what must be done, you will act haphazardly. Subject to error, you will have to retrace your steps; you will be farther removed from the goal than if you had been in less of a rush to reach it. Do not therefore act like the miser who loses a great deal for wanting not to lose anything. In the earliest age sacrifice time that you will regain with interest at a more advanced age. The wise doctor does not at first sight giddily give prescriptions but in the first place studies the constitution of his patient before prescribing anything to him. He may begin to treat the patient late but he cures him, whereas the doctor who is in too much of a rush kills him. (Rousseau 1979) p.94.

73. The greater or lesser facility or execution depends on countless circumstances that are impossible to determine otherwise than in a particular application of the method to this or that country, to this or that station. Now all these particular applications, not being essential to my subject, do not enter into my plan. (Rousseau 1979) p.35.

74. Do you wish to put order and regularity in the nascent passions? Extend the period during which they develop in order that they have the time to be arranged as they are born. Then it is not man who orders them; it is nature itself. Your care is only to let it arrange its work. If your pupil were alone, you would have nothing to do. But everything surrounding him influences his imagination. The torrent of prejudices carries him away. To restrain him, he must be pushed in the opposite direction. Sentiment must enchain imagination, and reason silence the opinion of men. The source of all the passions is sensibility; imagination determines their bent. (Rousseau 1979) p.219.

75. Young teacher, I am preaching a difficult art to you, that of governing without precepts and doing everything by doing nothing. This art, I agree, is not one that goes with your age; it is not fit to make your talents conspicuous from the outset nor to make an impression on fathers. But it is the only one fit for succeeding. You will never get to the point of producing wise men if you do not in the first place produce rascals. (Rousseau 1979) p.119.

76. Thus, the first education ought to be purely negative. It consists not at all in teaching virtue or truth but in securing the heart from vice and the mind from error. If you could do nothing and let nothing be done, if you could bring your pupil healthy and robust to the age of twelve without his knowing how to distinguish his right hand from his left, at your first lessons the eyes of his understanding would open up to reason. Without prejudice, without habit, he would have nothing in him which could hinder the effect of your care. Soon he would become in your hands the wisest of men; and in beginning by doing nothing, you would have worked an educational marvel. (Rousseau 1979) pp.93-94.

77. I shall add this one word which constitutes an important maxim: it is that usually one gets very surely and quickly what one is not in a hurry to get. I am almost certain that Emile will know how to read and write perfectly before the age of ten, precisely because it makes very little difference to me that he knows how before fifteen. But I would rather that he never knew how to read if this science has to be

bought at the price of all that can make it useful. Of what use will reading be to him if it has been made repulsive to him forever? (Rousseau 1979) p.117.

78. Dare I expose the greatest, the most important, the most useful rule of all education? It is not to gain time but to lose it. Common readers, pardon me my paradoxes. When one reflects, they are necessary and, whatever you may say, I prefer to be a paradoxical man than a prejudiced one. The most dangerous period of human life is that from birth to the age of twelve. This is the time when errors and vices germinate without one's yet having any instrument for destroying them; and by the time the instrument comes, the roots are so deep that it is too late to rip them out. If children jumped all at once from the breast to the age of reason, the education they are given might be suitable for them. But, according to the natural progress, they need an entirely contrary one. They ought to do nothing with their soul until all of its faculties have developed, because while the soul is yet blind, it cannot perceive the torch you are presenting to it or follow the path reason maps out across the vast plain of ideas, a path which is so faint even to the best of eyes. (Rousseau 1979) p.93.

79. Think through all the rules of your education; you will find them misconceived, especially those that concern virtues and morals. The only lesson of morality appropriate to childhood, and the most important for every age, is never to harm anyone. The very precept of doing good, if it is not subordinated to this one, is dangerous, false, and contradictory. Who does not do good? Everybody does it— the wicked man as well as others. He makes one man happy at the expense of making a hundred men miserable; and this is the source of all our calamities. The most sublime virtues are negative. They are also the most difficult, because they are without ostentation and above even that pleasure so sweet to the heart of man, the pleasure of sending someone away satisfied with us. O what good is necessarily done to his fellows by the one among them, if there is such a one, who never does them harm! What an intrepid soul, what a vigorous character he needs for that! It is not in reasoning about this maxim, but in trying to put it into practice, that one feels how great it is and how difficult of success. (Rousseau 1979) p.104.

80. I have said enough to make it understood that punishment as punishment must never be inflicted on children, but it should always happen to them as a natural consequence of their bad action. Thus you will not declaim against lying; you will not precisely punish them for having lied; but you will arrange it so that all the bad effects of lying—such as not being believed when one tells the truth, of being accused of the evil that one did not do although one denies it—come in league against them when they have lied. But let us explain what lying is for children. (Rousseau 1979) p.101.

81. There is an excess of rigor and an excess of indulgence, both equally to be avoided. If you let children suffer, you expose their health, their life. You make them miserable in the present. If by too much care you spare them every kind of discomfort, you are preparing great miseries for them; you make them delicate, sensitive; you cause them to leave man's estate to which they will return one day in spite of you. So, as not to expose them to some ills of nature, you are the artisan of those nature did not give them. (Rousseau 1979) pp.86-87.

82. The surest means of raising oneself above prejudices and ordering one's judgements about the true relations of things is to put oneself in the place of an isolated man and to judge everything as this man himself ought to judge of it with respect to his own utility. (Rousseau 1979) p.185.

83. As for me I do not intend to teach geometry to Emile; it is he who will teach

it to me; I will seek the relations, and he will find them, for I will seek them in such a way as to make him find them. For example, instead of using a compass to draw a circle, I shall draw it with a point at the end of a string turning on a pivot. After that, when I want to compare the radii among themselves, Emile will ridicule me and make me understand that the same string, always taut, cannot have drawn unequal distances. (Rousseau 1979) p.145.

84. What is the use of inscribing in their heads a catalogue of signs which represent nothing for them? In learning the things, will they not learn the signs? Why put them to the useless effort of learning the signs twice? And, meanwhile, what dangerous prejudices does one not begin to inspire in them by making them take for science words which have no sense for them? It is with the first word the child uses in order to show off, it is with the first thing he takes on another's word without seeing its utility himself, that his judgement is lost. He will have to shine in the eyes of fools for a long time in order to make up for such a loss. (Rousseau 1979) p.111-112.

85. If you want to instruct him by principles and teach him, along with the nature of the human heart, the external causes which are brought to bear on it and turn our inclinations into vices, you employ a metaphysic he is not in a condition to understand by thus transporting him all of a sudden from sensible objects to intellectual objects. You fall back into the difficulty so carefully avoided up to now of giving him lessons resembling lessons, of substituting in his mind the master's experience and authority for his own experience and the progress of his reason.

To remove both of these obstacles at once and to put the human heart in his reach without risk of spoiling his own, I would want to show him men from afar, to show him them in other times or other places and in such a way that he can see the stage without ever being able to act on it. This is the moment for history. It is by means of history that, without the lessons of philosophy, he will read the hearts of men; it is by means of history that he will see them, a simple spectator, disinterested and without passion, as their judge and not as their accomplice or as their accuser.

To know men, one must see them act. In society one hears them speak. They show their speeches and hide their actions. But in history their actions are unveiled, and one judges them on the basis of the facts. Even their talk helps in evaluating them; for in comparing what they do with what they say, one sees both what they are and what they want to appear to be. The more they disguise themselves, the better one knows them. (Rousseau 1979) p.237.

86. The exercise of the social virtues brings the love of humanity to the depths of one's heart. It is in doing good that one becomes good; I know of no practice more certain. Busy your pupil with all the good actions within his reach. Let the interest of indigents always be his. Let him assist them not only with his purse but with his care. Let him serve them, protect them, consecrate his person and his time to them. Let him be their representative; he will never again in his life fulfill so noble a function. (Rousseau 1979) p.250.

87. He must be touched and not hardened by the sight of human miseries. Long struck by the same sights, we no longer feel their impressions. Habit accustoms us to everything. What we see too much, we no longer imagine; and it is only imagination which makes us feel the ills of others. It is thus by dint of seeing death and suffering that priests and doctors become pitiless. Therefore, let your pupil know the fate of man and the miseries of his fellows, but do not let him witness them too often. A

single object well chosen and shown in a suitable light will provide him emotion and reflection for a month. (Rousseau 1979) p.231.

88. Those who want to guide the young soberly, in order to preserve them from the traps of the senses, make love disgusting to them and would gladly make it a crime for them to think of it at their age, as though love were made for the old. All these deceitful lessons, to which the heart gives the lie, are not persuasive. The young man, guided by a surer instinct, secretly laughs at the gloomy maxims to which he feigns acquiescence, and all he waits for is the occasion to discard them. All this is contrary to nature. By following an opposite route, I shall more surely arrive at the same goal. I shall not be afraid to indulge him in the sweet sentiment for which he has such a thirst. I shall depict it to him as the supreme happiness of life, because in fact it is. In depicting it to him, I want him to yield to it. In making him sense how much charm the union of hearts adds to the attraction of the sense, I shall disgust him with libertinism, and I shall make him moderate by making him fall in love. (Rousseau 1979) p.327.

89. How limited one must be to see only an obstacle to the lessons of reason in the nascent desires of a young man! I see in them the true means of making him amenable to these very lessons. One has a hold on the passions only by means of the passions. It is by their empire that their tyranny must be combated; and it is always from nature itself that the proper instruments to regulate nature must be drawn. (Rousseau 1979) p.327.

90. Now, a child, no more than a man, is not to be seen in a moment. Where are the observers who know how to grasp at first glance the traits which characterise him? Such observers exist, but they are few; and in a hundred thousand fathers not one of them will be found. (Rousseau 1979) p.162.

91. An error difficult to avoid is always to assume the child has the same taste for the activities about which the master is enthusiastic. When the entertainment of work carries you away, be careful that in the meantime he is not bored without daring to indicate it to you. The child ought to be wholly involved with the thing, but you ought to be wholly involved with the child—observing him, spying on him without letup and without appearing to do so, sensing ahead of time all his sentiments and forestalling those he ought not to have—in a word, busying him in such a way that he not only feels he is of use in the work but is pleased by dint of understanding well the purpose of that work. (Rousseau 1979) p.189.

92. Take the opposite of the practised path, and you will almost always do well. Since what is wanted is not to make a child out of a child but a doctor out of a child, fathers and masters can never soon enough scold, correct, reprimand, flatter, threaten, promise, instruct, talk reason. Do better: be reasonable, and do not reason with your pupil, especially to get his approbation for what displeases him. Bringing reason to bear on unpleasant things only makes reason tedious for him and discredits it early in a mind not yet in a condition to understand it. (Rousseau 1979) p.94.

93. Since we always proceed slowly from one idea based on the senses to another, we familiarize ourselves with one for a long time before going on to another, and finally, we never force our pupil to be attentive; it is a long way from this first lesson to knowledge of the path of the sun and the shape of the earth. (Rousseau 1979) p.170.

94. Never show the child anything he cannot see. While humanity is almost alien to him, and you are unable to raise him to man's estate, for his sake lower man

to the child's estate. In thinking about what can be useful to him at another age, speak to him only about things whose utility he sees right now. (Rousseau 1979) pp.183-184.

95. Judge whether the time for listening to grave lessons of wisdom is when the inflamed senses derange the understanding and tyrannize the will. Therefore, never talk reason to young people, even when they are at the age of reason, without first putting them in a condition to understand it. Most wasted speeches are wasted due to the fault of masters rather than of disciples. The pedant and the teacher say pretty much the same things, but the former says them on every occasion, while the latter says them only when he is sure of their effect. (Rousseau 1979) p.319.

96. One of the things that makes preaching most useless is that it is done indiscriminately to everyone without distinction or selectivity. How can one think that the same sermon is suitable to so many auditors of such diverse dispositions, so different in mind, humor, age, sex, station, and opinion? There are perhaps not even two auditors for whom what one says to all can be suitable; and all our affections are so inconstant that there are perhaps not even two moments in the life of each man when the same speech would make the same impression on him. (Rousseau 1979) p.319.

97. Although modesty is natural to the human species, naturally children have none. Modesty is born only with the knowledge of evil, and how could children, who do not and should not have this knowledge, have the sentiment which is its effect? To give them lessons in modesty and decency is to teach them that there are shameful and indecent things. It is to give them a secret desire to know those things. Sooner or later they succeed, and the first spark which touches the imagination inevitably accelerates the inflammation of the senses. Whoever blushes is already guilty. True innocence is ashamed of nothing. (Rousseau 1979) p.217.

98. How do we fail to see that if all the lessons given to a young man on this point are without success, it is because they are without reasons suitable to his age, and because it is important at every age to clothe reason in forms which will make it loved. Speak to him gravely when necessary, but let what you say always have an attraction that forces him to listen to you. Do not combat his desires with dryness. Do not stifle his imagination; guide it lest it engender monsters. (Rousseau 1979) p.325.

99. The issue is not to teach him the sciences but to give him the taste for loving them and methods for learning them when this taste is better developed. This is very certainly a fundamental principle of every good education. (Rousseau 1979) p.172 .

100. My principle aim in teaching him to feel and to love the beautiful of all sorts is to fix his affections and tastes on it, to prevent his natural appetites from becoming corrupted, and to see to it that he does not one day seek in his riches the means for being happy—means that he ought to find nearer to him. (Rousseau 1979) p.344.

101. Let the value of what he makes be drawn not from the worker but from the work. Let us never allow his work to be judged except by comparing it to that of good masters; let his work be valued for the work itself and not because it is his. Say of what is well made, "This is well made." But do not add, "Who made that?" If he himself says with a proud and self-satisfied air, "I made it," add coldly, "You or another, it makes no difference; in any event it is work well done." (Rousseau 1979) p.202.

102. Moreover, let there never be any comparisons with other children, no ri-

vals, no competitors, not even in running, once he has begun to be able to reason. I prefer a hundred times over that he not learn what he would only learn out of jealousy or vanity. However, every year I shall note the progress he has made; I shall compare it to that which he will make the following year. I shall tell him, "You have grown so many inches. That is the ditch you jumped over, the load you carried, the distance you threw a pebble, the course you ran before getting winded, etc. Let us now see what you will do." Thus I arouse him without making him jealous of anyone. He will want to outdo himself. He ought to. I see no problem in his being his own competitor. (Rousseau 1979) p.184.

103. It ought to be sensed that just as pain is often a necessity, pleasure is sometimes a need. There is, therefore, only one single desire of children which ought never be satisfied: that of being obeyed. From this it follows that in everything they ask for, attention must above all be paid to the motive which leads them to ask for it. So, as far as possible, grant them everything that can give them a real pleasure; always refuse them what they ask for only due to whim or in order to assert their authority. (Rousseau 1979) footnote on p.89.

104. Command him nothing, whatever in the world it might be, absolutely nothing. Do not even allow him to imagine that you might pretend to have any authority over him. Let him know only that he is weak and you are strong, that by his condition and yours he is necessarily at your mercy. Let him know it, learn it, feel it. Let his haughty head at an early date feel the harsh yoke which nature imposes on man, the heavy yoke of necessity under which every finite being must bend. Let him see this necessity in things, never in the caprice of men. Let the bridle that restrains him be force and not authority. Do not forbid him to do that from which he should abstain; prevent him from doing it without explanations, without reasonings. What you grant him, grant at his first word, without solicitations, without prayers—above all, without conditions. Grant with pleasure; refuse only with repugnance. But let all your refusals be irrevocable; let no importunity shake you; let 'no,' once pronounced, be a wall of bronze against which the child will have to exhaust his strength at most five or six times in order to abandon any further attempts to overturn it. (Rousseau 1979) p.91.

105. The worst education is to leave him floating between his will and yours and to dispute endlessly between you and him as to which of the two will be the master. I would a hundred times prefer that it were always he. (Rousseau 1979) p.91.

106. Thus, not seeing you eager to oppose him, not distrusting you, with nothing to hide from you, he will not deceive you, he will not lie to you, he will fearlessly show himself precisely as he is. You will be able to study him at your complete ease and arrange all around him the lessons you want to give him without his ever thinking he is receiving any. (Rousseau 1979) p.120.

107. One cannot teach children the danger of lying to men without being aware of the greater danger, on the part of men, of lying to children. A single proved lie told by the master to the child would ruin forever the whole fruit of the education. (Rousseau 1979) p.216.

108. Another error which I have already combated, but which small minds will never abandon, is that of always affecting magisterial dignity and wanting to pass for a perfect man in the mind of one's disciple. This method is misconceived. How can such masters fail to see that in wanting to strengthen their authority, they destroy it; to make yourself heard, you must put yourself in the place of those you are addressing, and you must be a man in order to know how to speak to the human heart? All

those perfect people are neither touching nor persuasive. One always tells oneself that it is quite easy for them to combat passions they do not feel. Show your weaknesses to your pupils if you want to cure his own. Let him see that you undergo the same struggles which he experiences. Let him learn to conquer himself by your example. And do not let him say as other pupils do: "These old men are spiteful because they are no longer young; they want to treat young people like old men; and because all their desires are extinguished, they treat ours as a crime." (Rousseau 1979) p.334.

109. Here I cannot prevent myself from mentioning the false dignity of governors who, in order stupidly to play wise men, run down their pupils, affect always to treat them as children, and always distinguish themselves from their pupils in everything they make them do. Far from thus disheartening your pupils' youthful courage, spare nothing to lift up their souls; make them your equals in order that they may become your equals; and if they cannot yet raise themselves up to you, descend to their level without shame, without scruple. Remember that your honour is no longer in you but in your pupil. Share his faults in order to correct them. (Rousseau 1979) p.246.

110. Now, if the master were to let himself be deceived like the disciple, he would lose the right to exact deference and to give his disciple lessons. Still less should the latter suppose that the master purposely lets him be ensnared and sets traps for his simplicity. What then must be done to avoid both of these difficulties at once? That which is best and most natural: be simple and true like him, warn him of the perils to which he is exposed, and show them to him clearly and sensibly, but without exaggeration, ill humor, pedantic display, and above all, without giving him your advice as an order until it has become one and this imperious tone is absolutely necessary. Is he obstinate after that, as he will very often be? Then say nothing more to him; leave him free; follow him; imitate him, and do it gaily and frankly. Let yourself go, enjoy yourself as much as he does, if it is possible. If the consequences become too great, you are always there to put a stop to them. And meanwhile, will not the young man, witnessing your foresight and your kindness, be at once greatly struck by the one and touched by the other? All his faults are so many bonds he provides you for restraining him in case of need. What here constitutes the master's greatest art is to provide occasions and to manage exhortations in such a way that he knows in advance when the young man will yield and when he will be obstinate. Thus the master can surround him on all sides with the lessons of experience without ever exposing him to too great dangers.

Warn him about his mistakes before he falls into them. When he has fallen into them, do not reproach him for them. You would only inflame his *amour-propre* and make it rebel. A lesson that causes revolt is of no profit. I know of nothing more inept than the phrase: "I told you so!" The best means of making him remember what one has told him is to appear to have forgotten it. Instead of reproaching him when you see him ashamed of not having believed you, gently efface this humiliation with good words. He will surely be more fond of you when he sees that you forget yourself for him, and that, instead of finishing the job of crushing him, you console him. But if you add reproaches to his sorrow, he will conceive a hatred of you and will make it a law unto himself not to listen to you anymore, as though to prove to you that he does not agree with you about the importance of your advice. (Rousseau 1979) pp.246-247.

111. Make yourself respectable to everyone. Begin by making yourself loved so

that each will seek to please you. You will not be the child's master if you are not the master of all that surrounds him; and this authority will never be sufficient if it is not founded on the esteem for virtue. It is not a question of emptying one's purse and spending money by the handful. I have never seen that money has made anyone loved. One ought not to be miserly and hard nor merely pity the poverty that one can relieve. But you can open your coffers all you want; if you do not also open your heart, others' hearts will always remain closed to you. It is your time, your care, your affection, it is you yourself that must be given. For no matter what you do, people never feel that your money is you. There are tokens of interest and benevolence which produce a greater effect and are really more useful than any gifts. How many unfortunate people, how many sick people need consolation more than alms! How many oppressed people need protection more than money! Reconcile people who have quarreled; forestall litigations; bring children to their duty, fathers to indulgence; encourage happy marriages; prevent harassment; use, lavish the influence of your pupil's parents in favor of the weak man to whom justice is denied and who is crushed by the powerful man. Loudly proclaim yourself the protector of the unfortunate. Be just, humane, and beneficent. Give not only alms; give charity. Works of mercy relieve more ills than does money. Love others, and they will love you. Serve them, and they will serve you. Be their brother, and they will be your children. (Rousseau 1979) p.95.

112. What I seek is, to elevate human nature to its highest, its noblest; and this I seek to do by love. Only in the holy power of love do I recognize the basis of the development of my [human] race to whatever of the divine and eternal lies within its nature. All the capacities for intellect, and art, and knowledge, which are within my nature, I hold to be only means for the divine elevation of the heart to love... Love is the only, the eternal foundation of the training of our race to humanity. (Pestalozzi 1859b) p.176.

113. Man will only become man through his inner and spiritual life. He becomes through it independent, free, and contented. Mere physical Nature leads him not hither. (Pestalozzi 1907) p.160.

114. Although the course of Nature in the development of man is laid down by God, nevertheless, when children are left entirely to themselves, only primitive instincts are awakened, whereas it is man's object—it is the aim of the Elementary Method, it is the aim of the wise and god-fearing—to call the human and Divine elements into life. (Pestalozzi 1912c) p.271.

115. Even before the child is born, the germs of future capacity are all there. Man's powers continue to develop through his whole life, just as in the case with the tree. His capacities are distinct from, and independent of, one another... His varied powers work together to a common end—manhood, the inner nature of which is not dependent upon the body. From (Green 1912) p.189.

116. Never forget this physical nearness or distance of all objects around you has an immense effect in determining your positive sense impressions [*Anschauung*], practical ability and even virtue. But even this law of your nature converges as a whole towards another. It converges towards the centre of our whole being, and we ourselves are this centre. Man! never forget it! All that you are, all you wish, all you might be, comes out of yourself. All must have a centre in your physical sense impression [*Anschauung*], and this again is yourself... (Pestalozzi 1907) pp.202-203.

117. Pestalozzi on why moral education is of fundamental importance, "The subordination of intellectual education to moral education follows on directly from

the recognition of the basic aim of education: the elevation of ourselves to a sense of the inner dignity of our nature, and of the pure higher, godly being, which lies within us. This sense is not developed by the power of our mind in thought, but is developed by the power of our heart in love." From (Heafford 1967) p.60.

118. [From Pestalozzi's address to his school on New Years Day 1809.] Amongst us, neither vanity nor fear, neither honor nor shame, neither reward nor punishment, as they are elsewhere almost universally used, purposely and as part of the method, are used to show you the path in which you are to go. The divine nature, which is in you, is counted holy in you. You are, among us, what the divine nature within you and without you summons you to be. We oppose no vile force against your gifts or your tendencies; we constrain them not—we only develop them. ...We do not instill into you what is ours, what exists in us as corrupted by ourselves; we develop in you what remains uncorrupted within yourselves... It is far from us to make you men as we are. It is far from us to make you such men as the majority of the men of the time are. Under our hands, you will become such men as your natures require; as the holy, the divine, within your natures require... From (Biber 1859) p.176.

119. Nature forms the child as an indivisible whole, as a vital organic unity with many-sided moral, mental, and physical capacities. She wishes that none of these capacities remain undeveloped. Where nature has influence and the child is well and truly guided by her, she develops the child's heart, mind, and body in harmonious unity. The development of the one is not only indivisibly linked with the development of the other, but each of these capacities is developed through and by means of the others." (Heafford 1967) pp.47-48.

120. A child is a being endowed with all the faculties of human nature, but none of them developed: *a bud not yet opened*. When the bud is unclosed, every one of the leaves unfolds, not one remains behind. Such must be the process of education.

No faculty in human nature but must be treated with the same attention; for their co-agency alone can ensure their success. (Pestalozzi 1827a) p.7.

121. Conversely, only that which affects man as an indissoluble unit is educative in our sense of that word. It must reach his hand and his heart as well as his head. No partial approach can be satisfactory. To consider any one capacity exclusively (head or heart or hand) is to undermine and destroy man's native equilibrium. It means unnatural methods of training, and produces partial human products. It is as wrong to think only of morality and religion as it is to have the intellect solely in mind...

The unity of human faculties is a Divine and permanent gift to the race. Respect for that unity is an essential condition of successful education. "What God has joined let no man put asunder." Whoever disregards this principle in the practice of education, in any way whatever, makes but half-men of us, in whom no satisfaction can be sought or found...

Want of balance, whether it is due to excessive emotional or to excessive intellectual development, brings ultimate discomfiture. (Pestalozzi 1912c) pp.268-269.

122. If I say that any subject will do for the purpose {of education}, I mean this literally. Not only there is not one of the little incidents in the life of a child, in his amusements and recreations, in his relation to his parents and friends and playfellows, but there is not actually anything within the reach of the child's attention, whether it belong to nature or to the employments and arts of life, that might not be made the object of a lesson by which some useful knowledge might be imparted, and, which is still more important, by which the child might not be familiarized with the habit of thinking on what he sees and speaking after he has thought.

The mode of doing this is not by any means to talk much *to* a child, but to enter into conversation *with* a child; ... *From Pestalozzi's Letters to James Pierrepont Greaves Letter XXIX, April 4, 1819* (Anderson 1931) pp.199-200.

123. Perhaps the most fearful gift that a fiendish spirit has made to this age is *knowledge without power of doing {Fertkgkeit} and insight without that power of exertion or of overcoming* that makes it possible and easy for our life to be in harmony with our inmost nature.

Man! needing much and desiring all, thou must, to satisfy thy wants and wishes, *know* and *think,* but for this thou must also *{can and} do.* And knowing and doing are so closely connected, that if one ceases the other ceases with it. (Pestalozzi 1907) p.173.

124. Whenever we put empty words into a child's mind, and impress upon his memory, as if they were real knowledge, or genuine means of acquiring it, even when neither his feelings nor his experience of things are in a position to furnish clues to their meaning, we are obviously deviating from the principle, "Life teaches"... We are sowing the seeds of callous insincerity and shallowness to which is due so much of he blundering arrogance which is characteristic of our time. *From Pestalozzi's The Swansong* in (Green 1912) p.293.

125. On the intellectual side, we accept the same fundamental principle, *Life Educates.* Just as moral education begins in inner experiences—i.e., in impressions which touch our feelings—so the education of the intellect results from the experience of objects which act as stimuli upon our senses. *From The Swansong* in (Green 1912) p.290.

126. But if a mother is to teach by THINGS, she must recollect also, that to the formation of ideas, more is requisite, than the bringing the object before the senses. Its qualities must be explained; its origin must be accounted for; its parts must be described, and their relation to the whole ascertained; its use, its effect or consequences, must be stated. (Pestalozzi 1827f) p.123.

127. To have a knowledge of words with no distinct idea of the things they represent enormously increases the difficulty of getting at the truth.... {children} should learn to read first in the Book of Nature. *From Pestalozzi's diary Feb. 2, 1774* (Russell 1926) p.17.

128. ...the first rule is to teach always by *things* rather than by *words*....

Whenever the knowledge of an abstract idea, which will not of course admit of any representation of that kind [representation by things rather than words], is to be communicated to the child, on the same principle an equivalent of that representation should be given by an exemplification through the medium of a fact laid before the child. This is the original intention and use of moral tales; and, this, too, agrees with the excellent old adage, "The way by precept is long and laborious, that by example short and easy." (Pestalozzi 1827f) pp.195-197.

129. In rainy weather toadstools grow fast on every dungheap; and in the same way definitions, not founded on sense-impression, produce, just as quickly, a fungus-like wisdom, which dies just as quickly in the sunlight, and which looks upon the clear sky as poison to it. The baseless, wordy show of such baseless wisdom produces men, who believe they have reached the end in all subjects, because their life is a tiresome babble about this end. (Pestalozzi 1907) p.58.

130. To the want of this distinction [*Things v. Words*—the title of the letter] I think we may safely ascribe much of the waste of time, and the deceptive exhibition of apparent knowledge, which is so frequent in schools, both of a higher and of a

lower character. ... No doubt a proceeding of this sort...is the most commodious system for the indolence or ignorance of those who practise upon it as a system of instruction. Add to which the powerful stimulus of vanity in the pupils—the hope of distinction and reward for some, the fear of exposure or punishment in others— and we shall have the principal motives before us owing to which this system, in spite of its wretchedness, has so long been patronized by those who do not think at all, and tolerated by those who do not sufficiently think for themselves. (Pestalozzi 1827f) p.195.

131. The mania for words and books, which pervades our whole system of popular education, has taught us at least this—that we can not remain as we are. Everything confirms me in my opinion that the only way of escaping the civil, moral, and religious degradation, is to have done with the superficiality, narrowness, and other errors of our popular instruction, and to recognize sense-impression as the real foundation of all knowledge. (Russell 1926) p.100.

132. I saw in this combination of unschooled ignorance a power of seeing [Anschauung], and a firm conception of the known and the seen of which our ABC puppets have no notion.

I learned from them—I must have been blind if I had not learned—to know the natural relation in which real knowledge stands to book-knowledge. I learnt from them what a disadvantage this one-sided letter-knowledge and entire reliance on words (which is only sound and noise when there is nothing behind them) must be. I saw what a real hindrance this may be to the real power of observation [Anschauung], and the firm conception of the objects that surround us. (Pestalozzi 1907) pp.18-19.

133. The possibility of a straight forward psychological achievement of this idea [simple stages of general human development in The Elementary Method] depends on the recognition of the difference between the method of unfolding man's fundamental capacities, which follow certain unchangeable laws, and the methods adopted in teaching special branches of knowledge and special dexterities in which those powers are applied.

... These last differ from each other as completely as the objects which we strive to know and put to use, and as completely as the position and circumstances of the individuals concerned differ. The Elementary Method proposes to avoid confusion by giving the first place to the methods of developing capacity. These are constant. (Green 1912) p.284.

... the problem of education ... does not consist in communicating special knowledge or special dexterities, but in developing the fundamental human powers. (Green 1912) p.196.

134. The general elevation of these inward powers of the human mind to a pure human wisdom, is the universal purpose of the education even of the lowest men. The practice, application and use of these powers and this wisdom, under special circumstances and conditions of humanity, is education for a profession or social condition. These must always be kept subordinate to the general object of human training....

To him who is not a Man, a man developed in his inmost powers, to him is wanting a basis for an education suited to his immediate destiny and to his special circumstances, such as no external elevation can excuse. (Pestalozzi 1859a) p.156.

135. Any method, that brands the brow of the learner with the stamp of completely stifled natural powers, and the want of common sense and mother-wit, is

condemned by me, whatever other advantages it may have. I do not deny that even *such* methods may produce good tailors, shoemakers, tradesmen, and soldiers; but I do deny that they can produce a tailor or a tradesman who is *a man* in the highest sense of the word. Oh! if men could only comprehend that the aim of all instruction is, and can be, no other but the development of human nature, by the harmonious cultivation of its powers and talents, and the promotion of manliness of life. (Pestalozzi 1907) pp.156-157.

136. We must bear in mind that the ultimate end of education is, not a perfection in the accomplishments of the school, but fitness for life; not the acquirement of habits of blind obedience and of prescribed diligence, but a preparation for independent action. We must bear in mind that, whatever class of society a pupil may belong to, whatever calling he may be intended for, there are certain faculties in human nature common to all, which constitute the stock of the fundamental energies of man. We have no right to withhold from anyone the opportunities of developing all their faculties... I repeat that we have no right to shut out the child from the development of those faculties also, which we may not for the present conceive to be very essential for his future calling or station in life. (Pestalozzi 1827c) p.85

137. *From Letters to James Pierrepont Greaves Letter XXXII April 25, 1819.* In order to give the character described here [a happy and fulfilled one] to the action and to the life of an individual, I consider it as necessary that all the faculties implanted in human nature should be properly developed. It is not that *virtuosity* ought to be attained in any direction, or that a degree of excellence ought to be anxiously aspired to which is the exclusive privilege of pre-eminent talent. But there is a degree of development of all the faculties which is far from the refinement of any; and of such a course that great advantage will be to prepare the mind for a more especial application to any line of studies congenial to its inclination, or connected with certain pursuits.

[*In a footnote Pestalozzi then quotes Locke,* "The business of education, in respect of knowledge, is not to perfect the learner in all or any one of the sciences; but to give his mind that disposition, and those habits, that may enable him to attain any part of knowledge he shall stand in need of in the future course of his life."] (Anderson 1931) p.211.

138. Men, fathers, force not the faculties of your children into paths too distant, before they have attained strength by exercise, and avoid harshness and over-fatigue.

When this right order of proceedings is anticipated, the faculties of the mind are weakened, and lose their steadiness, and the equipoise of their structure.

This you do when, before making them sensitive to truth and wisdom by the real knowledge of actual objects, you engage them in the thousand-fold confusions of word-learning and opinions; and lay the foundation of their mental character and of the first determination of their powers, instead of with truth and actual objects, with sounds and speech—and words. (Pestalozzi 1859a) p.157.

139. The child's own impulses induce free activity, and instruction must not hurry to interfere. It must only make demands for which the child is already prepared. When he *feels*, "I can do that now," then we may ask him to do it. The child must be allowed to take chalk, pencil, charcoal, etc., in his hand, and draw straight and crooked lines all over without attempting to interfere and correct. Only when the child begins of its own accord to imitate easy words, pleasant sounds , and to take pleasure in the changes and more accurate representation of his random strokes; only when he is stimulated to imitate a greater variety of words and sounds, and to

make his strokes more correct and varied, does the thought awaken in him: "My dear mother can help me to do this, which I very much want to do, but cannot do properly." *Then* is the time when instruction can be offered to the child in a natural way; then and then only should it be offered to him. In all departments of practical education the mode of procedure is the same. From (Green 1912) p.312.

140. The mechanism of Nature as a whole is great and simple. Man! imitate it. Imitate this action of great Nature, who out of the seed of the largest tree produces a scarcely perceptible shoot, then, just as imperceptibly, daily and hourly by gradual stages, unfolds first the beginnings of the stem, then the bough, then the branch, then the extreme twig on which hangs the perishable leaf.

Consider carefully this action of great Nature, how she tends and perfects every single part as it is formed, and joins on every new part to the permanent life of the old...

The mechanism of physical human nature is essentially subject to the same laws by which physical Nature generally unfolds her powers. (Pestalozzi 1907) pp. 202-203.

141. When I recommend to a mother to avoid *wearying* a child by her instructions, I do not wish to encourage the notion that instruction should always take the character of an amusement, or even of a play. I am convinced that such a notion, where it is entertained and acted upon by a teacher, will forever preclude solidity of knowledge, and from a want of sufficient exertions on the part of the pupils, will lead to that very result which I wish to avoid by my principle of a constant employment of the thinking powers.

A child must very early in life be taught a lesson which frequently comes too late, and is then a most painful one,—that exertion is indispensable for the attainment of knowledge. But a child should not be taught to look upon exertion as an unavoidable *evil*. (Pestalozzi 1827g) p.130.

142. Man is in general very incapable of comprehending great, general points of view, and, on the other hand, very apt in rightly comprehending a single definite object and in working himself into a thorough knowledge of it, and one can more easily find a thousand men who are in a position to abstract principles of education from the observation of their own children than a single one who through reflection on nature and the general needs of man makes himself capable in a particular case of educating a particular child for the demands of his particular situation. (Pestalozzi 1931a) pp.39-40.

143. You must generally distinguish between the laws of Nature and her course, that is, her single workings, and statements about those workings. In her laws she is eternal truth, and for us, the eternal standard of all truth; but in her modifications, in which her laws apply to every individual and to every case, her truth does not satisfy and content our race. The positive truth of the condition and circumstances of any individual case claims the same equal right of necessity, by virtue of eternal laws, as the common law of human nature itself. Consequently, the claim of necessity of both laws must be brought into harmony, if they are to work satisfactorily for men. (Pestalozzi 1907) pp.159-160.

144. But then indeed the individual circumstances of man are so infinitely various that it seems to me that if all the animals of earth had to be educated each to his career they would not have to be fitted for more dissimilar situations than has man alone. (Pestalozzi 1931a) p.37.

145. What makes me more assertive—and, I believe, more to be excused for being so—is that, instead of yielding to the systematic spirit, I grant as little as possible to reasoning and I trust only observation. I found myself not on what I have imagined but on what I have seen. It is true that I have not restricted my experience to the compass of a city's walls or to a single class of people. But after having compared as many ranks and peoples as I could see in a life spent observing them, I have eliminated as artificial what belonged to one people and not to another, to one station and not to another, and have regarded as incontestably belonging to man only what was common to all, at whatever age, in whatever rank, and in whatever nation. (Rousseau 1979) p.254.

146. Central point of life, individual destiny of man, thou art the book of nature. In thee lieth the power and the plan of that wise teacher; and every school education not erected upon the principles of human development, leads astray. (Pestalozzi 1859a) p.155.

It is to this end [finding a new approach to education] that I have devoted my whole time and attention, for this purpose I have endeavoured to trace nature to her source, and sought to find in her, the means, when properly applied, that will effectually relieve the powers of the mind from their Egyptian State of Bondage, that will awaken slumbering faculties, that will put the whole energies of the soul into a state of action, and will cause to germinate and fructify those seeds of Knowledge which the God of all Life has implanted in Man, and finally convert a physical corporal subject, into a rational thinking Being. The means which I come forward to offer, is not a system of Education, warp'd by the sophistry of Art, but one founded on the most simple Laws of nature.

After a life spent in the most minute researches and careful examination of elementary principles, I have the gratification to see the means that I have adopted, Which are faith and love themselves brought into action by natural simplicity, succeed in many points, not only in my own Establishment, but in that of numbers of others that have adopted and practiced my system. (Pestalozzi 1818) pp.3-4.

147. In my later years and especially since the founding of my boarding establishment I have, in cooperation with my friends, endeavored to organize the several means of developing the individual powers and capacities in a psychological sequence corresponding to the course through which nature herself develops these powers. The cultivation of these several powers, respectively, in accordance with the laws of nature has seemed to my house almost ever since its origin to be the problem the solution of which should be considered the task of the pedagogy of our time. (Pestalozzi 1931d) pp.131-132.

148. [in answer to his own question as to what is the art of education] I answer it is the art of the gardener under whose protective care a thousand trees grow and flourish. Notice that he contributes nothing to their growth in itself. Their growth depends essentially on themselves... So the educator. It is not he who endows man with capacity of any sort; he only sees to it that no external force should hinder or disturb natural course of development of any capacity... (Pestalozzi 1931d) pp.127-128.

149. The germ, out of which the feelings that are essential to religion and morality spring, is the same from which the whole spirit of my method of teaching arises. It begins entirely in the natural relation, which exists between the infant and its mother, and essentially rests on the Art of connection, instruction, from the

cradle upwards, with this natural relation, and building it with continuous Art upon a state of mind that resembles our dependence on the Author of our being. (Pestalozzi 1907) p.191.

150. I have recognised the Eternal *in myself.* I have *seen* the way of The Lord, I have *read* the laws of the Almighty in the dust, I have *sought* out the ways of His love in my heart I *know* in whom I *believe.* My trust in God becomes infinite through my self-knowledge, and through the insight germinated in it, of the laws of the moral world. (Pestalozzi 1907) p.196.

151. Thus, we find human being even at the earliest stages of boyhood fitted for the highest and most important concern of mankind, for the fulfillment of his destiny and mission, which is the representation of the divine nature within him. [This, he goes on to say, is the purpose of his educational program] (Froebel 1890) p.332.

152. The whole purpose of education must of necessity be to foster the realization of the divine principle in man. From (Lawrence 1952) p.190.

153. The only infallible remedy for counteracting any shortcoming and even wickedness is to find the originally good side of the human being that has been repressed, disturbed or misled into the shortcoming, and then foster, build up and properly guide the good side… From (Priestman 1952) p.157.

154. We grant space and time to young plants and animals because we know that, in accordance with the laws that live in them, they will develop properly and grow well; young animals and plants are given rest, and arbitrary interference with their growth is avoided, because it is known that the opposite practice would disturb their pure unfolding and sound development; but the young human is looked upon as a piece of wax, a lump of clay, which man can mold into what he pleases. O man, who roamest through garden and field, through meadow and grove, why dost thou close thy mind to the silent teaching of nature?… Thus, O parents, could your children on whom you force in tender years forms and aims against their nature, and who, therefore, walk with you in morbid and unnatural deformity—thus could your children, too, unfold in beauty and develop in all sided harmony! (Froebel 1890) pp. 8-9.

155. We find also three attitudes, spheres of work, and regions of the mind in man: 1.) the region of the soul, the heart, Feeling: 2.) the region of the mind, the head, Intellect; 3.) the region of the active life, the putting forth to actual deed, Will. As mental attitudes these three divisions seem the wider apart the more we contemplate them, as spheres of work and regions of mind they seem quite separate and perfect opposites… The need for the uniting link appears in almost every circumstance of life… To satisfy that need is the most imperative need now set before the human race, … Intellect, feeling and will would then unite, a many-sided power, to build up and constitute our life. From (Murray 1914) pp.15-16.

156. But every human being is born as a member of a family and a community and a nation, and he can achieve his own growth only as a harmonious part of these larger wholes, and they in turn represent different realms of unity through which it realizes by progressive stages its total growth toward the divine. From (Lawrence 1952) p.188.

157. Frobel, I think, was certainly carried away by his pantheism, and went to the full length of his contemporary Wordsworth, believing even in human pre-existence; the soul was "originally one with God" (Hayward 1904) p.29.

158. It is futile to object that the boy at this age, if he is to reach a certain degree

of skill and insight, ought to direct his whole strength to the learning of words, to verbal instruction, to intellectual culture. On the contrary, genuine experience shows that external, physical, productive activity interspersed in intellectual work strengthens not only the body but in a very marked degree the mind in its various phases of development, so that the mind, after such a refreshing work-bath (I can find no better name), enters upon its intellectual pursuits with new vigour and life. (Froebel 1890) p.237.

159. Play is the highest phase of child development—of human development at this period...

Play is the purest, most spiritual activity of man at this stage, and, at the same time, typical of human life as a whole—of the inner hidden natural life in man and all things... It holds the source of all that is good. A child that plays thoroughly, with self-active determination, persevering until physical fatigue forbids, will surely be a thorough, determined man, capable of self-sacrifice for the promotion of the welfare of himself and others.

As already indicated, play at this time is not trivial, it is highly serious and of deep significance. Cultivate and foster it, O mother; protect and guard it, O father! to the calm, keen vision of one who truly knows human nature, the spontaneous play of the a child discloses the future inner life of the man. (Froebel 1890) pp. 54-55.

160. Sharp limits and definite subdivisions with the continuous series of the years of development, withdrawing from attention the permanent continuity, the living connection, the inner living essence, are therefore highly pernicious, and even destructive in their influence. Thus, it is highly pernicious to consider the stages of human development—infant, child, boy or girl, youth or maiden, man or woman, old man or matron—as really distinct and not as life shows them, as continuous in themselves, in unbroken transitions; highly pernicious to consider the child or boy as something wholly different from the youth or man, and as something so distinct that the common foundations (human being) is seen but vaguely in the idea and word, and scarcely at all considered in life and for life. (Froebel 1890) p.28.

161. Therefore the child should, from the very time of his birth, be viewed in accordance with his nature, treated correctly, and given the free, all-sided use of his powers. By no means should the use of certain powers and members be enhanced at the expense of others, and these hindered in their development; the child should neither be partly chained, fettered, nor swathed; nor, later on, spoiled by too much assistance. (Froebel 1890) p.21.

162. Therefore, we ought to at last understand that we do great violence to boy-nature when we repress and supplant these normal many-sided tendencies in the growing human being; when, in the belief of doing service to God and man, and of promoting the future earthly prosperity, inner peace, and heavenly salvation of the boy, we cut off one or the other of these tendencies and graft others in their places.

God neither engrafts nor inoculates. He develops the most trivial and imperfect things in continuously ascending series and in accordance with eternal self-grounded and self-developing laws. (Froebel 1890) p.328.

163. It is my thesis that significant portions of the modern psychologies, and especially the clinical psychologies, are actually instances of religio-ethical thinking. They are, in fact, mixed disciplines which contain examples of religious, ethical, and scientific language. To state this about the modern psychologies is certainly to go against their own self-understanding.... But when many of these psychologies are

submitted to careful analysis one discovers that they have religious and moral horizons about which both they and the general public are unclear. (Browning 1987) p.8.

164. The achievement of personality means nothing less than the optimum development of the whole individual human being. ...Personality is the supreme realization of the innate indiosyncrasy of a living being. It is an act of high courage flung in the face of life, the absolute affirmation of all that constitutes the individual, the most successful adaptation to the universal conditions of existence coupled with the greatest possible freedom for self-determination. To educate a man to *this* seems to me no light matter. It is surely the hardest task the modern mind has set itself. (Jung 1954c) p.171 § 289.

165. As we know this question [of "making wholes"] has occupied the most adventurous minds of the East for more than two thousand years, and in this respect methods and philosophical doctrines have been developed which simply put all Western attempts along these lines into the shade. Our attempts have, with few exceptions, all stopped short at either magic (mystery cults, amongst which we must include Christianity) or intellectualism (philosophy from Pythagoras to Schopenhauer). It is only the tragedies of Goethe's *Faust* and Neitzschee's *Zarathustra* which mark the first glimmerings of a break-through of total experience in our Western hemisphere. [In a footnote he includes William Blake.] (Jung 1958b) pp.554-555 § 905.

166. Earlier, I raised the question of whether we have anything like satori in the West. If we discount the sayings of our Western mystics, a superficial glance discloses nothing that could be likened to it in even the faintest degree. ...In India it was yoga and in China Buddhism which supplied the driving force for these attempts to wrench oneself free from bondage to a state of consciousness that was felt to be incomplete. So far as Western mysticism is concerned, its texts are full of instructions as to how man can and must release himself from the "I-ness" of his consciousness, so that through knowledge of his own nature he may rise above it and attain the inner (godlike) man. (Jung 1958b) p.545 § 890.

167. Personality, as the complete realization of our whole being, is an unattainable ideal. But unattainability is no argument against the ideal, for ideals are only signposts, never the goal. (Jung 1954c) p.172 § 291.

168. [Jung, from an interview four days before his death] All that I have learned has led me step by step to an unshakable conviction of the existence of God. I only believe in what I know. And that eliminates believing. Therefore I do not take his existence on belief—I *know* that he exists. From (Sands 1961).

[Jung, answering the question, "Do you now believe in God."] I *know*. I don't need to believe. I know. (Jung 1957) p.4

169. Freud has unfortunately overlooked the fact that man has never yet been able single-handed to hold his own against the powers of darkness—that is, of the unconscious. Man has always stood in need of the spiritual help which his particular religion held out to him. ...It was to arm himself against this threat and to heal the damage done that he developed religious and magical practices. This is why the medicine-man is also the priest; he is the saviour of the soul as well as of the body, and religions are systems of healing for psychic illness. This is especially true of the two greatest religions of humanity, Christianity and Buddhism. Man is never helped in his suffering by what he thinks of for himself; only suprahuman, revealed truth lifts him out of his distress. (Jung 1958e) p.344 § 531.

170. Among all my patients in the second half of life—that is to say, over thirty-five—there has not been one whose problem in the last resort was not that of

finding a religious outlook on life. It is safe to say that every one of them fell ill because he had lost what the living religions of every age have given to their followers, and none of them has been really healed who did not regain his religious outlook. This of course has nothing whatever to do with a particular creed or membership of a church. (Jung 1958e) p.334 § 509.

Ordinary reasonableness, sound human judgement, science as a compendium of common sense, these certainly help us over a good part of the road, but they never take us beyond the frontiers of life's most commonplace realities, beyond the merely average and normal. They afford no answer to the question of psychic suffering and its profound significance. A psychoneurosis must be understood, ultimately, as the suffering of a soul which has not discovered its meaning. But all creativeness in the realm of spirit as well as every psychic advance of man arises from the suffering of the soul, and the cause of the suffering is spiritual stagnation, or psychic sterility. (Jung 1958e) p.331 § 497.

171. To the extent that a man is untrue to the law of his being and does not rise to personality, he has failed to realize his life's meaning. Fortunately, in her kindness and patience, Nature never puts the fatal question as to the meaning of their lives into the mouths of most people. And where no one asks, no one need answer. (Jung 1954c) p.183 § 314.

172. … it is only meaning that liberates. (Jung 1958e) p.330 § 496. (See fuller quotation in appendix note 188.)

173. The way of successive assimilation goes far beyond the curative results that specifically concern the doctor. It leads in the end to that distant goal which may perhaps have been the first urge to life: the complete actualization of the whole human being, that is, individuation. (Jung 1954h) p.160 § 352.

174. Since the ultimate authority of life lies within the individual, there is nothing more important in life than to develop the innate tendency of the psyche to realize its wholeness. The psyche demands to be developed and to be made whole; obedience to this command is the highest good and the ultimate concern of life. (Smith 1990) p.89.

175. The attainment of wholeness requires one to stake one's whole being. Nothing less will do; there can be no easier conditions, no substitutions, no compromises. (Jung 1958b) p.556 § 906.

176. I have called this wholeness which transcends consciousness the "self." The goal of the individuation process is the synthesis of the self. From another point of view the term "entelechy" might be preferable to "synthesis." There is empirical reason why "entelechy" is, in certain conditions, more fitting: the symbols of wholeness frequently occur at the beginning of the individuation process, indeed they can often be observed in the first dreams of early infancy. This observation says much for the *a priori* existence of potential wholeness, and on this account the idea of *entelechy* instantly recommends itself. (Jung 1959c) pp.164-165 § 278.

177. The culture of joy [Jungian and humanistic psychology]…sees the world as basically harmonious. It also sees human wants and needs as easily reconciled and coordinated in almost frictionless compatibility. This state is especially realized by people who are true to their own most basic natures. (Browning 1987) p.5.

178. [From a letter of Jung to D. Hoch, 28th May 1952] I am completely of your opinion that a man only lives, and lives ever completely, if he is related to God, who stands over him and defines him. From (Heisig 1979) p.78n.

179. The psychological interest of the present time is an indication that modern

man expects something from the psyche which the outer world has not given him: doubtless something which our religion ought to contain, but no longer does contain, at least for modern man. For him the various forms of religion no longer appear to come from within, from the psyche; they seem more like items from the inventory of the outside world. (Jung 1964b) p.83 § 168.

180. I want to make clear that by the term "religion" I do not mean a creed. It is, however, true that every creed is originally based on one hand upon the experience of the *numinosum* and on the other hand upon {Greek word for 'faith'}, that is to say, trust or loyalty, faith and confidence in a certain experience of a numinous nature and in the change of consciousness that ensues. The conversion of Paul is a striking example of this. We might say, then, that the term "religion" designates the attitude peculiar to a consciousness which has been changed by experience of the *numinosum*.

Creeds are codified and dogmatized forms of original religious experience. The contents of the experience have become sanctified and are usually congealed in a rigid, often elaborate, structure of ideas. ...The psychologist, if he takes up a scientific attitude, has to disregard the claim of every creed to be unique and eternal truth. He must keep his eye on the human side of the religious problem, since he is concerned with the original religious experience quite apart from what the creeds have made of it. (Jung 1958d) pp.8-9 § 9-10.

181. The tremendous effectiveness of these images [God images] is such that they not only give one the feeling of pointing to the *Ens realissimum*, but make one convinced that they actually express it and establish it as a fact. This makes discussion uncommonly difficult, if not impossible. It is, in fact, impossible to demonstrate God's reality to oneself except by using images which have arisen spontaneously or are sanctified by tradition, and whose psychic nature and effects the naïve-minded person has never separated from their unknowable metaphysical background. He instantly equates the effective image with the transcendental x to which it points. ...it must be remembered that the image and the statement are psychic processes which are different from their transcendental object; they do not posit it, they merely point to it. In the realm of psychic processes criticism and discussion are not only permissible but are unavoidable. (Jung 1958a) p.363 § 558.

182. It is a misunderstanding to accuse me of having made out of this an "immanent God" or a "God-substitute." I am an empiricist and as such I can demonstrate empirically the existence of a totality supraordinate to consciousness. Consciousness experiences this supraordinate totality as something numinous, as a *tremendum* or *fascinosum*. As an empiricist I am interested only in the experiential character of this totality, which in itself, ontologically considered, is indescribable. This "self" never at any time takes the place of God, though it may perhaps be a vessel for divine grace. (Jung 1964a) p.463 § 874.

183. As I have shown elsewhere, an experience of the self may be expected as a result of these psychotherapeutic endeavours, and quite often these experiences are numinous. It is not worth the effort to try to describe their totality character. Anyone who has experienced anything of the sort will know what I mean, and anyone who has not had the experience will not be satisfied by any amount of descriptions. Moreover there are countless descriptions of it in world literature. But I know of no case in which the bare description conveyed the experience. (Jung 1963) p.547 § 779.

184. One hopes to control the unconscious, but the past masters in the art of

self-control, the yogis, attain perfection in *samadhi,* a state of ecstasy, which so far as we know is equivalent to a state of unconsciousness. It makes no difference whether they call our unconscious a "universal consciousness"; the fact remains that in their case the unconscious has swallowed up ego-consciousness. ..."Universal consciousness" is logically identical with unconsciousness. It is nevertheless true that a correct application of the methods described in the Pali Canon or in the *Yoga-sutra* induces a remarkable extension of consciousness. But, with increasing extension, the contents of consciousness lose in clarity of detail. In the end, consciousness becomes all-embracing, but nebulous; an infinite number of things merge into an indefinite whole, a state in which subject and object are almost completely identical. This is all very beautiful, but scarcely to be recommended anywhere north of the Tropic of Cancer. (Jung 1959b) pp.287-288 § 520.

185. When I once remarked to Jung that his psychological insights and his attitude to the unconscious seemed to me to be in many respects the same as those of the most archaic religions—for example shamanism, or the religion of the Naskapi Indians who have neither priest nor ritual...—Jung answered with a laugh: "Well, that's nothing to be ashamed of. It is an honor!" ...The basis and substance of Jung's entire life and work do not lie in the traditions and religions which have become contents of collective consciousness, but rather in that primordial experience which is the final source of these contents: the encounter of the single individual with his own god or daimon, his struggle with the overpowering emotions, affects, fantasies and creative inspirations and obstacles which come to light from within. (von Franz 1975) pp.13-14.

186. Jung's discovery of the technique of active imagination is a return to the oldest known forms of meditation, as they existed *before* the subsequent development into yoga, Buddhistic meditation and Taoist alchemy. It was as if he had been carried back over the millennia, in one daring leap, to that world in which primordial man, completely naïve, first began to make contact with the world of the spirit. Unlike the shamans Jung did not enter this world in a trance-state, but rather in full consciousness and without any diminution of the individual moral responsibility which is one of the attainments of Western culture. This is something new and unique, something which cannot be compared with the earlier stages of culture which have been described. (von Franz 1975) pp.116-117.

187. In spite of his own self-understanding as a scientist taking a purely phenomenological approach to the study of psychology, Jung lapsed into both religious and ethical judgements at every turn. His psychological models quickly become metaphors orienting his readers to the meaning of life, and his descriptions of health and wholeness rapidly became moral prescriptions. (Browning 1987) p.164.

188. Even though the theories of Freud and Adler come much nearer to getting at the bottom of the neuroses than any earlier approach from the medical side, their exclusive concern with the instincts fails to satisfy the deeper spiritual needs of the patient. They are too much bound by the premises of nineteenth-century science, too matter of fact, and they give too little value to fictional and imaginative processes. In a word, they do not give enough meaning to life. And it is only meaning that liberates. (Jung 1958e) pp.330 § 496.

189. "Physical" is not the only criterion of truth: there are also *psychic* truths which can neither be explained nor proved nor contested in any physical way... Religious statements are of this type. They refer without exception to things that cannot be established as physical facts.

The psyche is an autonomous factor, and religious statements are psychic confessions which in the last resort are based on unconscious, i.e., on transcendental, processes. These processes are not accessible to physical perception but demonstrate their existence through the confession of the psyche. The resultant statements are filtered through the medium of human consciousness: that is to say, they are given visible forms which in their turn are subject to manifold influences from within and without. That is why whenever we speak of religious contents we move in a world of images that point to something ineffable. We do not know how clear or unclear these images, metaphors, and concepts are in respect of their transcendental object. If, for instance, we say "God," we give expression to an image or verbal concept which has undergone many changes in the course of time. We are, however, unable to say with any degree of certainty—unless it be by faith—whether these changes affect only the images and concepts, or the Unspeakable itself. ...There is no doubt that there is something behind these images that transcends consciousness and operates in such a way that the statements do not vary limitlessly and chaotically, but clearly all relate to a few basic principles or archetypes. These, like the psyche itself, or like matter are unknowable as such. All we can do is to construct models of them which we know to be inadequate, a fact which is confirmed again and again by religious statements. (Jung 1958a) pp.359-361§ 553-555.

190. I do not believe that I am going too far when I say that modern man, in contrast to his nineteenth-century brother, turns to the psyche with very great expectations, and does so without reference to any traditional creed but rather with a view to Gnostic experience. ...Modern man abhors faith and the religions based upon it. He holds them valid only so far as their knowledge-content seems to accord with his own experience of the psychic background. He wants to *know*—to experience for himself. (Jung 1964b) pp.83-84 § 171.

191. The common background of microphysics and depth-psychology is as much physical as psychic and therefore neither, but rather a third thing; a neutral nature which can at most be grasped in hints since in essence it is transcendental. (Jung 1963) p.538 § 768.

192. ...if you have insight "you use your inner eye, your inner ear, to pierce to the heart of things, and have no need of intellectual knowledge." [quoting Chaung-Tzu] This is obviously an allusion to the absolute knowledge of the unconscious. (Jung 1960e) p.489 § 923.

193. Religious experience is absolute; it is not to be disputed. You can only say that you have never had such an experience, whereupon your opponent will reply: "Sorry, I have." And there your discussion will come to an end. No matter what the world thinks about religious experience, the one who has it possesses a great treasure, a thing that has become for him a source of life, meaning, and beauty, and that has given a new splendour to the world and to mankind. He has *pistis* and peace. Where is the criterion by which you could say that such a life is not legitimate, that such an experience is not valid, and that such *pistis* is mere illusion? Is there, as a matter of fact, any better truth about the ultimate things than the one that helps you to live? That is the reason that I take careful account—*religio!*- of the symbols produced by the unconscious. They are the one thing that is capable of convincing the critical mind of modern man. And they are convincing for a very old-fashioned reason: They are *overwhelming*, which is precisely what the Latin word *convincere* means.... No one can know what the ultimate things are. We must therefore take them as we experience them. And if such experience helps to make life healthier, more beauti-

ful, more complete and more satisfactory to yourself and to those you love, you may safely say: "This is the grace of God." (Jung 1958d) pp.104-105 § 167.

194. For the practical work of dream-analysis one needs a special knack and intuitive understanding on the one hand, and a considerable knowledge of the history of symbols on the other. As in all practical work with psychology, mere intellect is not enough; one also needs feeling, because otherwise the exceedingly important feeling-values of the dream are neglected. Without these, dream-analysis is impossible. As the dream is dreamed by the whole man, it follows that anyone who tries to interpret the dream must be engaged as a whole man too. "Ars totum requirit hominem," says an old alchemist. Understanding and knowledge there must be, but they should not set themselves up above the heart, which in its turn must not give way to sentiment. (Jung 1954a) pp.106-107 § 198.

195. ...analytical psychology is a reaction against the exaggerated rationalization of consciousness which, seeking to control nature, isolates itself from her and so robs man of his own natural history. ...That quality of eternity which is so characteristic of the life of primitive man is entirely lacking. Hemmed round by rationalistic walls, we are cut off from the eternity of nature. Analytical psychology seeks to break though these walls by digging up again the fantasy-images of the unconscious which our rationalism has rejected. These images lie beyond the walls; they are part of the nature *in us*, which apparently lies buried in our past and against which we have barricaded ourselves behind the walls of reason. Analytical psychology tries to resolve the resultant conflict not by going "back to Nature" with Rousseau, but by holding on to the level we have successfully reached, and by enriching consciousness with a knowledge of man's psychic foundations. (Jung 1960a) pp.380-381 § 739.

196. One cannot just think up a system or truth which would give the patient what he needs in order to live, namely faith, hope, love, and understanding.

There for the highest achievements of human endeavour are so many gifts of grace, which are neither to be taught nor learned, neither given nor taken, neither withheld nor earned, since they come through experience, which is an irrational datum not subject to human will and caprice. Experiences cannot be *made*. They happen—yet fortunately their independence of man's activity is not absolute but relative. We can draw closer to them—that much lies within our human reach. There are ways which bring us nearer to living experiences, yet we should beware of calling these ways "methods." The very word has a deadening effect. The way to experience, moreover, is anything but a clever trick; it is rather a venture which requires us to commit ourselves with our whole being. (Jung 1958e) pp.331-332 § 500-501.

197. Unity and totality stand at the highest point on the scale of objective values because their symbols can no longer be distinguished from the *imago Dei*. Hence all statements about the God-image apply also to the empirical symbols of totality. ...If this insight were purely intellectual it could be achieved without much difficulty, for the world-wide pronouncements about God within us and above us, about Christ and the *corpus mysticum*, the personal and suprapersonal Atman, etc., are all formulations that can easily be mastered by the philosophic intellect. This is the common source of the illusion that one is then in possession of the thing itself. But actually one has acquired nothing more than its name, despite the age-old prejudice that the name magically represents the thing, and that it is sufficient to pronounce the name in order to posit the thing's existence. In the course of the millennia the reasoning mind has been given every opportunity to see through the futility of this conceit, though that has done nothing to prevent the intellectual mastery of a thing

from being accepted at its face value. It is precisely our experiences in psychology which demonstrates as plainly as could be wished that the intellectual "grasp" of a psychological fact produces no more than a concept of it, and that a concept is not more than a name, a *flatus vocis*... The intellect is undeniably useful in its own field, but it is a great cheat and illusionist outside of it whenever it tries to manipulate values.

...It is through the "affect" that the subject becomes involved and so comes to feel the whole weight of reality. The difference amounts roughly to that between a severe illness which one reads about in a textbook and the real illness which one has. In psychology one possesses nothing unless one has experienced it in reality. Hence a purely intellectual insight is not enough, because one knows only the words and not the substance of the thing from inside. (Jung 1959a) pp.31-33 § 60-61. 198.

198. All the old arguments against unreasonableness, self-deception, and immorality, once so potent, have lost their attraction. We are now reaping the fruit of nineteenth-century education. Throughout that period the Church preached to young people the merit of blind faith, while the universities inculcated an intellectual rationalism, with the result that today we plead in vain whether for faith or reason. Tired of the warfare of opinions, the modern man wishes to find out for himself how things are. ...It is no reckless adventure, but an effort inspired by deep spiritual distress to bring meaning once more into life on the basis of fresh and unprejudiced experience. (Jung 1958e) p.343 § 529.

199. In the East, mind is a cosmic factor, the very essence of existence; while in the West we have just begun to understand that it is the essential condition of cognition, and hence of the cognitive existence of the world. There is no conflict between religion and science in the East, because no science is there based upon the passion for facts, and no religion upon mere faith; there is religious cognition and cognitive religion. With us, man is incommensurably small and the grace of God is everything; but in the East, man is God and he redeems himself. (Jung 1958c) p.480 § 768.

200. *From the power that binds all creatures none is free*
Except the man who wins self-mastery!
Goethe from (Jung 1953b) p.227 § 380.

201. I have found that dominion and liberty are two incompatible words; therefore, I could be master of a cottage only in ceasing to be master of myself. (Rousseau 1979) p.472.

202. Individuation cuts one off from personal conformity and hence from collectivity. That is the guilt which the individuant leaves behind him for the world, that is the guilt he must endeavour to redeem. He must offer a ransom in place of himself, that is, he must bring forth values which are an equivalent substitute for his absence in the collective personal sphere. Without this production of values, final individuation is immoral and—more than that—suicidal. The man who can not create values should sacrifice himself consciously to the spirit of collective conformity. In so doing, he is free to choose the collectivity to which he will sacrifice himself. Only to the extent that a man creates objective values can he and may he individuate. Every further step in individuation creates new guilt and necessitates new expiation. Hence individuation is possible only so long as substitute values are produced. Individuation is exclusive adaptation to inner reality and hence an allegedly "mystical" process. The expiation is adaptation to the outer world. It has to be

offered to the outer world, with the petition that the outer world accept it. (Jung 1977a) p.451 § 1095.

203. This problem cannot be solved collectively, because the masses are not changed unless the individual changes. At the same time, even the best-looking solution cannot be forced upon him, since it is a good solution only when it is combined with a natural process of development. It is therefore a hopeless undertaking to stake everything on collective recipes and procedures. The bettering of a general ill begins with the individual, and then only when he makes himself and not others responsible. This is naturally only possible in freedom, but not under a rule of force, whether this be exercised by a self-elected tyrant or by one thrown up by the mob. (Jung 1959d) p.349 § 618.

204. Although the conscious achievement of individuality is consistent with man's natural destiny, it is nevertheless not his whole aim. It cannot possibly be the object of human education to create an anarchic conglomeration of individual existences. That would be too much like the unavowed ideal of extreme individualism, which is essentially no more than a morbid reaction against an equally futile collectivism. In contrast to all this, the natural process of individuation brings to birth a consciousness of human community precisely because it makes us aware of the unconscious, which unites and is common to all mankind. Individuation is an at-one-ment with oneself and at the same time with humanity. Once the individual is thus secured in himself, there is some guarantee that the organized accumulation of individuals in the State—even in one wielding greater authority—will result in the formation no longer of an anonymous mass but of a conscious community. The indispensable condition for this is conscious freedom and self-determination or there is no true community, and, it must be said, without such community even the free and self-secured individual cannot in the long run prosper. Moreover, the common weal is best served by independent personalities. (Jung 1954k) p.108 § 227.

205. That fact that the conventions always flourish in one form or another only proves that the vast majority of mankind do not choose their own way, but convention, and consequently develop not themselves but a method and a collective mode of life at the cost of their own wholeness. (Jung 1954c) p.174 § 296.

206. This process [the unconscious is the matrix out of which the conscious grows; for the conscious does not enter the world as a finished product, but is the end-result of small beginnings] continues throughout life, but from puberty onwards it becomes slower, and fewer and fewer fragments of the unconscious are added to consciousness. The greatest and most extensive development takes place during the period between birth and the end of psychic puberty, a period that may normally extend, for a man of our climate and race, to the twenty-fifth year. In the case of a woman it usually ends when she is about nineteen or twenty. ...We reinforce this process in children by education and culture. School is in fact a means of strengthening in a purposeful way the integration of consciousness. (Jung 1954b) p.52 § 104.

207. Just as the child in embryo is practically nothing but a part of the mother's body, and wholly dependent on her, so in early infancy the psyche is to a large extent part of the maternal psyche, and will soon become parental psyche as well. The prime psychological condition is one of fusion with the psychology of the parents, an individual psychology being only potentially present. Hence it is that the nervous and psychic disorders of children right up to school age depend very largely on

disturbances in the psychic world of the parents. All parental difficulties reflect themselves without fail in the psyche of the child, sometimes with pathological results. (Jung 1954b) p.53 § 106.

208. For all lovers of theory, the essential fact behind all this is that the things which have the most powerful effect upon children do not come from the conscious state of the parents but from their unconscious background. For the ethically minded person who may be a father or mother this presents an almost frightening problem, because the things we can manipulate more or less, namely consciousness and its contents, are seen to be ineffectual in comparison with these uncontrollable effects in the background, no matter how hard we may try. (Jung 1954f) p.42 § 84.

209. In this way neurotic states are often passed on from generation to generation, like the curse of Arteus. The children are infected indirectly through the attitude they instinctively adopt towards their parents' state of mind: either they fight against it with unspoken protest (though occasionally the protest is vociferous) or else they succumb to a paralysing and compulsive imitation. In both cases they are obliged to do, to feel, and to live not as *they* want, but as their parents want. The more "impressive" the parents are, and the less they accept their own problems (mostly on the excuse of "sparing the children"), the longer the children will have to suffer from the unlived life of their parents and the more they will be forced into fulfilling all the things that parents have repressed and kept unconscious. ...The only thing that can save the child from unnatural injury is the efforts of the parents not to shirk the psychic difficulties of life by deceitful manoeuvres or by remaining artificially unconscious, but rather to accept them as tasks, to be as honest with themselves as possible, and to shed a beam of light into the darkest corners of their souls. (Jung 1954a) p.78-79 § 154.

210. Generally speaking, all the life which the parents could have lived, but of which they thwarted themselves for artificial motives, is passed on to the children in substitute form. That is to say, the children are driven unconsciously in a direction that is intended to compensate for everything that was left unfulfilled in the lives of their parents. (Jung 1954g) p.191 § 328.

211. What usually has the strongest psychic effect on the child is the life which the parents (and ancestors too, for we are dealing here with the age-old psychological phenomenon of original sin) have not lived. This statement would be rather too perfunctory and superficial if we did not add by way of qualification: that part of their lives which *might have been* lived had not certain rather threadbare excuses prevented the parents from doing so. To put it bluntly, it is that part of life which they have always shirked, probably by means of a pious lie. That sows the most virulent germs. (Jung 1954f) p.43 § 87.

212. This [identification with parents] is an expression of primitive identity, from which the individual consciousness frees itself only gradually. In this battle for freedom the school plays a not unimportant part, as it is the first milieu the child finds outside his home. School comrades take the place of brothers and sisters; the teacher, if a man, acts as a substitute for the father, and, if a woman, for the mother. It is important that the teacher should be conscious of the role he is playing. He must not be satisfied with merely pounding the curriculum into the child; he must also influence him through his personality. This latter function is at least as important as the actual teaching, if not more so in certain cases. Though it is a misfortune for a child to have no parents, it is equally dangerous for him to be too closely bound to his family. An excessively strong attachment to the parents is a severe handicap in

his later adoption to the world, for a growing human being is not destined to remain forever the child of his parents. …Success [as a school] does not depend on the method, any more than that it is the exclusive aim of school life to stuff the children's heads with knowledge, but rather to make them real men and women. We need not concern ourselves so much with the amount of specific information a child takes away with him from school; the thing of vital importance is that the school should succeed in freeing the young man from the unconscious identity with his family, and should make him properly conscious of himself. Without this consciousness he will never know what he really wants, but will always remain dependent and imitative, with the feeling of being misunderstood and suppressed. (Jung 1954b) p.55-56 § 107.

213. I suspect our contemporary pedagogical and psychological enthusiasm for the child of dishonourable intentions: we talk about the child but we should mean the child in the adult. For in every adult there lurks a child—an eternal child, something that is always becoming, is never completed, and calls for unceasing care, attention, and education. That is the part of the human personality which wants to develop and become whole. But the man of today is far indeed from this wholeness. (Jung 1954c) p.169 § 286.

214. The fact is that the high ideal of educating the personality is not for children: for what is usually meant by personality—a well-rounded psychic whole that is capable of resistance and abounding in energy—is an *adult ideal*. It is only in an age like ours, when the individual is unconscious of the problems of adult life, or—what is worse—when he consciously shirks them, that people could wish to foist this ideal on to childhood. (Jung 1954c) p.169 § 286.

215. Analytical psychology has given considerable thought to the methods of aiding the adult in his psychic growth, …I must warn you again most emphatically that it would be very unsound to apply these methods directly to children. (Jung 1954b) p.58 § 111.

216. Through his historical development, the European has become so far removed from his roots that his mind was finally split into faith and knowledge, in the same way that every psychological exaggeration breaks up into its inherent opposites. He needs to return, not to Nature in the manner of Rousseau, but to his own nature. His task is to find the natural man again. Instead of this, there is nothing he likes better than systems and methods by which he can repress the natural man who is everywhere at cross purposes with him. (Jung 1958f) p.534 § 868.

217. There are, besides the gifts of the head, also those of the heart, which are no whit less important, although they may easily be overlooked because in such cases the head is often the weaker organ. And yet people of this kind sometimes contribute more to the well-being of society, and are more valuable, than those with other talents. (Jung 1954e) p.140 § 242.

218. [in reference to the 'child-god', the archetype of one who is "becoming"] The "child" is born out of the womb of the unconscious, begotten out of the depths of human nature, or rather out of living Nature herself. …The urge and compulsion to self-realization is a law of nature and thus of invincible power, even though its effect, at the start, is insignificant and improbable. (Jung 1959c) pp.170-171 § 289.

219. It is obvious that the purpose and inmost meaning of this new psychology [Jung's analytical psychology] is educational as well as medical. Since every individual is a new and unique combination of psychic elements, the investigation of

truth must begin afresh with each case, for each "case" is individual and not derivable from any preconceived formula. Each individual is a new experiment of life in her ever-changing moods, and an attempt at a new solution or new adaptation. We miss the meaning of the individual psyche if we interpret it on the basis of any fixed theory, however fond of it we may be. (Jung 1954a) p.93 § 173.

220. For the day will inevitably come when what the educator teaches by word of mouth no longer works, but only what he is. Every educator—and I use the term in its widest sense—should constantly ask himself whether he is actually fulfilling his teachings in his own person and in his own life, to the best of his knowledge and with a clear conscience. Psychotherapy has taught us that in the final reckoning it is not knowledge, not technical skill, that has a curative effect, but the personality of the doctor. And it is the same with education: it presupposes self-education. (Jung 1954e) p.140 § 240.

221. Your analytical knowledge should serve your own attitude as an educator first of all, because it is a well-known fact that children have an almost uncanny instinct for the teacher's personal shortcomings. They know the false from the true far better than one likes to admit. Therefore the teacher should watch his own psychic condition, so that he can spot the source of the trouble when anything goes wrong with the children entrusted to his care. He himself may easily be the unconscious cause of evil. ...It is not true that the educator is always the one who educates, and the child always the one to be educated. The educator, too, is a fallible human being, and the child he educates will reflect his failings. Therefore it is wise to be as clear-sighted as possible about one's subjective views, and particularly about one's faults. (Jung 1954a) pp.119-120 § 211.

222. The humanistic psychologists disapprove of the "pathology-centered" theories, i.e., those earlier psychological lines of thought which deduced motivation and personality theories, first and foremost, from more or less "psychic sick" people. The humanistic psychologists try to create motivation and personality theories which can also be applied to "psychic healthy" people. Accordingly, they are interested in areas of investigation which have been, in the past, neglected by psychologists, such areas as creativity, love and self-actualization. (Thorsen 1983) p.20.

223. [Characteristics of the self-actualizing person]
Superior perception of reality.
Increased acceptance of self, of other and of nature.
Increased spontaneity.
Increase in problem-centering.
Increased detachment and desire for privacy.
Increased autonomy, and resistance to enculturation.
Greater freshness of appreciation, and richness of emotional reaction.
Higher frequency of peak experiences.
Increased identification with the human species.
Changed (the clinician would say, improved) interpersonal relations.
More democratic character structure.
Greatly increased creativeness.
Certain changes in the value system.
...Being rather than Becoming (Maslow 1968) p.26.

224. A peak experience is a coming into the realization that what "ought to be" *is*, ...It tells human beings something about themselves and about the world that is the same truth, and that becomes the pivot of value and an ordering principle for

the hierarchy of meanings. It is the merging of subject and object, involving no loss of subjectivity but what seems its infinite extension. It is individuality freed of isolation. An experience of this sort gives the idea of transcendence an empirical ground. Its typical recurrence for his self-actualizers became for Maslow scientific evidence of what may be the normal psychological or inner life of persons who are fully human. (Geiger 1993) pp.xvi-xvii.

225. The new psychology also has a philosophy of health and sickness... Namely, that sickness comes from the denial of human potential. The good life is the seeking of this potential and daily leading the life that it encourages. This approach concerns the higher possibilities of human beings.... (Maslow 1996e) pp.116-117.

226. Man demonstrates *in his own nature* a pressure toward fuller and fuller Being, more and more perfect actualization of his humanness in exactly the same naturalistic, scientific sense that an acorn may be said to be "pressing toward" being an oak tree, or that a tiger can be observed to "push toward" being tigerish, or a horse toward being equine. Man is ultimately *not* molded or shaped into humanness or taught to be human. The role of the environment is ultimately to permit him or help him to actualize *his own* potentialities, not *its* potentialities. The environment does not give him potentialities and capacities; he *has* them in inchoate or embryonic form, just exactly as he has embryonic arms and legs. And creativeness, spontaneity, selfhood, authenticity, caring for others, being able to love, yearning for truth are embryonic potentialities belonging to his species-membership just as much as are his arms and legs and brain and eyes. (Maslow 1959b) p.130.

227. We can certainly now assert that at least a reasonable, theoretical, and empirical case has been made for the presence within the human being of a tendency toward, or need for, growing in a direction that can be summarized in general as self-actualization, or psychological health or maturation, and specifically as growth toward each and all of the sub-aspects of self-actualization. That is to say, the human being has within him a pressure (among other pressures) toward unity of personality, toward spontaneous expressiveness, toward full individuality and identity, toward seeing the truth rather than being blind, toward being creative, toward being good, and a lot else. That is, the human being is so constructed that he presses toward fuller and fuller being and this means pressing toward what most people would call good values, toward serenity, kindness, courage, knowledge, honesty, love, unselfishness, and goodness. (Maslow 1959b) pp.125-126.

228. It [the term "self-actualizing"] stresses "full-humanness," the development of the biologically based nature of man, and therefore is (empirically) normative for the whole species rather than for particular times and places, i.e., it is less culturally relative. It conforms to biological destiny, rather than to historically-arbitrary, culturally-local value-models as the terms "health" and "illness" often do. It also has empirical content and operational meaning. (Maslow 1968) p.vi.

229. The point of view that is rapidly developing now—that the highest spiritual values appear to have naturalistic sanctions and that supernatural sanctions for these values are, therefore, not necessary—raises some questions which have not been raised before in quite this form. For instance, why were supernatural sanctions for goodness, altruism, virtue, and love necessary in the first place?

... one important characteristic of the new "third" psychology is its demonstration of man's "higher nature." As we look back through the religious conceptions of human nature—and indeed we need not look back so very far because the same doctrine can be found in Freud—it becomes crystal clear that any doctrine of the innate depravity of man or any maligning of his animal nature very easily lead to some extra-human interpretation of goodness, saintliness, virtue, self-sacrifice, altruism, etc. If they can't be explained from within human nature—and explained they must be—then they must be explained from outside of human nature. The worse man is, the poorer a thing he is considered to be, the more necessary becomes a god. It can also be understood more clearly now that one source of the decay of belief in supernatural sanctions has been increasing faith in the higher possibilities of human nature (on the basis of new knowledge). (Maslow 1994) pp.36-37.

230. [From a paper sent by Maslow to Wilson on studying healthy people instead of sick ones.] When I started to explore the psychology of health, I picked out the finest, healthiest people, the best specimens of mankind I could find, and studied them to see what they were like. They were very different, in some ways startlingly different from the average...

I learned many lessons from these people. But one in particular is our concern now. I found that these individuals tended to report having had something like mystic experiences, moments of great awe, moments of the most intense happiness, or even rapture, ecstasy or bliss...

The little that I had ever read about mystic experiences tied them in with religion, with visions of the supernatural. And, like most scientists, I had sniffed at them with disbelief and considered it all nonsense, maybe hallucinations, maybe hysteria—almost surely pathological.

But the people telling me...about these experiences were not such people—they were the healthiest people! ...And I may add that it taught me something about the limitations of the small...orthodox scientist who won't recognize as knowledge, or as reality, any information that doesn't fit into the already existent science. From (Wilson 1972) pp.15-16.

231. This ability to become "lost in the present" seems to be a *sine qua non* for creativeness of any kind. But also certain *prerequisites* of creativeness—in whatever realm—somehow have something to do with this ability to become timeless, selfless, outside of space, of society, of history.

It has begun to appear strongly that this phenomenon is a diluted, more secular, more frequent version of the mystical experience that has been described so often as to have become what Huxley called *The Perennial Philosophy*...

It is always described as a loss of self or of ego, or sometimes as a transcendence of the self. There is a fusion with the reality being observed, ...a oneness where there was a twoness, and integration of some sort of the self with the nonself. There is universally reported a seeing of formerly hidden truth, a revelation in the strict sense, a stripping away of veils, and finally almost always, the whole experience is experienced as bliss, ecstasy, rapture, exaltation. (Maslow 1993) pp.59-60.

232. Most people lose or forget the subjectively religious experience, and redefine Religion as a set of habits, behaviors, dogmas, forms, which at the extreme becomes entirely legalistic and bureaucratic, conventional, empty, and in the truest meaning of the word, anti-religious. The mystic experience, the illumination, the great awakening, along with the charismatic seer who started the whole thing, are forgotten, lost, or transformed into their opposites. Organized Religion, the churches, finally may become the major enemies of the religious experience and the religious experiencer. This is the main thesis of this book. (Maslow 1994) p.viii.

233. We are learning that complete health means being available to yourself at all levels. We can no longer call this side "evil" rather than "good," lower rather than

higher, selfish rather than unselfish, beastly rather than human. Throughout human history and especially the history of Western civilization, and more especially the history of Christianity has there tended to be this dichotomy....

Once we transcend and resolve this dichotomy, once we can put these together into the unity in which they are originally, ...then we can recognize that the dichotomizing or the splitting is itself a pathological process. And then it becomes possible for one's civil war to end. This is precisely what happens in people that I call self-actualizing. (Maslow 1993) p.88.

234. The images of harmony fuse at points in Maslow's writings with what must be called virtually monistic metaphysical metaphors. By monistic images I mean symbols and metaphors that are used to paint an image of the world whose apparently independent parts are so interrelated, interdependent, and harmonious that they are all identified with one another and identical with the divine itself. ...[I]n the nooks and crannies of his [Maslow's] thought, and especially in his descriptions of peak-experiences, monistic images crop up. Monism is characterized by the idea that the sacred is a unified, motionless, timeless, unconditional, and self-caused perfection and, furthermore, that the human self in its depth is a manifestation of the divine life itself. (Browning 1987) p.81.

235. In a certain sense I see the acceptance of the prepotency and the logical priority of experience as another version of the spirit of empiricism itself. One of the beginnings of science, one of the roots from which it grew, was the determination not to take things on faith, trust, logic, or authority but to check and to see for oneself. Experience had shown how often the logic or the a priori certainty or Aristotle's authority failed to work in fact. The lesson was easy to draw. First, before everything else comes the seeing of nature with your own eyes, that is, experiencing it yourself. (Maslow 1966) p.69.

236. Many things in life cannot be transmitted well by words, concepts, or books. Colors that we see cannot be described to man born blind. ...Perhaps it is better to say that all of life must first be known experientially. There is no substitute for experience, none at all. All the other paraphernalia of communication and of knowledge—words, labels, concepts, symbols, theories, formulas, sciences—all are useful only because people already know experientially. The basic coin in the realm of knowing is direct, intimate, experiential knowing. Everything else can be likened to banks and bankers, to accounting systems and checks and paper money, which are useless unless there is real wealth to exchange, to manipulate, to accumulate, and to order.

...Words are fine for communicating and sharing experiences with those who have already experienced.... Even more, words and concepts are absolutely necessary for organizing and ordering the welter of experiences and the ultraexperiential word of which they appraise us. (Maslow 1966) pp.45-46.

237. Practically all scientists (of the impersonal) proceed on the tacit or explicit assumption that one studies classes or groups of things, not single things. Of course you actually look at one thing at a time.... But each one is treated as a sample of a species or of a class, and therefore as interchangeable....

Any one sample is just that, a sample; it is not itself. It stands for something. It is anonymous, expendable, not unique, not sacred, not *sine qua non*; it has no proper name all its own and is not worthwhile in itself as a particular instance. It is interesting only insofar as it represents something other than itself. (Maslow 1966) pp.8-9.

238. The Holistic Approach—If I want to learn something more about you as

an individual person, then I must approach you as a unit, as a one, as a whole. The customary scientific technique of dissection and reductive analysis that has worked so well in the inorganic world and not too badly even in the intrahuman world of living organisms, is just a nuisance when I seek knowledge of a person, and it has real deficiencies even for studying people in general. (Maslow 1966) p.11.

239. ...experiential knowledge is *sine qua non* but not all, i.e., it is necessary but not sufficient. Also we avoid thereby the trap of dichotomizing experiential knowledge from and against conceptual knowledge. My thesis is that experiential knowledge is prior to verbal-conceptual knowledge but that they are hierarchically-integrated and need each other. No human being dare specialize too much in either kind of knowing. (Maslow 1966) p.46.

240. ...experiential knowledge is not enough. Self-knowledge and self-improvement are not enough. The talk of knowing the world and of being competent within it still remains, and therefore also does the task of accumulating and ordering knowledge-about, that is, spectator knowledge, knowledge of the nonhuman.

...The two kinds of knowledge are necessary to each other and under good circumstances can be and should be intimately integrated with each other. (Maslow 1966) p.48.

241. Maslow thought that contemporary American education failed because it focused on extrinsic and coping behavior rather than on expressive behavior and intrinsic learning. ...Maslow blamed behaviorists for focusing exclusively on coping behavior, which, he argued, was the least significant part of personality. Coping behavior is functional, instrumental, adaptive, and the product of the interaction of the character-structure with the world. Coping behavior is learned or acquired in order to deal with specific environmental situations, and dies out if not rewarded or continuously bombarded with stimulus. Since the extrinsic knowledge ensuing from coping behavior is forcefully implanted by operant conditioning or indoctrination, it is never an integral part of personality and thus not perceived as meaningful. ...This type of learning focuses on techniques that are interchangeable and result in automatic habits such as driving or swimming. It is useful learning, but meaningless as far as growth and actualization of the inner character structure. ...In fact, understanding is inimical to behavioral operant conditioning. When conditioning ceases or people understand that they are victims of conditioning, they rebel and dispose of the enforced learning. Earning a degree, reward for scholarly achievement, and other similar practices are by-products of extrinsic education. (De Carvalho 1991) pp.101-102.

242. What is then the correct way of teaching people to be, e.g. engineers? It is quite clear that we must teach them to be creative persons, at least in the sense of being able to confront novelty, to improvise....

...We must develop a race of improvisers, of "here-now" creators. We must define the skillful person or the trained person, or the educated person in a very different way than we used to (i.e., *not* as one who has a rich knowledge of the past so that he can profit from past experiences in a future emergency). Much that we have called learning has become useless. Any kind of learning which is the simple application of the past to the present, or the use of past techniques in the present situation has become obsolete in many areas of life. Education can no longer be considered essentially or only a learning process; it is now also a character training, a person-training process....

All this adds up to increased emphasis on psychological health and strength. It means an increased valuing of the ability to pay the fullest attention to the here-now situation, to be able to listen well, to be able to see well in the concrete, immediate moment before us…

…Since in essence we are talking about a kind of person, a kind of philosophy, a kind of character, then the stress shifts away from stress on created products, and technological innovations and aesthetic products and innovations, etc. (Maslow 1993) pp.94-95.

243. Classroom learning often has as its unspoken goal the reward of pleasing the teacher. Children in the usual classroom learn very quickly that creativity is punished, while repeating a memorized response is rewarded, and concentrate on what the teacher wants them to say, rather than understanding the problem. (Maslow 1993) p.173.

244. The ideal, thus, was to integrate intrinsic learning with traditional extrinsic learning, such as training of professional skills or education for competence in any field. The main difference was whether this knowledge is sought out of personal need and meaning or as a response to rewarding or punishing stimuli. Knowledge gathered out of personal meaning translated into a lasting expressive behavior that is independent of reinforcing external stimuli. (De Carvalho 1991) p.104.

245. Healthy openness to the mysterious, the realistically humble recognition that we don't know much , the modest and grateful acceptance of gratuitous grace and of just plain good luck—all these can shade over into the anti-rational, the anti-empirical, the anti-scientific, the anti-verbal, the anti-conceptual. The peak-experience may then be exalted as the best or even the *only* path to knowledge, and thereby all the tests and verifications of the *validity* of the illumination may be tossed aside.

The possibility that the inner voices, the "revelations," may be mistaken, a lesson from history that should come through loud and clear, is denied, and there is then no way of finding out whether the voices within are the voices of good or evil. .. Spontaneity (the impulses from our best self) gets confused with impulsivity and acting out (the impulses from our sick self), and there is then no way to tell the difference. (Maslow 1994) pp.ix-x.

246. The better way to perceive [art] "style" is not to analyze or dissect it but to be receptive, global, intuitive….

…the prerequisite for holistic perception of qualities of wholeness I shall call "experiential naïveté," and I define it as a willingness and an ability to experience immediately without certain other ways of "knowing."

So those individuals who "know" art only in the analytic, atomistic, taxonomic, or historical sense are less able to perceive and enjoy. And the possibility must be admitted that education of a merely analytic sort may actually diminish originally present intuitiveness. (Maslow 1966) pp.62-63.

247. Their [humanistic psychologists'] clinical experiences have led them to conceive of the human being as having an essence, a biological nature, membership in a species. It is very easy to interpret the "uncovering" therapies as helping the person to *discover* his "identity," his "real self," in a word, his own subjective biology, which he can *then* proceed to actualize, to "make himself," to "choose." …it is implied, if not made explicit, by most of these writers that the organism, in the strictest sense, has *needs* which must be gratified in order to become fully human, to grow well, and to avoid sicknesses. This doctrine of a "real self" to be uncovered and actualized is also a total rejection of the *tabula rasa* notions of the behaviorists and associationists who often talk as if *anything* can be learned, *anything* can be taught, as

if the human being is a sort of passive clay to be shaped, controlled, reinforced, modified in any way that somebody arbitrarily decides.

We speak then of a self, a kind of intrinsic nature which is very subtle, which is not necessarily conscious, which has to be sought for, and which has to be uncovered and then built upon, actualized, taught, educated. The notion is that something is there but it's hidden, swamped, distorted, twisted, overlayed. The job of the psychotherapist (or the teacher) is to help a person find out what's already in him rather than to reinforce him or shape or teach him into a prearranged form, which someone else has decided upon in advance, *a priori*. (Maslow 1959a) pp.306-307.

248. Rogers and Maslow counterposed the understanding of human nature contained in the growth hypothesis to the positivistic philosophy of behaviorism, and believed that true learning is possible only when it is intrinsic, experiential, significant or meaningful. When one learns something, one is experiencing a process of discovery that is real and an integral part of the character structure. ...The essence of this type of learning is its personal intrinsic meaning. When one has a need to learn and is free to choose what to learn, the knowledge acquired becomes meaningful and a source of satisfaction. Self-initiated knowledge has the quality of personal involvement. Thus the purpose of education, according to Rogers and Maslow, was not external conditioning and enforcement of learning habits, as Skinner had argued, but rather to stimulate curiosity, the inner need to discover and explore, to facilitate personal involvement and, of course, to supply the necessary instructional resources. (De Carvalho 1991) pp.100-101.

They [Maslow and Rogers] believed that the ultimate goal of education was to facilitate the student's self-actualization and the fulfillment of their human potential. Both argued that the success of any educational system depends on its ability to involve students in the process of learning and to perceive meaning in the acquisition of knowledge. Without the student's wonder, curiosity, and personal need to learn, good teachers and well-funded schools will fail. Students are not rat-like organisms that learn technological knowledge and skills in response to rewarding stimuli. According to Maslow and Rogers, students instead learn only when they seek to actualize their human potential. The teacher should thus make an alliance with the students' natural curiosity and facilitate the process of self-discovery, so that the student may discover the vocation and skills that best suit their intrinsic abilities. Once this alliance has been made, it is also the educator's responsibility to make extrinsic knowledge available and teach specific skills. Teachers themselves should serve as role models, authentic, curious, and explorative; human beings intrigued by the wonders of their disciplines. (De Carvalho 1991) p.7.

249. Fusion-knowledge—These love relationships that can go over into the mystic experience of fusion with the world give us our end point (*beyond* knowledge through love for the object) of knowledge by fusion with the object, by becoming one with it. They can then be considered for theoretical purposes to become experiential knowledge, knowledge from within, by *being* what we are knowing. At least this is the ideal limit to which such knowledge approaches or tries to approach. (Maslow 1966) p.112.

250. In B-cognition the experience or object tends to be seen as a whole, as a complete unit, detached from relations, from possible usefulness, from expediency, and from purpose.

...We are reminded here of the absolute idealism of the 19th century, in which all the universe was conceived to be a unit.

When there is a B-cognition, the precept is exclusively and fully attended to. This may be called "total attention"...

This kind of perception is in sharp contrast to normal perception. Here the object is attended to simultaneously with attention to all else that is relevant. It is seen as imbedded in its relationships with everything else in the world, and as *part* of the world. ...Furthermore, in ordinary cognition, the object is seen not so much *per se* but as a member of a class, as an instance in a larger category. This kind of perception I have described as "rubricizing," and again would point out that this is not so much a full perception, as it is a kind of taxonomy, a classifying, a ticking off into one file cabinet or another.

To a far greater extent than we ordinarily realize, cognition involves also placing on a continuum. It involves a kind of automatic comparing or judging or evaluating. It implies higher than, less than, better than, taller than, etc.

B-cognition may be called non-comparing cognition or non-evaluating or non-judging cognition. (Maslow 1968) pp.74-75.

251. That is, we most categorize, schematize, classify, and abstract in our cognitive life. We do not so much cognize the nature of the world as it actually is, as we do the organization of our own inner world outlook. Most of experience is filtered through our system of categories, constructs, and rubrics... I was led to this differentiation by my studies of self-actualizing people, *finding in them simultaneously the ability to abstract without giving up concreteness and the ability to be concrete without giving up abstractness.* (Maslow 1968) pp.88-89.

252. What we [psychotherapists] have learned is that ultimately, the best way for a person to discover what he ought to do is to find out who and what he is, because the path to ethical and value decisions, to wiser choices, to oughtness, is via "isness," via discovery of facts, truth, reality, the nature of the particular person. (Maslow 1993) pp.106-107.

253. The word and the concept "contemplation" can, then, be understood as a form of nonactive, noninterfering witnessing and savoring. That is, it can be assimilated to Taoistic, nonintruding, receptivity to experience. In such a moment the experience happens instead of being made to happen. Since this permits it to be itself, minimally distorted by the observer, it is in certain instances a path to more reliable and more veridical cognition. (Maslow 1966) p.101.

254. In general we—the intellectuals, the philosophers, the scientists—have meant by it [the concept of "meaning"] that it integrates, coordinates, classifies, and organizes the chaos, the multiple, the creation of a whole. This whole and its parts then have the meaning that the parts did not hitherto have. "Organizing experience into meaningful patterns" implies that experience itself has not meaningfulness, that the organizer creates or imposes or donates the meaning, that his giving of meaning is an active process rather than a receptive one, that it is a gift from the knowner to the known.

In other words, "meaningfullness" of this kind is of the realm of classification and abstraction rather than of experience. (Maslow 1966) p.84.

255. Maslow assumes that there exists a reality independent of human beings' consciousness (*ontological realism*). He also assumes that there is some correspondence between human beings contents of consciousness and [independent reality] (*epistemological realism*). He belongs to empiricism within epistemology whose advocates assert that the genesis of knowledge of [independent reality] is brought through sense-experience and that this knowledge of [independent reality] is justified by

sense-experience. (Thorsen 1983) p.63.

256. The described characteristics of Being are also the values of Being. These Being-values are perceived as ultimate and as further unanalyzable (and yet they can each be defined in terms of each and all of the others). They are paralleled also by the characteristics of selfhood (identity) in peak-experiences; the characteristics of ideal art; the characteristics of ideal mathematical demonstration; of ideal experiments and theories; of ideal science and knowledge; the far goals of all ideal, uncovering (Taoistic, non-interfering) psychotherapies; the far goals of the ideal humanistic education; the far goals of the expression of some kinds of religion; the characteristics of ideally good environment and of the ideally good society. (Maslow 1994) p.91

257. If we were to accept as a major education goal the awakening and fulfillment of the B-values, which is simply another aspect of self-actualization, we would have a great flowering of a new kind of civilization. People would be stronger, healthier, and would take their own lives into their hands to a greater extent. With increased personal responsibility for one's personal life, and with a rational set of values to guide one's choosing, people would begin to actively change the society in which they lived. The movement toward psychological health is also the movement toward spiritual peace and social harmony. (Maslow 1993) pp.187-188.

258. Humanists for thousands of years have attempted to construct a naturalistic, psychological value system that could be derived from man's own nature, without the necessity of recourse to authority outside the human being himself....

These inadequate theories, most of them, rested on psychological assumptions of one sort or another. ...it is my belief that developments in the science and art of psychology, in the last few decades, make it possible for us for the first time to feel confident that this age-old hope may be fulfilled if we work hard enough. ...That is, we think that a scientific ethic may be possible, and we think we know how to go about constructing it. (Maslow 1959b) pp.119-120.

259. Just as each science was once a part of the body of organized religion but then broke away to become independent, so also it can be said that the same thing may now be happening to the problems of values, ethics, spirituality, morals. They are being taken away from the exclusive jurisdiction of the institutionalized churches and are becoming the "property," so to speak, of a new type of humanistic scientist who is vigorously denying the old claim of the established religions to be the sole arbiters of all questions of faith and morals. (Maslow 1994) p.12.

260. Healthy people seem to have clear impulse voices about matters of ethics and values, as well. Self-actualizing people have to a large extent transcended the values of their culture. They are not so much merely Americans as they are world citizens, members of the human species first and foremost. ...If an ultimate goal of education is self-actualizing, then education ought to help people transcend the conditioning imposed upon them by their own culture and become world citizens. (Maslow 1993) p.177.

261. Summarizing what we have said, that schools should be helping the children to look within themselves, and from this self-knowledge derive a set of values. (Maslow 1993) p.178.

262. Homeostasis—Hundreds of experiments have been made that demonstrate a universal inborn ability in all sorts of animals to select a beneficial diet if enough alternatives are presented from among which they are permitted free choice. This wisdom of the body is often retained under less usual conditions, *e.g.,* adrena-

lectomized animals can keep themselves alive by readjusting their self-chosen diet, pregnant animals will nicely adjust their diets to the needs of the growing embryo, etc. {for support Maslow cites W.B. Cannon, *Wisdom of the Body,* Norton, 1932} (Maslow 1959b) p.120.

It seems quite clear that all organisms are more self-governing, self-regulating and autonomous than we thought 25 years ago. The organism deserves a good deal of trust, and we are learning steadily to rely on this internal wisdom of our babies with reference to choice of diet, time of weaning, amount of sleep, time of toilet training, need for activity, and a lot else. (Maslow 1968) pp.150-151.

263. ...[individuated, self-actualized] people, when they feel strong, if *really* free choice is possible, tend spontaneously to choose the true rather than the false, good rather than evil, beauty rather than ugliness, integration rather than dissociation, joy rather than sorrow, aliveness rather than deadness, uniqueness rather than stereotypy [sterotype?], and so on for what I have already described as the B-values.

A subsidiary hypothesis is that tendencies to choose these same B-values can be seen weakly and dimly in all or most human beings, i.e., that these may be species-wide values which are seen most clearly and unmistakeably, most strongly in healthy people, and that in these healthy people these higher values are least alloyed either by defensive (anxiety-instigated) values, or by what I shall refer to below as healthy-regressive, or "coating" values.

...Another very likely hypothesis is this; what healthy people choose is on the whole what is "good for them" in biological terms certainly, but perhaps also in other senses ("good for them" here means "conducing to their and others' self-actualization").

To spell out only one implication here, these propositions affirm the existence of the highest values within human nature itself, to be discovered there. This is in sharp contradiction to the older and more customary beliefs that the highest values can come only form a supernatural God, or from some other source outside human nature itself. (Maslow 1968) pp.168-170.

264. The last few decades of clinical and experimental psychology have brought into clearer focus the logically prior need, before knowing, to be a good knower. The distorting power not only of the various psychopathologies but also of the more "normal" ungratified needs, hidden fears, characteristic defenses, i.e., of the "normal" or average personality, are far greater than mankind ever thought before this century. In my opinion we have learned from clinical and personological experience (1) that improvement of psychological health makes the person a better knower, even a better scientist, and (2) that a very good path to improved and fuller human-ness or health has been via self-knowledge, insight, and honesty with oneself. (Maslow 1966) p.48.

265. My general thesis is that many of the communication difficulties between persons are the byproduct of communication barriers *within* the person; and that communication between the person and the world, to and fro, depends largely on their isomorphism (i.e., similarity of structure and form); that the world can commu-nicate to a person only that of which he is worthy, that which he deserves or is "up to"; that to a large extent, he can receive from the world, and give to the world, only that which he himself is...

...Of course I take communication here in the very broadest sense. I include all the processes of perception and of learning, and all the forms of art and of cre-ation. And I include primary-process cognition (archaic, mythological, metaphorical, poetic cognition) as well as verbal, rational, secondary-process communication.

...A main consequence of this general thesis—that difficulties with the outer parallel difficulties within the inner—is that we should expect communication with the outer world to improve along with improvement in the development of the personality, along with its integration and wholeness, and along with freedom from civil war among the various portions of the personality, i.e., perception of reality should improve. (Maslow 1993) pp.149-150.

266. The empirical fact is that self-actualizing people, our best experiencers, are also our most compassionate, our great improvers and reformers of society, our most *effective* fighters against injustice, inequality, slavery, cruelty, exploitation, (and also our best fighters *for* excellence, effectiveness, competence). And it also becomes clearer and clearer that the best "helpers" are the most fully human persons. What I may call the bodhisattvic path is an *integration* of self-improvement and social zeal, i.e., the best way to become a better " helper" is to become a better person. (Maslow 1994) p.xii.

267. The uniqueness of Maslow's 'philosophy' lies in its breadth of application. Marxism is a social philosophy that ignores the individual; existentialism is an individual philosophy that has nothing much to say about society as a whole. Koestler spoke about the fundamental irreconcilableness of the yogi and the commissar; the yogi thinks in terms of personal salvation, the commissar in terms of what is good for society as a whole; and they seem to be unable to find any common ground. Maslow, without making any undue fuss about it, has bridged the gap. ...With Maslow's hierarchy of values, the problem vanishes. (Wilson 1972) pp.188-189.

268. Personal salvation and what is good for the person alone cannot be really understood in isolation. Social psychology is, therefore, necessary. The good of other people must be invoked, as well as the good for oneself, even though it must be demonstrated how these are—or may be—synergic. To some extent, the individual's interests and those of his or her team or organization, culture, or society may be at odds—even though an overall principle of *synergy* may prevail. But in any case, it is quite clear that a purely intrapsychic, individualistic psychology, without reference to other people and social conditions, is not adequate. (Maslow 1996b) pp.31-32.

269. The steps and the choices are taken out of pure spontaneity, from within outward. The healthy infant or child, just Being, as *part* of his Being, is randomly, and spontaneously curious, exploratory, wondering, interested. ...*Exploring, manipulating, experiencing,* being interested, choosing, delighting, *enjoying* can all be seen as attributes of pure Being, and yet lead to Becoming, though in a serendipitous way, fortuitously, unplanned, unanticipated. (Maslow 1968) p.45.

270. So far as motivational status is concerned, healthy people has sufficiently gratified their basic needs for safety, belongingness, love, respect and self-esteem so that they are motivated primarily by trends to self-actualization. (Maslow 1968) p.25.

271. My thesis is, then: we can, in principle, have a descriptive, naturalistic science of human values; that the age-old mutually exclusive contrast between "what is" and "what ought to be" is in part a false one; that we can study the highest values or goals of human beings as we study the values of ants or horses or oak trees, or for that matter, Martians. We can discover (rather than create or invent) which values men tend toward, yearn for, struggle for, as they improve themselves, and which values they lose as they get sick. (Maslow 1968) p.167.

272. Generated by this new humanistic philosophy is also a new conception of learning, of teaching, and of education. Stated simply, such a concept holds that the

function of education, the goal of education—the human goal, the humanistic goal, the goal so far as human beings are concerned—is ultimately the "self-actualization" of a person, the becoming fully human, the development of the fullest height that the human species can stand up to or that the particular individual can come to. (Maslow 1993) p.162.

273. We know ....that the initiation of such learning [significant learning] rests not upon the teaching skill of the leader, not upon scholarly knowledge of the field, not upon curricular planning, not upon use of audiovisual aids, not upon the programmed learning used, not upon lectures and presentations, not upon an abundance of books, though each of these might at one time or another be utilized as an important resource. No, the facilitation of significant learning rests upon certain attitudinal qualities that exist in the personal *relationship* between the facilitator and the learner. (Rogers 1983) p.121.

274. It appears that the person who emerges from a theoretically optimal experience of personal growth, whether through client-centered therapy or some other experience of learning and development, is then a fully functioning person. He is able to live life fully in and with each and all of his feelings and reactions. He is making use of all his organic equipment to sense, as accurately as possible, the existential situation [living in the moment] within and without. He is using all of the data his nervous system can thus supply, using it in awareness, but recognizing that his total organism may be, and often is, wiser than his awareness. He is able to permit his total organism to function in all of its complexity in selecting, from the multitude of possibilities, that behavior which in this moment of time will be most generally and genuinely satisfying. He is able to trust his organism in this functioning, not because it is infallible, but because he can be fully open to the consequences of each of his actions and correct them if they prove to be less than satisfying.

He is able to experience all of his feelings, and is afraid of none of his feelings; he is his own sifter of evidence, but is open to evidence from all sources; he is completely engaged in the process of being and becoming himself, and thus discovers that he is soundly and realistically social; he lives completely in this moment, but learns that this is the soundest living for all times. He is a fully functioning organism, and because of the awareness of himself which flows freely in and through his experience, he is a fully functioning person. (Rogers 1983) p.290.

275. The fact can scarcely have escaped the notice of the social scientist with a feeling for the history of ideas that Sigmund Freud inherits the tradition of Augustine in his belief that man is basically and fundamentally hostile, anti-social, and carnal.

It has been less frequently recognized, apparently, by writers concerned with the theoretical aspects of counseling that Carl Rogers, in the same sense, is the successor to Rousseau. Recall that Rousseau began his classic presentation in *Emile* with the observation that every man comes from the hand of his Maker a perfect being. This pristine splendor is corrupted, said Rousseau, by an imperfect society.

In his counseling theory Carl Rogers seems to have subtly refurbished the conception of man as basically good. ...For Rogers, man is basically good in that he has within himself a drive to health and adjustment which operates more or less automatically once obstacles are removed.

...The counseling process is one in which the counselee ideally grows in the desirable direction of health, integration, and stability. A part of this process seems to be the development of an increasing ability to trust one's basic impulses:

...This trust in basic impulses is not then, we may presume, a characteristic "conditioned" into a person by another—something imposed. It is a matter of coming to recognize that one's basic nature is something to be relied upon, trusted and not feared. (Walker 1956) p.89.

276. Here then is my theoretical model of the person who emerges from therapy or from the best of education, the individual who has experienced optimal psychological growth—a person functioning freely in all the fullness of his organismic potentialities; a person who is dependable in being realistic, self-enhancing, socialized, and appropriate in his behavior; a creative person who is ever-changing, ever developing, always discovering himself and the newness in himself in each succeeding moment of time.

Let me stress, however, that what I have described is a person who does not exist. He is the theoretical goal, the end-point of personal growth. We see persons moving *in this direction* from the best of experiences in education, from the best experiences in therapy, from the best of family and group relationships. (Rogers 1983) pp. 295-296.

277. [The experience of learning to be free] is a deeply compelling phenomenon for anyone who has observed it, or who has lived it.

The experience to which I am referring is a central process or central aspect of psychotherapy. It is the experience of becoming a more autonomous, more spontaneous, more confident person. It is the experience of freedom to be one's self. ...The client begins to realize, "I am not compelled to be simply the creation of others, molded by their expectancies, shaped by their demands. I am not compelled to be a victim of unknown forces in myself. I am less and less a creature of influences in myself which operate beyond my ken in the realms of the unconscious. I am increasingly the architect of the self. I am free to will and choose. I can, through accepting my individuality, my 'isness,' become more of my uniqueness, more of my potentiality." (Rogers and Stevens 1973) pp.47-48.

278. It is such experiences in individual and group psychotherapy which lead us to believe that we have here an important dynamic for modern education. We may have here the essential core of a process by which we might facilitate the production, through our educational system, of persons who will be adaptive and creative, able to make responsible choices, open to the kaleidoscopic changes in their world, worthy citizens of a fantastically expanding universe. It seems at least a possibility that in our schools and colleges, in our professional schools and universities, individuals could learn to be free. (Rogers and Stevens 1973) p.56.

279. Humans have within themselves an organismic basis for valuing. To the extent that we can be freely in touch with this valuing process in ourselves, we will behave in ways that are self-enhancing. (Rogers 1983) p.268.

280. **Propositions Regarding the Outcomes of the Valuing Process**

In persons who are moving toward greater openness to their experiencing, there is an organismic commonality of value directions.

These common value directions are of such kinds as to enhance the development of the individual, of others in the community, and to contribute to the survival and evolution of his species.

Let me indicate a few of these value directions, as I see them in my clients as they move in the direction of personal growth and maturity

♦ They tend to move away from façades. Pretense, defensiveness, putting up a front tend to be negatively valued.

♦ They tend to move away from "oughts."

♦ They tend to move away from meeting the expectations of others.

♦ Being real is positively valued.

♦ Self-direction is positively valued.

♦ One's self, one's own feelings come to be positively valued.

♦ Being a process is positively valued.

♦ Perhaps more than all else, the client comes to value an openness to all of her inner and outer experiences.

♦ Sensitivity to others and acceptance of others is positively valued.

♦ Finally, deep relationships are positively valued.

...A corollary of what I have been saying is that in *any* culture, given a climate of respect and freedom in which she is valued as a person, the mature individual would tend to choose and prefer these same value directions.

Finally, it appears that we have returned to the issue of the universality of values, but by a different route. Instead of universal values "out there," or a universal value system imposed by some group—philosophers, rulers, or priests—we have the possibility of universal human value directions emerging from the experiencing of the human organism. Evidence from therapy indicates that both personal and social values emerge as natural, and experienced, when the individual is close to her own organismic valuing process. The tentative conclusion is that though modern humans no longer trust religion or science or philosophy or any system of beliefs to *give* them their values, they can find an organismic valuing base deep within themselves, which, if they can learn to be in touch with it, will prove to be an organized, adaptive, and social approach to the perplexing value issues which face all of us. (Rogers and Freiberg 1994) pp.288-291.

281. [Answering the question: What kind of person is the person who becomes?] First of all I would say that in this process the individual becomes more open to his experience. ...It seems that the person increasingly discovers that his own organism is trustworthy, that it is a suitable instrument for discovering the most satisfying behavior in each immediate situation. ...The individual increasingly comes to feel that this locus of evaluation [of choices and decisions, or evaluative judgements] lies within himself. Less and less does he look to others for approval or disapproval; for standards to live by; for decisions and choices. He recognizes that it rests within himself to choose; that the only question which matters is, "Am I living in a way which is deeply satisfying to me, and which truly expresses me?" This I think is perhaps *the* most important question for the creative individual. (Rogers 1961) pp.115-119.

282. If the purpose of teaching is to promote learning, then we need to ask what we mean by that term. Here I become passionate. I want to talk about *learning*. But *not* the lifeless, sterile, futile, quickly forgotten stuff that is crammed into the mind of the poor helpless individual tied into his seat by ironclad bonds of conformity! I am talking about LEARNING—the insatiable curiosity that drives the adolescent boy to absorb everything he can see or hear or read about gasoline engines in order to improve the efficiency and speed of his "cruiser." I am talking about the student who says, " I am discovering, drawing in from outside, and making that which is drawn in a real part of *me*." (Rogers 1983) pp.18-19.

283. [Of 'significant learning'] *It has the quality of personal involvement*—the whole person in both feeling and cognitive aspects of being *in* the learning event. It is *self-initiated*. Even when the impetus or stimulus comes from the outside, the sense of

discovery, of reaching out, of grasping and comprehending, comes from within. *It is pervasive.* It makes a difference in the behavior, the attitudes, perhaps even the personality of the learner. *It is evaluated by the learner.* She knows whether it is meeting her need, whether it leads toward what she *wants* to know, whether it illuminates the dark area of ignorance she is experiencing. The locus of evaluation, we might say, resides definitely in the learner. *Its essence is meaning.* (Rogers 1983) p.20.

284. You may be thinking that "facilitator of learning" is just a fancy name for a teacher and that nothing at all would be changed. If so, you are mistaken. There is *no* resemblance between the traditional function of teaching and the function of the facilitator of learning.

The traditional teacher—the *good* traditional teacher—asks her or himself questions of this sort: "What do I think would be good for a student to learn at this particular age and level of competence? How can I plan a proper {136} curriculum for this student? How can I inculcate motivation to learn this curriculum? How can I instruct in such a way that he or she will gain the knowledge that should be gained? How can I best set an examination to see whether this knowledge has actually been taken in?"

On the other hand, the facilitator of learning asks questions such as these, not of self, but of the *students*: "What do you want to learn? What things puzzle you? What are you curious about? What issues concern you? What problems do you wish you could solve?" When he or she has the answers to these questions, further questions follow. "Now how can I help him or her find the resources—the people, the experiences, the facilities, the books, the knowledge in myself—which will help them learn in ways that will provide answers to the things that concern them, the things they are eager to learn?" And, then later, "How can I help them evaluate their own progress and set future learning goals based on this self-evaluation?" (Rogers 1983) pp.135-136.

285. Generic modes are produced by a functional analysis of what is taken to be the underlying features necessary to the performance of a skill, task, practice or even area of work. (Bernstein 1996a) p.67

286. Carl Rogers listed mistaken assumptions he felt are imbedded in mainstream education. His second and third assumptions are ones that many holistic educators would agree are wrong, and are relevant to the present issue.

> A second implicit assumption is that presentation equals learning. This is evident in every curriculum, every lesson plan. It is especially clear if one observes a faculty committee trying to decide what topics a course shall 'cover.' It is clear that what is presented or 'covered' is what is learned. Anyone who has used any method which taps the actual experience of students in a class knows that this assumption could not be further from the truth; yet it persists.

> A third and very basic assumption is that the aim of education is to accumulate brick upon brick of factual knowledge. There must be a 'foundation of knowledge.' These clearly defined building blocks must be assimilated before the student can proceed to learn on his own. Though this assumption flies in the face of everything we know about the curve of forgetting, it remains an unquestioned assumption. (Rogers 1967).

287. Ivan Illich and John Holt were early proponents of 'deschooling' and their many books always advocated allowing a child's interests to dictate learning. Any-

thing else was described as not only without meaning, but as constituting an abuse of a child's natural learning process. Their work has inspired many in holistic education to seek out and follow what is meaningful for the individual children in their care. From Holt:

> Children do not need to be made to learn, told what to learn, or shown how. If we give them access to enough of the world, including our own lives and work in the world, they will see clearly what things are truly important to us and to others, and they will make for themselves a better path into that world than we could make for them.
>
> A few good principles to keep in mind: (1) Children do not need to be 'taught' in order to learn; they will learn a great deal, and probably learn best, without being taught. (2) Children are enormously interested in our adult world and what we do there. (3) Children learn best when things are embedded in a context of real life, are part of what George Dennison, in *The Lives of Children,* called 'the continuum of experience.' (4) Children learn best when their learning is connected with an immediate and serious purpose. (Holt 1982).

288. Wexler's latest book presents an interesting discussion of the 'self' as a focus for education in the new age as a natural response away from the postmodern malaise of mainstream education.

> By focusing on the self in educational change, we not only move away from the superficial rationalization of the current performance-oriented, outcome-governed corporatism. Instead, I try to understand the directions of subjectivity within the historical, macrosociocultural changes that occur in the transition from postmodernism to resacralization. (Wexler 1997) p.114-115.
>
> The model of the dynamic context that frames my interpretation of self/educational processes is one that I am drawn to after a rejection of postmodernisms as either analytics or ethics, and one that colleagues will identify as rejecting rather than reflexively preserving modernity, in favor of a premodern, if not ancient, understanding of individual and collective transformations. (Wexler 1997) p.118.

289. Carl Rogers' influential comments on the traditional teachers' role in determining curriculum:

> One of the most obvious and pervasive assumptions is that the student cannot be trusted to pursue his own learning. The attitude of most teachers and faculty members tends to be one of mistrustful guidance. They look suspiciously on the student's aims and desires and devote their energies to guiding him along the pathway he "should" follow. I believe it is extremely rare that students have the feeling that they are being set free to learn, on their own. (Rogers 1967).

290. There is also the view that students and adults are essentially 'in the same boat.' Both groups need to learn about themselves, make meaningful connections between things thought and things lived, and discover how to meet the challenges of living more deeply. While there are some differences due to background and experiences, the similarities outweigh the differences. For the most articulate proponent of this see the educational work of J. Krishnamurti (Krishnamurti 1953; Krishnamurti

1970; Krishnamurti 1974; Krishnamurti 1975; Krishnamurti 1981; Krishnamurti 1985; Krishnamurti 1993a; Krishnamurti 1993b; Krishnamurti 1994).

291. However, this idealism of competence, a celebration of what we are in contrast to what we have become, is bought at a price: that is, the price of abstracting the individual from the analysis of distributions of power and principles of control which selectively specialize modes of acquisition and realizations. Thus the announcement of competence points away from such selective specialisations and so points away from the macro blot on the micro context. (Bernstein 1996a) p.56.

292. Recognition and realization rules for legitimate texts are implicit. The emphasis is upon the realization of competences that acquirers already possess, or are thought to possess. Differences between displaces stratification of acquirers: classification is weak. (Bernstein 1996a) p. 58.

293. Recognition and realization rules for legitimate texts are explicit. Acquirers have relatively less control over selection, sequence and pace. Acquirers' texts (performances) are graded, and stratification displaces differences between acquirers. Classifications are strong. (Bernstein 1996a) pp.58-59.

294. From Roger's list of assumptions in mainstream education that is so often quoted in holistic education literature.

> Another undeniable assumption, evident in all of our educational operations, is that constructive and creative citizens develop from passive learners. There seems to be a great unanimity in the verbalized aim of producing good citizens, able to act constructively, with an independence and originality adequate to the main virtue encouraged in our classrooms, at all levels, is that of passive learning material which is presented by the instructor, which in turn has been selected by some educational group as being material important for the student to learn. This is clearly the way in which we assume that an independent citizenry is developed. (Rogers 1967).

295. This issue of the regulation of pedagogical space is probably the most consistently vitriolic topic in holistic education. Possibly the most forceful of all current speakers on the topic is John Taylor Gatto, a teacher of almost thirty years in New York City, and a winner of several awards for excellence in teaching. He makes a convincing case that there are special interests which want a population that has learned to be obedient and passive. Gatto explains that as a teacher recognized for the excellence of his teaching, there were seven essential things that he (and every other excellent teacher) taught:

> The first lesson I teach is confusion. Everything I teach is out of context. I teach un-relating of everything. I teach dis-connections.
> The second lesson I teach is class position. I teach that students must stay in the class where they belong. I don't know who decides my kids belong there but that's not my business. The children are numbered so that if any get away they can be returned to the right class.
> The third lesson I teach is indifference. I teach children not to care too much about anything, even though they want to make it appear that they do.
> The fourth lesson I teach is emotional dependence. By stars and red checks, smiles and frowns, prizes, honors, and disgraces, I teach kids to surrender their will to the predestined chain of command. Rights may be granted or withheld by any authority without appeal, because rights do not

exist inside a school—not even the right of free speech, as the Supreme Court has ruled—unless school authorities say they do.

The fifth lesson I teach is intellectual dependency. Good students wait for a teacher to tell them what to do. It is the most important lesson, that we must wait for other people, better trained than ourselves, to make the meanings of our lives.

The sixth lesson I teach is provisional self-esteem. If you've ever tried to wrestle into line kids whose parents have convinced them to believe they'll be loved in spite of anything, you know how impossible it is to make self-confident spirits conform.

The seventh lesson I teach is that one can't hide. I teach students that they are always watched, that each is under constant surveillance by myself and my colleagues. (Gatto 1992) pp.2-11.

296. Most holistic educators would feel that, once again, Carl Rogers speaks for them in his sixth assumption he feels is imbedded in mainstream education.

One final and very pervasive assumption, especially in American education, is that evaluation is education and education is evaluation. Taking examinations and preparing for the next set of exams is a way of life for students. There is little or no thought of intrinsic goals, since the extrinsic have become all-important. Rarely does the student ask himself, "What aspect of this particular subject or this book interests me?" of "How could I find out about this particular aspect of life?" The sole question is, "What do you suppose will be asked on the examination?" It has gradually come to be assumed by teachers, by students, and by their parents, that report cards and grades constitute education. When a faculty member asked a student what he got out of a certain course, the student's response was what one would expect in this system: "I got a B." (Rogers 1967).

297. ...regulative discourse criteria (criteria of conduct and manner, and relation) are likely to be more explicit [in competence based pedagogy than performance based pedagogy]. (Bernstein 1996a) p. 60.

298. Possibly the greatest impact has been made by a Professor of Political Science at Rutgers University who wrote a book called *An Aristocracy of Everyone* after developing a program for citizenship started in 1988. His program received recognition from President Clinton and praise from many states which subsequently built on his work. Many holistic educators welcomed his book and his program as legitimising what they had been saying for years, but which had been criticised as unrealistic.

...the crucial democratic relationship between rights and responsibilities, which have too often been divorced in our society, can only be made visible in a setting of experiential learning where academic discussion is linked to practical activity. In other words, learning about the relationship between civic responsibility and civic rights means exercising the rights and duties of membership in an actual community, whether that community is a classroom, a group project or community service team, and or the university/college at large. (Barber 1992) p.254.

299. ...focus on procedural commonalities shared within a group. In the cases we have analysed the group is children but the procedural commonalities may well

be shared with other categories, e.g., ethnic communities, social class groups. From this point of view competence models are predicated on fundamental 'similar to' relations. Differences between acquirers are not subject to stratification but can be viewed as complementary to the actualization of a common potential. (Bernstein 1996a) p.64.

300. From Ron Miller, generally considered the best historian of holistic education:

> A basic premise of holistic education is the belief that our lives have a meaning and purpose greater than the mechanistic laws described by science, and greater than the "consensus consciousness" of any one culture. This transcendent purpose is a creative, self-guiding energy which we ought not attempt to suppress....
>
> ...two quite different languages have been used to describe this spiritual attitude. One is primarily religious and theistic, and describes the transcendent in terms such as "God," "divine" and "soul" ...The other is a more empirical, down-to-earth language, taken from twentieth century psychology, which uses terms such as "archetype" and "individuation" and "self-actualization". There are significant and interesting differences between these two conceptions. For example, religious approaches tend to seek the transcendent through various *disciplines*, and holistic education methods developed in these traditions (such as Waldorf, Montessori, and schools affiliated with religious sects) are often quite highly structured and disciplined. On the other hand, empirical psychological approaches are more interested in the *spontaneity* of creative expression, and educators who draw upon this point of view (Neef, Ferrer, Neil, Goodman, Holt, etc.) are the "child-centered" libertarians in holistic tradition. (Miller 1992) pp.154-155.

301. Foresight! Foresight, which takes us ceaselessly beyond ourselves and often places us where we shall never arrive. This is the true source of all our miseries. What madness for a fleeting being like man always to look far into a future which comes so rarely and to neglect the present of which he is sure. It is a madness all the more destructive since it increases continuously with age; and old men, always distrustful, full of foresight, and miserly, prefer to deny themselves what is necessary today so as not to lack it a hundred years from now. Thus, we are attached to everything, we cling to everything—times, places, men, things; everything which is, everything which will be, is important to each of us. Our individual persons are now only the least part of ourselves. Each one extends himself, so to speak, over the whole earth and becomes sensitive over this entire large surface. Is it surprising that our ills are multiplied by all the points where we can be wounded? How many princes grieve over the loss of a country they have never seen? How many merchants are there whom it suffices to touch in India in order to make them scream in Paris? (Rousseau 1979) pp.82-83.

302. Conscious and unconscious do not make a whole when one of them is suppressed and injured by the other. If they must contend, let it at least be a fair fight with equal rights on both sides. Both are aspects of life. Consciousness should defend its reason and protect itself, and the chaotic life of the unconscious should be given that chance of having its way too—as much of it as we can stand. This

means open conflict and open collaboration at one. That, evidently, is the way human life should be....

This, roughly, is what I mean by the individuation process. (Jung 1959b) p.288 § 522-523.

303. ...the mystical (or experiential) also has its traps which I have not stressed sufficiently. As the more Apollonian type can veer toward the extreme of being reduced to the merely behavioral, so does the mystical type run the risk of being reduced to the merely experiential. Out of the joy and wonder of his ecstasies and peak-experiences he may be tempted to *seek* them, *ad hoc*, and to value them exclusively, as the only or at least the highest goods of life, giving up other criteria of right and wrong. Focused on these wonderful subjective experiences, he may run the danger of turning away from the world and from other people in his search for triggers to peak-experiences, *any* triggers. (Maslow 1994) p. viii.

304. It is the overstress on the conscious and the rational and the underestimation of the wisdom of our total reacting organism that prevent us from living as unified, whole human beings.

Yet I can testify from personal experience that it is not easy for people whose lives have been dichotomized for decades to achieve this unity. (Rogers 1990a) p.369.

305. ...the school and instruction are to lead the boy to the threefold, yet in itself one, knowledge—to the knowledge of himself in all his relations, and thus to the knowledge of man as such; to the knowledge of God, the eternal condition, cause and source of his being, and of the being of all things; and to the knowledge of nature and the outer world as proceeding from the Eternal Spirit and depending thereupon. (Froebel 1890) p.137.

306. ...there is no longer the illusion that we can gain *certain* knowledge. Instead, by a variety of means and methods, we can gain new knowledge and this new knowledge has a degree of truth value that depends on the methods and circumstances of the particular research study. It is refreshing to find that we need to use our judgment to discriminate between those findings and conclusions that have a high degree of validity and those that have a lesser degree of validity. There is a full recognition that we will never have certain knowledge. (Rogers 1990c) p.284.

307. The Christian West considers man to be wholly dependent upon the grace of God, or at least upon the Church as the exclusive and divinely sanctioned earthly instrument of man's redemption. The East, however, insists that man is the sole cause of his higher development, for it believes in "self-liberation."

In spite of everything, the West is thoroughly Christian as far as its psychology is concerned. ...Grace comes from elsewhere; at all events from outside. Every other point of view is sheer heresy. Hence it is quite understandable why the human psyche is suffering from undervaluation. Anyone who dares to establish a connection between the psyche and the idea of God is immediately accused of "psychologism" or suspected of morbid "mysticism." (Jung 1958c) pp.481-482 § 770-771.

308. It follows, therefore, that, in order to incline a young man to humanity, far from making him admire the brilliant lot of others, one must show him the sad sides of that lot, one must make him fear it. Then, by an evident inference, he ought to cut out his own road to happiness, following in no one else's tracks. (Rousseau 1979) p.223.

Bibliography

A Foreigner, (three years resident of Yverdon). 1823. *Hints to Mothers on the Cultivation of the Minds of Children in the Spirit of Pestalozzi's Method*. London: Longman, Hurst, Rees, Orme, and Brown.

Anderson, Lewis Flint. 1931. *Pestalozzi*. Edited by E. H. Reisner, *McGraw-Hill Education Classics*. New York: McGraw-Hill Book Company.

Anderson, Rob, and Kenneth N. Cissna, eds. 1997. *The Martin Buber—Carl Rogers Dialogue: A new transcript with commentary*. Albany: State University of New York Press.

Baldwin, Alfred, Joan Kalhorn, and Fay Huffman Breese. 1945. Patterns of Parent Behavior. *Psychological Monographs* 58 (no. 268).

Barber, Benjamin. 1992. *An Aristocracy Of Everyone: The Politics Of Education And The Future Of America*. Oxford: Oxford University Press.

Barnard, Henry, ed. 1859. *Pestalozzi and Pestalozzianism: Life, educational principles, and methods of John Henry Pestalozzi with biographical sketches from several of his assistants and disciples*. New York: F.C. Browness.

Berlin, Isaiah. 1999. *The Roots of Romanticism*. London: Chatto and Lindus.

Bernstein, Basil. 1996a. *Pedagogy Symbolic Control and Identity: Theory, Research, Critique*. Edited by A. Luke, *Critical Perspectives on Literacy and Education*. London: Taylor & Francis.

Bernstein, Basil. 1996b. Sociology of Education Series. Oxford: Nuffield College.

Bernstein, Basil. 1997. From personal discussions.

Biber. 1859. Pestalozzi, Teaching as the Father of a Family. In *Pestalozzi and Pestalozzianism: Life, educational principles, and methods of John Henry Pestalozzi with biographical sketches of several of his assistants and disciples*. Edited by H. Barnard. New York: F.C. Brownell.

Bohm, David. 1980. *Wholeness and the Implicate Order*. London: Routledge & Kegan Paul.

Bohm, David. 1993. *On Dialogue*: Transcripts of dialogues that occurred in 1989.

Bohm, David. 1994. *Thought As A System*. London: Routledge.

Boutin, Gerard. 1976. Le Concept de Nature Humaine et ses Implications Pedagogiques chez Burrhus F. Skinner et Carl R. Rogers. PhD, Faculte des Lettres, Universite de Fribourg, Fribourg, Switzerland.

Boyd, William. 1963. *The Educational Theory of Jean-Jacques Rousseau*. New York: Russell & Russell.

Browning, Don S. 1987. *Religious Thought and the New Psychologies*. Philadelphia: Fortress Press.

Burman, Erica. 1994. *Deconstructing Developmental Psychology.* London: Routledge.

Cajete, Gregory A. 1994. *Look To The Mountain: An Ecology Of Indigenous Education.* Durango, Colorado: Kivaki Press.

Campbell, Joseph. 1949. *The Hero of a Thousand Faces.* Princeton: Princeton University Press.

Carter, Forrest. 1976. *The Education Of Little Tree.* Albuquerque: University of New Mexico Press.

Central. 1997. Central Park East Secondary School. 1573 Madison Avenue: New York, NY 10029.

City. 1997. City and Country School. 146 West 13th Street: New York, NY 10011.

Claxton, Guy. 1998. *Hare Brain Tortoise Mind: Why intelligence increases when you think less.* London: Fourth Estate Ltd.

Coupland, Nikolas, and Jon F. Nussbaum. 1993. *Discourse and Lifespan Identity.* Edited by H. Giles. Vol. 4, *Language and Language Behaviors.* Newbury Park, CA: Sage Publications.

Coward, Harold, ed. 1985. *Jung and Eastern Thought.* Edited by R. D. Mann and J. B. Mann, *SUNY Series in Transpersonal and Humanistic Psychology.* Albany: State Universtiy of New York Press.

Darling, John. 1994. *Child-centred Education and Its Critics.* London: Paul Chapman Publishing.

De Carvalho, Roy Jose. 1991. *The Growth Hypothesis in Psychology: The humanistic psychology of Abraham Maslow and Carl Rogers.* San Francisco: EMText.

Dearden, R.F. 1968. *The Philosophy of Primary Education.* Edited by J. W. Tibble, *The Students Library of Education.* London: Routledge & Kegan Paul.

d'Entrevèves, A. P. 1963. *Natural Law: An introduction to legal philosophy.* London: Hutchinson.

Diesterweg. 1859. Pestalozzi and the Schools of Germany. In *Pestalozzi and Pestalozzianism: Life, educational principles, and methods of John Henry Pestalozzi with biographical sketches of several of his assistants and disciples.* Edited by H. Barnard. New York: F.C. Brownell.

Dodge, K.A. 1986. A social information-processing model of social competence in children. In *Minnesota Symposium on Child Psychology.* Edited by M. Perlmutter. Vol. 18. Hillsdale, NJ: Erlbaum.

Dudty, David , and Helen Dudty, eds. 1994. *Holistic Education: Some Australian Explorations* "Belconnen, ACT": Australian Curriculum Studies Association.

Duveen, Gerard, and Barbara Lloyd. 1990. *Social Representations and the Development of Knowledge.* Cambridge: Cambridge University Press.

Egan, Kieran. 1989. *Teaching as Story Telling.* Chicago: University of Chicago Press.

Egan, Kieran. *Conceptions of Development in Education* Philosophy of Education Society Yearbook, 1998 [cited 1999] . Available from http://www.ed.uiuc.edu/EPS/PES-Yearbook/1998/egan.html.

Eliade, Mircea. 1959. *The Sacred and The Profane: The nature of religion.* Translated by Willard R. Trask. New York: Harcourt Brace Jovanovich.

Elk, Black. 1988. *Black Elk Speaks.* Nebraska: University of Nebraska Press.

Ellenberger, Henri F. 1970. *The Discovery of the Unconscious: The history and evolution of dynamic psychiatry.* London: Basic Books.

Ergardt, Jan T. 1983. The Concept of *Citta* in Some Early Buddhist Texts and Jung's Analytical Psychology. In *Buddhist and Western Psychology.* Edited by N. Katz. Boulder, Colorado: Prajna Press.

Eysenck, H. 1964. *Crime and Personality*. London: Routledge and Kegan Paul.

Freedman, B.J., L. Rosenthal, C.P. Donahoe, D.G. Schlundt, and R.M. McFall. 1978. A social-behavioral analysis of skills deficits in deliquent and non-delinquent adolescent boys. *Journal of Consulting and Clinical Psychology* 46 (1448-62).

Freire, Paulo. 1995a. *Pedagogy Of The Oppressed*. New York: The Continuum Publishing Company.

Friere, Paulo. 1995b. *Pedagogy Of Hope: Reliving Pedagogy Of The Oppressed*. New York: Continuum Publishing.

Froebel, Friedrich. 1890. *The Education of Man*. Translated by W.N. Hailman. Edited by W. T. Harris. 15 vols. Vol. 5, *International Education Series*. New York: D. Appleton and Company.

Furst, Lilian R., and Peter N. Skrine. 1971. *Naturalism*. Edited by J. D. Jump, *The Critical Idiom*. London: Methuen &Co. Ltd.

Gardner, Howard. 1983. *Frames of Mind: The theory of multiple intelligneces*. New York: Harper and Row.

Gardner, Howard. 1993. *The Unschooled Mind: How Children Think And How Schools Should Teach*. London: Fontana Press.

Gardner, John W. 1987. *Excellence: Can We Be Equal and Excellent Too?* New York: W.W. Norton & Company.

Gatto, John Taylor. 1992. *Dumbing Us Down: The Hidden Curriculum of Compulsory Schooling*. Philadelphia, PA: New Society Publishers.

Geiger, Henry. 1993. Introduction. In *The Farther Reaches of Human Nature*. Edited by A. Maslow. Harmondsworth: Arkana.

Goffman, Erving. 1997. The Self and Social Roles. In *The Goffman Reader*. Edited by C. Lemert and A. Branaman. Oxford: Blackwell.

Goleman, Daniel. 1995. *Emotional Intelligence*. London: Bloomsbury Publishing.

Green, J.A. 1912. *Pestalozzi's Educational Writings*. Edited by J. W. Anderson, *Educational Classics*. London: Edward Arnold.

Grimsley, Ronald. 1968. *Rousseau and the Religious Quest*. Oxford: Clarendon Press.

Grimsley, Ronald. 1969. *Jean-Jacques Rousseau: A study in self-awareness*. 2nd ed. Cardiff: University of Wales Press.

Grotberg, Edith. 1995. *A Guide To Promotion of Resilience in Children: Strengthening the human spirit, Early Childhood Development: Practice and Reflections*. The Hague: Bernard van Leer Foundation.

Hamilton, H.A. 1952. The Religious Roots of Froebel's Philosophy. In *Friedrich Froebel and English Education*. Edited by E. Lawrence. London: Routledge & Kegan Paul.

Hanson, Barbara Gail. 1995. *General Systems Theory: Beginning with wholes*. First ed. Toronto, Ontario: Taylor & Francis.

Hayward, F.H. 1904. *The Educational Ideal of Pestalozzi and Froebel*. London: Ralph Holland & Co.

Heafford, Michael. 1967. *Pestalozzi: His thought and relevance today*. Edited by C. H. Dobinson, *The Library of Educational Thought*. London: Methuen & Co. Ltd.

Heisig, James W. 1979. *Imago Dei: A study of Jung's psychology of religion*. Edited by J. Hillman, *Studies in Jungian Thought*. Lewisburg: Bucknell University Press.

Hirschi, T., and M.J. Hindelang. 1977. Intelligence and delinquency: A revisionist review. *American Sociological Review* (42):571-587.

Holt, John. 1982. *How Children Fail*. Second ed. London: Penguin Books.

Hooks, Bell. 1994. *Teaching To Transgress: Education As The Practice Of Freedom*. New York: Routledge.

Huxley, Aldous. 1946. *The Perennial Philosophy*. London: Chatto and Windus.

Jennings, W.S., R. Kilkenny, and L. Kohlberg. 1983. Moral development theory and practice for youthful and adult offenders. In *Personality Theory, Moral Development and Criminal Behavior*. Edited by W. S. Laufer and J. M. day. Lexington, Mass.: Lexington Books/D.C.Heath.

Jung, C.G. 1953a. The Psychology of the Unconscious. In *Two Essays on Analytical Psychology*. Translated by R.F.C. Hull. 20 vols. Vol. 7, *The Collected Works of C.G. Jung*. London: Routledge & Kegan Paul.

Jung, C.G. 1953b. The Relations Between the Ego and the Unconscious. In *Two Essays on Analytical Psychology*. Translated by R.F.C. Hull. 20 vols. Vol. 7, *The Collected Works of C.G. Jung*. London: Routledge & Kegan Paul.

Jung, C.G. 1954a. Analytical Psychology and Education. In *The Development of Personality*. Translated by R.F.C. Hull Edited by H. Read, M. Fordham and G. Adler. 20 vols. Vol. 17, *The Collected Works of C.G. Jung*. London: Routledge & Kegan Paul.

Jung, C.G. 1954b. Child Development and Education. In *The Development of Personality*. Translated by R.F.C. Hull Edited by H. Read, M. Fordham and G. Adler. 20 vols. Vol. 17, *The Collected Works of C.G. Jung*. London: Routledge & Kegan Paul.

Jung, C.G. 1954c. The Development of Personality. In *The Development of Personality*. Translated by R.F.C. Hull Edited by H. Read, M. Fordham and G. Adler. 20 vols. Vol. 17, *The Collected Works of C.G. Jung*. London: Routledge & Kegan Paul.

Jung, C.G. 1954d. Fundamental Questions in Psychotherapy. In *The Practice of Psychotherapy*. Translated by R.F.C. Hull Edited by H. Read, M. Fordham and G. Adler. 20 vols. Vol. 16, *The Collected Works of C.G. Jung*. London: Routledge & Kegan Paul.

Jung, C.G. 1954e. The Gifted Child. In *The Development of Personality*. Translated by R.F.C. Hull Edited by H. Read, M. Fordham and G. Adler. 20 vols. Vol. 17, *The Collected Works of C.G. Jung*. London: Routledge & Kegan Paul.

Jung, C.G. 1954f. Introduction to Wickes's "Analyse der Kinderseele". In *The Development of Personality*. Translated by R.F.C. Hull Edited by H. Read, M. Fordham and G. Adler. 20 vols. Vol. 17, *The Collected Works of C.G. Jung*. London: Routledge & Kegan Paul.

Jung, C.G. 1954g. Marriage as a Psychological Relationship. In *The Development of Personality*. Translated by R.F.C. Hull Edited by H. Read, M. Fordham and G. Adler. 20 vols. Vol. 17, *The Collected Works of C.G. Jung*. London: Routledge & Kegan Paul.

Jung, C.G. 1954h. The Pratical Use of Dream Analysis. In *The Practice of Psychotherapy*. Translated by R.F.C. Hull Edited by H. Read, M. Fordham and G. Adler. 20 vols. Vol. 16, *The Collected Works of C.G. Jung*. London: Routledge & Kegan Paul.

Jung, C.G. 1954i. Problems of Modern Psychotherapy. In *The Practice of Psychotherapy*. Translated by R.F.C. Hull Edited by H. Read, M. Fordham and G. Adler. 20 vols. Vol. 16, *The Collected Works of C.G. Jung*. London: Routledge & Kegan Paul.

Jung, C.G. 1954j. The Psychology of Transference. In *The Practice of Psychotherapy*. Translated by R.F.C. Hull Edited by H. Read, M. Fordham and G. Adler. 20 vols. Vol. 16, *The Collected Works of C.G. Jung*. London: Routledge & Kegan Paul.

Jung, C.G. 1954k. Psychotherapy Today. In *The Practice of Psychotherapy*. Translated by R.F.C. Hull Edited by H. Read, M. Fordham and G. Adler. 20 vols. Vol. 16, *The Collected Works of C.G. Jung*. London: Routledge & Kegan Paul.

Jung, C.G. 1954l. The Significance of the Unconscious in Individual Education. In

The Development of Personality. Translated by R.F.C. Hull Edited by H. Read, M. Fordham and G. Adler. 20 vols. Vol. 17, *The Collected Works of C.G. Jung.* London: Routledge & Kegan Paul.

Jung, C. G. 1957. *Face to Face.* Transcript of television interview with John Freeman.

Jung, C.G. 1958a. Answer to Job. In *Psychology and Religion.* Translated by R.F.C. Hull Edited by H. Read, M. Fordham and G. Adler. 20 vols. Vol. 11, *The Collected Works of C.G. Jung.* London: Routledge & Kegan Paul.

Jung, C.G. 1958b. Forward to Suzuki's Introduction to Zen Buddhism. In *Psychology and Religion.* Translated by R.F.C. Hull Edited by H. Read, M. Fordham and G. Adler. 20 vols. Vol. 11, *The Collected Works of C.G. Jung.* London: Routledge & Kegan Paul.

Jung, C.G. 1958c. Psychological Commentary on "The Tibetan Book of the Great Liberation". In *Psychology and Religion.* Translated by R.F.C. Hull. 20 vols. Vol. 11, *The Collected Works of C.G. Jung.* London: Routledge & Kegan Paul.

Jung, C.G. 1958d. Psychology and Religion. In *Psychology and Religion.* Translated by R.F.C. Hull. 20 vols. Vol 11, *The Collected Works of C.G. Jung.* London: Routledge & Kegan Paul.

Jung, C.G. 1958e. Psychotherapists or the Clergy. In *Psychology and Religion.* Translated by R.F.C. Hull Edited by H. Read, M. Fordham and G. Adler. 20 vols. Vol. 11, *The Collected Works of C.G. Jung.* London: Routledge & Kegan Paul.

Jung, C.G. 1958f. Yoga and the West. In *Psychology and Religion.* Translated by R.F.C. Hull. 20 vols. Vol. 11, *The Collected Works of C.G. Jung.* London: Routledge & Kegan Paul.

Jung, C.G. 1959a. *Aion: Researches into the Phenomenology of the Self.* Translated by R.F.C. Hull. Edited by H. Read, M. Fordham and G. Adler. 2nd ed. 20 vols. Vol. 9, ii, *The Collected Works of C.G. Jung.* London: Routledge & Kegan Paul.

Jung, C.G. 1959b. Conscious, Unconscious, and Individuation. In *The Archetypes and the Collective Unconscious.* Translated by R.F.C. Hull. 20 vols. Vol. 9, i, *The Collected Works of C.G. Jung.* London: Routledge & Kegan Paul.

Jung, C.G. 1959c. The Psychology of the Child Archetype. In *The Archetypes and the Collective Unconscious.* Translated by R.F.C. Hull. 20 vols. Vol. 9, i, *The Collected Works of C.G. Jung.* London: Routledge & Kegan Paul.

Jung, C.G. 1959d. A Study in the Process of Individuation. In *The Archetypes and the Collective Unconscious.* Translated by R.F.C. Hull. 20 vols. Vol. 9, i, *The Collected Works of C.G. Jung.* London: Routledge & Kegan Paul.

Jung, C.G. 1960a. Analytical Psychology and 'Weltanschauung'. In *The Structure and Dynamics of the Psyche.* Translated by R.F.C. Hull. 20 vols. Vol. 7, *The Collected Works of C.G. Jung.* London: Routledge & Kegan Paul.

Jung, C. G. 1960b. On Psychic Energy. In *The Structure and Dynamics of the Psyche.* 20 vols. Vol. 8, *The Collected Works of C. G. Jung.* London: Routledge & Kegan Paul.

Jung, C. G. 1960c. The Psychological Foundations of Belief in Spirits. In *The Structure and Dynamics of the Psyche.* . 20 vols. Vol. 8, *The Collected Works of C. G. Jung.* London: Routledge & Kegan Paul.

Jung, C. G. 1960d. The Stages of Life. In *The Structure and Dynamics of the Psyche.* 20 vols. Vol. 8, *The Collected Works of C. G. Jung.* London: Routledge & Kegan Paul.

Jung, C.G. 1960e. Synchronicity: An Acausal Connecting Principle. In *The Structure and Dynamics of the Psyche.* Translated by R.F.C. Hull. 20 vols. Vol. 8, *The Collected Works of C.G. Jung.* London: Routledge & Kegan Paul.

Jung, C. G. 1960f. The Transcendent Function. In *The Structure and Dynamics of the*

Psyche. 20 vols. Vol. 8, *The Collected Works of C. G. Jung.* London: Routledge & Kegan Paul.

Jung, C.G. 1963. *Mysterium Coniunctionis.* Translated by R.F.C. Hull. Edited by H. Read, M. Fordham and G. Adler. 2nd ed. 20 vols. Vol. 14. London: Routledge & Kegan Paul.

Jung, C.G. 1964a. Good and Evil in Analytical Psychology. In *Civilization in Transition.* Translated by R.F.C. Hull Edited by H. Read, M. Fordham and G. Adler. 20 vols. Vol. 10, *The Collected Works of C.G. Jung.* London: Routledge & Kegan Paul.

Jung, C.G. 1964b. The Spiritual Problem of Modern Man. In *Civilization in Transition.* Translated by R.F.C. Hull Edited by H. Read, M. Fordham and G. Adler. 20 vols. Vol. 10, *The Collected Works of C.G. Jung.* London: Routledge & Kegan Paul.

Jung, C.G. 1964c. The Swiss Line in the European Spectrum. In *Civilization in Transition.* Translated by R.F.C. Hull Edited by H. Read, M. Fordham and G. Adler. 20 vols. Vol. 10, *The Collected Works of C.G. Jung.* London: Routledge & Kegan Paul.

Jung, C.G. 1964d. The Undiscovered Self: Present and future. In *Civilization in Transition.* Translated by R.F.C. Hull Edited by H. Read, M. Fordham and G. Adler. 20 vols. Vol. 10, *The Collected Works of C.G. Jung.* London: Routledge & Kegan Paul.

Jung, C.G. 1967. The Visions of Zosimos. In *Alchemical Studies.* Translated by R.F.C. Hull. 20 vols. Vol. 13, *The Collected Works of C.G. Jung.* London: Routledge & Kegan Paul.

Jung, C.G. 1971a. The Apollinian and Dionysian. In *Psychological Types.* Translated by R.F.C. Hull. 20 vols. Vol. 6, *The Collected Works of C.G. Jung.* London: Routledge & Kegan Paul.

Jung, C.G. 1971b. *Psychological Types.* Translated by R.F.C. Hull. Edited by H. Read, M. Fordham and G. Adler. 20 vols. Vol. 6, *The Collected Works of C.G. Jung.* London: Routledge & Kegan Paul.

Jung, C.G. 1971c. Schiller's Ideas on the Type Problem. In *Psychological Types.* Translated by R.F.C. Hull Edited by H. Read, M. Fordham and G. Adler. 20 vols. Vol. 6, *The Collected Works of C.G. Jung.* London: Routledge & Kegan Paul.

Jung, C.G. 1977a. Adaptation, Individuation, Collectivity. In *The Symbolic Life: Miscellaneous writings.* Translated by R.F.C. Hull Edited by H. Read, M. Fordham and G. Adler. 20 vols. Vol. 17, *The Collected Works of C.G. Jung.* London: Routledge & Kegan Paul.

Jung, C.G. 1977b. Answers to "Mishmar" on Adolf Hitler. In *The Symbolic Life: Miscellaneous writings.* Translated by R.F.C. Hull Edited by H. Read, M. Fordham and G. Adler. 20 vols. Vol. 17, *The Collected Works of C.G. Jung.* London: Routledge & Kegan Paul.

Jung, C.G. 1977c. Attitude Change Conducive to World Peace. In *The Symbolic Life: Miscellaneous writings.* Translated by R.F.C. Hull Edited by H. Read, M. Fordham and G. Adler. 20 vols. Vol. 17, *The Collected Works of C.G. Jung.* London: Routledge & Kegan Paul.

Jung, C.G. 1977d. Depth Psychology and Self-Knowledge. In *The Symbolic Life: Miscellaneous writings.* Translated by R.F.C. Hull Edited by H. Read, M. Fordham and G. Adler. 20 vols. Vol. 17, *The Collected Works of C.G. Jung.* London: Routledge & Kegan Paul.

Jung, C.G. 1977e. Foreword to Spier: "The Hands of Children". In *The Symbolic Life: Miscellaneous writings.* Translated by R.F.C. Hull Edited by H. Read, M. Fordham and G. Adler. 20 vols. Vol. 17, *The Collected Works of C.G. Jung*. London: Routledge & Kegan Paul.

Jung, C.G. 1977f. Foreword to the Hebrew Edition of Jung: "Psychology and Education". In *The Symbolic Life: Miscellaneous writings*. Translated by R.F.C. Hull Edited by H. Read, M. Fordham and G. Adler. 20 vols. Vol. 17, *The Collected Works of C.G. Jung*. London: Routledge & Kegan Paul.

Jung, C.G. 1977g. Forward to Abergg: "Ostasien Denkt Anders". In *The Symbolic Life: Miscellaneous writings*. Translated by R.F.C. Hull Edited by H. Read, M. Fordham and G. Adler. 20 vols. Vol. 17, *The Collected Works of C.G. Jung*. London: Routledge & Kegan Paul.

Jung, C.G. 1977h. Religion and Psychology: A reply to Martin Buber. In *The Symbolic Life: Miscellaneous writings*. Translated by R.F.C. Hull Edited by H. Read, M. Fordham and G. Adler. 20 vols. Vol. 17, *The Collected Works of C.G. Jung*. London: Routledge & Kegan Paul.

Jung, C.G. 1977i. The Rules of Life. In *The Symbolic Life: Miscellaneous writings*. Translated by R.F.C. Hull Edited by H. Read, M. Fordham and G. Adler. 20 vols. Vol. 17, *The Collected Works of C.G. Jung*. London: Routledge & Kegan Paul.

Kaplan, H.B. 1980. *Deviant Behavior in Defense of Self*. New York: Academic Press.

Krishnamurti. 1953. *Education And The Significance Of Life*. London: Victor Gollancz Ltd.

Krishnamurti. 1962. unpublished transcript, 10th public talk, 12th August, at Saanen, Switzerland.

Krishnamurti. 1970. *Talks With American Students*. Wassenaar, Holland: Servire.

Krishnamurti. 1974. *On Education*. Pondicherry, India: All India Press.

Krishnamurti. 1975. *Beginnings of Learning*. London: Victor Gollancz Ltd.

Krishnamurti. 1981. *Letters To The Schools: Volume One*. Den Haag, Holland: Mirananda.

Krishnamurti. 1985. *Letters To The Schools: Volume Two*. Den Haag, Holland: Mirananda.

Krishnamurti. 1993a. *A Flame Of Learning*. Den Haag, Holland: Mirananda.

Krishnamurti. 1993b. *Krishnamurti At Rajghat*. Madras, India: Krishnamurti Foundation India.

Krishnamurti. 1994. *On Learning And Knowledge*. San Francisco: HarperSanFrancisco.

Langer, Ellen J. 1989. *Mindfulness*. Reading, Massachusetts: Addison-Wesley Publishing Company.

Langer, Ellen J. 1997. *The Power of Mindful Learning*. Reading, Massachusetts: Addison-Wesley.

Lawrence, Evelyn. 1952. Frobel's Educational Philosophy in 1952. In *Friedrich Froebel and English Education*. Edited by E. Lawrence. London: Routledge & Kegan Paul.

Liedloff, Jean. 1989. *The Continuum Concept*. 4th ed. Middlesex: Arkana.

Lincoln, Yvonna S. 1993. I and Thou: Method, Voice, and Roles in Research with the Silenced. In *Naming Silenced Lives: Personal narratives and the process of educational change*. Edited by D. McLaughlin and W. G. Tierney. London: Routledge.

Luvmour, Sambhava , and Josette Luvmour. 1997. *Metamorphosis: A Guide to Family, Individual and Community Awakening Through Rites of Passage* manuscript.

Maslow, Abraham, ed. 1959a. *New Knowledge in Human Values*. New York: Harper & Brothers.

Maslow, Abraham. 1959b. Psychological Data and Value Theory. In *New Knowledge in Human Values*. Edited by A. Maslow. New York: Harper & Brothers.

Maslow, Abraham. 1966. *The Psychology of Science, The John Dewey Society Lectureship Series*. New York: Harper & Row.

Maslow, Abraham. 1968. *Toward a Psychology of Being*. New York: Van Nostrand Reinhold Company.

Maslow, Abraham. 1993. *The Farther Reaches of Human Nature*. Harmondsworth: Arkana.

Maslow, Abraham. 1994. *Religions, Values, and Peak-Experiences*. New York: Arkana.

Maslow, Abraham. 1996a. Acceptance of the Beloved in Being-Love. In *Future Visions: The unpublished papers of Abraham Maslow*. Edited by E. Hoffman. Thousand Oaks, CA: Sage Publications.

Maslow, Abraham. 1996b. Critique of Self-Actualization Theory. In *Future Visions: The unpublished papers of Abraham Maslow*. Edited by E. Hoffman. Thousand Oaks, CA: Sage Publications.

Maslow, Abraham. 1996c. Humanistic Biology: Elitist implications of the concept of "Full Humanness". In *Future Visions: The unpublished papers of Abraham Maslow*. Edited by E. Hoffman. Thousand Oaks, CA: Sage Publications.

Maslow, Abraham. 1996d. Limits, Controls, and the Safety Needs in Children. In *Future Visions: The unpublished papers of Abraham Maslow*. Edited by E. Hoffman. Thousand Oaks, CA: Sage Publications.

Maslow, Abraham. 1996e. Science, Psychology, and the Existential Outlook. In *Future Visions: The unpublished papers of Abraham Maslow*. Edited by E. Hoffman. Thousand Oaks, CA: Sage Publications.

Miller, John P. 1993. *The Holistic Teacher*. Toronto, Ontario: The Ontario Institute for Studies in Education.

Miller, J.P., J.R. Bruce Cassie, and S.M. Drake. 1990. *Holistic Learning: A Teachers Guide to Integrated Studies*. Toronto, Ontario: OISE.

Miller, Ron. 1992. *What Are Schools For?: Holistic Education In American Culture*. Second ed. Brandon, VT: Holistic Education Press.

Mintz, Jerry, R. Solomon, and S. Solomon, eds. 1994. *The Handbook of Alternative Education*. New York: Macmillan Publishing.

Mitchell, Robert. 1994. *Nurturing Souls*. Unpublished manuscript.

Morss, John R. 1992. On the Necessity of an Anti-Developmental Psychology. unpublished paper.

Murray, E.R. 1914. *Frobel as a Pioneer in Modern Psychology*. London: George Philip & Sons.

Noll, Richard. 1996. *The Jung Cult: Origins of a charismatic movement*. London: Fontana Press.

Nunes, T., A.-L. Schliemann, and D. Carraher. 1993. *Street Mathematics and School Mathematics*. New York: Cambridge Universtiy Press.

Nunn, Chris. 1996. *Awareness: What it is, What it does*. London: Routledge.

O'Brien, George L. 1997. Government Schools in Crisis, edited by G. Erikson. 1800 Market St., San Francisco, CA 94102: International Society for Individual Liberty.

Paterson, Alice. 1914. *The Edgeworths: A study in later eighteenth century education*. London: University Tutorial Press Ltd.

Pestalozzi, Johan Henirich. 1818. *The Address of Pestalozzi to the British Public*. Translated by unknown. Yverdon, Switzerland: Ls. Fiva, son.

Pestalozzi, Johan Heinrich. 1827a. Letter III, October 7, 1818. In *Letters on Early Education Addressed to J.P. Greaves, Esq*. Translated by unknown. London: Sherwood, Gilbert and Piper.

Pestalozzi, Johan Heinrich. 1827b. Letter XVI, December 31, 1818. In *Letters on*

Early Education Addressed to J.P. Greaves, Esq. . London: Sherwood, Gilbert and Piper.

Pestalozzi, Johan Heinrich. 1827c. Letter XXI, February 4, 1819. In *Letters on Early Education Addressed to J.P. Greaves, Esq.* . London: Sherwood, Gilbert and Piper.

Pestalozzi, Johan Heinrich. 1827d. Letter XXIII, February 18, 1819. In *Letters on Early Education Addressed to J.P. Greaves, Esq.* . London: Sherwood, Gilbert and Piper.

Pestalozzi, Johan Heinrich. 1827e. Letter XXIX, April 4, 1819. In *Letters on Early Education Addressed to J.P. Greaves, Esq.* . London: Sherwood, Gilbert and Piper.

Pestalozzi, Johan Heinrich. 1827f. Letter XXVIII, March 27, 1819. In *Letters on Early Education Addressed to J.P. Greaves, Esq.* . London: Sherwood, Gilbert and Piper.

Pestalozzi, Johan Heinrich. 1827g. Letter XXX, April 10, 1819. In *Letters on Early Education Addressed to J.P. Greaves, Esq.* . London: Sherwood, Gilbert and Piper.

Pestalozzi, Johan Heinrich. 1827h. Letter XXXIII, May 1, 1819. In *Letters on Early Education Addressed to J.P. Greaves, Esq.* . London: Sherwood, Gilbert and Piper.

Pestalozzi, Johan Heinrich. 1859a. Evening Hour of the Hermit. In *Pestalozzi and Pestalozzianism: Life, educational principles, and methods of John Henry Pestalozzi with biographical sketches of several of his assistants and disciples.* Edited by H. Barnard. Vol. 2. New York: F.C. Brownell.

Pestalozzi, Johan Heinrich. 1859b. Pestalozzi's Address to His School on New Year's Day 1809. In *Pestalozzi and Pestalozzianism: Life, educational principles, and methods of John Henry Pestalozzi with biographical sketches of several of his assistants and disciples.* Edited by H. Barnard. Vol. 2. New York: F.C. Brownell.

Pestalozzi, Johan Heinrich. 1907. *How Gertrude Teaches Her Children: An attempt to help mothers to teach their own children.* Translated by Lucy E. Holland and Francis C. Turner. 4th ed. London: Swan, Sonnenshein & Co.

Pestalozzi, Johan Heinrich. 1912a. 3rd Letter for Revision of How Gertrude Teaches Her Children, begun 1805. In *Pestalozzi's Educational Writings.* Edited by J. A. Green, *Educational Classics.* London: Edward Arnold.

Pestalozzi, Johan Heinrich. 1912b. 8th Letter for Revision of How Gertrude Teaches Her Children, begun 1805. In *Pestalozzi's Educational Writings.* Edited by J. A. Green, *Educational Classics.* London: Edward Arnold.

Pestalozzi, Johan Heinrich. 1912c. The Swansong. In *Pestalozzi's Educational Writings.* Edited by J. A. Green, *Educational Classics.* London: Edward Arnold.

Pestalozzi, Johan Heinrich. 1931a. Article from Ein Schweizer-Blat, issue 28, no. 2, published 1782. In *Pestalozzi.* Edited by L. F. Anderson, *McGraw-Hill Education Classics.* New York: McGraw-Hill Book Company.

Pestalozzi, Johan Heinrich. 1931b. Letters to James Pierrepont Greaves Letter XXXII April 25, 1819. In *Pestalozzi.* Edited by L. F. Anderson, *McGraw-Hill Education Classics.* New York: McGraw-Hill Book Company.

Pestalozzi, Johan Heinrich. 1931c. Letters to James Pierrepont Greaves, Letter XXXIII May 1, 1819. In *Pestalozzi.* Edited by L. F. Anderson, *McGraw-Hill Education Classics.* New York: McGraw-Hill Book Company.

Pestalozzi, Johan Heinrich. 1931d. Pestalozzi's Address to his House on the Occasion of his Seventy Second Birthday, January 12, 1818. In *Pestalozzi.* Edited by L. F. Anderson, *McGraw-Hill Education Classics.* New York: McGraw-Hill Book Company.

Pestalozzi, Johan Heinrich. 1931e. Views and Experiences. In *Pestalozzi.* Edited by L.

F. Anderson, *McGraw-Hill Education Classics*. New York: McGraw-Hill Book Company.

Piaget, Jean. 1971. *Science of Education and the Psychology of the Child*. London: Longman.

Priestman, O.B. 1952. The Influence of Froebel on the Independent Preparatory Schools of Today. In *Friedrich Froebel and English Education*. Edited by E. Lawrence. London: Routledge & Kegan Paul.

Purpel, David E. 1989. *The Moral and Spiritual Crisis in Education: A curriculum for justice and compassion in education*. New York: Bergin & Garvey.

Raumer, Karl von. 1859. Memoir of Pestalozzi. In *Pestalozzi and Pestalozzianism: Life, educational principles, and methods of John Henry Pestalozzi with biographical sketches of several of his assistants and disciples*. Edited by H. Barnard. New York: F.C. Brownell.

Rogers, Carl. 1961. *On Becoming a Person: A therapist's view of psychotherapy*. London: Constable & Company Ltd.

Rogers, Carl. 1967. The Facilitation of Significant Learning. In *Some Contemporary Viewpoints of Instruction*. Edited by L. Siegel, *Chandler Publications in Educatioanl Psychology*. San Francisco: Chandler Publishing Co.

Rogers, Carl. 1983. *Freedom to Learn for the 80's*. Columbus, OH: Charles E. Merrill Publishing Co.

Rogers, Carl. 1990a. Can I Be a Facilitative Person in a Group? In *The Carl Rogers Reader*. Edited by H. Kirschenbaum and V. L. Henderson. London: Constable & Co. Ltd.

Rogers, Carl. 1990b. A Note on 'The Nature of Man'. In *The Carl Rogers Reader*. Edited by H. Kirschenbaum and V. L. Henderson. London: Constable & Co. Ltd.

Rogers, Carl. 1990c. Some Thoughts Regarding the Current Presuppositions of the Behavioral Sciences. In *The Carl Rogers Reader*. Edited by H. Kirschenbaum and V. L. Henderson. London: Constable & Co. Ltd.

Rogers, Carl, and H. Jerome Freiberg. 1994. *Freedom to Learn*. Third ed. New York: Merrill.

Rogers, Carl, and Barry Stevens. 1973. *Person to Person: The problem of being human*. London: Souvenir Press (Educational & Academic) Ltd.

Rousseau, Jean-Jacques. 1790. *Du Contrat Social: ou Principe du droit politique suive des considerations sur le gouvernment de Pologne, et sur sa reformation projettee*. Paris: Defer de Maisonneuve.

Rousseau, Jean-Jacques. 1967. Lettre á Dr. Theodore Tronchin, 26 Novembre 1758. In *Correspondence Complete de Jean Jacque Rousseau*. Edited by R. A. Leigh. Vol. 5. Geneva: Publications de L'Institute et Musee Voltaire.

Rousseau, Jean Jacques. 1979. *Emile: or On Education*. Translated by Allan Bloom. London: Penguin Books.

Russell, John. 1926. *Pestalozzi: Educational Reformer 1746—1827*. Seventh ed. London: George Allen & Unwin Ltd.

Sands, Fredrich. 1961. Why I believe in God. *Good Housekeeping (American Edition)* 64 (December):139-141.

Sells, Michael A. 1994. *Mystical Languages of Unsaying*. Chicago: Universtiy of Chicago Press.

Senge, Peter. 1990. *The Fifth Discipline*. First ed. New York: Doubleday Currency.

Smetana, J. 1990. Morality and conduct disorders. In *Handbook of Developmental Psychopathology*. Edited by M. Lewis and S. M. Miller. New York: Plenum.

Smith, Curtis D. 1990. *Jung's Quest for Wholeness: A religious and historical perspective.* Albany, New York: State University of New York Press.

Smith, Steve. 1997. *The Education Liberator* Vol.3 (No. 3).

Spence, S.H. 1981. Differences in social skills performances between institutionalized juvenile male offenders and a comparable group of boys without offence records. *British Journal of Social and Clinical Psychology* 20:163-71.

Storr, Anthony. 1999. Personal correspondence.

Sugarman, Leonie. 1986. *Life-Span Development: Concepts, theories and iterventions.* London: Routledge.

Taylor, Charles. 1989. *Sources of The Self: The making of the modern identity.* Cambridge: Cambridge University Press.

Thorsen, Hakan. 1983. *Peak Experience, Religion and Knowledge: A philosophical inquiry into some main themes in the writings of Abraham H. Maslow.* Edited by D. Haglund and H. Hof, *Studia Philosophiae Religionis.* Stockholm: CWK Gleerup.

Tillich, Paul. 1957. *Dynamics of Faith.* New York: Harper & Row.

Ullich, Robert. 1935. *A Sequence of Educational Influences: Traced through unpublished writings of Pestalozzi, Frobel, Diesterweg, Horace Mann and Henry Barnard.* Cambridge, MA: Harvard University Press.

von Franz, Marie-Louise. 1975. *C. G. Jung: His myth in our time.* Translated by William H. Kennedy. London: Hodder and Stoughton.

Walker, Donald E. 1956. Carl Rogers and the Nature of Man. *Journal of Counseling Psychology* 3 (2):89—93.

Wexler, Philip. 1997. *Holy Sparks; Social theory, education, and religion.* Basingstoke, Hampshire: Macmillan Press.

White, Victor. 1952. *God and the Unconscious.* London: Harvill.

White, Victor. 1960. *Soul and Psyche: An enquiry into the relationship of psychotherapy and religion.* London: Collins and Harvill.

Wickes, Fances G. 1977. *The inner World of Childhood: A study in Analytical Psychology.* London: Coventure Ltd.

Wilson, Colin. 1972. *New Pathways in Psychology: Maslow and the post-Freudian revolution.* London: Victor Gollancz. Ltd.

Winch, Peter. 1990. *The Idea of Social Science and its Relation to Philosophy.* Second ed. London: Routledge.

Wittgenstein, Ludwig. 1953. *Philosophical Investigations.* Translated by Anscombe, G.E.M. Second ed. Oxford: Blackwell.

Woodham-Smith, P. 1952a. The History of the Froebel Movement in England. In *Friedrich Froebel and English Education.* Edited by E. Lawrence. London: Routledge & Kegan Paul.

Woodham-Smith, P. 1952b. The Origin of the Kindergarten. In *Friedrich Froebel and English Education.* Edited by E. Lawrence. London: Routledge & Kegan Paul.

Index

Note: Topics that are associated with particular "Authors" are listed as subcategories for each of the six "Authors." Topics that cross different "Authors" are listed as main topics within the index, and readers are cautioned to take care in noticing the differing and particular meanings that each "Author" may give to the words used.

About the Author

Scott H. Forbes is an American who has lived in Europe off and on since he was a boy, and has spent most of his life there. He has worked for more than 30 years in the field of holistic education. For 20 years he worked at the Brockwood Park Krishnamurti Educational Centre in England where he was principal for ten years. During those years he lectured widely in Europe, the Far East, and in many countries formerly under the Soviet Union. Dr. Forbes earned his doctorate from the University of Oxford for his work establishing an intellectual basis for holistic education. He has been involved with founding holistic schools, doing educational research in holistic education, and conducting teacher development programs to help teachers of any school make their practice more holistic. Dr. Forbes is currently founding a holistic school in Portland, Oregon, as well as a center for other activities to further holistic education. Dr. Forbes and the various activities he is involved with can be reached at www.holistic-education.net.